Computer Accounting
with
QuickBooks® 2015

Seventeenth Edition

Donna Kay, MBA, PhD, CPA, CITP

QuickBooks Pro 2015
QuickBooks Premier 2015
QuickBooks Accountant 2015

COMPUTER ACCOUNTING WITH QUICKBOOKS® 2015, SEVENTEENTH EDITION

Published by McGraw-Hill Education, 2 Penn Plaza, New York, NY 10121. Copyright © 2016 by McGraw-Hill Education. All rights reserved. Printed in the United States of America. Previous editions © 2015, 2014, and 2013. No part of this publication may be reproduced or distributed in any form or by any means, or stored in a database or retrieval system, without the prior written consent of McGraw-Hill Education, including, but not limited to, in any network or other electronic storage or transmission, or broadcast for distance learning.

Some ancillaries, including electronic and print components, may not be available to customers outside the United States.

This book is printed on acid-free paper.

3 4 5 6 7 QTN/QTN 19 18 17 16

ISBN 978-1-259-18386-7
MHID 1-259-18386-6

Senior Vice President, Products & Markets: *Kurt L. Strand*
Vice President, General Manager, Products & Markets: *Marty Lange*
Vice President, Content Design & Delivery: *Kimberly Meriwether David*
Managing Director: *Tim Vertovec*
Marketing Director: *Brad Parkins*
Brand Manager: *Steve Schuetz*
Director, Product Development: *Rose Koos*
Director of Digital Content: *Patricia Plumb*
Lead Product Developer: *Ann Torbert*
Product Developer: *Jonathan Thornton*
Marketing Manager: *Michelle Nolte*
Digital Product Developer: *Kevin Moran*
Digital Product Analyst: *Xin Lin*
Director, Content Design & Delivery: *Linda Avenarius*
Program Manager: *Daryl Horrocks*
Content Project Manager: *Dana M. Pauley*
Buyer: *Susan K. Culbertson*
Design: *Debra Kubiak*
Content Licensing Specialists: *Keri Johnson*
Cover Image: *Getty Images*
Compositor: *S4Carlisle Publishing Services*
Printer: *Quad/Graphics*

www.mhhe.com

Why QuickBooks?

MILLIONS OF USERS

95%

of Small Business Entrepreneurs
Choose QuickBooks Financial Software

ARE YOU READY?

What's New?

QUICKBOOKS USER CERTIFICATION

QuickBooks User Certification
Ask your instructor about the QuickBooks User Certification Exam

1
Complete *Computer Accounting with QuickBooks*
Chapters 1 - 12

2
Review *Section 3: Quick Guide*
using the Review Guide Data Starter File

3
Try *Chapters 1- 12 Online Practice Quizzes*
at the Online Learning Center

4
Try *QuickBooks User Certification Practice Exams*

5
When ready, take the *QuickBooks User Certification Examination*

Updated! QuickBooks User Certification Guide

Computer Accounting with QuickBooks 2015 gives you an updated Quick Guide to streamline your review for the QuickBooks User Certification examination. See the Quick Guide in Section 3 for more detailed information about developing your action plan to review for QuickBooks User Certification.

What's New?

QuickBooks Online

New! Chapter 14

Computer Accounting with QuickBooks 2015 gives you an integrated approach to teach and learn QuickBooks desktop and QuickBooks Online.

What's New?

HOT ARROWS

Step 3: When the following *Preferences* window appears, click the **Accounting** icon in the left scrollbar.

Step 4: Then select the **Company Preferences** tab.

Step 5: Select **Use account numbers** to display the account numbers in the Chart of Accounts.

Step 6: Then click **OK**.

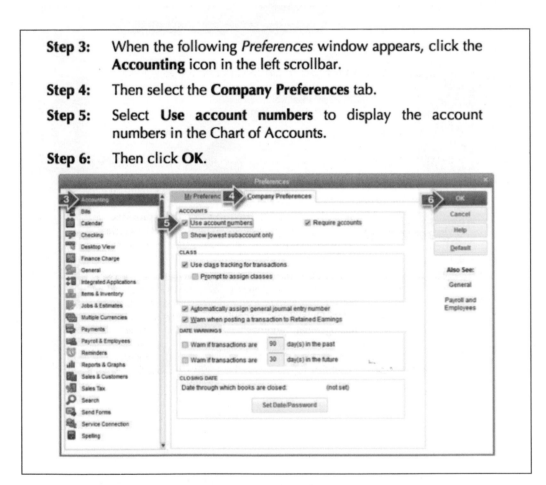

New! Hot Arrows Streamline Learning

Matching step-by-step instructions, hot arrows on screen captures make learning QuickBooks even faster and easier.

What's New?
GO BEYOND THE FLIPPED CLASSROOM

CHAPTER 13
QUICKBOOKS LIVE CONSULTING PROJECT

SCENARIO

Chapter 13 provides an opportunity to apply the knowledge and skills you have acquired thus far to an authentic QuickBooks project. You will assume the role of a consultant providing QuickBooks consulting services to a client. This project provides an opportunity for realistic, valuable practical experience to better prepare you for professional employment as well as enhance your resume.

The chapter contains a project management framework to guide you through the development of an accounting system for entrepreneurs or not-for-profits using QuickBooks accounting software. The project management approach divides the project into milestones for system development that can be used with various types of organizations, allowing for flexibility to customize the system to meet the specific needs of the entrepreneur or not-for-profit.

Live QuickBooks Consulting Project

Go beyond the flipped classroom. See Chapter 13 for a Live QuickBooks Consulting Project where your instructor becomes your QuickBooks coach. Use a Live Consulting Project that offers an effective mastery opportunity, provides a project management framework and bolsters your resume with professional experience.

Why Choose the Leading Text to Learn the World's Leading Small Business Financial Software?

- **By design, this text makes learning QuickBooks efficient and effective**

- **QuickBooks Accountant 2015 software** ($495 value) packaged with a new text, *free* to use for 140 days

- **Student data starter files** make it easy to start assignments

- **Online Learning Center** with slide presentations, data starter files, and online practice quizzes for chapters 1 – 12

- **Online Practice Tests** available on the Online Learning Center, automatically graded so you receive immediate feedback

- **Mobile QuickBooks apps** coverage so you can stay mobile and still connect to your QuickBooks software

- **www.My-QuickBooks.com** website with updates, issue resolution tips, Go Digital Excel templates, and more

- **Go Digital** with free Excel templates and instructions for your QuickBooks assignments, available at www.My-QuickBooks.com

- **QuickBooks for your Mac** offers options to run QuickBooks software on your Mac (see Appendix E and www.My-QuickBooks.com)

- **QuickBooks Issue Resolution** for assistance in navigating software issues and correcting errors (see Appendix C and www.My-QuickBooks.com)

- **Time-saving Workflow** approach to QuickBooks software for use at home or on campus

- **QuickBooks Live Consulting Project** (Chapter 13) guides you through the development of a Live QuickBooks consulting project to go beyond the *flipped classroom*

- **Expanded assignments** with 12 QuickBooks projects and 4 QuickBooks cases

- **QuickBooks QuickGrader** automatically grades QuickBooks reports exported to Excel (denoted with *)

- **Quick Guide** summarizes easy step-by-step explanations covering frequently used tasks (Section 3)

- **QuickBooks User Certification Review Guide** updated to streamline your review for the QuickBooks User Certification examination (Section 3)

How Do I Learn More about Becoming a QuickBooks Certified User?

Computer Accounting with QuickBooks 2015 offers you a Quick Guide to streamline your review for the QuickBooks User Certification examination.

What is the QuickBooks User Certification examination?

The QuickBooks User Certification examination is an online exam that is proctored at authorized testing centers. The QuickBooks User Certification is a certification focused on QuickBooks users. The QuickBooks ProAdvisor certification is a different certification that is focused more on accountants who provide advisory services to QuickBooks clients.

Why consider the QuickBooks User Certification?

Passing the QuickBooks User Certification examination can add another credential to your resume. Employers often look for credentials that indicate skill and knowledge level as a baseline for employment.

What is covered on the QuickBooks User Certification examination?

The QuickBooks User Certification exam covers the 10 domains listed in the following table. The Quick Guide provided in Section 3 of *Computer Accounting with QuickBooks 2015* is a review guide for the exam. The Quick Guide streamlines your review since it is mapped to the 10 domains covered on the QuickBooks User Certification exam. Chapters 1 through 12 of this text use a tutorial approach for learning QuickBooks effectively. The Quick Guide is designed to guide you in quickly reviewing key material efficiently.

How do I obtain more information about the QuickBooks User Certification exam?

For more information, see:

- www.certiport.com
- www.My-QuickBooks.com, QB Certified User
- Quick Guide (Section 3)

How Is this Text Mapped to the QuickBooks User Certification?

How is Computer Accounting with QuickBooks 2015 mapped to the QuickBooks User Certification?

Each domain of the Quick Guide contained in Section 3 of *Computer Accounting with QuickBooks 2015* is mapped to one of the 10 domains of the QuickBooks User Certification. Quick Guide mapping to the QuickBooks User Certification follows.

Quick Guide Section	QuickBooks User Certification Domain
1	QuickBooks Setup
2	QuickBooks Utilities and General Product Knowledge
3	List Management
4	Items
5	Sales
6	Purchases
7	Payroll
8	Reports
9	Basic Accounting
10	Customization and Saving Time

See the Quick Guide in Section 3 for more detailed information about developing your action plan to review for QuickBooks User Certification.

Dear QuickBooks Student

Give yourself a competitive advantage – learn the leading financial software for entrepreneurs using Computer Accounting with QuickBooks. This text streamlines learning QuickBooks because it focuses on you—the learner—designed using the most effective way to learn QuickBooks.

Using a hands-on approach, this text integrates understanding accounting with mastery of QuickBooks software. Proven instructional techniques are incorporated throughout the text to make your mastery of QuickBooks as effortless as possible. Designed for maximum flexibility to meet your needs, *Computer Accounting with QuickBooks* can be used either in a QuickBooks course or independently at your own pace.

This text uses a highly effective three-step approach to streamline your learning:

1. *Chapter Tutorials.* Providing numerous screen shots and detailed instructions, chapters in *Computer Accounting with QuickBooks* are designed as tutorials for you to initially learn the accounting software features. All chapters are based on realistic, virtual company cases to enhance your understanding of the business environment in which QuickBooks is used.

2. *Learning Activities.* To improve long-term retention of your software skills and mastery of QuickBooks, learning activities are included at the end of the chapters. Designed with fewer instructions to test your understanding and, when needed, to develop your skills at quickly seeking out additional information to complete tasks, the activities consist of exercises, projects and web quests. JIT Learning, the ability to seek out information as needed, is an increasingly important skill in a rapidly changing business environment. *Computer Accounting with QuickBooks* is designed to seamlessly facilitate your development of this crucial skill. In addition, the virtual cases challenge you to apply and develop both software and problem-solving skills.

3. *Reflection.* Reflection improves learning and retention. A reflection exercise, *A Wish and A Star*, appears at the end of each chapter to enhance and reinforce what you learned.

QuickBooks 2015 includes a Quick Guide in Section 3 to streamline your review for the QuickBooks User Certification examination, and Chapter 14 adds QuickBooks Online Accountant information so you can compare the popular QuickBooks desktop software with the new QuickBooks Online Accountant.

Best wishes for your continued success,

Meet the Author

Donna Kay is Associate Professor of Accounting and Accounting Systems & Forensics at Maryville University in Saint Louis, Missouri, where she teaches both undergraduate and graduate accounting. Dr. Kay earned B.S. and MBA degrees from Southern Illinois University at Edwardsville before receiving a Ph.D. from Saint Louis University, where she conducted action research on the perceived effectiveness of instructional techniques in the computer classroom. Named to Who's Who Among American Women, Dr. Kay holds certifications as both a Certified Public Accountant (CPA) and Certified Informational Technology Professional (CITP) and is an active member of the American Institute of Certified Public Accountants (AICPA), the Missouri Society of CPAs (MSCPA), and the American Accounting Association (AAA). Dr. Kay has served on the Information Technology Committee of the MSCPA and a Strategic and Emerging Technologies subcommittee of the AAA.

Acknowledgments

It takes a dedicated team to make each edition of this text possible.
Special thanks to:

- *The McGraw-Hill team who continue to strive to continually improve this text to meet student and professor needs: Steve Schuetz, Jonathan Thornton, Michelle Nolte*

- *A phenomenal QuickBooks team:*
  Becky Cornell for her cheerful, careful accuracy checking and editing,
  Matt Harrer for his innovative application development of the QuickBooks SpeedGrader

- *Brian Behrens for always being in my corner with prompt and greatly appreciated support*

- *The RubinBrown team for their cheerful assistance: Steve Newstead, Justin Lee, Nancy Rehkemper, Steven Harris, Jackie Jacquin, Janet Colombo, Mike Ferman, and Matt Hartman*

- *The Clayton on the Park team, especially Mike Larson for his assistance*

- *Mike Whalen for his support and unfaltering encouragement*

- *All the QuickBooks educators who share ideas, comments, suggestions, and encouragement. Special recognition to:*
  Lanny Nelms, Gwinnett Technical College
  Michael Goldfine, Brooklyn College
  Miriam Lefkowitz, Brooklyn College
  Amy Browning, Ivy Tech Distance Education
  James Capone, Kean University
  Nancy Schrumpf, Parkland College
  Paige Paulsen, Salt Lake Community College
  Carol Thomas, West Virginia University Parkersburg
  Ed Siepp, Southwestern Illinois College
  Dawn Peters, Southwestern Illinois College
  Brian Voss, Austin Community College – Eastview
  Joel Peralto, Hawaii Community College
  Vicki Williams, University of Alaska – Juneau
  Larry Herring, Texas State University – San Marcos
  Teri Grimmer, Portland Community College
  Mike Fritz, Portland Community College
  David Packard, Elgin Community College

Daniel Jenkins, Albany Technical College

Cecile Roberti, Community College of Rhode Island – Warwick

Natalie Waddell, Central Georgia Technical College

Rebecca Butler, City College of San Francisco

Deborah Hudson, Gaston College

John Kelly, Manchester Community College

Amy Chataginer, Mississippi Gulf Coast Community College – Jackson County

Donna Parker, Mississippi Gulf Coast Community College – Jefferson Davis

Linda Kropp, Modesto Junior College

Cathy Scott, Navarro College

Sara Barritt, Northeast Community College

Aaron Reeves, St Louis Community College

CONTENTS

CONTENTS

SECTION 2 QUICKBOOKS ACCOUNTING FOR ENTREPRENEURS

xx ● Contents

SECTION 3 QUICK GUIDE

SECTION 4 QUICKBOOKS EXTRAS

INDEX

CONTENTS OVERVIEW

Designed as hands-on tutorials for initially learning QuickBooks, *Computer Accounting with QuickBooks* chapters provide screen captures with hot arrows and detailed instructions. To improve long-term retention of your software skills, end-of-chapter learning activities are designed with fewer instructions to test your understanding and, when needed, to develop your skills to quickly seek out additional information to complete the task. The ability to find information as needed, or JIT Learning, is an increasingly important skill in a rapidly changing business environment. The design of *Computer Accounting with QuickBooks* seamlessly facilitates your development of this crucial skill. Each chapter concludes with *Reflection: A Wish and A Star* to further reinforce and improve your retention of chapter material. Additionally, a virtual company case runs throughout the text, enabling you to better understand how various transactions and activities are interrelated in the business environment.

Designed in four sections, this text offers:

SECTION 1 EXPLORING QUICKBOOKS WITH ROCK CASTLE CONSTRUCTION focuses on learning the basics of entering transactions and generating reports using the sample company, Rock Castle Construction.

SECTION 2 QUICKBOOKS ACCOUNTING FOR ENTREPRENEURS builds upon Section 1, covering the entire accounting cycle, including new company setup as well as QuickBooks advanced features for accountants. Paint Palette, a case that runs throughout the second section, starts out as a sole proprietor service business, then expands to become a merchandising corporation. Using a progressive approach, the text gradually introduces advanced features while maintaining continuity and interest.

SECTION 3 QUICK GUIDE provides a Review Guide for the QuickBooks User Certification. As a Quick Resource Guide, it provides step-by-step instructions for frequently used customer, vendor, and employee tasks in a convenient, user-friendly resource.

SECTION 4 QUICKBOOKS EXTRAS are appendices including Install & Register QuickBooks Software, Back Up and Restore QuickBooks Files, QuickBooks Issue Resolution, Go Digital with QuickBooks, and more.

SECTION 1 EXPLORING QUICKBOOKS WITH ROCK CASTLE CONSTRUCTION INCLUDES:

CHAPTER 1 QUICK TOUR OF QUICKBOOKS. This chapter provides a guided tour of the software using QuickBooks Navigation tools and introduces the QuickBooks sample company, Rock Castle Construction. Other topics include the *Workflow* and *Restart & Restore* approaches for backup files.

CHAPTER 2 CUSTOMIZING QUICKBOOKS AND THE CHART OF ACCOUNTS. This chapter introduces how to customize QuickBooks and the Chart of Accounts to meet specific business needs. Other topics include customizing QuickBooks security.

CHAPTER 3 BANKING. This chapter focuses on the checking account and check register for a small business. Topics include making deposits, writing checks, and reconciling a bank statement.

CHAPTER 4 CUSTOMERS AND SALES. Chapter 4 demonstrates how to record customer transactions. Topics include how to create invoices, record sales, record customer payments, and print customer reports.

CHAPTER 5 VENDORS, PURCHASES, AND INVENTORY. This chapter focuses on recording vendor transactions, including creating purchase orders, paying bills, and printing vendor reports.

CHAPTER 6 EMPLOYEES AND PAYROLL. Chapter 6 covers time tracking, billing tracked time, and processing payroll using QuickBooks payroll service. Manual payroll preparation is covered in Chapter 11.

CHAPTER 7 REPORTS AND GRAPHS. In this chapter, you complete the accounting cycle by creating a trial balance and entering adjusting entries. In addition, you learn how to create a variety of reports and graphs using QuickBooks.

SECTION 2 QUICKBOOKS ACCOUNTING FOR ENTREPRENEURS INCLUDES:

CHAPTER 8 NEW COMPANY SETUP. Chapter 8 covers how to use the EasyStep Interview feature to set up a new company in QuickBooks. You also learn how to create customer, vendor, and item lists.

CHAPTER 9 ACCOUNTING FOR A SERVICE COMPANY. Chapter 9 records transactions for an entire year using the company created in Chapter 8. Expanded end-of-chapter learning activities include a short exercise setting up a new company and entering transactions. Project 9 and QuickBooks Case 9 provide opportunities to integrate all the QuickBooks skills covered thus far in a comprehensive fashion.

CHAPTER 10 MERCHANDISING CORPORATION: SALES, PURCHASES AND INVENTORY. After learning how to set up a merchandising corporation with inventory, you record transactions for the first month of operations. Project 10 and QuickBooks Case 10 are comprehensive assignments for a merchandising corporation.

CHAPTER 11 MERCHANDISING CORPORATION: PAYROLL. Chapter 11 covers how to set up and record payroll using QuickBooks manual payroll approach. Project 11 continues and builds upon Project 10. QuickBooks Case 11 is a continuation of QuickBooks Case 10.

CHAPTER 12 ADVANCED QUICKBOOKS FEATURES FOR ACCOUNTANTS. This chapter covers the advanced features of QuickBooks software including budgets, estimates, progress billing, credit card sales, accounting for bad debts, memorized reports, the audit trail, and accountant's copy. Using the advanced features of QuickBooks, Project 12 is a continuation of Project 9. QuickBooks Case 12 is a continuation of QuickBooks Case 9.

CHAPTER 13 QUICKBOOKS LIVE CONSULTING PROJECT. This chapter outlines the project management milestones for development of a QuickBooks accounting system. Providing you with an opportunity to apply QuickBooks software to a live consulting project gives you hands-on professional experience for your resume.

CHAPTER 14 QUICKBOOKS ONLINE ACCOUNTANT. Chapter 14 integrates coverage of QuickBooks desktop and QuickBooks Online. QuickBooks user options and QuickBooks accountant options are presented.

SECTION 3 QUICK GUIDE INCLUDES:

QUICKBOOKS SETUP. Instructions and resources for installing your QuickBooks software and setting up a new company.

QUICKBOOKS UTILITIES AND GENERAL PRODUCT KNOWLEDGE. Find step-by-step instructions for frequently used company commands including back up and restore, password protect, and customizing QuickBooks with preferences.

LIST MANAGEMENT. Step-by-step instructions for managing QuickBooks lists including add, delete, edit and merge list entries.

ITEMS. Instructions for how to add, edit and use different types of QuickBooks items.

SALES (CUSTOMER TRANSACTIONS). Instructions about customer transactions including how to invoice customers, receive customer payments, and deposit customer payments.

PURCHASES (VENDOR TRANSACTIONS). Instructions about vendor transactions including how to create purchase orders, receive items, enter bills, and pay bills.

PAYROLL (EMPLOYEE TRANSACTIONS). Instructions about payroll transactions including how to set up payroll, add and edit payroll items, track time, and pay employees.

REPORTS. Quickly locate instructions for creating QuickBooks reports.

BASIC ACCOUNTING. Review tasks related to the chart of accounts and learn about various journal entries used with QuickBooks including adjusting and correcting entries.

CUSTOMIZATION/SAVING TIME AND SHORTCUTS. Review how to memorize transactions, set up multiple users in QuickBooks, create custom fields for lists, and customize an invoice.

Section 4 QuickBooks Extras includes:

Appendix A Install & Register QuickBooks Software. This appendix provides step-by-step instructions for installing and registering your QuickBooks software.

Appendix B Back Up & Restore QuickBooks Files. Save time using the streamlined *Workflow* and *Restart & Restore* approaches for saving QuickBooks files. Detailed instructions for backing up and restoring your QuickBooks files are included.

Appendix C QuickBooks Issue Resolution. This appendix provides you with valuable tips and frequently asked questions to troubleshoot QuickBooks issues.

Appendix D Go Digital with QuickBooks. Consistent with sustainability and paperless initiatives on many college campuses today, *Computer Accounting with QuickBooks* offers you three easy ways to go Digital with QuickBooks. Check out this appendix to learn more.

Appendix E QuickBooks & My Mac. Consistent with today's trend toward Macs on college campuses and in the business environment, this appendix directs you to resources for running QuickBooks on your Mac.

Appendix F www.My-QuickBooks.com. A student website www.My-QuickBooks.com is offered with *Computer Accounting with QuickBooks 2014*. View QuickBooks videos, download go Digital templates, and much more.

YOUR ROADMAP TO VIRTUAL CASES

What is the most effective way to learn QuickBooks software? Virtual company cases provide you with a realistic context and business environment to enhance your understanding of QuickBooks.

Your roadmap to related learning activities follows.

ROCK CASTLE CONSTRUCTION
- Chapter 1 & Exercises
- Chapter 2 & Exercises
- Chapter 3 & Exercises
- Chapter 4 & Exercises
- Chapter 5 & Exercises
- Chapter 6 & Exercises
- Chapter 7 & Exercises

LARRY'S LANDSCAPING
- Project 1
- Project 2
- Project 3
- Project 4
- Project 5
- Project 6
- Project 7

PAINT PALETTE

- Chapter 8
- Exercise 8.1
- Chapter 9
- Exercise 9.1
- Exercise 9.2
- Exercise 9.3
- Exercise 9.4
- Exercise 9.5
- Chapter 12

ALEXANDRA LLC
- Exercise 9.6

PAINT PALETTE STORE
- Chapter 10
- Chapter 11

BRITTANY'S YARNS
- Exercise 10.1
- Exercise 11.1

DOMINIC CONSULTING
- Project 8
- Project 9
- Project 12

RONEN ENTERPRISES
- Project 10
- Project 11

TUSCANY LANDSCAPES
- QuickBooks Case 9
- QuickBooks Case 12

TOMASO'S MOWERS & MORE
- QuickBooks Case 10
- QuickBooks Case 11

©McGraw-Hill Education, 2016

NOTES:

SECTION 1
EXPLORING QUICKBOOKS WITH ROCK CASTLE CONSTRUCTION

CHAPTER 1
QUICK TOUR OF QUICKBOOKS

SCENARIO

Mr. Rock Castle, owner of Rock Castle Construction, called to hire you as his accountant. His former accountant unexpectedly accepted a job offer in Hawaii, and Rock Castle Construction needs someone immediately to maintain its accounting records. Mr. Castle indicates they use QuickBooks to maintain the company's accounting records. When you tell him that you are not familiar with QuickBooks software, Mr. Castle reassures you, *"No problem! QuickBooks is easy to learn. Stop by my office this afternoon."*

When you arrive at Rock Castle Construction, Mr. Castle leads you to a cubicle as he rapidly explains Rock Castle's accounting.

"Rock Castle needs to keep records of transactions with customers, vendors, and employees. We must keep a record of our customers and the sales and services we provide to those customers. Also, it is crucial for the company to be able to bill customers promptly and keep a record of cash collected from them. If we don't know who owes Rock Castle money, we can't collect it.

"Rock Castle also needs to keep track of the supplies, materials, and inventory we purchase from vendors. We need to track all purchase orders, the items received, the invoices or bills received from vendors, and the payments made to vendors. If we don't track bills, we can't pay our vendors on time. And if Rock

Castle doesn't pay its bills on time, the vendors don't like to sell to us.

"Also, we like to keep our employees happy. One way to do that is to pay them the right amount at the right time. So Rock Castle must keep track of the time worked by its employees, the amounts owed to the employees, and the wages and salaries paid to them.

"QuickBooks permits Rock Castle to keep a record of all of these transactions. Also, we need records so we can prepare tax returns, financial reports for bank loans, and reports to evaluate the company's performance and make business decisions.

"Your first assignment is to learn more about QuickBooks." Mr. Castle tosses you a QuickBooks training manual as he rushes off to answer a phone call.

Slightly overwhelmed by Mr. Castle's rapid-fire delivery, you sink into a chair. As you look around your cubicle, you notice for the first time the leaning tower of papers stacked beside the computer, waiting to be processed. No wonder Mr. Castle wanted you to start right way.

Mr. Castle bursts back into your cubicle quickly tossing something onto your cluttered desk. "And here's your new company smartphone—that way I can reach you anytime I need you!"

Noticing your startled expression, Mr. Castle pauses and then reassuringly says, "Don't worry—IT has already set up security for your new phone so that all financial communications will be secure."

Recalling your favorite college professor's advice, you remind yourself to **Focus & Work Smarter**. Opening the QuickBooks training manual, you see the following page.

CHAPTER 1
LEARNING OBJECTIVES

In Chapter 1, you will learn about the following QuickBooks features:

ACCOUNTING INFORMATION SYSTEMS

Accounting is the language of business. Learning accounting is similar to learning a foreign language. As you use this text, you will learn terms and definitions that are unique to accounting.

QuickBooks is accounting software that provides an easy and efficient way to collect and summarize accounting information. In addition, QuickBooks creates many different reports that are useful when managing a business.

The objective of an accounting system is to collect, summarize, and communicate information to decision makers. Accounting information is used to:

- Prepare tax returns for federal and state tax agencies.

- Prepare financial statements for banks and investors.

- Prepare reports for managers and owners to use when making decisions. Such decisions include: Are our customers paying their bills on time? Which of our products are the most profitable? Will we have enough cash to pay our bills next month?

TRANSACTIONS

An accounting system collects information about *transactions*. As a company conducts business, it enters into transactions (or exchanges) with other parties such as customers, vendors, and employees. For example, when a business sells a product to a customer, there are two parts to the transaction:

1. The business *gives* a product to the customer.
2. In exchange, the business *receives* cash (or a promise to pay later) from the customer.

Business

Cash   Product

Customer

DOUBLE-ENTRY ACCOUNTING

Double-entry accounting has been used for over 500 years. In Italy in the year 1494, Luca Pacioli, a Franciscan monk, wrote a mathematics book that described double-entry accounting. At that time, the merchants of Venice used the double-entry system to record what was given and received when trading.

Double-entry accounting is used to record what is exchanged in a transaction:

1. The amount *received*, such as equipment purchased, is recorded with a *debit*.

2. The amount *given*, such as cash or a promise to pay later, is recorded with a *credit*.

For a debit and credit refresher, see Chapter 3.

Each entry must balance; debits must equal credits. In a manual accounting system, accountants make debit and credit entries in a Journal using paper and pencil. When using QuickBooks for your accounting system, you can enter accounting information in two different ways: (1) onscreen Journal, and (2) onscreen forms.

1. **Onscreen Journal.** You can make debit and credit entries in an onscreen Journal shown below. Notice the similarities between the onscreen Journal and a manual Journal.

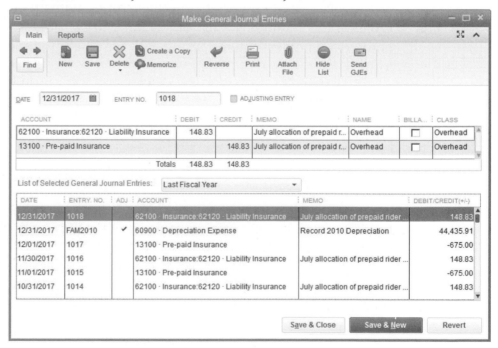

Instead of using the onscreen Journal, you can use onscreen forms to enter information in QuickBooks.

2. **Onscreen forms.** You can enter information about transactions using *onscreen forms* such as the onscreen check and the onscreen invoice shown below.

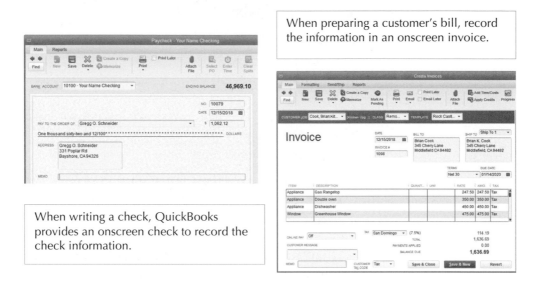

When preparing a customer's bill, record the information in an onscreen invoice.

When writing a check, QuickBooks provides an onscreen check to record the check information.

QuickBooks automatically converts information entered in onscreen forms into double-entry accounting entries with debits and credits. QuickBooks maintains a list of journal entries for all the transactions entered—whether entered using the onscreen Journal or onscreen forms.

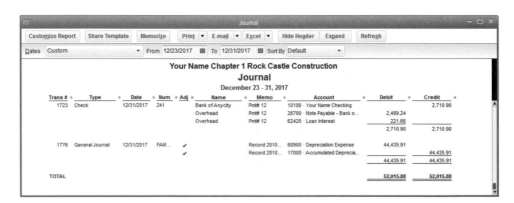

QUICKBOOKS ACCOUNTING SYSTEM

Steps to create an accounting system using QuickBooks are:

Step 1: **Set up a new company data file.** QuickBooks uses an EasyStep Interview that asks you questions about your business. QuickBooks then automatically creates a company data file for your business. In Section 1 of this text, Exploring QuickBooks with Rock Castle Construction, you will use a sample company data file that has already been created for you. In Section 2, you will set up a new company using the EasyStep Interview. To learn how to set up a company file, see Chapter 8.

Step 2: **Create a Chart of Accounts.** A Chart of Accounts is a list of all the accounts for a company. Accounts are used to sort and track accounting information. For example, a business needs one account for cash, another account to track amounts customers owe (Accounts Receivable), and yet another account to track inventory. QuickBooks automatically creates a Chart of Accounts in the EasyStep Interview. QuickBooks permits you to modify the Chart of Accounts later, after completing the EasyStep Interview.

Step 3: **Create lists.** QuickBooks uses lists to record and organize information about:

- **Customers**.
- **Vendors**.
- **Items** (items purchased and items sold, such as inventory).
- **Employees**.
- **Other** (such as owners).

Step 4: **Enter transactions.** Enter transaction information into QuickBooks using the onscreen Journal or onscreen forms (such as onscreen invoices and onscreen checks).

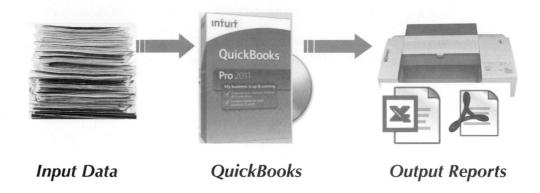

Input Data   ***QuickBooks***   ***Output Reports***

Step 5: **Prepare reports.** Reports summarize and communicate information about a company's financial position and business operations. Financial statements are standardized financial reports that summarize information about past transactions. Financial statements are provided to external users, such as bankers and investors. Internal users, such as managers, also may use financial statements. The primary financial statements for a business are:

- **Balance Sheet**: summarizes what a company owns and owes on a particular date.

- **Profit & Loss Statement** (or **Income Statement**): summarizes what a company has earned and the expenses incurred to earn the income.

- **Statement of Cash Flows**: summarizes cash inflows and cash outflows for operating, investing, and financing activities of a business.

Additional financial reports are used by internal users (managers) to assist in making decisions. An example of such a report is a cash budget that projects amounts of cash that will be collected and spent in the future.

Section 1: Exploring QuickBooks with Rock Castle Construction covers Step 2: creating a Chart of Accounts; Step 3: creating lists; Step 4: entering transactions; and Step 5: preparing reports. *Section 2: QuickBooks Accounting for Entrepreneurs* covers how to set up a new company in QuickBooks and reviews Steps 2 through 5.

INSTALL QUICKBOOKS

If you are using the trial version of QuickBooks software that is packaged with your text, see *Appendix A: Install & Register QuickBooks Software* for instructions to install and register the software. After installing the software, **you must register the software** with Intuit or you will be locked out of the software. If registered, you will be able to use the QuickBooks software for 140 days.

START QUICKBOOKS

To start QuickBooks software, click the **QuickBooks** icon on your desktop. If a QuickBooks icon does not appear on your desktop, from Microsoft® Windows® click **Start** button **> Programs > QuickBooks > QuickBooks Premier Accountant Edition 2015**.

OPEN COMPANY

After starting QuickBooks software, the following *Let's get your business set up quickly!* window appears. From this screen you can:

1. Use Express Start to set up a new QuickBooks company file.

2. Use Detailed Start to control the setup and fine-tune a new QuickBooks company file.

3. Create a new company file based on an existing one.

4. Open an existing QuickBooks company file.

!
Register your QuickBooks software! Failure to register your QuickBooks trial version software will result in the software no longer functioning.

QuickBooks Accountant 2015 software is packaged with your text. QuickBooks data files are packaged on the CD on the back cover of your text.

QuickBooks Accountant 2015 includes all the features of QuickBooks Pro plus features for client services. If you use QuickBooks Pro, your screens may appear slightly different than those appearing in this text.

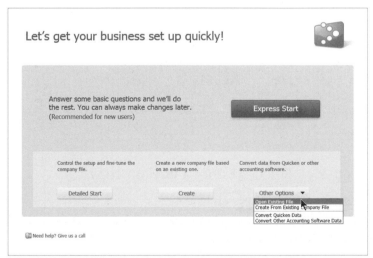

Let's get your business set up quickly!

Answer some basic questions and we'll do the rest. You can always make changes later. (Recommended for new users)

Express Start

Control the setup and fine-tune the company file.

Detailed Start

Create a new company file based on an existing one.

Create

Convert data from Quicken or other accounting software.

Other Options ▼

Open Existing File
Create From Existing Company File
Convert Quicken Data
Convert Other Accounting Software Data

Need help? Give us a call

To open the QuickBooks data file for Chapter 1:

Step 1: **Copy Chapter 1 DATA STARTER.QBB** file from the data file CD to your desktop. If you prefer, you can download the **Chapter 1 DATA STARTER.QBB** file from the Online Learning Center (OLC) to your desktop.

> For your convenience, QuickBooks (.QBB) data files accompany *Computer Accounting with QuickBooks 2015*. You will find the data files on the CD packaged on the back cover of your text. Before using the data files on the CD, you must copy the files to your desktop. Or you can download the data files from the Online Learning Center at www.mhhe.com/kay2015.

Step 2: From the *Let's get your business set up quickly!* window, select **Other Options > Open Existing File**.

If your QuickBooks software has been used before, the following window will appear. Select **Open or restore an existing company**.

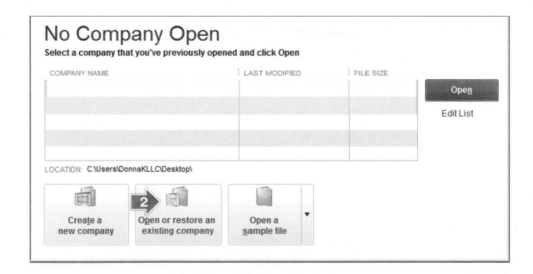

Step 3: Select **Restore a backup copy**.

Step 4: Click **Next**.

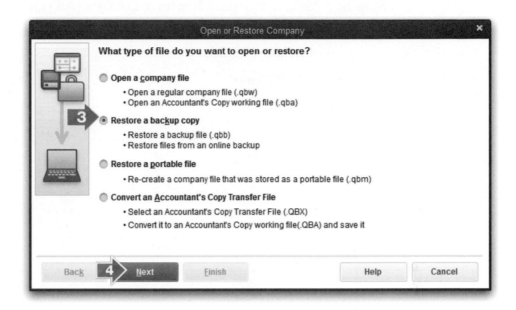

Step 5: When the following *Open or Restore Company* window appears, select **Local backup**.

Step 6: Click **Next**.

Step 7: Identify the location of the Chapter 1 DATA STARTER.QBB file. If you copied the Chapter 1 DATA STARTER file to your desktop, select the ***Look in*** field to find the location of the .QBB file on your desktop.

Step 8: Select the file: **Chapter 1 DATA STARTER.QBB.**

Step 9: The *Files of type* field should automatically display: **QBW Backup (*.QBB)**.

Step 10: Click **Open**.

Your Windows settings determine whether the .QBB filename extension appears after the filename.

Step 11: When the following window appears, click **Next**.

Step 12: Identify the file name and location of the new company file (.QBW) file. You can save the .QBW (working file) on your desktop. Select the location to save in: **Desktop**. (Or another option is to save your QBW files to **Users > Public > Public Documents > Intuit > QuickBooks > Company Files**. Be sure you have permissions to save to a folder.)

Step 13: File name: **YourName Chapter 1**. Insert your name in the file name so you can identify your files.

Step 14: The *Save as type* field should automatically appear as **QuickBooks Files (*.QBW)**.

Step 15: Click **Save**.

QBW files can also be saved to your storage device if there is adequate storage space.

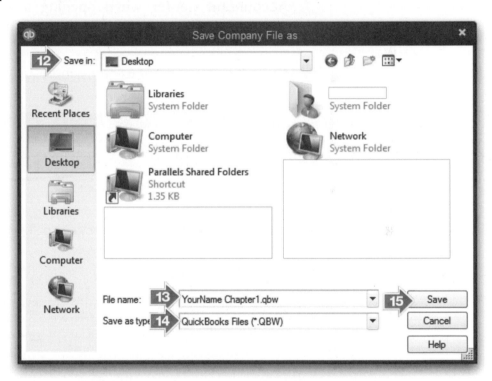

Step 16: Click **OK** when the following window appears.

If an *Update Company* window appears, select **Yes**.

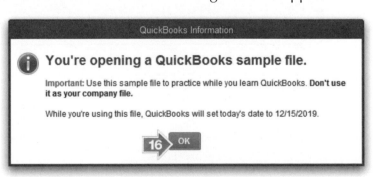

Step 17: Click **OK** if the following *QuickBooks Information* window appears.

Step 18: If the *Accountant Center* window appears, *uncheck* **Show Accountant Center when opening a company file**. The Accountant Center is a feature for organizing QuickBooks accountant tools.

Step 19: **Close** the *Accountant Center* window.

CHANGE COMPANY NAME

In order to identify your printouts, add your name to the company name. When you create reports and checks, your name will then automatically appear on your printouts.

To change a company name in QuickBooks, complete the following:

Step 1: From the Menu bar, select **Company**.

Step 2: Select **My Company**.

Step 3: When the following *My Company* window appears, select **Edit**.

Step 4: Update the *Company Information* window, update *Company Name* field to: **YourName Chapter 1 Rock Castle Construction**.

The company name that appears in the Title bar of the QuickBooks window and on reports can differ from the backup company filename.

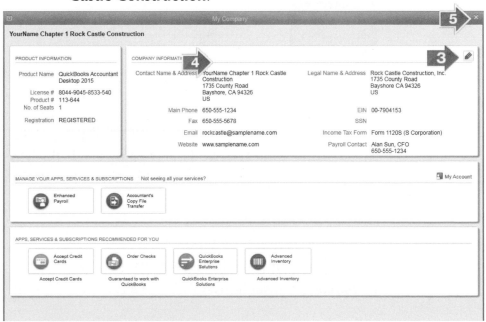

Step 5: **Close** the *My Company* window.

QUICKBOOKS NAVIGATION

Taking a few minutes to learn QuickBooks navigation will make learning QuickBooks easier. QuickBooks offers three different ways to navigate QuickBooks 2015 software:

- Home page

- Icon bar (My Shortcuts)

- Menu bar

> **Home page:** Click the Home icon on the Icon bar to reveal flowcharts of frequently used tasks.

> **Menu bar:** Click on the Menu bar to reveal a drop-down menu for each area.

> **Icon bar:** Click on icons to display customer, vendor, and employee centers and frequently used windows, such as customer invoices.

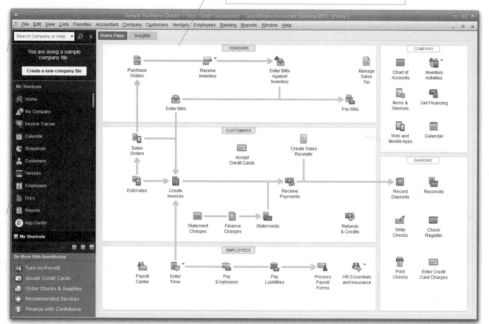

HOME PAGE

To view the QuickBooks Home page, click the **Home** icon in the Icon bar. The Home page contains the main categories of transactions and tasks:

1. *Customer* or sales transactions
2. *Vendor* or purchase transactions
3. *Employee* or payroll transactions
4. *Banking* transactions

5. *Company* tasks

CUSTOMERS

The *Customers* section is a flowchart of the main activities associated with sales and customers. You can:

- Create estimates.

- Create invoices to bill customers.

- Record refunds and credits for merchandise returned by customers.

- Record payments received from customers (cash, check, and credit card payments).

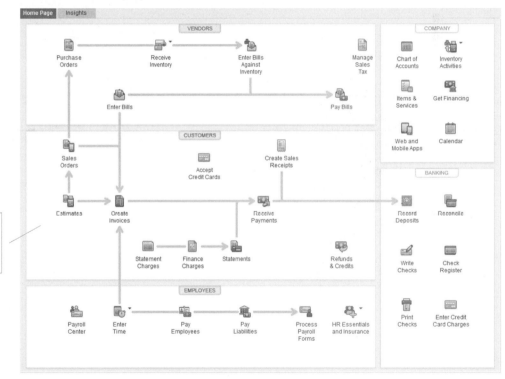

Flowchart of **customer** and sales transactions.

VENDORS

From the *Vendors* flowchart, you can record:

- Purchase orders (orders placed to purchase items).
- Inventory received.
- Bills received.
- Bills paid.
- Sales tax paid.

Flowchart of **vendor** and purchase transactions.

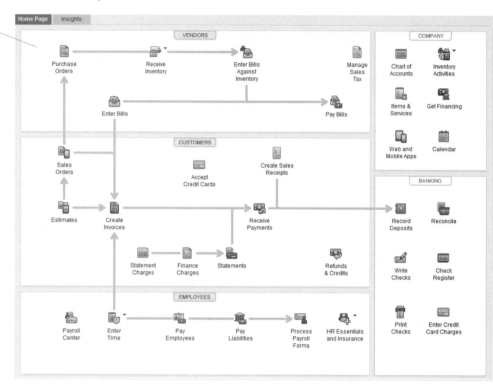

EMPLOYEES

From the *Employees* flowchart, you can:

- Enter time worked.

- Pay employees.

- Pay payroll tax liabilities.

- Process payroll forms.

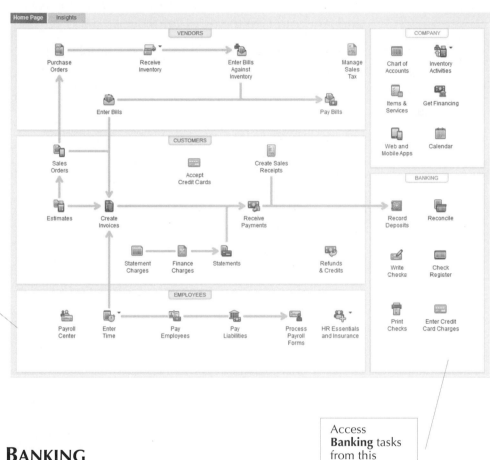

Flowchart of **employee** and payroll transactions.

Access **Banking** tasks from this section.

BANKING

From the *Banking* section, you can:

- Record deposits.

- Write checks.

- Reconcile your bank statement.

- Open your check register.

COMPANY

From the *Company* section, you can access:

- Chart of Accounts. A list of accounts a company uses to track accounting information.

- Items & Services. A list of items and services that a company buys and/or sells.

- QuickBooks Web and Mobile Apps. A QuickBooks service that permits you to connect your mobile devices (iOS and Android OS) to your QuickBooks data.

- Calendar. View your to do list and reminders in a calendar form.

Access the Chart of Accounts from the **Company** section.

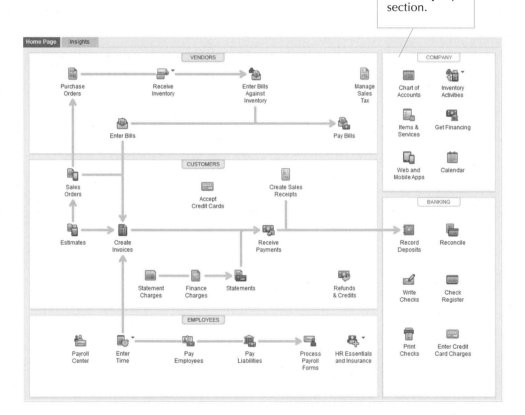

INSIGHTS

A new feature of QuickBooks 2015 is called Insights.

Select the **Insights** tab next to the Home Page tab to view a digital dashboard of relevant financial data. The digital dashboard can be customized for the specific business user. This is a new feature of QuickBooks 2015.

QuickBooks Icon Bar

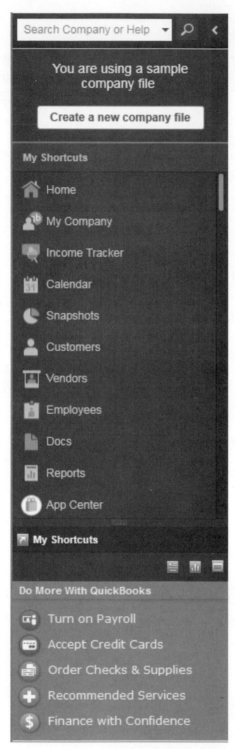

The QuickBooks Icon bar with My Shortcuts is a toolbar that can be customized for frequently used activities. The Icon bar can be displayed either beneath the Menu bar or on the left side of the QuickBooks window.

To display the Icon bar if it does not appear on your screen:

Step 1: Click **View** on the Menu bar.

Step 2: Select **Left Icon Bar**.

The Icon bar can be customized to display the tasks that you use most frequently. To customize the Icon bar:

Step 1: Click **View** on the Menu bar.

Step 2: Select **Customize Icon Bar**.

Step 3: Reorder the tasks in the following order and then click the **OK** button.

- Home
- My Company
- Calendar
- Snapshots
- Customers
- Vendors
- Employees
- Reports
- Docs
- App Center

To use My Shortcuts for the *My Company* window:

Step 1:   Select **My Company** on the Icon bar.

Step 2:   Select **Edit** to make changes to the *My Company* window.

Step 3:   **Close** the *My Company* window.

To use My Shortcuts to access the *Income Tracker* window:

Step 1:   Select **Income Tracker** on the Icon bar.

Step 2:   In the *Income Tracker* window, view summaries of amounts for Unbilled, Unpaid, and Paid amounts.

To use My Shortcuts to access the *Calendar* window:

Step 1:   Select **Calendar** on the Icon bar.

Step 2:   To add a task to the calendar, select **Add To Do**.

To view and customize snapshots of company information:

Step 1: Click **Snapshots** to display summaries of financial information about the company, payments, and customers.

Step 2: To customize the snapshots for specific business requirements, select **How do I customize this page?**

Snapshots provides an overview, summarizing information such as:

- Customers Who Owe Money
- Vendors to Pay
- Account Balances
- Reminders of Due Dates and Amounts

To view the Customer Center:

Step 1: Click **Customers** on the Icon bar to display the following Customer Center.

Step 2: Toggle between customer and transaction information.

You can also access the Customer Center by clicking on the **Customers** button in the *Customers* section of the Home page.

The Customer Center summarizes information about customers, jobs, and customer transactions. The information can be printed or exported to Excel or Word.

To view the Vendor Center:

Step 1: Click **Vendors** on the Icon bar to display the Vendor Center.

Step 2: Toggle between vendor and transaction information.

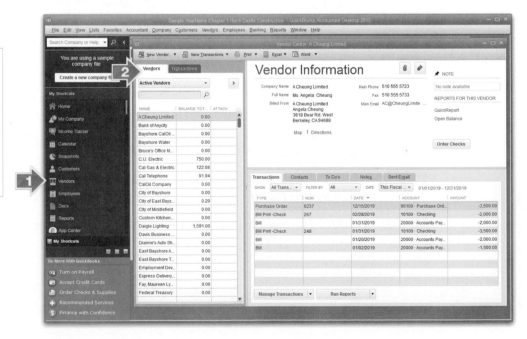

You can also access the Vendor Center by clicking on the **Vendors** button in the *Vendors* section of the Home page.

The Vendor Center summarizes information about vendors and vendor transactions. The information can be printed or exported to Excel.

To view the Employee Center:

Step 1: Click **Employees** on the Icon bar to display the Employee Center.

Step 2: From the Employee Center you can toggle between employee, transaction, and payroll information.

You can also access the Employee Center by clicking on the **Employees** button in the *Employees* section of the Home page.

To view the Doc Center:

Step 1: Click **Docs** to display the Doc Center.

Step 2: Use the Doc Center to add a document from your computer or scan a document into QuickBooks. You can even attach the document, such as a receipt, to a specific transaction.

To view the Report Center:

Step 1:   Click **Reports** on the Icon bar to view the Report Center.

Step 2:   You can select from Standard, Memorized, Favorites, Recent, or Contributed reports. In a later section of this chapter, you will learn how to prepare a report.

Contributed Reports are specialized reports shared by other QuickBooks users.

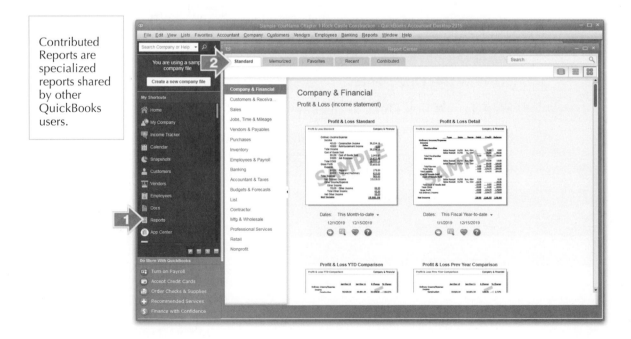

To display the Intuit App Center:

Step 1:   Select **App Center** on the Icon bar to view the Intuit App Center for organizing apps that work with your QuickBooks software and data.

Step 2:   Click **Learn more** to learn more about apps that connect with QuickBooks.

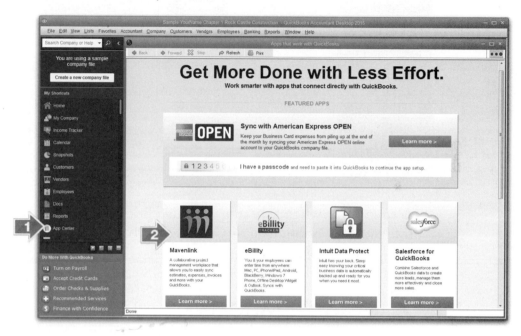

To move between open windows in QuickBooks:

Step 1:   Select **Open Windows** on the Icon bar to view all open windows. Use this feature when you need to switch back and forth between open windows quickly.

Step 2:   Then select the **Report Center**.

Step 3:   **Close** all open windows except the Home page.

> Open Windows is a time-saving technique to use when completing your QuickBooks assignments.

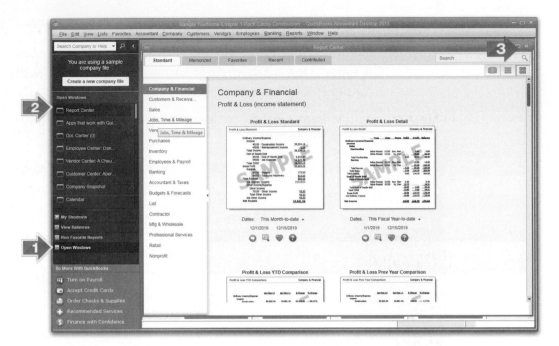

To save time when working in QuickBooks, you can organize and arrange My Shortcuts on the Icon bar to suit your specific QuickBooks needs.

QUICKBOOKS MENUS

You can also access tasks using the Menu bar across the top of the *QuickBooks* window.

Step 1: Click **File** on the Menu bar and the following drop-down menu will appear.

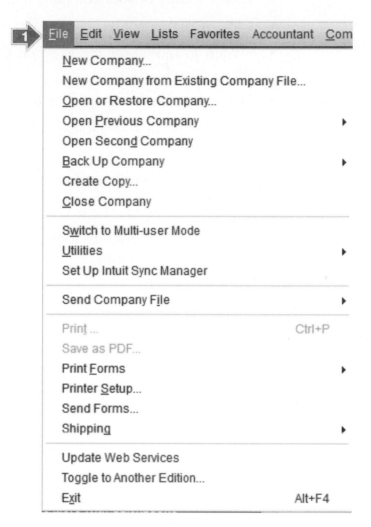

From the File drop-down menu, you can perform tasks including the following:

- Create a new company file.

- Create a new company from an existing company file.

- Open or restore an existing company file.

- Open a previous company file.

- Open a second company file, permitting you to have two QuickBooks company files open at the same time.

- Back up your company file.

- Create a copy of your company file.

- Close a company file.

- Switch to multi-user mode when QuickBooks is used on a network.

- Use utilities such as importing and exporting files.

- Send a copy of your QuickBooks company file to your accountant.

QuickBooks output tasks include:

- Print or save as a Portable Document Format (PDF) file.

- Print Forms for printing forms, such as invoices, sales receipts, and tax forms.

- Printer Setup to select a printer as well as fonts and margins.

- Send Forms to email various QuickBooks forms, such as sending invoices to customers.

- Ship using FedEx, UPS, and USPS.

In QuickBooks Accountant Edition, the File menu displays Toggle to Another Edition. This command allows you to switch to another QuickBooks edition, such as QuickBooks Pro.

To remove the File drop-down menu from the screen, click anywhere outside the drop-down menu or press the **Esc** (Escape) key.

Step 2: Click **Edit** on the Menu bar and the following drop-down menu appears:

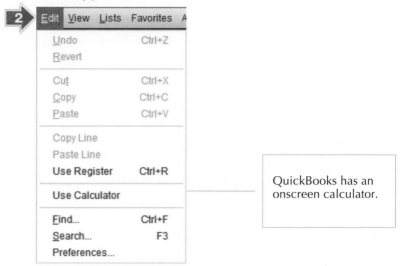

QuickBooks has an onscreen calculator.

From the Edit drop-down menu, you can undo, cut, copy, paste, and edit information entered in QuickBooks.

The Edit menu changes based upon which windows are open. For example:

- Click the **Home** icon to display the Home page, then click the **Purchase Orders** icon in the *Vendors* section to display the purchase order form.

Step 3: Click **Edit** menu. Now the Edit menu will appear as follows:

The Edit menu now contains: New Purchase Order, Duplicate Purchase Order, Memorize Purchase Order, and Change Account Color.

Step 4: Click **Lists** on the Menu bar to display the following drop-down menu.

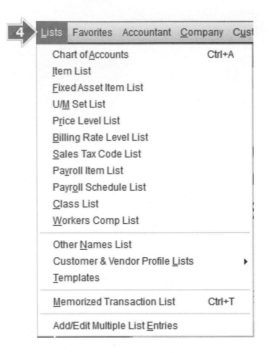

From the Lists drop-down menu, you can access various lists of information.

- **Chart of Accounts**. A list of accounts used to record transactions.

- **Item List**. A list of inventory items that you buy and sell or a list of services provided to customers.

- **Payroll Item List**. A list of items related to payroll checks and company payroll expense such as salary, hourly wages, federal and state withholding, unemployment taxes, Medicare, and Social Security.

- **Templates**. A list of templates for business forms, such as invoices and purchase orders.

- **Memorized Transaction List**. A list of recurring transactions that are memorized or saved. For example, if your company pays $900 in rent each month, then the rent payment transaction can be memorized to eliminate the need to reenter it each month.

Step 5: Click **Accountant** on the Menu bar to display the drop-own menu.

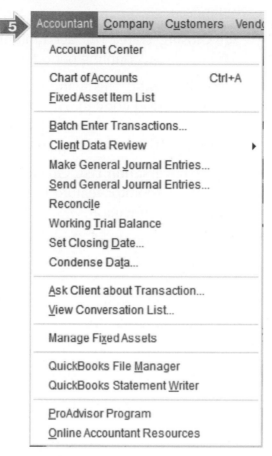

From the Accountant drop-down menu, you can access features accountants use for client services.

- **Accountant Center**. A central location to organize accountant tools in QuickBooks.

- **Chart of Accounts**. A list of accounts used to record transactions.

- **Client Data Review**. This tool streamlines client file cleanup tasks.

- **Make General Journal Entries**. An onscreen journal for the accountant to make correcting and adjusting entries.

- **Reconcile**. The accountant can reconcile client bank statements.

- **Working Trial Balance.** The accountant can use this to review beginning balances, adjustments, and ending balances.

- **Set Closing Date.** The accountant can set the closing date for the accounting period.

- **Condense Data.** This feature permits the accountant to create a period copy of a client's QuickBooks files. For example, an accountant might create a period copy of a client's 2015 accounting year to provide to the IRS.

- **View Conversation List.** QuickBooks 2015 introduces a Client Collaborator feature to facilitate accountant and client communication.

- **Online Accountant Resources.** QuickBooks offers desktop and online accounting solutions. See Section 3 of this text for more information about QuickBooks Online Accountant.

Step 6: Click **Company** on the Menu bar to display the drop-down menu.

From the Company menu, you can:

- Access company information and, for example, change the company name.

- Set up users and restrict access to certain parts of QuickBooks.

- Change your password.

- Set up budgets and use planning decision tools.

- Create a To Do List and Reminders.

- Access the Chart of Accounts and onscreen Journal.

- Enter vehicle mileage.

- Set up mobile access to access your QuickBooks data online on your mobile device.

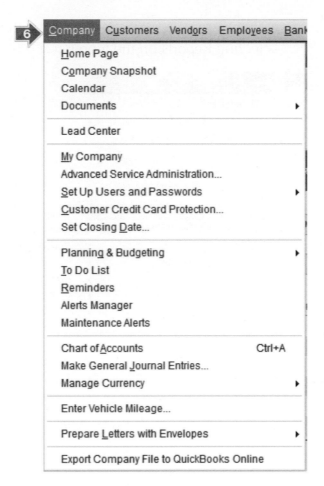

Step 7: The next four items on the Menu bar display drop-down menus listing various activities related to the four major types of transactions for a company:

- Customer

- Vendor

- Employee

- Banking

Some of the frequently used activities on these drop-down menus can also be accessed from the Home page.

Step 8: Click **Reports** on the Menu bar to display the list of reports that QuickBooks can create for your company. These reports can also be accessed from the Report Center by selecting Reports on the Icon bar.

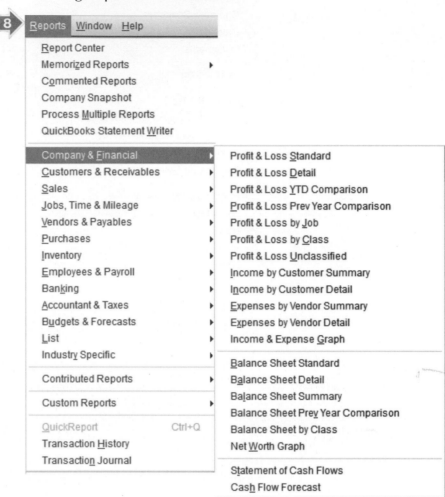

Step 9: Click **Window** on the Menu bar to display the drop-down menu. From this menu you can switch between windows to display onscreen.

Step 10: If not already selected, select **Create Purchase Orders** from the drop-down menu.

Step 11: **Close** the *Create Purchase Orders* window by clicking the ☒ in the upper right corner of the *Create Purchase Orders* window.

QUICKBOOKS REPORTS

Preparing reports is an important aspect of an accountant's role. QuickBooks offers many different types of reports that can be customized to meet business needs. To prepare a QuickBooks trial balance report for Rock Castle Construction:

Step 1: To view the Report Center, select **Reports** in the *My Shortcuts* section of the Icon bar.

Step 2: Select **Accountant & Taxes** from the report categories on the left of the window.

Step 3: Select **Carousel View**.

Step 4: Select **Trial Balance** report.

Step 5: Select the date range: **11/01/2019** To **11/30/2019**.

Step 6: Select **Run** icon.

 Total Debits equal $1,061,566.46.

Step 7: Prepare the Go Digital **Excel Reports Template** for Chapter 1 as follows:

To keep your Desktop neat, consider adding a Folder to your Desktop: *QB Excel Reports Templates.* Then download the Excel Reports Templates to that folder.

- Go to **www.My-QuickBooks.com**.

- Select the **QB2015** link.

- **Download** the Go Digital **Excel Reports Template** for **Chapter 1** to your Desktop.

- **Open** the Excel workbook.

- Select **File > Save As**.

- Enter file name: **YourLastName FirstName CH1 REPORTS**

- The filename extension should be: **.xls** or **.xlsx**

- **Close** the Excel workbook.

Step 8: To export the Trial Balance from the QuickBooks software, with the Trial Balance report displayed on your screen, select **Excel.**

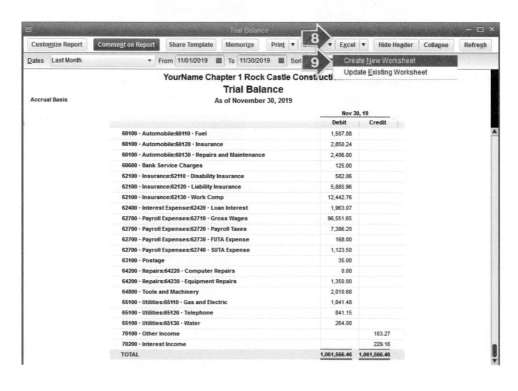

Step 9: Select **Create New Worksheet**.

Step 10: When the following *Send Report to Excel* window appears, select **Replace an existing worksheet**.

Step 11: Click the **Browse** button and select your **CH1 REPORTS** Excel file**.**

Step 12: From the drop-down list, select the sheet: **CH1 TB**.

Step 13: Click the **Advanced** button.

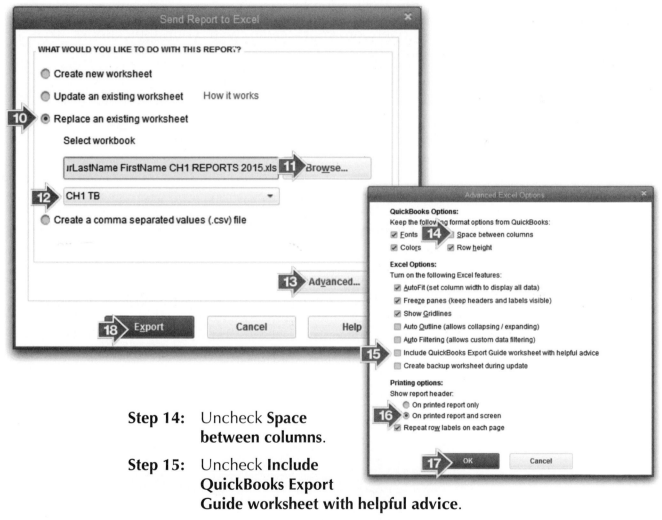

Step 14: Uncheck **Space between columns**.

Step 15: Uncheck **Include QuickBooks Export Guide worksheet with helpful advice**.

Step 16: Select **On printed report and screen**.

Step 17: Click **OK**.

Step 18: Click **Export**.

Step 19: When the following *Export Report Alert* window appears, select **Do not display this message in the future**.

Step 20: Select **Yes**.

Excel should open on your screen with your QuickBooks Trial Balance inserted.

Step 1: Select the **1 REPORTS** sheet tab.

With some Excel versions, you may be asked to close the workbook before you can insert another report.

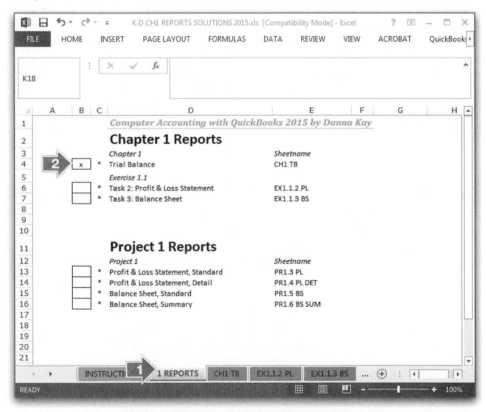

Step 2: Mark the report sheet you completed by inserting an "**x**".

Step 3: Save your **CH1 REPORTS** Excel workbook using the filename: **YourLastName FirstName CH1 REPORTS**.

Step 4: (Optional) If you would like to print the Trial Balance report, with the Trial Balance displayed on your QuickBooks screen, select **Print** to print the report.

Step 5: Click the ☒ in the upper right corner of the *Trial Balance* window to close this report. If asked if you would like to memorize the report, click **No**.

QUICKBOOKS HELP MENU

QuickBooks has several Help features to assist you in using QuickBooks software.

Step 1: Click **Help** on the Menu bar to display the drop-down menu of Help features.

+
See **Correcting Errors** in *Appendix C: QuickBooks Issue Resolution* for information about fixing errors.

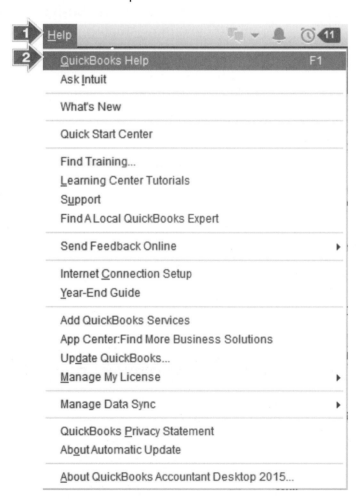

Help features of QuickBooks include:

- **QuickBooks Help** with search, relevant topics, and online forum

- **Ask Intuit** contains online support for Intuit, Community, and IRS results to your questions

- **Quick Start Center** with videos about using QuickBooks

- **Learning Center Tutorials** offer tutorials to learn QuickBooks

- **Support** links to online QuickBooks support and resource centers

- **Year-End Guide** offers assistance in closing the accounting period

- **App Center: Find More Business Solutions** links to a website containing small business software applications

- **Register QuickBooks** permits you to register your QuickBooks software

Step 2: Select **QuickBooks Help** from the Help menu, and the following *Have a Question?* window will appear.

At the top of the window, you can type in your question. Results can be viewed as:

- **Answers in Help**. Links to relevant help topics appear in this section.

- **Answers from Community**. This acclaimed QuickBooks online forum permits QuickBooks users to share questions and answers to QuickBooks questions.

- **Still need help?** This option includes Ask our community of experts where you can post your question to QuickBooks' live community of experts and superusers.

Next, you will use QuickBooks Search to search for information about exporting QuickBooks reports to Excel software.

Step 3: In the *Search* field, type: **export to Excel**.

Step 4: Click the **search** icon.

Step 5: Select **Export a report to Excel**.

!
Ask your instructor if you should Go Digital or use paper printouts. See Appendix D for more information about going digital.

Step 6: Read about how to export QuickBooks reports to Excel. To print the Help information, click the **Print** icon, then select your printer and click **Print**.

SAVE COMPANY FILES

Two types of QuickBooks files you will use are:

1. **.QBW file.** The QuickBooks <u>w</u>orking file in which you can enter accounting data and transactions.

2. **.QBB file.** The QuickBooks <u>b</u>ackup file used to move a QuickBooks file to another computer or if the working file (.QBW) fails. The data files provided for you with this text are .QBB files. Because .QBB files are compressed, the .QBB file must be restored (unzipped) using QuickBooks software. *Unlike Excel files, for example, .QBB files cannot be opened by clicking on the file.*

The .QBW file is the only QuickBooks file in which you can enter data and transactions. When you enter transactions into a .QBW file, the information is automatically saved. The typical workflow for a business is to use the .QBW file to record transactions and periodically back up to a .QBB (backup) file.

> .QBM files, QuickBooks movable files, also called a portable file, can be used to email or move a company file to another computer.

A sound disaster recovery plan includes a backup system. For example, a good backup system is to have a different backup for each business day: Monday backup, Tuesday backup, Wednesday backup, and so on. Then if it is necessary to use the backup file and the Wednesday backup, for example, fails, the company has a Tuesday backup to use. Furthermore, it is recommended that a business store at least one backup at a remote location.

> Two types of QuickBooks files used by accountants are:
> 1. Accountant's Copy Transfer File (.QBX)
> 2. Accountant's Copy Working File (.QBA)

Typically, the backup file is used only if the company's working file (.QBW) fails. Then the backup file (.QBB) can be restored and used. So it is important that the backup copy is as up to date as possible in case it must be used to replace lost company data. The backup file (.QBB) is compressed and must be restored to a working file (.QBW) before you can use it to enter data or transactions.

For your backup schedule, you will save a .QBB file at the end of each chapter, exercise, project, or case.

To complete your *Computer Accounting with QuickBooks* assignments, you can use *one* of the following two approaches:

If you have questions about which approach to use, check with your instructor.

1. **Workflow Approach.** Saves you time if you are using the same computer.

2. **Restart & Restore Approach.** Required if you are switching computers.

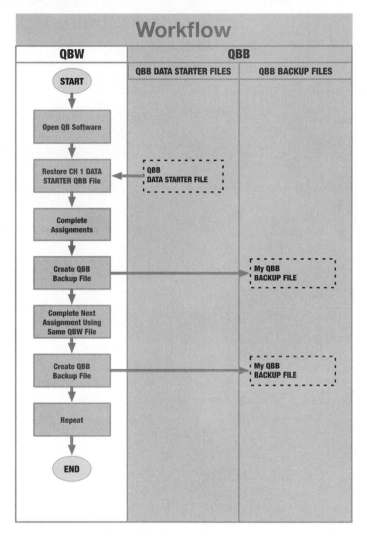

WORKFLOW APPROACH

Use the Workflow approach if you will be using the same computer to complete your QuickBooks assignments. Just as in a business workflow, since you are using the same computer, you can continue to use the same .QBW file. You will make backups at the end of each chapter and exercise. You will only use the backup if your .QBW file fails you.

 Look for this Workflow icon for instructions for this approach.

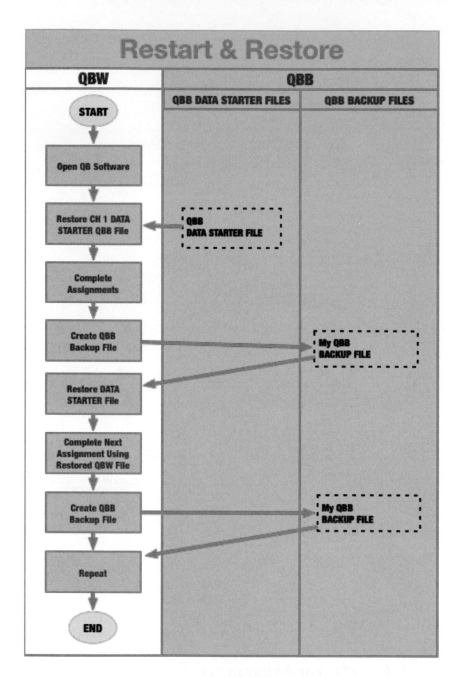

RESTART & RESTORE APPROACH

Use the Restart & Restore approach if you will be moving between campus and home computers. When you finish your QuickBooks work session, you will back up to a .QBB file in order to move the QuickBooks file to another computer.

When you restart your work session on another computer, you will restore the backup (.QBB) file.

There are actually two ways you can do this:

- Restore your own .QBB file. The advantage to using your own file is that your name is already included in the company name.

- Restore the .QBB data file that comes with the Computer Accounting *with QuickBooks* text (available on CD or download from the Online Learning Center). There is a .QBB data file for each chapter except chapters 8, 10, and 13. The advantage to using the data file provided with your text is that you avoid carrying forward any errors in your company file.

Look for this Restart & Restore icon for instructions for this approach.

QuickBooks Backup (.QBB) Files

Look for this Backup icon to remind you to back up your QuickBooks file.

To save a backup (.QBB) file:

Step 1: With your QuickBooks file (*.QBW) open, click **File**.

Step 2: Select **Back Up Company**.

Step 3: Select **Create Local Backup**.

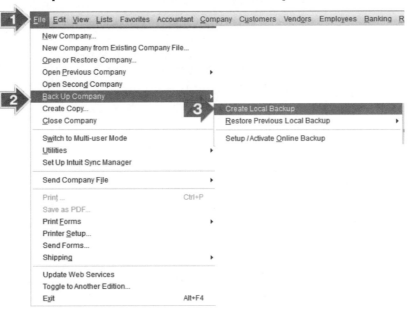

Step 4: When the following window appears, select **Local backup**.

Step 5: Select **Next**.

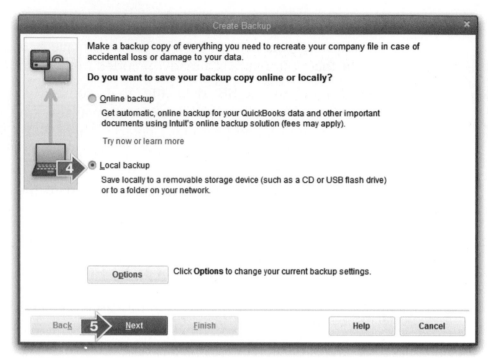

+

Instructions for backing up QuickBooks files are also contained in *Appendix B: Back Up & Restore QuickBooks Files.*

You can schedule a backup at regular intervals or every time you close a QuickBooks company file.

Step 6: If the following *Backup Options* window appears, to make it easier to find your backup files, click the **Browse** button.

Step 7: Select **Desktop**.

Step 8: Click **OK** to close the *Browse for Folder* window. Click **OK** again to close the *Backup Options* window.

+

Create a **QBB Backup Folder** on your Desktop. Then save your QBB files to that Desktop folder.

Backup files can also be saved using QuickBooks Online Backup service.

Step 9: Select **Use this Location** if a *QuickBooks* warning window appears.

Step 10:   Select **Save it now**.

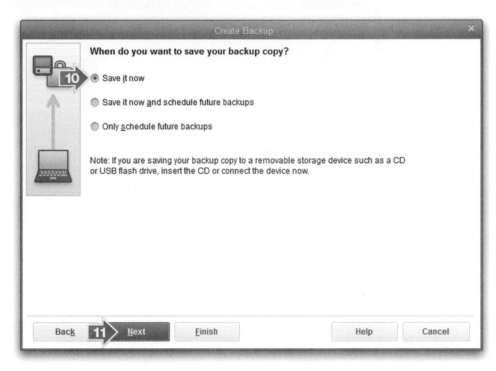

Step 11:   Select **Next**.

Step 12:   When the following *Save Backup Copy* window appears, the *Save in* field should automatically show: **Desktop**.

Step 13:   Update the *File name* field as shown to: **YourName Chapter 1 (Backup)**. Depending on your operating system settings, the file extension .QBB may appear automatically. If the .QBB extension does not appear, ***do not type it.***

Step 14:   The *Save as type* field should automatically appear as **QBW Backup (*.QBB).**

Step 15:   Click **Save**.

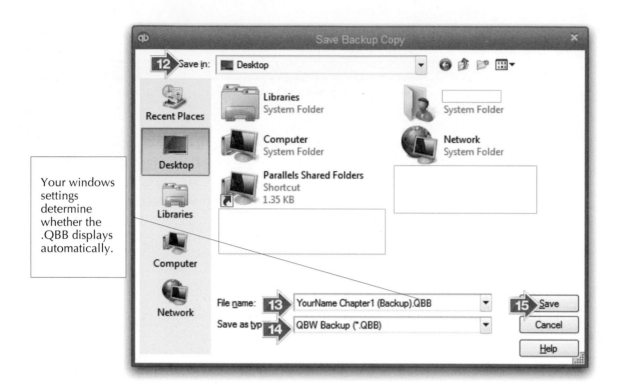

Your windows settings determine whether the .QBB displays automatically.

Step 16: When the following message appears, click **OK**.

 If you are using the workflow approach, leave your .QBW file open and proceed directly to Exercise 1.1.

 If you are using the Restart & Restore approach and are ending your computer session now, use the following directions to close the company file and exit QuickBooks. When you restart, you will restore your backup file to complete Exercise 1.1.

CLOSE COMPANY

To close a QuickBooks company file:

Step 1:   From the Menu bar, select **File**.

Step 2:   Click **Close Company**.

If the company file is left open when you exit QuickBooks, the next time anyone uses the QuickBooks software, the company file might still be open, permitting access to your company accounting records.

EXIT QUICKBOOKS

To exit QuickBooks, click the ⊠ in the upper right corner of the *QuickBooks* window, *or* click **File** menu **> Exit**.

WWW.MY-QUICKBOOKS.COM

Go to www.My-QuickBooks.com to view additional QuickBooks resources including Excel Reports Templates, QuickBooks videos, and QuickBooks Hot Arrows and Hot Topics. The Hot Topics can be viewed on your computer or tablet and feature frequently used QuickBooks tasks. Bookmark www.My-QuickBooks.com for your future use.

MULTIPLE-CHOICE PRACTICE TEST

A **Multiple-Choice Practice Test** for Chapter 1 is on the *Computer Accounting with QuickBooks* Online Learning Center at www.mhhe.com/kay2015. Try the Practice Test and see how many questions you answer correctly.

EXTRAS!

Section 3: Quick Guide contains quick, easy step-by-step directions for frequently used QuickBooks tasks, including correcting errors. You can find *Quick Guide* at the back of your text

Quick Check is a list of the reports and documents that you are to deliver to your instructor for grading. You can find the Chapter 1 Quick Check at the end of the chapter or online at www.mhhe.com/kay2015. Staying organized saves time. Use the checklist to organize your reports, checking off the reports as completed. Then include the checklist with your reports for grading.

Go Digital using Excel templates. Download Excel templates at www.My-QuickBooks.com. See *Appendix D: Go Digital with QuickBooks* for instructions about how to save your QuickBooks reports in Excel or your QuickBooks documents in PDF. Check with your instructor to see if you should go digital.

LEARNING ACTIVITIES

Important: Ask your instructor whether you should Go Digital to complete the following assignments (see Appendix D: Go Digital with QuickBooks) or print.

EXERCISE 1.1: PRINT FINANCIAL STATEMENTS

SCENARIO

> **+**
> See *Section 3: Quick Guide* for step-by-step directions.

While working at your computer, you notice Mr. Castle heading toward you. Adding another stack of papers to your overflowing inbox, he says, *"I need a profit & loss statement and a balance sheet for November as soon as possible. I haven't seen any financial statements since our former accountant left."*

As he walks away, Mr. Castle calls over his shoulder, *"From now on I'd like a P&L and balance sheet by the first of each month."*

TASK 1: OPEN COMPANY FILE

WORKFLOW

If you will be using the same computer and the same Chapter 1.QBW file, you can use the Workflow approach.

- If your Chapter 1.QBW file is not already open, open it by selecting **File > Open Previous Company**. Select your **Chapter 1 .QBW file.** If a *QuickBooks Information* window appears with a message about the sample company file, click **OK**.

- Add **YourName Exercise 1.1** to the company name by selecting **Company** menu **> My Company**.

RESTART & RESTORE

If you are not using the same computer that you used in Chapter 1, you must use the Restart and Restore approach.

- Restore your **Chapter 1 Backup.QBB** file using the directions in *Appendix B: Back Up & Restore QuickBooks Files.*

- After restoring the file, add **YourName Exercise 1.1** to the company name by selecting **Company** menu **> My Company**. If a *QuickBooks Information* window appears with a message about the sample company file, click **OK**.

> The company name appears on reports and can differ from the file name. See **Quick Guide** for additional instructions for changing the company name.

TASK 2: PRINT PROFIT & LOSS STATEMENT

The Profit & Loss Statement (also called the Income Statement) lists income earned and expenses incurred to generate income. Summarizing the amount of profit or loss a company has earned, the Profit & Loss Statement is one of the primary financial statements given to bankers and investors.

Prepare the Profit & Loss Statement for Rock Castle Construction by completing the following steps:

Step 1: Click **Reports** in the Icon bar.

Step 2: Select type of report: **Company & Financial**.

Step 3: Select report: **Profit & Loss Standard**.

Step 4: Select the date range: **Last Month**. The *Dates* field will now be: **11/01/2019** To **11/30/2019**. Select the **Run** icon.

+

See *Appendix D: Go Digital with QuickBooks* for instructions.

Step 5: Export the report to **Excel** using the Go Digital Excel Reports template or **print** the report as follows:

- Click the **Print** button at the top of the *Profit & Loss* window. Select **Report**.

- Select **Portrait** orientation.

- Select **Fit report to 1 page(s) wide**.

- Click **Print** to print the Profit & Loss Statement.

Step 6: Click the ☒ in the upper right corner of the *Profit & Loss* window to close the window.

 Net income is $16,507.99.

Step 7: **Highlight** the single largest income item appearing on the Profit & Loss Statement for the month of November.

Step 8: **Highlight** the single largest expense item appearing on the Profit & Loss Statement for the month of November.

TASK 3: PRINT BALANCE SHEET

The Balance Sheet is the financial statement that summarizes the financial position of a business. Listing assets, liabilities, and equity, the Balance Sheet reveals what a company owns and what it owes.

To prepare the Balance Sheet for Rock Castle Construction at November 30, 2019, complete the following steps:

Step 1: From the *Report Center* window, select type of report: **Company & Financial**.

Step 2: Select report: **Balance Sheet Standard**.

Step 3: Select date range: **Last Month** with *Dates* field From **11/01/2019** To **11/30/2019**. Select the **Run** icon.

Step 4: Export the Balance Sheet to **Excel** using the Go Digital Excel Reports template or **print** the Balance Sheet.

Step 5: Click the ☒ in the upper right corner of the *Balance Sheet* window to close the window.

  Total Assets equal $652,098.45.

Step 6: **Highlight** the single largest asset listed on Rock Castle Construction's November 30, 2019 Balance Sheet.

 ## TASK 4: SAVE EXERCISE 1.1 FILE

Save a backup of your Exercise 1.1 file. Use the file name: **YourName Exercise 1.1 Backup.QBB**. See *Appendix B: Back Up & Restore QuickBooks Files* for instructions.

Leave your QuickBooks .QBW file open if you are completing Exercise 1.2 now.

 ## WORKFLOW

If you are proceeding to Chapter 2 and using the same computer, you can leave your .QBW file open and use it for Chapter 2.

 ## RESTART & RESTORE

If you are stopping your QuickBooks work session and changing computers, you will need to restore your .QBB file when you restart.

EXERCISE 1.2: QUICKBOOKS HELP

In this exercise, you will use QuickBooks Help to obtain additional information about using QuickBooks.

Step 1: Use QuickBooks Help to search for an answer to the question: **When do I use a backup vs. a portable company file?**

Step 2: **Print** the information you find.

Step 3: **Circle** or **highlight** the information on the printout about differences between backup files and portable files.

EXERCISE 1.3: QUICKBOOKS HELP

In this exercise, you will use QuickBooks Help to obtain additional information about using QuickBooks.

Step 1: Use QuickBooks Help to search for information about a QuickBooks feature of your choice.

Step 2: **Print** the information.

Step 3: **Circle** or **highlight** the information on the printout that you find the most useful.

EXERCISE 1.4: WEB QUEST

Intuit Marketplace offers a variety of apps that work with QuickBooks data. To explore some of these apps, complete the following steps.

Step 1: Go to the website: apps.intuit.com.

Step 2: On the Intuit Apps website, what apps do you find the most useful? Print information about the app you would rate the highest.

Due to Web page updates, websites in the Web Quests are subject to change.

CHAPTER 1 QUICK CHECK
NAME:
INSTRUCTIONS:
1. CHECK OFF THE ITEMS YOU COMPLETED.
2. ATTACH THIS PAGE TO YOUR PRINTOUTS.

!
Ask your instructor if you should Go Digital (Excel* or PDF) or use paper printouts.

* Export these reports to CH1 REPORTS Excel template.

Items without * **cannot** be exported to Excel. Such items must be saved as PDF or printed. Ask your instructor.

NOTE TO INSTRUCTORS
* Identifies assignments exported to Excel that can be speedgraded using the QuickBooks QuickGrader.

CHAPTER 1
- [ ] * Trial Balance
- [ ] Export to Excel Help

EXERCISE 1.1
- [ ] * Task 2: Profit & Loss Statement
- [ ] * Task 3: Balance Sheet

EXERCISE 1.2
- [ ] Help Topic Printout

EXERCISE 1.3
- [ ] Your Choice Help Topic Printout

EXERCISE 1.4
- [ ] Intuit App Printout

 Download Go Digital Excel templates at www.My-QuickBooks.com.
* Export these reports to CH1 REPORTS template.

 # REFLECTION: A WISH AND A STAR

Reflection improves learning and retention. Reflect on what you have learned after completing Chapter 1.

A Star:

What did you like best that you learned about QuickBooks in Chapter 1?

A Wish:

If you could pick one thing, what do you wish you knew more about when using QuickBooks?

PROJECT 1 LARRY'S LANDSCAPING

SCENARIO

Larry's Landscaping just hired you as an accounting consultant to maintain its accounting records using QuickBooks financial software. The QuickBooks company file for Larry's Landscaping has already been created and transactions have been entered. Your assignment is to complete the following steps to export reports to Excel and then email them to the finance director at Larry's.

To complete this project, download the Go Digital Reports Excel template for Chapter 1 at www.My-QuickBooks.com. To ensure your success at going digital, carefully follow the instructions provided in the Excel template.

1. Restore the Project 1 data file (.QBB file) for Larry's Landscaping. Update the Company Name to: **YourName Project 1 Larry's Landscaping**.

2. Download the Go Digital Reports Excel template for Chapter 1. Save the Excel file using the file name: **YourLastName FirstName CH1 REPORTS**. (If you have already downloaded the Chapter 1 Reports Excel template for prior Chapter 1 assignments, you will use that template for this project assignment.)

3. Using the Chapter 1 Reports Excel template, export to **Excel** the Profit & Loss Standard for Larry's Landscaping for the last fiscal year, October 1, 2018 through September 30, 2019. **Highlight** the single largest income item. (*Important*: Remember to **uncheck** *Space between columns*, **uncheck** *Include QuickBooks Export Guide worksheet with helpful advice*, and **select** *Show report header: On printed report and screen*.)

4. Export to **Excel** the Profit & Loss Detail for Larry's Landscaping for the last fiscal year, October 1, 2018 through September 30, 2019. Which type of landscaping service produces more revenue for Larry's: Installation or Maintenance & Repairs? **Highlight** your answer.

5. Export to **Excel** the Balance Sheet Standard for Larry's Landscaping for the last fiscal year ending September 2019. **Highlight** the largest liability on the balance sheet.

6. Export to **Excel** the Balance Sheet Summary for Larry's Landscaping for the last fiscal year, ending September 2019. **Highlight** the largest asset.

7. Mark the reports completed on the 1 REPORTS sheet. Save your Excel file.

8. Save a .QBB backup of your work.

PROJECT 1 QUICK CHECK
NAME:
INSTRUCTIONS:
1. CHECK OFF THE ITEMS YOU COMPLETED.
2. ATTACH THIS PAGE TO YOUR PRINTOUTS.

!
Ask your instructor if you should Go Digital (Excel* or PDF) or use paper printouts.

NOTE TO INSTRUCTORS
* Identifies assignments that can be speedgraded using the QuickBooks QuickGrader.

PROJECT 1

☐ * Profit & Loss Statement, Standard
☐ * Profit & Loss Statement, Detail
☐ * Balance Sheet, Standard
☐ * Balance Sheet, Summary

Download Go Digital Excel templates at www.My-QuickBooks.com.

* Export these reports to CH1 REPORTS template.

NOTES:

CHAPTER 2
CUSTOMIZING QUICKBOOKS
AND THE CHART OF ACCOUNTS

SCENARIO

The next morning when you arrive at work, Mr. Castle is waiting for you, pacing in the aisle outside your cubicle.

He looks at you over the top of his glasses, his voice tense when he asks, *"Do you have the P&L and balance sheet ready?"*

"Yes sir!" you reply, handing him the financial statements.

You hit the *Send* button on your smartphone. *"And I'm sending you a link so you can also view the financials in a spreadsheet."*

The creases in Mr. Castle's brow disappear as his eyes run down the statements, murmuring to himself as he walks away, *"The banker waiting in my office should like this…."*

As he rounds the corner, he calls back to you, *"See your inbox for account changes we need to make. And password protect that QuickBooks file so every Tom, Dick, and Harry can't get into our accounting records!"*

Wondering who Tom, Dick, and Harry might be, you dive into learning how to password protect QuickBooks files.

CHAPTER 2
LEARNING OBJECTIVES

In Chapter 2, you will learn about the following QuickBooks features:

INTRODUCTION

> **!**
> Failure to register your QuickBooks trial version software will result in the software no longer functioning.

In Chapter 2, you will see how to customize QuickBooks to meet entrepreneurs' specific accounting needs. You will see how to customize a company's Chart of Accounts, a list of all the accounts used by a company to collect accounting information. In Chapter 2, you will learn how to restrict access to your QuickBooks accounting records using passwords to improve security and controls. Finally, you can customize a digital dashboard for your company using the QuickBooks feature, Company Snapshot.

Start QuickBooks by clicking on the **QuickBooks desktop icon** or click **Start > Programs > QuickBooks > QuickBooks Premier Accountant Edition 2015**.

WORKFLOW APPROACH

Use the Workflow approach if you are using the same computer and the same .QBW file from the prior chapter. Just as in a business, since you are using the same computer, you can continue to use the same .QBW file.

Step 1: If your .QBW file is not already open, open it by selecting **File > Open Previous Company**. Select your most recent **.QBW file.**

Step 2: Add **YourName Chapter 2** to the company name by selecting **Company** menu **> My Company**.

RESTART & RESTORE APPROACH

Use the Restart & Restore approach if you are moving your QuickBooks files between campus and home computers. When you restart your work session, first you will restore the backup (.QBB) file.

Step 1: Restore the **Backup.QBB** file using the directions in *Appendix B: Back Up & Restore QuickBooks Files*.

You can restore using one of two different .QBB files.

1. Restore your own .QBB file from the last exercise completed in the previous chapter. For example, in this case you would restore the backup file: [Your Name] Exercise 1.1 Backup.QBB. The advantage to using your

own file is that your name is already included in the company name.

2. Restore the Chapter 2 DATA STARTER.QBB file that comes with *Computer Accounting with QuickBooks* (available on CD or download from the Online Learning Center). The advantage to using the data file provided with your text is that you avoid carrying forward any errors in your company file.

Step 2: After restoring the .QBB file, add **YourName Chapter 2** to the company name by selecting **Company** menu **> My Company**.

CUSTOMIZE QUICKBOOKS

QuickBooks is an accounting system that permits a company to conveniently collect accounting information and store it in a single file. QuickBooks has streamlined the way that many entrepreneurs maintain accounting records. QuickBooks offers a number of ways to customize QuickBooks to meet entrepreneurs' specific accounting needs.

1. Customize with QuickBooks Editions

2. Customize QuickBooks using Preferences

3. Customize QuickBooks Favorites

4. Customize the QuickBooks Chart of Accounts

5. Customize security access for QuickBooks files

CUSTOMIZE WITH QUICKBOOKS EDITIONS

Intuit offers the following different editions of QuickBooks to meet specific business needs.

1. *QuickBooks Pro* is designed for small businesses that do not require industry-specific features.

2. *QuickBooks Premier* offers more advanced features than QuickBooks Pro and permits you to customize QuickBooks by selecting a version with industry-specific features. QuickBooks Premier has six industry versions from which you can choose.

- Contractor
- Manufacturing and Wholesale
- Nonprofit
- Professional Services
- Retailers
- General Business

3. *QuickBooks Accountant* is designed for accounting firms that provide QuickBooks services to multiple clients. This QuickBooks edition lets you toggle between different versions of QuickBooks. (Select File menu > Toggle to Another Edition.) This permits the accountant to view whatever edition of QuickBooks the particular client uses.

4. *QuickBooks Enterprise Solutions* is designed for mid-size companies that have outgrown QuickBooks Premier. QuickBooks Enterprise can be used to track inventory at multiple locations and consolidate reports from multiple companies.

5. *QuickBooks Online* provides accounting solutions in the cloud that can be accessed using the Internet and a browser. Currently, QuickBooks Online does not offer all the features of QuickBooks desktop accounting solutions.

6. *QuickBooks Online iPad App* syncs with QuickBooks Online and lets you stay mobile with your iPad and QuickBooks. To learn more, see Chapter 14, *QuickBooks Online Accountant*.

7. *QuickBooks Online Accountant* is designed for accounting firms that provide services to clients using QuickBooks Online. QuickBooks Online Accountant is accessed using the Internet and a browser and permits the accountant to collaborate with several different clients. See Chapter 14 to learn more about *QuickBooks Online Accountant*.

CUSTOMIZE QUICKBOOKS USING PREFERENCES

QuickBooks can be customized using QuickBooks preferences. To customize QuickBooks preferences:

Step 1: Select **Edit** menu.

+
To save you time, try the Open Window List. To view all open windows, select **Open Windows** on the Icon bar or from the Menu bar select **View > Open Window List**.

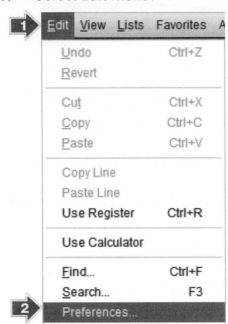

Step 2: Select **Preferences**.

Step 3: To customize the default date for new transactions, select **General** in the *Preferences* scrollbar window.

Step 4: Select **My Preferences** tab.

Step 5: Select Default Date to Use for New Transactions: **Use the last entered date as default**.

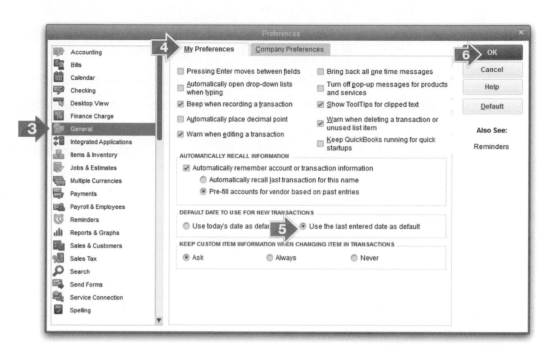

Step 6:   Click **OK** to close the *Preferences* window and save your changes.

As you can see from the *Preferences* window, there are many areas of QuickBooks that you can customize to meet the specific needs of your particular company. For example, QuickBooks now offers the ability to use multiple currencies as seen in the preceding *Preferences* scrollbar.

CUSTOMIZE QUICKBOOKS FAVORITES

QuickBooks 2015 offers a Favorites menu that you can customize with up to 30 of your favorite QuickBooks menu items.

To customize the Favorites menu:

Step 1:   Select **Favorites** menu.

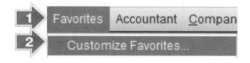

Step 2:   Select **Customize Favorites**.

Step 3: Select the item in the *Customize Your Menus* window. In this case, select **Chart of Accounts**.

Step 4: Click **Add**.

Step 5: Click **OK** to close the *Customize Your Menus* window.

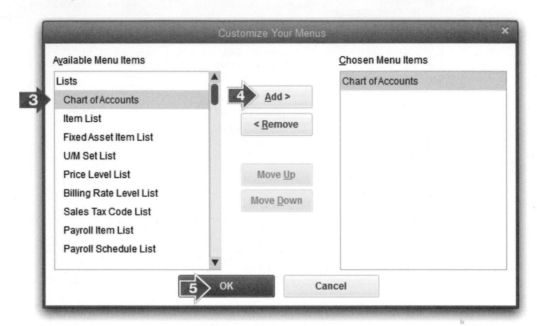

Next, you will learn about customizing the QuickBooks Chart of Accounts.

CHART OF ACCOUNTS

The Chart of Accounts is a list of accounts and account numbers. A company uses accounts to record transactions in the accounting system. Accounts (such as the Cash account or Inventory account) permit you to sort and track information.

QuickBooks will automatically create a Chart of Accounts when you set up a new company. Then you may customize the Chart of Accounts, adding and deleting accounts as necessary to suit your company's specific needs. QuickBooks also permits you to use subaccounts.

Accounts can be categorized into the following groups:

**Balance Sheet
Accounts**

Assets

Liabilities

Equity

**Profit & Loss
Accounts**

Income (Revenue)

Expenses

Non-Posting Accounts

Purchase Orders

Estimates

BALANCE SHEET ACCOUNTS

The Balance Sheet is a financial statement that summarizes what a company owns and what it owes. Balance Sheet accounts are accounts that appear on the company's Balance Sheet.

Review the Balance Sheet you printed in Exercise 1.1 for Rock Castle Construction. Three types of accounts appear on the Balance Sheet:

1. Assets
2. Liabilities
3. Owners' (or Stockholders') Equity

> **ASSETS = LIABILITIES + OWNERS' EQUITY**

1. **Assets** are resources that a company owns. These resources are expected to have *future benefit*.

    Asset accounts include:

    - Cash.

    - Accounts receivable (amounts to be *received* from customers in the future).

    - Inventory.

    - Other current assets (assets likely to be converted to cash or consumed within one year).

    - Fixed assets (property used in the operations of the business, such as equipment, buildings, and land).

    - Intangible assets (such as copyrights, patents, trademarks, and franchises).

2. **Liabilities** are amounts a company owes to others. Liabilities are *obligations*. For example, if a company borrows $10,000 from the bank, the company has an obligation to repay the $10,000 to the bank. Thus, the $10,000 obligation is shown as a liability on the company's Balance Sheet.

    Liability accounts include:

    - Accounts payable (amounts that are owed and will be *paid* to suppliers in the future).

    - Sales taxes payable (sales tax owed and to be *paid* in the future).

    - Interest payable (interest owed and to be *paid* in the future).

+
If you are unsure whether an account is an asset account, ask the question: *Does this item have future benefit?* If the answer is yes, the item is probably an asset.

+
If you are unsure whether an account is a liability account, ask the question: *Is the company obligated to do something, such as pay a bill or provide a service?* If the answer is yes, the item is probably a liability.

> The difference between a note payable and a mortgage payable is that a mortgage payable has real estate as collateral.

- Other current liabilities (liabilities due within one year).

- Loan payable (also called notes payable).

- Mortgage payable.

- Other long-term liabilities (liabilities due after one year).

3. **Owners' equity** accounts (stockholders' equity for a corporation) represent the net worth of a business. Equity is calculated as assets (resources owned) minus liabilities (amounts owed).

   Different types of business ownership include:

   - Sole proprietorship (an unincorporated business with one owner).

   - Partnership (an unincorporated business with more than one owner).

   - Corporation (an incorporated business with one or more owners).

   Owners' equity is increased by:

   - Investments by owners. For a corporation, owners invest by buying stock.

   - Net profits retained in the business rather than distributed to owners.

   Owners' equity is decreased by:

   - Amounts paid to owners as a return for their investment. For a sole proprietorship or partnership, these are called withdrawals. For a corporation, they are called dividends.

> OWNERS' EQUITY = ASSETS - LIABILITIES

   - Losses incurred by the business.

The following QuickBooks Learning Center graphic shows the relationship of assets, liabilities, and owners' equity accounts.

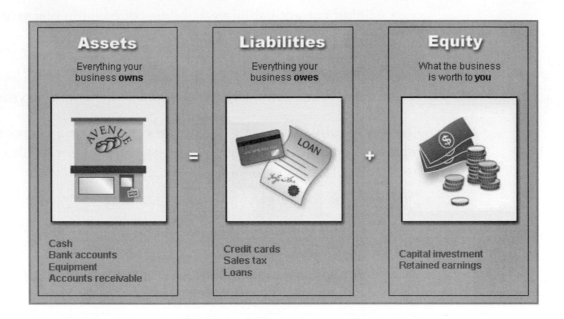

Balance Sheet accounts are referred to as *permanent accounts*. Balances in permanent accounts are carried forward from year to year. Thus, for a Balance Sheet account, such as Cash, the balance at December 31 is carried forward and becomes the opening balance on January 1 of the next year.

INCOME STATEMENT (PROFIT & LOSS) ACCOUNTS

The Income Statement (also called the Profit and Loss Statement or P&L Statement) reports the results of a company's operations, listing income and expenses for a period of time. Income Statement accounts are accounts that appear on a company's Income Statement.

Review the Income Statement you printed in Exercise 1.1 for Rock Castle Construction. QuickBooks uses two different Income Statement accounts:

1. Income accounts
2. Expense accounts

1. **Income** accounts record sales to customers and other revenues earned by the company. Revenues are the prices charged customers for goods and services provided.

Examples of Income accounts include:

- Sales or revenues.

- Fees earned.

- Interest income.

- Rental income.

- Gains on sale of assets.

2. **Expense** accounts record costs that have expired or been consumed in the process of generating income. Expenses are the costs of providing goods and services to customers.

Examples of Expense accounts include:

- Cost of goods sold expense.

- Salaries expense.

- Insurance expense.

- Rent expense.

- Interest expense.

> INCOME (OR REVENUE)
> - EXPENSES
> = NET INCOME

Net income is calculated as income (or revenue) less cost of goods sold and other expenses. Net income is an attempt to match or measure efforts (expenses) against accomplishments (revenues).

Income Statement accounts are called *temporary* accounts because they are used for only one year. At the end of each year, temporary accounts are closed (the balance reduced to zero).

For example, if an Income Statement account, such as Advertising Expense, had a $5,000 balance at December 31, the $5,000 balance would be closed or transferred to owners' equity at year-end. The opening balance on January 1 for the Advertising Expense account would be $0.00.

The following QuickBooks Learning Center graphic summarizes the five types of accounts in the Chart of Accounts.

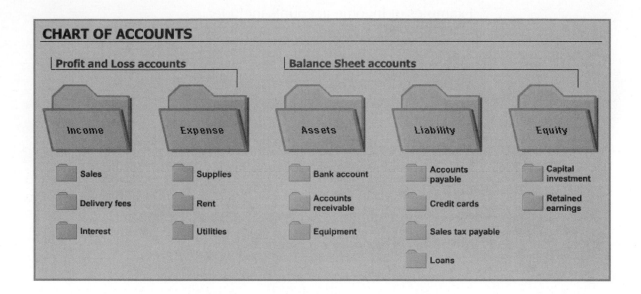

NON-POSTING ACCOUNTS

Non-posting accounts are accounts that do not appear on the Balance Sheet or Income Statement. However, these accounts are needed to track information necessary for the accounting system.

Examples of non-posting accounts include:

- Purchase orders: documents that track items that have been ordered from suppliers.

- Estimates: bids or proposals submitted to customers.

LISTS

QuickBooks uses lists to provide additional supporting detail for selected accounts.

QuickBooks lists include:

1. **Customer List.** Provides information about customers, such as customer name, customer number, address, and contact information.

2. **Vendor List.** Provides information about vendors, such as vendor name, vendor number, and contact information.

3. **Employee List.** Provides information about employees for payroll purposes including name, Social Security number, and address.

4. **Item List.** Provides information about the items or services sold to customers, such as hours worked and types of items.

5. **Payroll Item List.** Tracks detailed information about payroll, such as payroll taxes and payroll deductions. The Payroll Item List permits the use of a single or limited number of payroll accounts while more detailed information is tracked using the Item List for payroll.

6. **Class List.** Permits income to be tracked according to the specific source (class) of income. An example of a class might be a department, store location, business segment, or product line.

Lists are used so that information can be entered once in a list and then reused as needed. For example, information about a customer, such as address, can be entered in the Customer List. This customer information then automatically appears on the customer invoice.

CUSTOMIZE CHART OF ACCOUNTS

+

Obtain a copy of the tax form for your business at www.irs.gov. Then modify your Chart of Accounts to track the information needed for your tax return.

When you set up a new company, QuickBooks automatically creates a Chart of Accounts. Then you can customize the Chart of Accounts to suit your specific needs by adding, deleting, and editing accounts.

DISPLAY CHART OF ACCOUNTS

You can display the Chart of Accounts in three different ways:
1. From the Company menu
2. From the *Company Snapshot* window
3. From the *Company* section of the Home page

To view the Chart of Accounts for Rock Castle Construction from the Home page, complete the following steps:

Step 1: To display the *Chart of Accounts* window, click the **Chart of Accounts** icon in the *Company* section of the Home page.

Step 2: For each account, the account name, type of account, and the balance of the account are listed.

The **Account** button at the bottom of the window displays a drop-down menu for adding, editing, and deleting accounts. Or you can right-click in the *Chart of Accounts* window to display a pop-up menu to add and edit accounts.

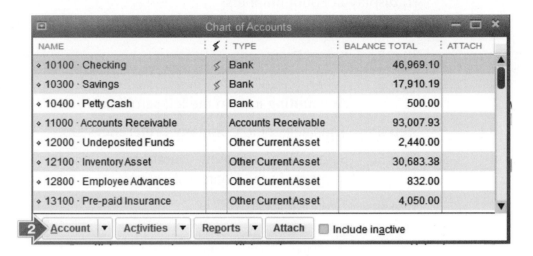

DISPLAY ACCOUNT NUMBERS

Account numbers are used to uniquely identify accounts. Usually account numbers are used as a coding system to also identify the account type. For example, a typical numbering system for accounts might be as follows.

Account type determines whether the account appears on the Balance Sheet or Income Statement.

Account Type	Account No.
Asset accounts	10000 – 19999
Liability accounts	20000 – 29999
Equity accounts	30000 – 39999
Revenue (income) accounts	40000 – 49999
Expense accounts	50000 – 59999

QuickBooks preferences will determine whether the account number is displayed in the Chart of Accounts. If account numbers are not displayed in Rock Castle Construction's Chart of Accounts, select the QuickBooks preference to view account numbers as follows.

To display account numbers:

Step 1: Select **Edit** menu.

Step 2: Select **Preferences**.

Step 3: When the following *Preferences* window appears, click the **Accounting** icon in the left scrollbar.

Step 4: Then select the **Company Preferences** tab.

Step 5: Select **Use account numbers** to display the account numbers in the Chart of Accounts.

Step 6: Then click **OK**.

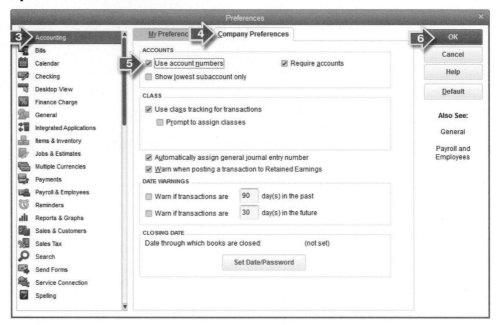

Step 7: If the Chart of Accounts does not appear on your screen, click **Window** menu **> Chart of Accounts**.

The Chart of Accounts should now list account numbers preceding the account name.

ADD NEW ACCOUNTS

You can customize the Chart of Accounts by adding, deleting, and editing accounts as needed to meet your company's specific and changing needs.

Rock Castle Construction has decided to begin advertising and would like to add an Advertising Expense account to the Chart of Accounts.

To add a new account to the Chart of Accounts:

Step 1: Click the **Account** button at the bottom of the *Chart of Accounts* window to display a drop-down menu.

Step 2: Select **New**.

Step 3: Select Account Type: **Expense**.

Step 4: Click **Continue**.

Step 5: In the *Add New Account* window, verify the Account Type: **Expense**.

Step 6: Enter the new Account Number: **60400**.

Step 7: Enter the Account Name: **Advertising Expense**.

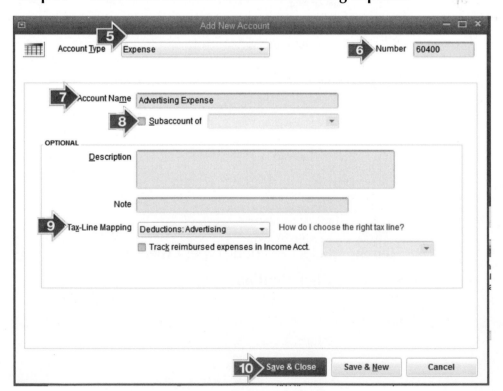

Selecting the appropriate Tax Line ensures that QuickBooks provides the information needed to complete your tax return.

Step 8: Leave Subaccount unchecked. Subaccounts are subcategories of an account. For example, Rock Castle Construction has an Automobile Expense account (Account No. 60100) with three Automobile Expense subaccounts:

- Fuel (Account No. 60110)
- Insurance (Account No. 60120)
- Repairs and Maintenance (Account No. 60130)

Step 9: Select Tax-Line Mapping: **Deductions: Advertising**. This indicates the Advertising Expense account balance will appear as a deduction on Rock Castle Construction's tax return.

Step 10: Click **Save & Close** to save the changes and close the *Add New Account* window.

Notice that Account 60400 Advertising Expense now appears on the Chart of Accounts.

If the new account had been a Balance Sheet account (an asset, liability, or equity account), QuickBooks would ask you for the opening account balance as of your QuickBooks start date. Since Advertising Expense is an Expense account that appears on the Income Statement and not the Balance Sheet, QuickBooks did not ask for the opening balance.

DELETE ACCOUNTS

Occasionally you may want to delete unused accounts from the Chart of Accounts. You can only delete accounts that are not being used. For example, if an account has been used to record a transaction and has a balance, it cannot be deleted. If an account has subaccounts associated with it, that account cannot be deleted.

Rock Castle Construction would like to delete an account it does not plan to use, the Printing and Reproduction Expense account.

To delete an account:

Step 1: Display the *Chart of Accounts* window.

Step 2: Select the account to delete. In this case, click **63300: Printing and Reproduction**.

Step 3:   Click the **Account** button at the bottom of the *Chart of Accounts* window.

Step 4:   Click **Delete Account**.

Step 5:   Click **OK** to confirm that you want to delete the account.

EDIT ACCOUNTS

Next, you will edit an account. Rock Castle Construction would like to change the name of the Advertising Expense account to Advertising & Promotion.

To change the name of the Advertising Expense account to Advertising & Promotion:

Select **View** menu > **Open Window List** to display all open windows. From the Open Window List, select the *Chart of Accounts* window.

Step 1:   From the *Chart of Accounts* window, select the account to edit: **60400 Advertising Expense**.

Step 2:   Click the **Account** button in the lower left corner of the *Chart of Accounts* window or **right-click** the mouse to display the pop-up menu.

Step 3:   From the pop-up menu, select **Edit Account** to open the *Edit Account* window.

Step 4:   Make changes to the account information. In this case, change Account Name to: **Advertising & Promotion**.

You cannot change the Account Type if there are subaccounts associated with the account.

Step 5:   Click **Save & Close** to save the changes. Advertising Expense should now appear as Advertising & Promotion in the *Chart of Accounts* window.

PRINT CHART OF ACCOUNTS

QuickBooks provides an Account Listing report that lists the Chart of Accounts plus the account balances.

To print the Account Listing report:

Step 1:   Display the *Chart of Accounts* window.

Step 2:   Select the **Account** button.

Step 3:   Select **Re-sort List**.

> You can also display the Account Listing report by selecting the **Reports** button > **Accounting Listing**.

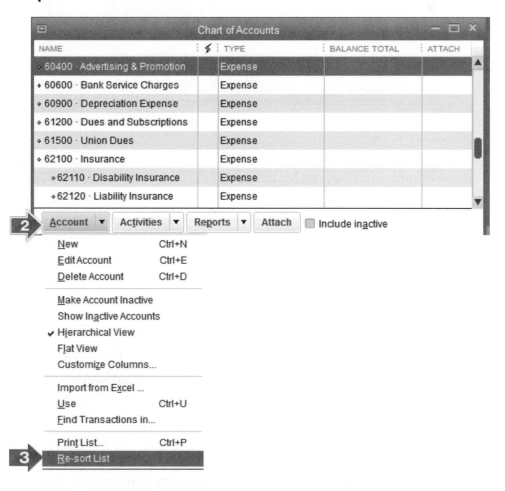

Step 4:   When the *Re-sort List?* Window appears, select **OK**.

Step 5: **Close** the *Chart of Accounts* window.

Step 6: To open the Report Center, select **Reports** in the *My Shortcuts* section of the Icon bar.

> Also see
> ***Appendix D: Go Digital with QuickBooks*** for instructions to export reports to Excel.

Step 7: Select **Accountants & Taxes > Account Listing**. Select date range: **12/15/2019**.

Step 8: To export the Account Listing report to Excel, at the top of the *Account Listing* window select **Excel**.

Step 9: Select **Create New Worksheet**

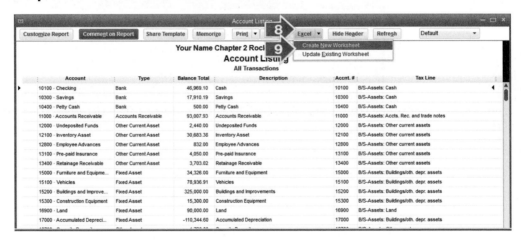

Step 10: When the following *Send Report to Excel* window appears, select **Replace an existing worksheet**.

Step 11: Browse for **YourLastName FirstName CH2 REPORTS Excel** file.

Step 12: From the drop-down list, select the sheet: **CH2 COA**.

Step 13: Select the **Advanced** button.

Step 14: Uncheck **Space between columns**.

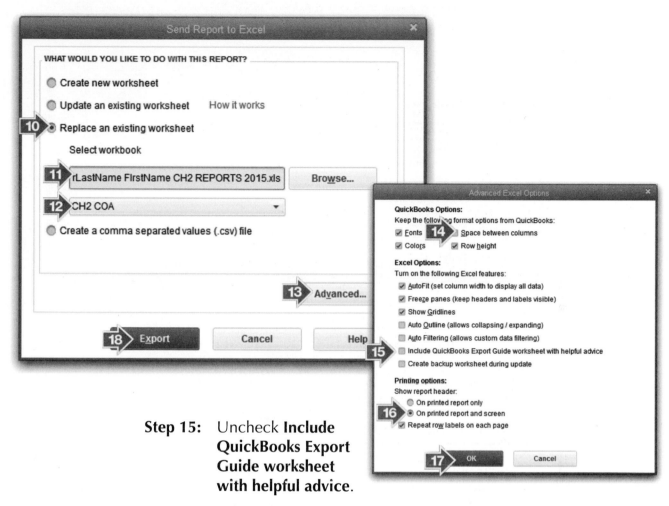

Step 15: Uncheck **Include QuickBooks Export Guide worksheet with helpful advice**.

Step 16: Select Show report header: **On printed report and screen**.

Step 17: Click **OK**.

Step 18: Click **Export**.

Step 19: If the *Export Report Alert* window appears, select **Do not display this message in the future**. Then select **Yes**.

Excel software should open on your screen with your QuickBooks report.

Step 1: Select the **2 REPORTS** sheet tab.

Step 2: Mark the report you have completed by inserting an "**X**".

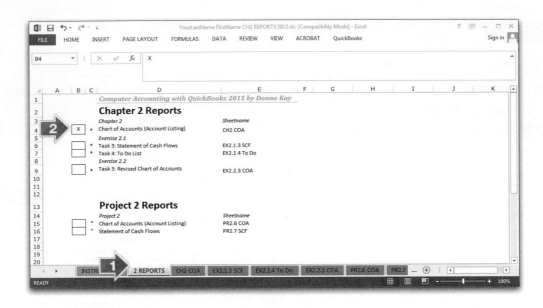

Step 3: **Save** your **CH2 REPORTS** Excel workbook using the filename: **YourLastName FirstName CH2 REPORTS**.

Step 4: **Close** the *Account Listing* window.

CUSTOMIZE QUICKBOOKS SECURITY

QuickBooks permits a company to conveniently collect accounting information and store it in a single file. Much of the accounting information stored in QuickBooks is confidential, however, and a company often wants to limit employee access.

Password protection can be used to customize and limit access to company data and improve security and control.

Two ways to restrict access to accounting information stored in a QuickBooks company data file are:

1. Password protect the company file so individuals must enter a user ID and password to open the company file.

2. Limit access to selected areas of the company's accounting data. For example, a user may access accounts receivable to view customer balances but not be able to access payroll or check writing.

Only the QuickBooks Administrator can add users with passwords and grant user access to selected areas of QuickBooks. The

QuickBooks Administrator is an individual who has access to all areas of QuickBooks.

To add a new user and password protection to your company file:

Step 1:   Select **Company** menu.

Step 2:   Select **Set Up Users and Passwords**.

Step 3:   Select **Set Up Users**.

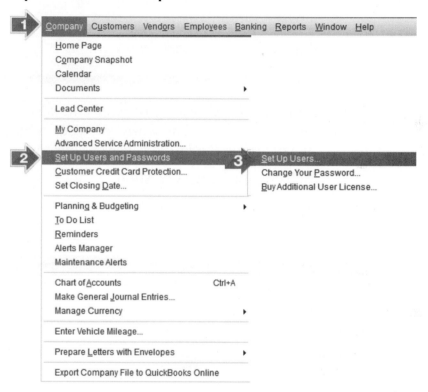

<table>
<tr><td>If Admin does not appear in the User List window, select Add User, then add Admin.</td></tr>
</table>

Step 4:   First, set up a QuickBooks Administrator who has access to all areas of QuickBooks. The Administrator can then add new users. To add the Administrator password, from the *User List* window, select **Admin**.

Step 5:   Select **Edit User**.

Step 6: On the *Change user password and access* window, enter and confirm a **Password** of your choice. ***Write the password on the inside cover of your text.***

Step 7: Select a **Challenge Question**.

Step 8: Enter your **Challenge Answer**.

Step 9: Click **Next**.

> **!**
> **Write your password on the inside of your book cover.**
> You will not be able to access your company file without your password.

Step 10: Click **Finish**.

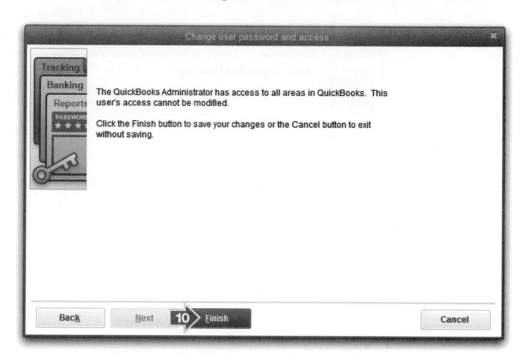

Step 11: Only the QuickBooks Administrator can add new users. To add another user, click **Add User**.

Step 12: In the following *Set up user password and access* window, enter **YourName** in the *User Name* field.

Step 13: At this point, if you were adding another employee as a user, you would ask the employee to enter and confirm his or her password. In this instance, enter and confirm a **password** of your choice. *Write the password on the inside cover of your book.*

Step 14: Click **Next**.

Step 15: In the following window, you can restrict user access to selected areas of QuickBooks or give the user access to all areas of QuickBooks. Select: **All areas of QuickBooks**.

Step 16: Click **Next**.

Step 17: Select **Yes** to confirm that you want to give access to all areas of QuickBooks.

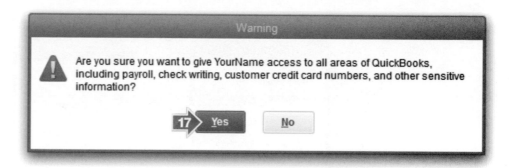

Step 18: The next window summarizes the user's access for each QuickBooks area, indicating access to create documents, print, and view reports. Click **Finish**.

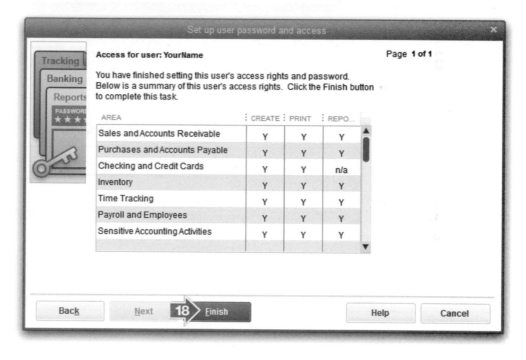

+
Notice User Access Rights are set by Areas: Create, Print, Reports

Step 19: If you receive a warning message about Intuit Sync Manager, click **OK**.

Step 20: Two names (Admin and YourName) should appear on the User List. Click **Close** to close the *User List* window.

!
If you use data files provided with the text for later chapters, use the Admin log in and Leave the password blank.

Now whenever you open the company file for Rock Castle Construction, you will be asked to enter your user name and password.

CUSTOMIZE QUICKBOOKS SNAPSHOTS

QuickBooks Snapshots gives you an overview of key information for your company and lets you perform key tasks.

Customize QuickBooks by using Snapshots to:

- Choose which accounts to view

- Track accounts receivable owed to you

- Receive payments

- Select which reminders to see

A vital aspect of maintaining an accounting system is tracking due dates for tax and vendor payments. In addition, billing and collections of customer payments must be scheduled in a timely manner to ensure adequate cash flows to operate the business. QuickBooks has four different features to assist in tracking tasks:

1. **Reminders.** Shows only those tasks that are currently due, including tasks from the To Do List.

2. **To Do List.** Tracks all tasks to be completed. You can add items to the To Do List, mark items complete, and print the list.

3. **Alerts Manager.** Lists tasks and due dates related to taxes and regulations. These alerts will appear as Reminders as they become due.

4. **Calendar.** The Calendar feature permits you to track tasks and due dates in a calendar format.

If you are responsible for maintaining an accounting system, you can view Reminders or the Calendar feature regularly to see what accounting tasks require your attention.

Next, you will learn how to customize Snapshots to display Reminders to assist you in tracking tasks.

Step 1: To open the *Company Snapshot* window, from the *My Shortcuts* section of the Icon bar, select **Snapshots**.

Snapshots summarizes:

- Account Balances
- Customers Who Owe Money
- Vendors to Pay
- Reminders

Step 2: To customize Snapshots, select **Add Content**.

Step 3: Add **Vendors to Pay**.

Step 4: Add **Reminders**.

Step 5: Select **Done**.

CUSTOMIZE QUICKBOOKS CALENDAR

The QuickBooks Calendar provides a user friendly way to track tasks and due dates.

Step 1: To open QuickBooks Calendar, from the Home page, select the **Calendar** icon in the *Company* section.

Step 2: In the *Calendar* window, select **December 15**. A list of transactions due and entered for the date selected appears below the calendar.

Step 3: You can customize your QuickBooks Calendar to suit your preferences. For example, at the top of the calendar is a Today button. Select the **Today** button to view just the current day.

Step 4: Also at the top of the calendar are three icons that permit you to view the calendar in a daily, weekly, or monthly format. Select the **Weekly** icon to view only one week. Then select the **Monthly** icon to return to the monthly calendar view.

Step 5: At the top of the calendar, you can also select which transactions to show. Select the drop-down list to view the different transactions that can be selected to show on your calendar. Select **All Transactions**.

To the right of the calendar is a list of red-flagged past due items, including any items on your To Do list.

Step 6: **Close** the QuickBooks Calendar.

In Chapter 2 you learned a few ways to customize QuickBooks to meet your specific needs. QuickBooks can be customized further using additional Preferences features.

SAVE CHAPTER 2

 Save a backup of your Chapter 2 file using the file name: **YourName Chapter 2 Backup.QBB**. See *Appendix B: Back Up & Restore QuickBooks Files* for instructions.

WORKFLOW

If you are using the Workflow approach, leave your .QBW file open and proceed directly to Exercise 2.1.

RESTART & RESTORE

If you are using the Restart & Restore approach and ending your computer session now, close your .QBW file and exit QuickBooks. When you restart, you will restore your backup file to complete Exercise 2.1.

WWW.MY-QUICKBOOKS.COM

Go to www.My-QuickBooks.com to view additional QuickBooks resources including Excel Reports Templates, QuickBooks videos, and QuickBooks Hot Arrows and Hot Topics. The Hot Topics can be viewed on your computer or tablet and feature frequently used QuickBooks tasks. Bookmark www.My-QuickBooks.com for your future use.

MULTIPLE-CHOICE PRACTICE TEST

A **Multiple-Choice Practice Test** for Chapter 2 is on the *Computer Accounting with QuickBooks* Online Learning Center at www.mhhe.com/kay2015. Try the Practice Test and see how many questions you answer correctly.

EXTRAS!

Section 3: Quick Guide contains quick, easy step-by-step directions for frequently used QuickBooks tasks, including correcting errors. You can find *Quick Guide* at the back of your text or online at www.mhhe.com/kay2015. *Check it out!*

Quick Check is a list of the reports and documents that you are to deliver to your instructor for grading. You can find the Chapter 2 Quick Check at the end of the chapter or online at www.mhhe.com/kay2015. Staying organized saves time. Use the checklist to organize your reports, checking off the reports as completed. Then include the checklist with your reports for grading.

Go Digital using Excel templates. See *Appendix D: Go Digital with QuickBooks* for instructions about how to save your QuickBooks reports electronically. Download Excel templates at www.My-QuickBooks.com. Check with your instructor to see if you should deliver your reports electronically.

LEARNING ACTIVITIES

Important: Ask your instructor whether you should complete the following assignments by printing reports or by exporting to Excel templates (see Appendix D: Go Digital with QuickBooks).

EXERCISE 2.1: TO DO LIST

SCENARIO

When you return to your cubicle after lunch, you find the following note stuck to your computer screen.

In addition to printing out the Statement of Cash Flows, you decide to add a task to your QuickBooks To Do List to remind you to print out the financial statements for Rock Castle each month.

TASK 1: OPEN COMPANY FILE

WORKFLOW

If you are using the Workflow approach, you will use the same .QBW file.

- If your QBW file is not already open, open it by selecting **File > Open Previous Company**. Select your **.QBW file.**

- Add **YourName Exercise 2.1** to the company name by selecting **Company** menu **> My Company**.

RESTART & RESTORE

If you are not using the same computer, you must use the Restart and Restore approach.

- Restore your **Chapter 2 Backup.QBB** file using the directions in *Appendix B: Back Up & Restore QuickBooks Files.*

- After restoring the file, add **YourName Exercise 2.1** to the company name (select **Company** menu **> My Company**).

TASK 2: ADD A TASK TO THE TO DO LIST

To help you keep track of the financial statements that Mr. Castle would like prepared each month, add a task to your To Do List that automatically appears in your QuickBooks Calendar and Snapshots Reminder when due. You will add the task for December and January.

To add a task to the To Do List, complete the following steps:

Step 1: Select the **Calendar** icon on the Home page to display the *Calendar* window.

Step 2: As shown in the following *Calendar* window, select **Add To Do**.

Step 3:   From the *Add To Do* window, select Type: **Task**

Step 4:   Priority: **High**

Step 5:   Due: **12/12/2019**

Step 6:   Time: **08:00 AM**

Step 7:   Details: **Print financial statements for Mr. Castle.**

Step 8:   Status: **Active**

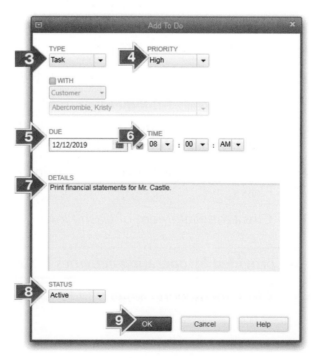

Step 9: Click **OK** to close the Add *To Do* window. Notice that under Past Due as of Today list, the To Do item you just added now appears as 3 days past due.

Step 10: Select **Add To Do** again and enter the January task: **Print financial statements for Mr. Castle**. Due: **01/01/2020 at 08:00 AM**.

Step 11: Click **OK** to save the task and close the window. Leave the *Calendar* window open.

TASK 3: PRINT STATEMENT OF CASH FLOWS

The Statement of Cash Flows summarizes a company's cash inflows and cash outflows. The cash flows are grouped by activity:

- Cash flows from operating activities. Cash flows related to the operations of the business—providing goods and services to customers.

- Cash flows from investing activities. Cash flows that result from investing (buying and selling) long-term assets, such as investments and property.

- Cash flows from financing activities. Cash flows that result from borrowing or repaying principal on debt or from transactions with owners.

See *Appendix D: Go Digital with QuickBooks* for instructions to export reports to Excel.

Print the Statement of Cash Flows for Rock Castle Construction by completing the following steps:

Step 1: Click **Reports** in the Icon bar.

Step 2: Select type of report: **Company & Financial**.

Step 3: Select report: **Statement of Cash Flows**. Select the date range: **Last Month**. The dates should now be: **11/01/2019** and **11/30/2019**. Select **Run**.

Step 4: **Export** the report to Excel or **print** the Statement of Cash Flows.

Step 5: **Close** the *Statement of Cash Flows* window.

✓ | *Net cash provided by operating activities is $25,016.93.*

Step 6: **Close** the *Report Center* window.

Step 7: **Highlight** the net change in cash for the period on the Statement of Cash Flows printout.

TASK 4: MARK TASK COMPLETE

Mark the task to print November financial statements completed as follows:

Step 1: From the *Calendar* window, double-click on the past due task: Print financial statements for Mr. Castle.

Step 2: When the *Edit To Do* window appears, change the Status from Active to **Done**.

Step 3: Click **OK**.

Step 4: Export the To Do List to Excel as follows:

- Click **Reports** in the Icon bar.

- Select type of report: **List**

- Select report: **To Do Notes**

- Select Dates: **Today 12/15/2019**

- Select **Run**.

- Export to your **CH2 REPORTS** Excel workbook.

Step 5: **Highlight** the task you completed.

TASK 5: SAVE EXERCISE 2.1

Save a backup of your Exercise 2.1 file using the file name: **YourName Exercise 2.1 Backup.QBB**. See *Appendix B: Back Up & Restore QuickBooks Files* for instructions.

WORKFLOW

If you are proceeding to Exercise 2.2 and using the same computer, you can leave your .QBW file open and use it for Exercise 2.2.

RESTART & RESTORE

If you are stopping your QuickBooks work session and changing computers, you will need to restore your .QBB file when you restart.

EXERCISE 2.2: EDIT CHART OF ACCOUNTS

SCENARIO

When you return to your cubicle after your afternoon break, another note is stuck to your computer screen.

Beginning January 1, I want a report listing advertising costs and promotion costs separately so we can track effectiveness.

RC

In order to track advertising costs separately from promotion costs, you decide to make the following changes to the Chart of Accounts.

1. Rename Account 60400 Advertising & Promotion account to: Selling Expense.

2. Add two subaccounts: 60410 Advertising Expense and 60420 Promotion Expense.

After these changes, the Chart of Accounts should list the following accounts:

*   Account 60400: Selling Expense
*   Subaccount 60410: Advertising Expense
*   Subaccount 60420: Promotion Expense

TASK 1: OPEN COMPANY FILE

WORKFLOW

If you are using the Workflow approach, you will use the same .QBW file.

*   If your QBW file is not already open, open it by selecting **File > Open Previous Company**. Select your **.QBW file.**

- Add **YourName Exercise 2.2** to the company name by selecting **Company** menu **> My Company**.

 ## RESTART & RESTORE

If you are using the Restart and Restore approach, restore your backup file using the directions in *Appendix B: Back Up & Restore QuickBooks Files*. After restoring the file, add **YourName Exercise 2.2** to the company name (select **Company** menu **> My Company**).

TASK 2: EDIT ACCOUNT

Edit the Chart of Accounts to change the name of Account 60400 from Advertising & Promotion to Selling Expense.

Step 1: Open the *Chart of Accounts* window by clicking the **Chart of Accounts** icon in the *Company* section of the Home page.

Step 2: Select account: **60400 Advertising & Promotion**.

Step 3: Click the **Account** button at the bottom of the *Chart of Accounts* window, then select **Edit Account** from the drop-down menu (or right-click and select Edit Account from the menu).

Step 4: Change the account name from Advertising & Promotion to: **Selling Expense**.

Step 5: Click **Save & Close** to save the changes.

TASK 3: ADD SUBACCOUNTS

Add two subaccounts to the Selling Expense account:
1. Advertising Expense
2. Promotion Expense

Step 1: Click the **Account** button at the bottom of the *Chart of Accounts* window, then select **New** to open the *Add New Account* window.

Step 2: Select Account Type: **Expense**. Click **Continue**.

Step 3: Enter Account Number: **60410**

Step 4: Enter Account Name: **Advertising Expense**.

Step 5: **Check** the box in front of the *Subaccount of* field.

Step 6: From the drop-down list, select subaccount of: **60400 Selling Expense**.

Step 7: From the drop-down list for Tax-Line Mapping, select **Deductions: Advertising**.

Step 8: Click **Save & New**.

Step 9: Using the preceding instructions, add the next subaccount: **60420 Promotion Expense**. Click **Save & Close**.

Step 10: Using the Reports center, export to Excel or **print** the revised Chart of Accounts.

Step 11: **Highlight** the accounts that you changed or added.

TASK 4: SAVE EXERCISE 2.2

Save a backup of your Exercise 2.2 file using the file name: **YourName Exercise 2.2 Backup.QBB**. See *Appendix B: Back Up & Restore QuickBooks Files* for instructions.

WORKFLOW

If you are using the Workflow approach, you can leave your .QBW file open and use it for the next chapter.

RESTART & RESTORE

If you are stopping your QuickBooks work session and changing computers, you will need to restore your .QBB file when you restart.

EXERCISE 2.3: QUICKBOOKS EDITIONS

In this exercise, you will choose two industry-specific sample companies to explore and evaluate.

Step 1: From the opening QuickBooks screen, select **Open a sample file**.

Step 2: Pick two of the sample companies (other than the sample product-based business and sample service-based business). Open the sample company files you picked and prepare a list of the features that you see are different in these industry-specific editions.

EXERCISE 2.4: WEB QUEST

When setting up a Chart of Accounts for a business, it is often helpful to review the tax form that the business will use. Then a company's Chart of Accounts can be customized to track information needed for the tax form. The tax form used by the type of organization is listed below.

Type of Organization	Tax Form
Sole Proprietorship	Form 1040 Schedule C
Partnership	Form 1065
Corporation	Form 1120
S Corporation	Form 1120S

In this exercise, you will download tax forms from the Internal Revenue Service website.

Step 1:   Go to the Internal Revenue Service website: www.irs.gov.

Step 2:   As shown in the preceding table, a sole proprietorship files tax form Schedule C that is attached to the individual's Form 1040 tax form.

- **Print** or PDF the tax form Schedule C: Profit or Loss From Business (Sole Proprietorship).

- **Highlight** Advertising Expense on the Schedule C.

Step 3:   An S Corporation files Form 1120S.

- **Print** or PDF Form 1120S (U.S. Income Tax Return for an S Corporation).

- **Highlight** Advertising Expense on Form 1120S.

CHAPTER 2 QUICK CHECK

NAME:

INSTRUCTIONS:

1. CHECK OFF THE ITEMS YOU COMPLETED.
2. ATTACH THIS PAGE TO YOUR PRINTOUTS.

> **!**
> Ask your instructor if you should go Digital (Excel or PDF) or use paper printouts.

CHAPTER 2
- ☐   *   Chart of Accounts (Account Listing)

EXERCISE 2.1
- ☐   *   Task 3: Statement of Cash Flows
- ☐   *   Task 4: To Do List

EXERCISE 2.2
- ☐   *   Task 3: Revised Chart of Accounts

EXERCISE 2.3
- ☐   Your Choice: List of Industry-Specific Features

EXERCISE 2.4
- ☐   Schedule C Tax Form
- ☐   1120S Tax Form

Download Go Digital Excel templates at www.My-QuickBooks.com.

* Export these reports to CH2 REPORTS template.

REFLECTION: A WISH AND A STAR

Reflection improves learning and retention. Reflect on what you have learned after completing Chapter 2.

A Star:

What did you like best that you learned about QuickBooks in Chapter 2?

A Wish:

If you could pick one thing, what do you wish you knew more about when using QuickBooks?

PROJECT 2 LARRY'S LANDSCAPING

To complete this project, use the Go Digital Excel template for Chapter 2 at www.My-QuickBooks.com. Follow the instructions provided in the Excel template.

Complete the following for Larry's Landscaping.

1. Use either your QuickBooks company file (.QBW file) or backup file (.QBB file) that you completed for Project 1. (If you have issues with your QuickBooks file, contact your instructor.) Add **YourName Project 2** to the company name.

2. Download the Go Digital Excel template for Chapter 2. Save the Excel file using the file name: **YourLastName FirstName CH2 REPORTS**.

3. Using QuickBooks preferences, select **Use the last entered date as default**.

4. Using QuickBooks preferences, select **Use account numbers** to display account numbers in the Chart of Accounts.

5. Customize Larry's Chart of Accounts as follows. **Re-sort** the Chart of Accounts.

Account No.	Account Title	Account Type	Subaccount of:	Tax Line
7310	Supplies	Expense	N/A	Schedule C: Supplies (not from COGS)
7320	Computer Supplies	Expense	N/A	Schedule C: Supplies (not from COGS)
7430	Professional Design Fees	Expense	7400 Professional Fees	Schedule C: Legal and professional fees
6710	Section 179	Expense	6700 Depreciation	Schedule C: Other business expenses
7754	Internet Provider	Expense	7750 Utilities	Schedule C: Office expenses

6. Export to **Excel** the Chart of Accounts for Larry's Landscaping using the Account Listing report at December 15, 2019. **Highlight** the accounts that you added.

7. Export to **Excel** the Statement of Cash Flows for Larry's Landscaping for the last fiscal year, October 1, 2018 to September 30, 2019. **Highlight** any item on the statement that you might classify differently than shown on the report.

8. Mark the reports completed on the 2 REPORTS sheet. Save your Excel file.

9. Save a .QBB backup of your work.

PROJECT 2 QUICK CHECK
NAME:
INSTRUCTIONS:
1. CHECK OFF THE ITEMS YOU COMPLETED.
2. ATTACH THIS PAGE TO YOUR PRINTOUTS.

> **!**
> Ask your instructor if you should go Digital (Excel or PDF) or use paper printouts.

PROJECT 2

☐   *   Chart of Accounts (Account Listing)

☐   *   Statement of Cash Flows

Download Go Digital Excel templates at www.My-QuickBooks.com.

* Export these reports to CH2 REPORTS template.

CHAPTER 3
BANKING

SCENARIO

The next morning as you pass the open door of Mr. Castle's office, you notice he is looking at the financial statements you prepared. You try to slip past his door unnoticed, but you take only a few steps when you hear him curtly call your name.

You turn to see Mr. Castle charging toward you with documents in hand.

"I need you to keep an eye on the bank accounts. Cash is the lifeblood of a business. A business can't survive if it doesn't have enough cash flowing through its veins to pay its bills. So it's very important that someone keep an eye on the cash in our bank accounts—the cash inflows into the accounts and the cash outflows from the accounts. That is your job now."

Handing you more documents, Mr. Castle continues, *"We fell behind on our bank reconciliations. Here is last month's bank statement that needs to be reconciled."*

After you master QuickBooks bank reconciliations, you send Mr. Castle the following quick text.

CHAPTER 3
LEARNING OBJECTIVES

In Chapter 3, you will learn about the following QuickBooks features:

INTRODUCTION

In Chapter 3, you will learn about using QuickBooks to perform banking tasks, such as making deposits, writing checks, reconciling bank statements, and online banking.

Start QuickBooks by clicking on the **QuickBooks desktop icon** or click **Start > Programs > QuickBooks > QuickBooks Premier Accountant Edition 2015**.

WORKFLOW

Use the Workflow approach if you are using the same computer and the same .QBW file from the prior chapter. Just as in a business, since you are using the same computer, you can continue to use the same .QBW file. Although you will make backups, you will not need to use the backup files unless your .QBW file fails.

Step 1: If your .QBW file is not already open, open it by selecting **File > Open Previous Company**. Select your most recent **.QBW file.**

Step 2: Update Company Name to include **YourName Chapter 3**.

RESTART & RESTORE

Use the Restart & Restore approach if you are moving your QuickBooks files between computers.

Step 1: Restore the **Backup.QBB** file using the directions in *Appendix B: Back Up & Restore QuickBooks Files*. You can restore using one of two different .QBB files.

1. Restore your own .QBB file from the last exercise completed in the previous chapter.

2. Restore the Chapter 3 DATA STARTER.QBB file that comes with *Computer Accounting with QuickBooks* (available on CD or download from the Online Learning Center).

   If the *QuickBooks Login* window appears:

   - Leave the *User Name* field as **Admin**.

   - Leave the *Password* field **blank**.

Step 2: After restoring the file, update Company Name to include **YourName Chapter** 3.

BANKING NAVIGATION

If necessary, click the **Home** icon in the Icon bar to display the Home page.

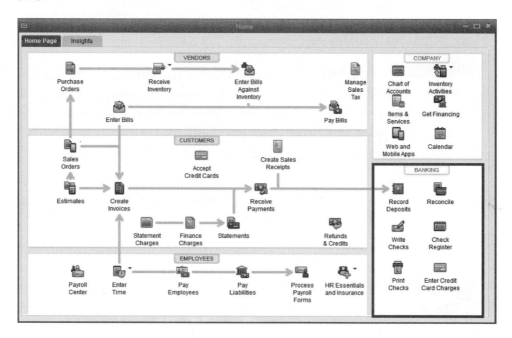

From the *Banking* section of the Home page, you can:

- Record deposits (cash flowing into the Checking account).
- Write checks (cash going out of the Checking account).
- Print checks.
- Reconcile bank statements.
- View Check Register.
- Enter credit card charges.

A business should establish a ***business*** checking account completely separate from the owner's ***personal*** checking account. The company's business checking account should be used *only* for business transactions, such as business insurance and mortgage payments for the company's office building. An owner should maintain a completely separate checking account for personal transactions, such as mortgage payments for the owner's home.

VIEW AND PRINT CHECK REGISTER

The Check Register is a record of all transactions affecting the Checking account. The QuickBooks onscreen Check Register looks similar to a checkbook register used to manually record deposits and checks.

To view the QuickBooks Check Register:

Step 1:   Click the **Check Register** icon in the *Banking* section of the Home page.

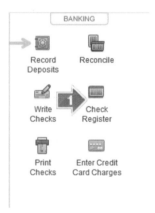

Step 2:   The following window will appear asking you to specify a bank account. Select **10100 Checking**.

Step 3:   Click **OK**.

The following *Check Register* window should appear on your screen. Notice there are separate columns for:

- Payments (checks)
- Deposits
- Balance

If necessary, scroll up or down to locate the 11/15/2019 Sergeant Insurance entry or use the Go To feature.

Split indicates that a payment is split between two or more accounts.

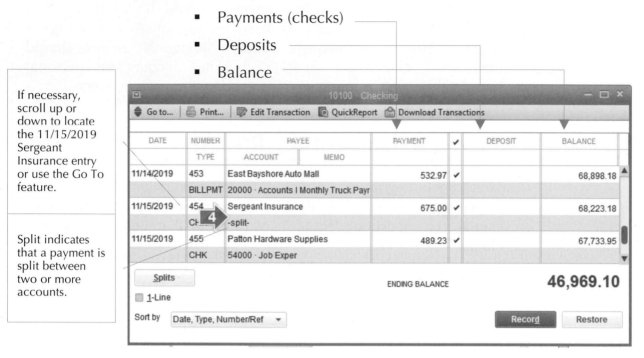

Small enterprises that have strictly cash-based operations sometimes simply use the Check Register to record all transactions. Such enterprises record payments and deposits directly into the Check Register using the Record button. However, most business enterprises require the more advanced features of the QuickBooks accounting software that are covered in the following chapters.

Step 4: QuickBooks drill-down feature permits you to double-click some items to drill-down and view the supporting documents. To view the check for the Sergeant Insurance transaction, double-click the **Sergeant Insurance** entry on **11/15/2019** in the Check Register.

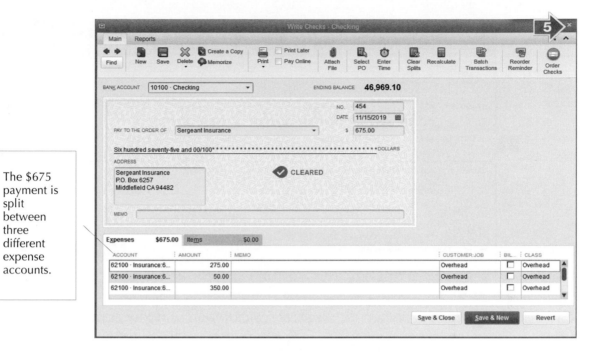

The $675 payment is split between three different expense accounts.

Step 5: The check is stamped *Cleared*, indicating it has already cleared the bank with funds paid to Sergeant Insurance.

Close the *Write Checks* window by clicking on the ⊠ in the upper right corner of the window.

If you wanted to double check to make certain the Sergeant Insurance bill had not been erroneously paid twice, you can use the QuickReport feature of the Check Register to view all payments to Sergeant Insurance.

Step 1: Display the Check Register. In the register, click on the **11/15/2019 Sergeant Insurance** payment for $675 to select it.

Step 2: Select the **QuickReport** button at the top of the *Check Register* window.

Step 3:   When the *Register QuickReport* window appears:

- Enter Dates: **All**.

- Export the report to **Excel** or **print**.

> ✓ *This fiscal year's total for Sergeant Insurance is $-21,698.98.*

Step 4:   **Highlight** Check No. 454 to Sergeant Insurance dated 11/15/2019 on the printout.

Step 5:   **Close** the *Register QuickReport* window and then the *Check Register* window by clicking the ☒ in the upper right corner of each window.

You can record deposits and checks directly in the Check Register or use the *Make Deposits* window and the *Write Checks* window.

MAKE DEPOSITS

Deposits are additions to the Checking account. Any cash coming into a business should be recorded as a deposit to one of the company's accounts.

QuickBooks classifies deposits into two types:

1. Payments from customers.

2. Nonsales receipts (deposits other than customer payments) such as:

  ▪ Cash received from loans.

  ▪ Investments from owners.

  ▪ Interest earned.

  ▪ Other income, such as rental income.

Payments from customers are entered using the *Customers* section of the Home page. For more information about recording payments from customers, see Chapter 4: Customers and Sales. Deposits other than customer payments are recorded using the *Banking* section of the Home page.

Mr. Castle wants to invest an additional $72,000 in the business by depositing his $72,000 check in Rock Castle Construction's Checking account.

To record nonsales receipts (a deposit other than a customer payment):

Step 1: From the *Banking* section of the Home page, click the **Record Deposits** icon.

Step 2: The following *Payments to Deposit* window will appear. QuickBooks uses a two-step process to record payments received:

  1. Record the payment received but not yet deposited (undeposited funds).

  2. Record the deposit.

The payments listed in the *Payments to Deposit* window are undeposited funds that have been recorded as received but not yet deposited in the bank. Since these amounts will be deposited at a later time, confirm that none of the payments have been selected for deposit, then click **OK**.

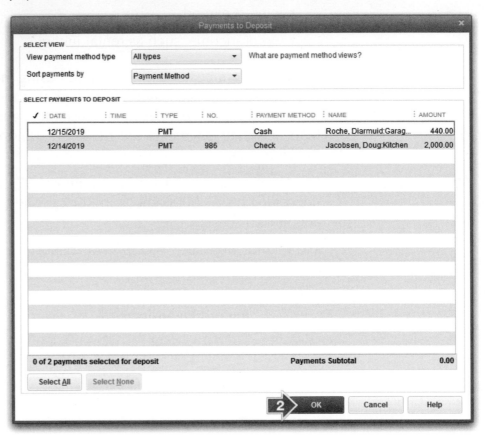

Step 3: When the following *Make Deposits* window appears, record Mr. Castle's $72,000 deposit. Select Deposit To: **10100 Checking.**

Step 4: Select Date: **12/15/2019**.

> Select the account from the drop-down list or type **30100** and QuickBooks automatically completes the account title.

Step 5: Click in the *Received From* column and type: **Rock Castle**. Press the **Tab** key.

Step 6: When prompted, select **Quick Add** to add the name to the Name List.

Step 7: Select Name Type: **Other**.

Step 8: Click **OK**.

Step 9:   Click in the *From Account* column. From the drop-down list of accounts, select **30100 Capital Stock**. Press **Tab**.

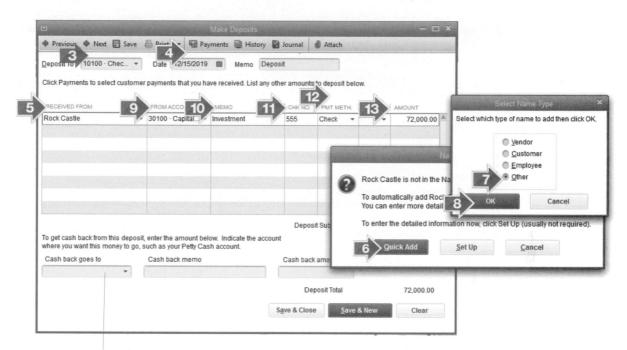

Cash back can be used to keep cash out for Petty Cash. However, a better approach is to deposit the full amount and then write a check for Petty Cash.

Step 10:   Enter Memo: **Investment**.

Step 11:   Enter Check No.: **555** (the number of Mr. Castle's check).

Step 12:   From the Payment Method drop-down list, select **Check**.

Step 13:   Enter Amount: **72000**. (QuickBooks will automatically enter the comma in the amount.)

Step 14:   QuickBooks permits you to print a deposit slip using a QuickBooks preprinted form and a deposit summary. To print a summary of the deposit you just recorded, select the **Print** arrow at the top of the *Make Deposits* window.

Step 15:   Select **Deposit Summary**.

Select the appropriate printer or PDF printer, then click **Print**. The deposit summary should list the $72,000 check from Mr. Castle.

Mr. Castle's $72,000 investment in the company has now been recorded as a deposit in Rock Castle Construction's Checking account.

Step 16:   Close the *Make Deposits* window by clicking the **Save & Close** button.

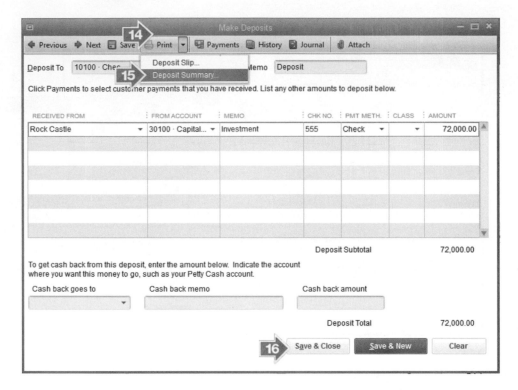

WRITE CHECKS

A business needs to track all cash paid out of the company's checking account. Examples of payments include purchases of inventory, office supplies, employee salaries, rent payments, and insurance payments.

Supporting documents (source documents) for payments include canceled checks, receipts, and paid invoices. These source documents provide proof that the transaction occurred; therefore, source documents should be kept on file for tax purposes.

QuickBooks provides two ways to pay bills:

One-step approach to bill paying:

❶ Record and pay the bill at the same time. When using this approach, the bill is paid when it is received.

Two-step approach to bill paying:

❶ Record the bill when it is received.

❷ Pay the bill later when it is due.

ONE-STEP APPROACH TO BILL PAYING

<table>
<tr>
<td>
Covered in Chapter 3: Banking.
</td>
<td>

</td>
<td>
❶ **Pay Bills When Received:**
Record bill and print check to pay bill.

QuickBooks:
1. Records an expense (debit).
2. Reduces the Checking account (credit).
</td>
</tr>
</table>

TWO-STEP APPROACH TO BILL PAYING

<table>
<tr>
<td>
Covered in Chapter 5: Vendors, Purchases, and Inventory.
</td>
<td>
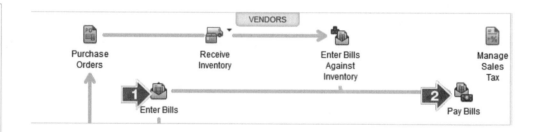
</td>
</tr>
</table>

❶ **Enter Bills:** Record bills for services, such as utilities.

QuickBooks:
1. Records an expense (debit).
2. Records an obligation (liability) to pay later (credit).

❷ **Pay Bills:** Select bills to pay, then print checks.

When the bill is paid and the obligation fulfilled, QuickBooks:
1. Reduces the liability (debit).
2. Reduces the Checking account (credit).

The *Write Checks* window (One-Step Approach) should **not** be used to pay:

1. Paychecks to employees for wages and salaries. Instead, from the *Employees* section of the Home page, use the *Pay Employees* window.

2. Payroll taxes and liabilities. From the *Employees* section, use the *Pay Liabilities* window.

3. Sales taxes. From the *Vendors* section, use the Manage Sales Tax icon and the *Pay Sales Tax* window.

4. Bills already entered in the *Enter Bills* window. From the *Vendors* section, use the *Pay Bills* window.

The *Write Checks* window (One-Step Approach) can be used to pay:

1. Expenses, such as rent, utilities, and insurance.

2. Non-inventory items, such as office supplies.

3. Services, such as accounting or legal services.

In this chapter, you will use the *Write Checks* window (One-Step Approach) to pay a computer repair service bill for Rock Castle Construction.

To use the *Write Checks* window to pay bills:

Step 1:   From the *Banking* section of the Home page, click the **Write Checks** icon and an onscreen check will appear.

You can also open the *Write Checks* window by clicking the **Check** icon on the Icon bar My Shortcuts.

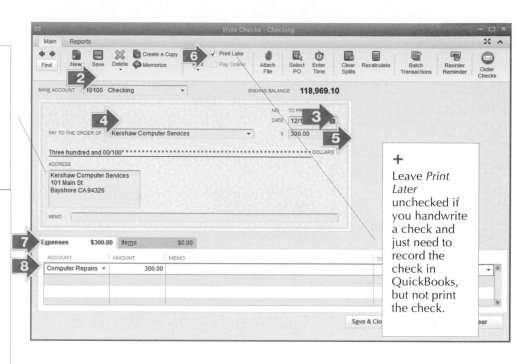

QuickBooks automatically completes the address using address information from the Vendor List.

If you use handwritten *and* computer-printed checks, to keep check numbers in sequence, set up two subaccounts for the Checking account:
1. Computer-printed checks subaccount.
2. Handwritten checks subaccount.

If you use more than one Checking account, change the check color:
1. Edit menu.
2. Change Account Color.

Leave *Print Later* unchecked if you handwrite a check and just need to record the check in QuickBooks, but not print the check.

Step 2: To enter the check information, select Bank Account: **Checking**.

Step 3: Select Date: **12/15/2019**.

Step 4: For the *Pay to the Order of* field, select: **Kershaw Computer Services**. (Select Kershaw from the drop-down list or type the first few letters of the name.)

Step 5: Enter the check amount: **300**.

Step 6: Click the checkbox preceding **Print Later** so that a check mark appears. This tells QuickBooks to both record and print the check. The *Check No.* field will now display: To Print. Notice there is also an option to Pay Online.

Step 7: Next, to record the payment in the correct account using the lower portion of the *Write Checks* window, select the **Expenses** tab.

Step 8: If not already selected, select Account: **64220 Computer Repairs**. Account 64200 Repairs: 64220 Computer Repairs should appear in the *Account* column and $300 should automatically appear in the expense *Amount* column.

FYI: If the payment was related to a specific customer or job, you could enter that information in the *Customer: Job* column and select Billable.

Step 9: To print the check, select the **Print** button located at the top of the *Write Checks* window.

Step 10: Enter Check No.: **517**.

<table>
<tr><td>Instead of printing one check at a time, you can record all your checks and then print them all at once:
1. File menu
2. Print Forms
3. Checks</td></tr>
</table>

Step 11: Click **OK**.

Step 12: If you are using the preprinted check forms, insert check forms in the printer now.

- Select Check Style: **Standard**.
- Select: **Print company name and address**.
- Select the appropriate printer or PDF printer.
- Click **Print**.

Step 13: Click **OK** if your check printed correctly. If you need to reprint any, select the appropriate checks, then click OK.

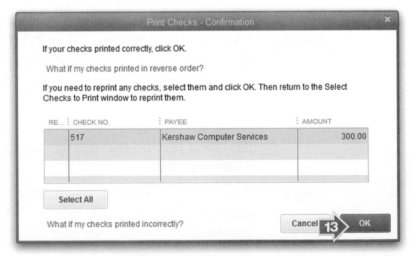

Step 14: Click **Save & Close** to close the *Write Checks* window. QuickBooks automatically records the check in the Check Register.

PRINT JOURNAL

QuickBooks uses two different ways to enter information:

1. Onscreen forms, such as the onscreen check you just completed.

2. An onscreen Journal using debits and credits.

When you enter information into an onscreen form, QuickBooks automatically converts that information into a journal entry with debits and credits.

To view the journal entry for the check that you just recorded:

Step 1: Click **Reports** in the Icon bar to open the *Report Center* window.

Step 2: Select: **Accountant & Taxes**.

Step 3: Select: **Journal**.

Step 4: Select Dates: **Today** From: **12/15/2019** To: **12/15/2019**.

Step 5: Select **Run**.

Step 6: Your *Journal* window should appear as follows. Double-click on a journal entry, to *drill down* to the related source document. If you double-click on the journal entry that records the computer repair, the *Write Checks* window appears, displaying the onscreen check that you just prepared. **Close** the *Write Checks* window.

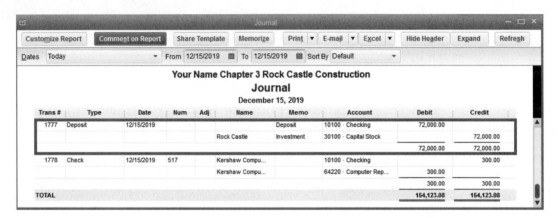

Step 7: Notice that the journal entry to record the deposit of Mr. Castle's $72,000 check includes a debit to the Checking account and a credit to Account 30100 Capital Stock.

Five different types of accounts are listed below along with the effects that debits and credits have on them.

Account Type	Debit/Credit	Effect on Balance
Asset	Debit	Increase
Liability	Credit	Increase
Equity	Credit	Increase
Revenues (Income)	Credit	Increase
Expenses	Debit	Increase

Notice that the *debit* to Rock Castle Construction Checking account increased the balance. The *credit* to the Capital Stock account for $72,000 increased the Capital Stock account balance.

Account	Account Type	Debit/ Credit	Effect on Balance
Checking	Asset	Debit	Increase
Capital Stock	Equity	Credit	Increase

Step 8: View the entry on 12/15/2019 to record the check written to Kershaw Computers for computer repair services. This entry debits (increases) the balance of the expense account, Computer Repairs, and credits (decreases) the Checking account balance.

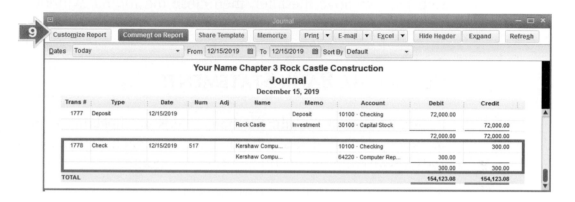

Step 9: Next, to create a report filter, select **Customize Report** at the top of the report window.

Step 10: Click the **Filters** tab.

Step 11: Choose Filter: **Name**.

Step 12: From the drop-down Name List, select: **Kershaw Computer Services**.

Step 13: Click **OK** to close the *Modify Report: Journal* window.

Step 14: Export to **Excel** or **print** the Journal report.

Step 15: Remove the filter, then **close** the *Journal* window and the *Report Center* window.

RECONCILE BANK STATEMENTS

Typically once a month, the bank sends a Checking account bank statement to you. The bank statement lists each deposit, check, and withdrawal from the account during the month.

A bank reconciliation is the process of comparing, or reconciling, the bank statement with your accounting records for the Checking account. The bank reconciliation has two objectives: (1) to detect errors and (2) to update your accounting records for unrecorded items listed on the bank statement (such as service charges).

Differences between the balance the bank reports on the bank statement and the balance the company shows in its accounting records usually arise for two reasons:

1. **Errors** (either the bank's errors or the company's errors).

2. **Timing differences.** This occurs when the company records an amount before the bank does or the bank records an amount before the company does. For example, the company may record a deposit in its accounting records, but the bank does not record the deposit before the company's bank statement is prepared and mailed.

Timing differences include:

Items the bank has not recorded yet, such as:

- **Deposits in transit:** deposits the company has recorded but the bank has not.

- **Outstanding checks:** checks the company has written and recorded but the bank has not recorded yet.

Items the company has not recorded yet, such as:

- **Unrecorded charges:** charges that the bank has recorded on the bank statement but the company has not recorded in its accounting records yet. Unrecorded charges include service charges, loan payments, automatic withdrawals, and ATM withdrawals.

- **Interest earned on the account:** interest the bank has recorded as earned but the company has not recorded yet.

The following bank statement lists the deposits and checks for Rock Castle Construction according to the bank's records as of November 20, 2019.

BANK STATEMENT		

Rock Castle Construction		11-20-2019
1735 County Road		Checking
Bayshore, CA 94326		

Previous Balance	10-20-2019	$71,452.58
+ Deposits	0	0.00
- Checks	4	4,161.56
- Service Charge		10.00
+ Interest Paid		0.00
Ending Balance	11-20-2019	$67,281.02

Deposits	
Date	**Amount**
	0.00

Checks Paid		
Date	**No.**	**Amount**
10-31-2019	433	712.56
10-31-2019	436	24.00
11-14-2019	451	3,200.00
11-19-2019	460	225.00
Thank you for banking with us!		

To reconcile this bank statement with Rock Castle's QuickBooks records, complete the following steps:

Step 1:   From the *Banking* section of the Home page, click the **Reconcile** icon to display the *Begin Reconciliation* window shown below.

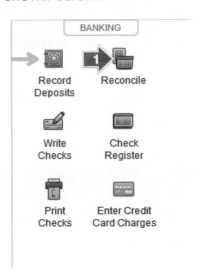

Step 2:   Select Account to Reconcile: **Checking**.

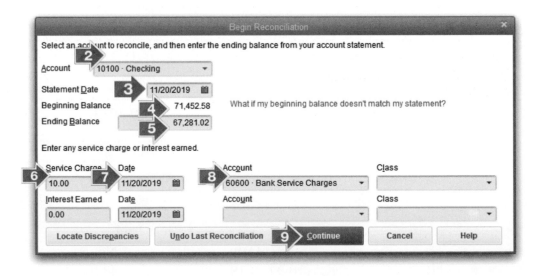

Step 3:   Enter date shown on the bank statement: **11/20/2019**.

Step 4: Compare the amount shown in the *Beginning Balance* field with the beginning (previous) balance of **$71,452.58** on the bank statement.

Step 5: In the *Ending Balance* field, enter the ending balance shown on the bank statement: **$67,281.02**.

Step 6: In the *Service Charge* field, enter the bank's service charge: **$10.00**.

Step 7: Change the date to **11/20/2019**.

Step 8: Select the Account: **Bank Service Charges**.

Step 9: Click **Continue**.

Step 10: To mark deposits that have been recorded by the bank, simply click on the deposit in the *Deposits and Other Credits* section of the *Reconcile* window.

Step 11: To mark checks and payments that have cleared the bank, simply click on the check in the *Checks and Payments* section of the *Reconcile* window.

Step 12: After marking all deposits and checks that appear on the bank statement, compare the Ending Balance and the Cleared Balance at the bottom of the *Reconcile* window.

The Difference amount in the lower right corner of the Reconcile window should equal $0.00.

Step 13: If the difference is $0.00, click **Reconcile Now**.

If there is a difference between the Ending Balance and the Cleared Balance, then try to locate the error or use QuickBooks Locate Discrepancies feature from the *Begin Reconciliation* window.

Click on deposits and checks that have cleared the bank and are listed on the bank statement.

If you use Online Banking, click the **Matched** button to reconcile online transactions and mark online transactions as cleared.

If you are not finished and plan to return to this bank reconciliation later, click **Leave**.

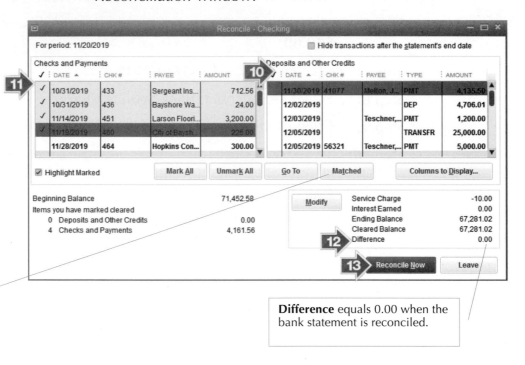

Difference equals 0.00 when the bank statement is reconciled.

Step 14: When the *Select Reconciliation Report* window appears, select type of Reconciliation Report: **Detail**.

Step 15: Click **Display**. Then select **Print** or **Excel** to generate the report.

Step 16: **Highlight** the items on the bank reconciliation report that you marked as cleared for the November bank reconciliation.

You have now completed the November bank reconciliation for Rock Castle Construction.

+

After you click **Reconcile Now**, you can view the Bank Reconciliation by selecting **Reports** menu > **Banking** > **Previous Reconciliation**.

If you need to make changes to the bank reconciliation:
1. To return to the reconciliation screen to make changes, from the *Begin Reconciliation* window, click **Locate Discrepancies**.
2. Another way to change the status of a cleared item: Display the Check Register, then click the Cleared Status column until the appropriate status (cleared or uncleared) appears.

 # ONLINE BANKING

QuickBooks offers an online banking feature so that you can conduct banking transactions online using the Internet. View online banking features through the Banking menu.

The steps for using online banking with QuickBooks are:

1. Set up account for a participating financial institution.

2. Enter transactions in QuickBooks and flag online payments.

3. Download transactions into the QuickBooks bank feeds center.

4. Match or add downloaded transactions into QuickBooks.

You can access QuickBooks online banking features from the Banking menu shown next.

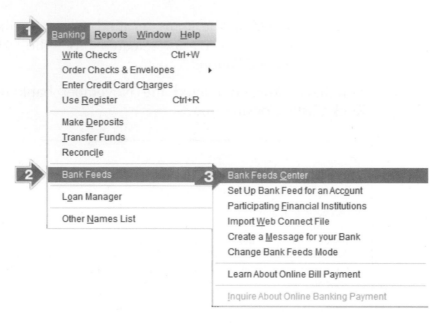

Step 1: Select **Banking** from the Menu bar.

Step 2: Select **Bank Feeds**.

Step 3: Select **Bank Feeds Center**.

Step 4: In the *Bank Feeds* window, select the Bank Account: **ANYTIME Financial Account ending in ***1235**.

Step 5: Select: **Transactions List**.

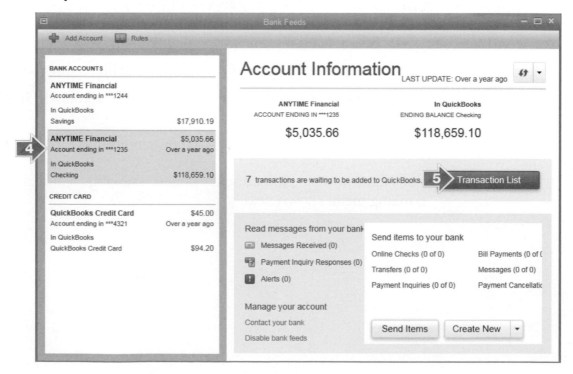

Step 6: In *Tell QuickBooks how to handle these bank transactions*, **check** the transaction for **Anton Teschner**. In the *Action* column, select **Approve**.

Step 7: **Close** the *Transactions List* window and the *Bank Feeds* window.

ENTER CREDIT CARD CHARGES

QuickBooks offers businesses the ability to enter credit card charges into QuickBooks and then to download card charges to update and match QuickBooks records.

To enter a credit card charge for a $50.00 trackpad purchased from Kershaw Computer Services:

Step 1: From the *Banking* section of the Home page, click the **Enter Credit Card Charges** icon.

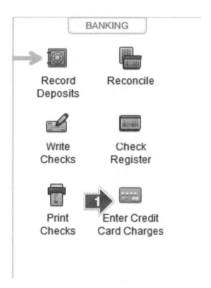

Step 2: From the following *Enter Credit Card Charges* window, select **Purchase/Charge**.

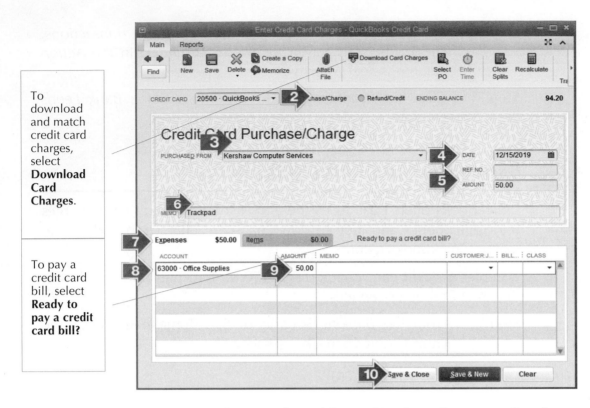

To download and match credit card charges, select **Download Card Charges**.

To pay a credit card bill, select **Ready to pay a credit card bill?**

Step 3: Select Purchased From: **Kershaw Computer Services**.

Step 4: Enter Date: **12/15/2019**.

Step 5: Enter Amount: **50.00**.

Step 6: Enter Memo: **Trackpad**.

Step 7: Select the **Expenses** tab.

Step 8: In the *Account* field, enter account number: **63000 - Office Supplies**.

Step 9: The *Amount* field should automatically display the amount of 50.00 dollars.

Step 10: Click **Save & Close**.

SAVE CHAPTER 3

Save a backup of your Chapter 3 file using the file name: **YourName Chapter 3 Backup.QBB**. See *Appendix B: Back Up & Restore QuickBooks Files* for instructions.

WORKFLOW

If you are using the Workflow approach, leave your .QBW file open and proceed directly to Exercise 3.1.

RESTART & RESTORE

If you are using the Restart & Restore approach and are ending your computer session now, close your .QBW file and exit QuickBooks. When you restart, you will restore your backup file to complete Exercise 3.1.

WWW.MY-QUICKBOOKS.COM

Go to www.My-QuickBooks.com to view additional QuickBooks resources including Excel Reports Templates, QuickBooks videos, and QuickBooks Hot Arrows and Hot Topics. The Hot Topics can be viewed on your computer or tablet and feature frequently used QuickBooks tasks. Bookmark www.My-QuickBooks.com for your future use.

MULTIPLE-CHOICE PRACTICE TEST

Try the **Multiple-Choice Practice Test** for Chapter 3 on the *Computer Accounting with QuickBooks* Online Learning Center at www.mhhe.com/kay2015.

GO DIGITAL!

Go Digital using Excel templates. See *Appendix D: Go Digital with QuickBooks* for instructions about how to save your QuickBooks documents and reports electronically. Visit www.My-QuickBooks.com to download the Excel reports templates.

LEARNING ACTIVITIES

Important: Ask your instructor whether you should complete the following assignments by printing reports or exporting them to Excel (see Appendix D: Go Digital with QuickBooks).

Exercise 3.1:
Make Deposit, Void Check, and Write Check

Scenario

As you glance up from your work, you notice Mr. Castle charging past your cubicle with more documents in hand. He tosses a hefty stack of papers into your creaking inbox. *"Here is another deposit to record. Also, Washuta called to say they did not receive the check we sent them. You will need to void that check—I believe it was check no. 470. I have already called the bank and stopped payment. Also, here are more bills to pay."*

Task 1: Open Company File

Workflow

If you are using the Workflow approach, you will use the same .QBW file.

- If your QBW file is not already open, open it by selecting **File > Open Previous Company**. Select your **.QBW file.**

- Update Company Name to include **YourName Exercise 3.1**.

Restart & Restore

If you are not using the same computer, you must use the Restart and Restore approach.

- Restore your **Chapter 3 Backup.QBB** file using the directions in *Appendix B: Back Up & Restore QuickBooks Files*.

- After restoring the file, update Company Name to include **YourName Exercise 3.1**.

Task 2: Make Deposit

Step 1: Record the deposit for Mr. Castle's $1,000 check (No. 556). Record the deposit in Account 30100 Capital Stock with a deposit date of 12/15/2019. Use Memo: Investment.

Step 2: **Print** the deposit summary.

Task 3: Find Check

Find Check No. 470 made out to Washuta & Son Painting in the QuickBooks Check Register by completing the following steps.

Step 1: View the Check Register. (Click **Check Register** icon in the *Banking* section of the Home page.)

Step 2: Next, search the Check Register for Check No. 470 using the Go To feature. Click the **Go to** button in the upper left corner of the *Check Register* window.

Step 3: In the *Go To* window:
- Select Which Field: **Number/Ref.**
- Enter Search For: **470**.

Step 4: Click the **Next** button. If asked if you want to search from the beginning, click **Yes**.

Step 5: Check No. 470 on 11/28/2019 to Washuta & Son Painting should appear in the *Check Register* window.

Step 6: **Close** the *Go To* window.

Step 7: To view Check No. 470, double-click on the Check Register entry for Washuta & Son Painting to drill down to the check. After viewing the check, **close** the *Check* window.

Task 4: Void Check

The next task is to void Check No. 470. There are two ways to remove a check amount from the Check Register:

1. Delete the check: This removes all record of the transaction.

2. Void the check: QuickBooks changes the amount deducted in the Check Register to zero, but the voided check still appears in the Check Register, thus leaving a record of the transaction. Should questions arise later about the transaction, a voided check provides a better record than a deleted check.

For Check No. 470 you want to maintain a record of the transaction, so you want to void the check rather than delete it.

Void Check No. 470 by completing the following steps:

Step 1: Select **Check No. 470** in the Check Register.

Step 2: With your cursor over Check No 470, **right-click** and from the pop-up menu select **Void Bill Pmt - Check**. VOID should now appear next to Check No. 470 in the Check Register and the Payment amount should now be $0.00.

Step 3: Click the **Record** button in the lower right corner of the *Check Register* window.

Step 4: When asked if you are sure you want to record the voided check, click **Yes**.

Step 5: With your cursor on the voided check No 470, select **QuickReport**. Export to **Excel** or **print** the Register QuickReport.

Step 6: **Highlight** Check No. 470 on the Check Register report and verify that Check No. 470 is void, showing a check amount of $0.00.

Step 7: **Close** the *Check Register* window.

TASK 5: WRITE CHECKS

Step 1: Write checks to pay the following bills and save.

Check No.	Select: Print Later
Date	12/15/2019
Vendor	Express Delivery Service
Amount	$45.00
Expense Account	54520 Freight & Delivery

Check No.	Select: Print Later
Date	12/15/2019
Vendor	Davis Business Associates
Amount	$200.00
Expense Account	60410 Advertising Expense

Step 2: **Print** checks in a batch as follows:

- Click the down arrow by the **Print** button in the *Write Checks* window. Select **Batch**.

- When the *Select Checks to Print* window appears, **select only the preceding two checks that you entered**. Your total for checks to print should be $245.00

- First Check Number is **518**.

- Click **OK**.

- Select **Standard** check style.

- Select **Print company name and address**.

- Click **Print.**

TASK 6: SAVE EXERCISE 3.1

Save a backup of your Exercise 3.1 file using the file name: **YourName Exercise 3.1 Backup.QBB** . See *Appendix B: Back Up & Restore QuickBooks Files* for instructions.

WORKFLOW

If you are proceeding to Exercise 3.2 and using the same computer, you can leave your .QBW file open and use it for Exercise 3.2.

RESTART & RESTORE

If you are stopping your QuickBooks work session and changing computers, you will need to restore your .QBB file when you restart.

EXERCISE 3.2: BANK RECONCILIATION

SCENARIO

When you arrive at work the next morning, Rock Castle Construction's December bank statement is on your desk with the following note from Mr. Castle attached.

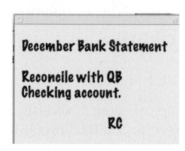

TASK 1: OPEN COMPANY FILE

WORKFLOW

If you are using the Workflow approach, you will use the same .QBW file. If your QBW file is not already open, open it by selecting **File > Open Previous Company**. Select your **.QBW file.** Update Company Name to include **YourName Exercise 3.2**.

RESTART & RESTORE

If you are using the Restart and Restore approach, restore your backup file using the directions in *Appendix B: Back Up & Restore QuickBooks Files*. After restoring the file, update Company Name to include **YourName Exercise 3.2**.

TASK 2: PRINT PREVIOUS BANK STATEMENT

Prepare the previous bank reconciliation as follows:

Step 1: Click **Reports > Banking > Previous Reconciliation.** If necessary, select **Run**.

Step 2: Select Type of Report: **Summary**.

Step 3: Select: **Transactions cleared plus any changes made to those transactions since the reconciliation**.

Step 4: Click **Display**. If a *Reconciliation Report* window appears, click **OK**.

Step 5: Export to **Excel** or **print** the Reconciliation Summary report.

TASK 3: RECONCILE BANK STATEMENT

Reconcile Rock Castle's December bank statement that appears on the following page. If necessary, change the Statement Date and Service Charge Date to **12/20/2019**.

!
If the difference between the Ending Balance and the Cleared Balance is not zero, and you want to return to the bank reconciliation later, do NOT click *Reconcile Now*. Instead, click **Leave**.

In the Reconcile window (lower left corner) "Items you have marked cleared" should agree with the December bank statement:

Deposits and Other Credits	***$58,413.56***
Checks and Payments	***$15,996.28***
Ending Balance	***$109,688.30***
Cleared Balance	***$109,688.30***
Difference	***$ 0.00***

TASK 4: PRINT BANK RECONCILIATION REPORT

Export to **Excel** or **print** a Reconciliation Summary report.

+

After you click **Reconcile Now**, you can return to this Bank Reconciliation by selecting **Reports** menu > **Banking** > **Previous Reconciliation**.

Another way to change the status of a cleared item:
1. Display the Check Register.
2. Click the Cleared Status column until the appropriate status (cleared or uncleared) appears.

BANK STATEMENT		
Rock Castle Construction	12-20-2019	Checking Account
Previous Balance	11-20-2019	$67,281.02
+ Deposits	10	58,413.56
- Checks	12	15,996.28
- Service Charge	1	10.00
+ Interest Paid		0.00
Ending Balance	12-20-2019	$109,688.30

Deposits	
Date	**Amount**
11-30-2019	4,135.50
12-02-2019	4,706.01
12-03-2019	1,200.00
12-05-2019	5,000.00
12-05-2019	25,000.00
12-10-2019	102.65
12-10-2019	1,000.00
12-12-2019	4,936.12
12-14-2019	4,700.00
12-15-2019	7,633.28

Checks Paid		
Date	**No.**	**Amount**
11-28-2019	464	300.00
11-28-2019	465	500.00
11-28-2019	466	600.00
11-28-2019	467	800.00
11-28-2019	468	6,790.00
11-28-2019	469	2,000.00
11-30-2019	471	24.00
11-30-2019	472	656.23
11-30-2019	473	686.00
11-30-2019	474	218.00
11-30-2019	475	2,710.90
12-01-2019	476	711.15

Thank you for banking with us!

TASK 5: SAVE EXERCISE 3.2

Save a backup of your Exercise 3.2 file using the file name: **YourName Exercise 3.2 Backup.QBB**. See *Appendix B: Back Up & Restore QuickBooks Files* for instructions.

WORKFLOW

If you are using the Workflow approach, you can leave your .QBW file open and use it for the next chapter.

RESTART & RESTORE

If you are stopping your QuickBooks work session and changing computers, you will need to restore your .QBB file when you restart.

EXERCISE 3.3: WEB QUEST

The Website listed is subject to change.

Various preprinted check forms and deposit slips are available from Intuit. These preprinted forms can be used with your printer to create checks and deposit slips.

Step 1: Go to www.quickbooks.com.

Step 2: Locate and **print** information about the security features of basic voucher checks versus Secure Plus voucher checks.

EXERCISE 3.4: ONLINE FINANCIAL SECURITY

Online financial services, although convenient, can present security risks. To learn more about security for online financial services, use the QuickBooks Help feature to explore this topic.

Step 1: Use QuickBooks Help to search for: **Security of online services**.

Step 2: **Print** the information you find.

Chapter 3 Quick Check

Name:

Instructions:

1. **Check off the items you completed.**
2. **Turn in this page with your printouts.**

! Ask your instructor if you should Go Digital (Excel* or PDF) or use paper printouts.

Chapter 3

- ☐ * Check Register QuickReport
- ☐ Deposit Summary
- ☐ Check
- ☐ * Journal
- ☐ * Bank Reconciliation Report

Exercise 3.1

- ☐ Task 2: Deposit Summary
- ☐ * Task 4: Check Register
- ☐ Task 5: Checks

Exercise 3.2

- ☐ * Task 2: Previous Bank Statement Report
- ☐ * Task 4: Bank Reconciliation Report

Exercise 3.3

- ☐ QuickBooks Preprinted Forms

Exercise 3.4

- ☐ Online Financial Security Printout

Download Go Digital Excel templates at www.My-QuickBooks.com.

* Export these reports to CH3 REPORTS template.

 # Reflection: A Wish and A Star

Reflection improves learning and retention. Reflect on what you have learned after completing Chapter 3 that you did not know before you started the chapter.

A Star:

What did you like best that you learned about QuickBooks in Chapter 3?

A Wish:

If you could pick one thing, what do you wish you knew more about when using QuickBooks?

PROJECT 3 LARRY'S LANDSCAPING

To complete this project, download the Go Digital Reports Excel template for Project 3 at www.My-QuickBooks.com. Follow the instructions provided in the Excel template.

Complete the following for Larry's Landscaping.

1. Use either your QuickBooks company file (.QBW file) or backup file (.QBB file) that you completed for Project 2. (If you have issues with your QuickBooks file, contact your instructor.) Update Company Name to: **YourName Project 3 Larry's Landscaping**.

2. Download the Go Digital Reports Excel template for Chapter 3. Save the Excel file using the file name: **YourLastName FirstName CH3 REPORTS**.

3. Make the following deposits for Larry's Landscaping. Record all deposits occurring on the same day on the same deposit form.

Date	Received From	Account	Memo	Amount	Cash/Check No.
12/16/2019	Larry Wadford	3020 Owner's Contributions	Owner Investment	$1,000.00	Check No. 1558
12/16/2019	Gussman's Nursery	4300 Other Income	Storage Rental Revenue	$270.00	Cash
12/17/2019	Conner Garden Supplies	4300 Other Income	Storage Rental Revenue	$580.00	Check No. 2200
12/18/2019	Gussman's Nursery	4300 Other Income	Storage Rental Revenue	$360.00	Cash
12/18/2019	Bank of Anycity	4300 Other Income	Interest Revenue	$127.00	Check No. 11818

4. Using your saved Reports Excel template for Chapter 3, export to **Excel** the Deposit Detail report for December 16 through 18, 2019. (Hint: Report Center > Banking.)

5. Write the following checks for Larry's Landscaping.

Date	To	Account		Amount	Check No.
12/16/2019	Computer Services by DJ	7552 Computer Repairs	Computer Repair	$180.00	1464
12/17/2019	Computer Services by DJ	7320 Computer Supplies	External Hard Disk	$127.00	1465
12/17/2019	Mike Scopellite	7430 Professional Design Fees	Professional Design Consulting	$360.00	1466
12/18/2019	Sowers Office Equipment	7300 Office Supplies	Special Order	$250.00	1467
12/18/2019	Nye Properties	7500 Rent (Expense)	Rent	$800.00	1468

6. Export to **Excel** the Check Detail report for December 16 through 18, 2019. (Hint: Report Center > Banking)

7. Reconcile the following bank statement.

BANK STATEMENT

Larry's Landscaping	11-30-2019
1045 Main Street	Checking
Bayshore, CA 94326	

Beginning Balance	10-30-2019	$238,625.29
+ Deposits	2	5,775.80
- Checks	8	2,865.51
- Service Charge		25.00
+ Interest Paid		0.00
Ending Balance	11-30-2019	$241,510.58

Deposits

Date	Amount
11-25-2019	5,000.00
11-30-2019	775.80

Checks Paid

Date	No.	Amount
10-22-2019	1459	244.13
10-28-2019	1461	550.00
11-22-2019	1460	244.13
11-28-2019	1462	550.00
11-29-2019	1112	177.25
11-30-2019	1113	125.00
11-30-2019	1114	375.00
11-30-2019	1115	600.00

Thank you for banking with us!

8. Export to **Excel** the bank reconciliation summary report.

9. Export to **Excel** the bank reconciliation detail report. Highlight the checks and deposits cleared for the November bank statement.

10. Export to **Excel** the Journal report for December 16 through 18, 2019.

11. Mark the reports completed on the 3 REPORTS sheet. Save your Excel file.

12. Save a .QBB backup of your work.

PROJECT 3 QUICK CHECK

NAME:

INSTRUCTIONS:

1. CHECK OFF THE ITEMS YOU COMPLETED.
2. ATTACH THIS PAGE TO YOUR PRINTOUTS.

!
Ask your instructor if you should Go Digital (Excel* or PDF) or use paper printouts.

PROJECT 3

☐ * Deposit Detail

☐ * Check Detail

☐ * Bank Reconciliation Summary

☐ * Bank Reconciliation Detail

☐ * Journal

Download Go Digital Excel templates at www.My-QuickBooks.com.

* Export these reports to CH3 REPORTS template.

CHAPTER 4
CUSTOMERS AND SALES

Just as you are finishing the last bank reconciliation and checking bank reconciliations off your smartphone reminders, Mr. Castle reappears. He always seems to know just when you are about to finish a task.

"While cash flow is crucial to our survival," he says, *"we also need to keep an eye on profits. We are in the business of selling products and services to our customers. We have to be certain that we charge customers enough to cover our costs and make a profit."*

Mr. Castle pulls out a pen and begins scribbling on a sheet of paper on your desk:

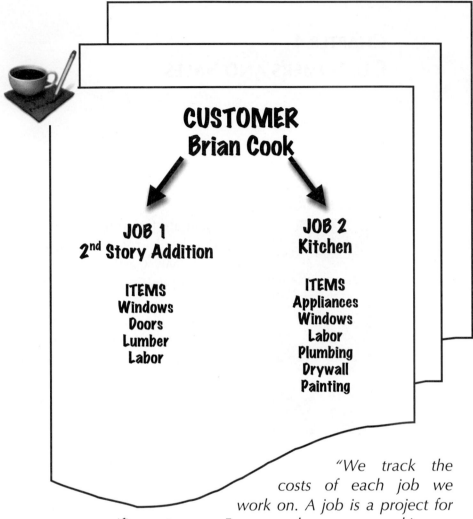

CUSTOMER
Brian Cook

JOB 1
2ⁿᵈ Story Addition

ITEMS
Windows
Doors
Lumber
Labor

JOB 2
Kitchen

ITEMS
Appliances
Windows
Labor
Plumbing
Drywall
Painting

"We track the costs of each job we work on. A job is a project for a specific customer. For example, we are working on two jobs for Brian Cook: Job 1 is a second story addition and Job 2 is a kitchen remodeling job.

"In QuickBooks we use items to track the products and services we use on each project. On the 2ⁿᵈ story addition job we used four different items."

Pushing a stack of papers toward you, Mr. Castle says, *"Here are some customer transactions that need to be recorded in QuickBooks."*

CHAPTER 4
LEARNING OBJECTIVES

In Chapter 4, you will learn about the following QuickBooks features:

INTRODUCTION

In Chapter 4, you will learn how to use QuickBooks software to record customer transactions, including sales to customers and collection of customer payments. Furthermore, you will learn about financial reports that will help you manage your sales.

Start QuickBooks by clicking on the **QuickBooks desktop icon** or click **Start > Programs > QuickBooks > QuickBooks Premier Accountant Edition 2015**.

WORKFLOW

Use the Workflow approach if you are using the same computer and the same .QBW file from Exercise 3.2 of the prior chapter.

Step 1: If your .QBW file is not already open, open it by selecting **File > Open Previous Company**. Select your **.QBW file.**

Step 2: Update Company Name to include **YourName Chapter 4**.

RESTART & RESTORE

Use the Restart & Restore approach if you are restarting your work session.

Step 1: Restore the **Backup.QBB** file using the directions in *Appendix B: Back Up & Restore QuickBooks Files*.

You can restore your .QBB file from the previous chapter or the Chapter 4 DATA STARTER.QBB file that comes with the *Computer Accounting with QuickBooks* text (available on CD or download from the Online Learning Center).

If the *QuickBooks Login* window appears:

- Leave the *User Name* field as **Admin**.

- Leave the *Password* field **blank**.

- Click **OK**.

Step 2: After restoring the file, update Company Name to include **YourName Chapter 4**.

CUSTOMER NAVIGATION

If necessary, click the **Home** icon in the Icon bar to display the Home page.

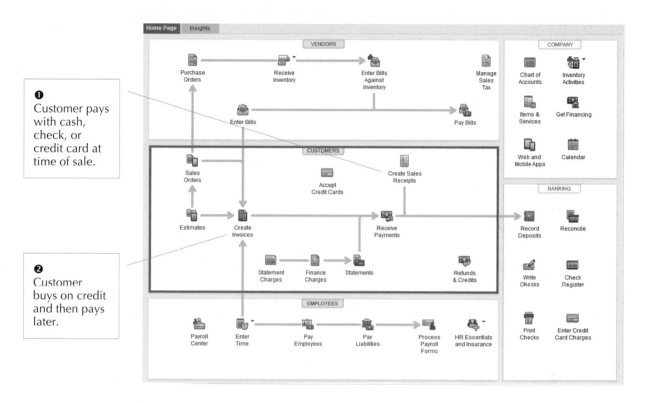

The *Customers* section of the Home page is a flowchart of customer transactions. As the flowchart indicates, Rock Castle Construction can record a customer sale in two different ways:

❶ **Create Sales Receipts.** The customer pays when Rock Castle Construction provides the good or service to the customer. The customer pays with cash, check, or credit card at the time of sale. The sale is recorded on a sales receipt.

❷ **Create Invoices/Receive Payments.** The sale is recorded on an invoice when the good or service is provided to the customer. The customer promises to pay later. These customer promises are called *accounts receivable* — amounts that Rock Castle Construction expects to *receive* in the future. The customer may pay its account with cash, check, credit card, or online payment.

Other QuickBooks features available from the *Customers* section include:

- **Finance Charges**. Add finance charges to customer bills whenever bills are not paid by the due date.

- **Statements**. Prepare billing statements to send to customers.

- **Refunds and Credits**. Record refunds and credits for returned or damaged merchandise.

- **Accept Credit Cards**. Accept customer credit cards in payment for products and services.

The first step in working with customer transactions is to enter customer information in the Customer List.

CUSTOMER LIST

The Customer List contains customer information such as address, telephone number, and credit terms. Once customer information is entered in the Customer List, QuickBooks automatically transfers the customer information to the appropriate forms, such as sales invoices and sales returns. This feature enables you to enter customer information only once instead of entering the customer information each time a form is prepared.

The Customer List in QuickBooks also tracks projects (jobs) for each customer. For example, Rock Castle Construction is working on two projects for Brian Cook:

Job 1: 2nd Story Addition

Job 2: Kitchen

VIEW CUSTOMER LIST

To view the Customer List for Rock Castle Construction:

Step 1:   Click **Customers** in the Icon bar.

Step 2:   The following *Customer Center* window appears, listing customers and jobs. Notice the two jobs listed for Brian Cook:
- 2nd story addition

- Kitchen

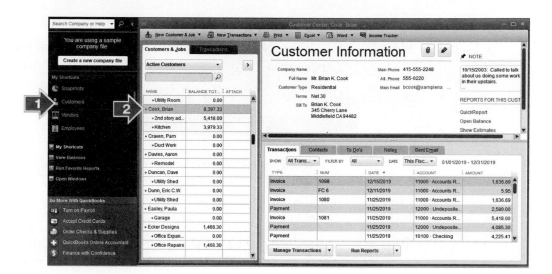

The Customers & Jobs List displays:

- Customer name

- Job name

- Balance for each job

To view additional information about a customer, click the customer or job name. The *Customer/Job Information* window displays:

- Customer address and contact information

- Transaction information for the customer

- Estimate information (if an estimate for the job was prepared)

- Notes about the job

ADD NEW CUSTOMER

Rock Castle Construction needs to add a new customer, Tom Whalen, to the Customer List.

To add a new customer to the Customer List:

Step 1: Click the **New Customer & Job** button at the top of the Customer Center.

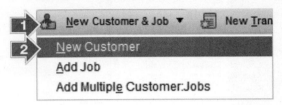

Step 2: Click **New Customer** on the drop-down menu.

Step 3: A blank *New Customer* window should appear. Select the **Address Info** tab. Enter the following information in the *New Customer | Address Info* window.

Customer Name	Whalen, Tom
Mr./Ms./...	Mr.
First Name	Tom
Last Name	Whalen
Main Phone	415-555-1234
Mobile	415-555-5678
Address Details **Bill To / Ship To**	100 Sunset Drive Bayshore, CA 94326

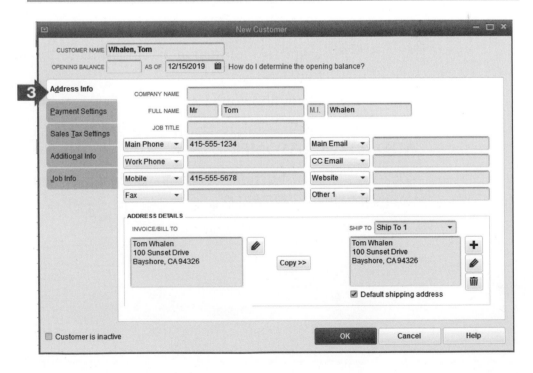

Step 4: To enter payment information for the customer, click the **Payment Settings** tab. Enter the following information in the *Payment Settings* fields:

Account No.	7890
Credit Limit	50,000
Payment Terms	Net 30
Preferred Payment	Check

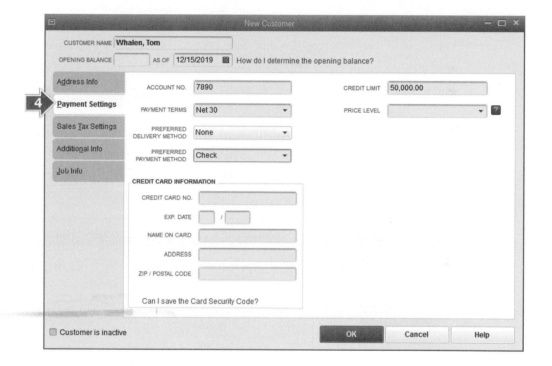

Step 5: To enter sales tax information for the customer, click the **Sales Tax Settings** tab. Enter the following information in the *Sales Tax Settings* fields:

Tax Code	Tax
Tax Item	San Tomas

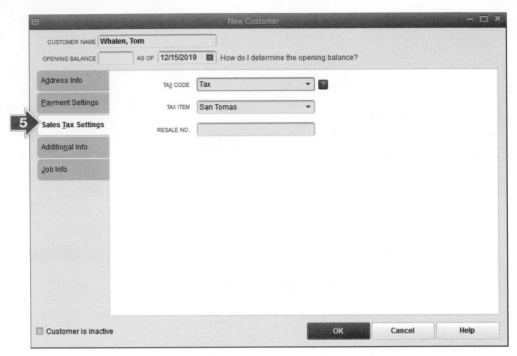

Step 6: Click the **Additional Info** tab to display another customer information window. Enter the following information in the *Additional Info* field.

Customer Type	Residential

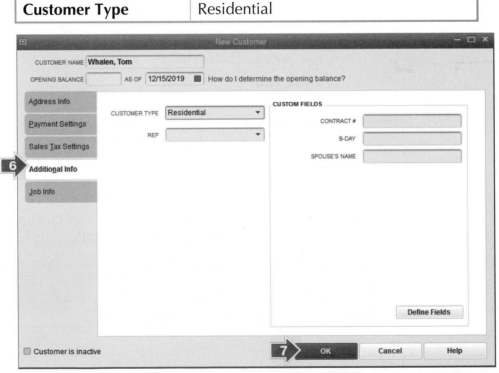

Step 7: Click **OK** to add the new customer to Rock Castle Construction's Customer List.

Step 8: To sort the Customer List, with your cursor over the Customer List:

- **Right-click** to display the pop-up menu.
- Select: **Re-sort List**.

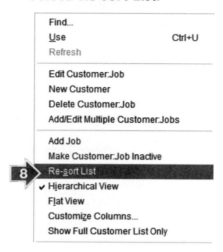

EDIT CUSTOMER INFORMATION

Enter the email address for Tom Whalen by editing the customer information as follows:

Or **Right-click >
Edit Customer:
Job.**

Step 1: Select **Tom Whalen** in the *Customers & Jobs* window.

Step 2: Click the **Edit Customer** icon in the *Customer Information* window.

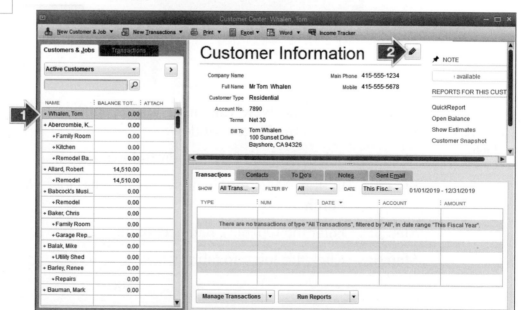

Step 3:   When the *Edit Customer* window appears, enter or revise the customer or job information as needed. In this instance, click the **Address Info** tab. Then enter the Main Email: **twhalen@www.com**.

Step 4:   Click **OK** to record the new information and close the *Edit Customer* window.

ADD A JOB

To add a Screen Porch job for Tom Whalen, complete the following steps:

Step 1:   Click on the customer, **Tom Whalen**, in the *Customers & Jobs* window.

Step 2:   Click the **New Customer & Job** button at the top of the *Customer Center* window.

> Or **Right-click** > **Add Job.**

Step 3:   Select **Add Job** from the drop-down menu.

Step 4:   In the *New Job* window, enter the Job Name: **Screen Porch**.

Step 5:   Enter the Opening Balance: **0.00**.

Step 6:   Click the **Job Info** tab.

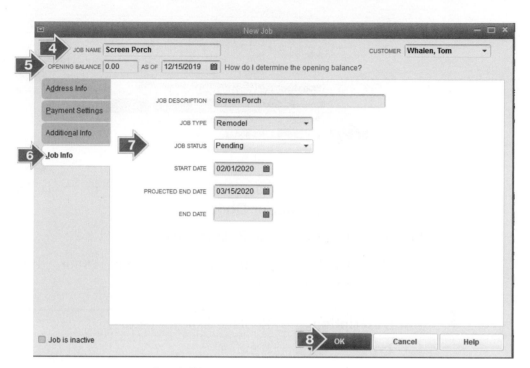

Step 7:   Enter the following information in the *Job Info* fields:

Job Description	Screen Porch
Job Type	Remodel
Job Status	Pending
Start Date	02/01/2020
Projected End Date	03/15/2020

Step 8:   Click **OK** to close the *New Job* window.

Tom Whalen tells Rock Castle Construction that he will hire them to do the screen porch job on one condition—he needs Rock Castle Construction as soon as possible to replace a damaged exterior door that will not close. Rock Castle sends a workman out to begin work on replacing the door right away.

To add the Exterior Door job:

Step 1:   Click on the customer, **Tom Whalen**, in the *Customers & Jobs* window.

Step 2:   **Right-click > Add Job**.

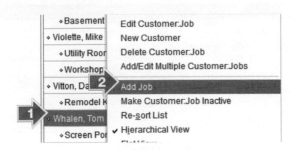

Step 3: In the *Job Name* field at the top of the *New Job* window, enter: **Exterior Door**.

Step 4: Enter Opening Balance: **0.00**.

Step 5: Click the **Job Info** tab, then enter the following information.

Job Description	Replace Exterior Door
Job Type	Repairs
Job Status	Awarded
Start Date	12/15/2019
Projected End	12/18/2019

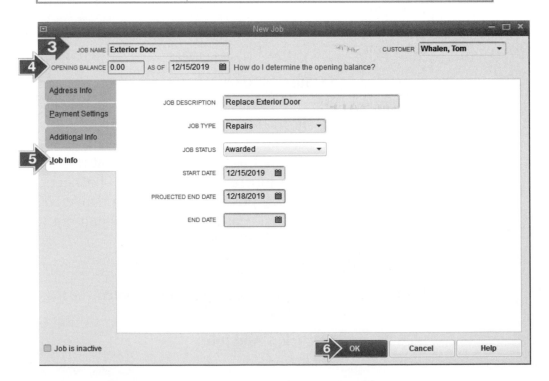

Step 6:   Click **OK** to record the new job and close the *New Job* window.

Step 7:   As shown below, Rock Castle Construction's Customer List should now list two jobs for Tom Whalen: Exterior Door and Screen Porch. **Close** the *Customer Center* window.

Whalen, Tom	0.00
Exterior Door	0.00
Screen Porch	0.00

RECORDING SALES IN QUICKBOOKS

How you record a sale in QuickBooks depends upon how the customer pays for the goods or services. There are three possible ways for a customer to pay for goods and services:

- Cash sale: Customer pays cash (or check) at the time of sale.

- Credit sale: Customer promises to pay later.

- Credit card sale: Customer pays using a credit card.

The diagrams on the following pages summarize how to record sales transactions in QuickBooks. This chapter covers how to record cash and credit sales. Chapter 12 covers credit card sales.

CASH SALES

When a customer pays for goods or services at the time the good or service is provided, it is typically called a cash sale.

Recording a cash sale in QuickBooks requires two steps:

1. **Create Sales Receipts.** Create a sales receipt to record the cash sale.

2. **Record Deposits.** Record the bank deposit.

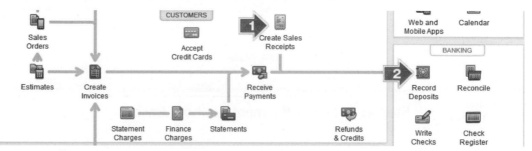

One of Rock Castle Construction's customers, Ernesto Natiello, wants to purchase an extra set of cabinet pulls that match the cabinets that Rock Castle Construction installed. Ernesto pays $10 in cash for the extra cabinet pulls.

To record the cash sale in QuickBooks:

Step 1: From the *Customers* section of the Home page, click **Create Sales Receipts** to display the *Enter Sales Receipts* window. If asked if you would like to complete the Payment Interview, select **No**.

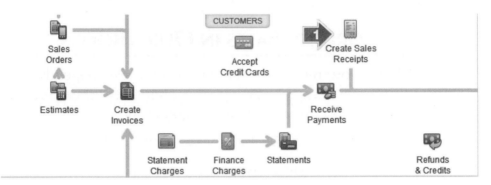

Step 2: In the *Enter Sales Receipts* window, enter Customer: **Natiello, Ernesto**.

Step 3: Select Date: **12/15/2019**.

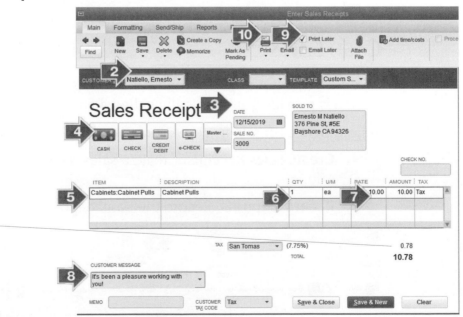

Since type of customer (an individual) and item are subject to tax, QuickBooks automatically calculates and adds the sales tax.

Step 4: Select Payment Method: **Cash**.

Step 5:   Select Item: **Cabinet Pulls**.

Step 6:   Select Quantity: **1**.

Step 7:   Enter Rate: **10.00**.

Step 8:   Select Customer Message: **It's been a pleasure working with you!**

Step 9:   Select **Print Later** checkbox.

Step 10: Select **Print > Preview**. If the company name does not print properly on the invoice or sales receipt, reduce the font size as follows:

- Select the **Formatting** tab in the *Enter Sales Receipts* window. Select **Customize Data Layout > Basic Customization**.

- Select Change Font For: **Company Name > Change Font**.

- Select font size **10**.

- Close the customization windows.

Step 11: **Print** the sales receipt:

- Click the **Print** button at top of the *Enter Sales Receipts* window.

- Select Print on: **Blank paper**.

- If necessary, uncheck: **Do not print lines around each field**.

- Select the appropriate printer or PDF printer, then click **Print**.

Step 12: Click **Save & Close** to record the cash sale and close the *Enter Sales Receipts* window.

QuickBooks will record the $10.78 as undeposited funds. Later, you will record this as a bank deposit to Rock Castle's Checking account.

CREDIT SALES

Credit sales occur when Rock Castle Construction provides goods and services to customers and in exchange receives a promise that the customers will pay later. This promise to pay is called an account receivable because Rock Castle expects to *receive* the account balance in the future.

Recording a credit sale in QuickBooks requires three steps:

1. **Create Invoices.** Create an invoice to bill the customer for the product or service provided. QuickBooks records accounts receivable and the sales amount.

2. **Receive Payments.** Receive payment from the customer. QuickBooks reduces accounts receivable and increases undeposited funds.

3. **Record Deposits.** Deposit the customer's payment in the bank.

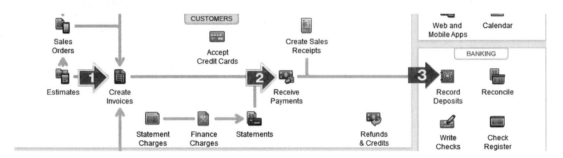

CREDIT SALES: CREATE INVOICES

For more information about time tracking, see Chapter 6.

An invoice is used to record sales on credit when the customer will pay later. An invoice is a bill that contains detailed information about the items (products and services) provided to a customer.

If QuickBooks' time-tracking feature (tracking time worked on each job) is *not* used, then time worked on a job is entered directly on the invoice. In this chapter, assume that time tracking is not used and that time worked on a job is entered on the invoice form.

+
Click the **Estimates** icon to create a customer estimate using QuickBooks.

Next, you will create an invoice for Rock Castle Construction. Rock Castle sent a workman to the Whalen residence immediately after receiving the phone call from Tom Whalen requesting an exterior door replacement as soon as possible. The workman spent one hour at the site the first day.

In this instance, Rock Castle Construction was not asked to provide an estimate before starting the work. Charges for products and labor used on the Whalen door replacement job will be recorded on an invoice.

To create an invoice to record charges:

Step 1:   In the *Customers* section of the Home page, click the **Create Invoices** icon to display the *Create Invoices* window.

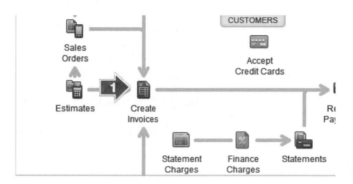

Step 2:   Select the Template: **Rock Castle Invoice**.

Step 3:   Enter the Customer:Job by selecting **Whalen, Tom: Exterior Door** from the drop-down Customer & Job List. Make certain to select the customer name and the correct job: Exterior Door.

+
To add new customers from the *Create Invoices* window: Select **Add New** from the Customer drop-down list.

No sales tax on labor.

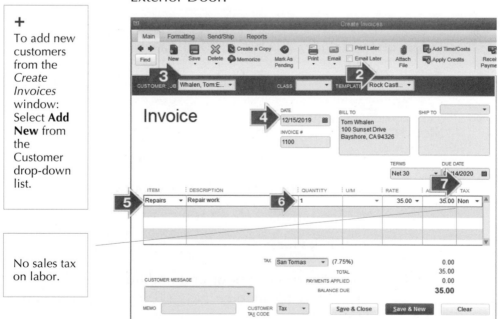

Step 4:   Select Date: **12/15/2019**.

Step 5: Enter charges for the service provided the customer. Enter Item: **Repairs.** Press **Tab.** Description should automatically display: Repair work.

Step 6: Enter Quantity: **1** (hour).

- The Rate should automatically display $35.00.
- The Amount should automatically display $35.00.

Step 7: From the drop-down list, select Tax: **Non-Taxable Sales.**

Step 8: You will wait until the job is complete to print the invoice. In the meantime, mark the invoice as pending:

- **Right-click** to display the pop-up menu.
- Select: **Mark Invoice As Pending**.

Step 9: If you wanted to enter another invoice, you would click **Save & New**. Instead, click **Save & Close** to close the *Create Invoices* window.

Later in the day on December 15, 2019, one of the Rock Castle Construction crews located an exterior door and finished installing the new door at the Whalen residence. The following additional products and services were used:

Exterior wood door	1 @ $120	Taxable Sales	
Repair work	4 hours	Non-Taxable Sales	

Step 1: To display the invoice for the Exterior Door job again:

- Click the **Create Invoices** icon.
- When the *Create Invoices* window appears, click **Find**.
- Enter Invoice No.: **1100**.
- Click **Find**.

Step 2: Enter the exterior door and additional repair labor as new line items on Invoice No. 1100 for the Whalen Exterior Door job.

Step 3: Mark the invoice as final as follows:

+

A **Progress Invoice** is used if the customer is billed as the work progresses rather than when the work is fully completed.

!

See *Correcting Errors* in *Appendix C: QuickBooks Issue Resolution* if you would like assistance correcting mistakes.

To print envelopes for invoices and shipping labels, click the down arrow by the Print icon.

- **Right-click** to display the pop-up menu.
- Select: **Mark Invoice As Final.**

Step 4: Select **Print Preview**. If the company name does not display properly on the invoice, reduce the font size.

Step 5: With Invoice No. 1100 displayed, print the invoice as follows:

- Select the **Print** icon. If asked if you want to record your changes, select **Yes**.
- Select Print on: **Blank paper**.
- If necessary, uncheck: **Do not print lines around each field**.
- Select the appropriate printer or PDF printer, then click **Print**.

Step 6: Click **Save & Close** to close the *Create Invoices* window. If asked if you want to record your changes, select **Yes**.

QuickBooks will record the sale and record an account receivable for the amount to be received from the customer in the future.

> **+**
> If the company name does not print properly on the invoice or sales receipt, reduce the font size as follows:
> 1. Select the **Formatting** tab > **Customize Data Layout > Basic Customization**.
> 2. Select **Company Name > Change Font**.
> 3. Select font size **10**.

The Invoice Total is $304.30. Notice that the Exterior Door is a taxable item and QuickBooks automatically calculates and adds sales tax of $9.30 for the door.

ONLINE BILLING

QuickBooks has the capability to email invoices to customers. Customer email addresses are filled in automatically from the Customer List information. You can email single invoices or send a batch of invoices.

Although you cannot email invoices from the sample company files, to demonstrate how to email invoices:

Step 1: Open Invoice No. 1100 on your screen. (Click the **Create Invoices** icon. Click **Previous** until the invoice appears, or click the **Find** button and enter Invoice No. **1100**.)

Step 2: Select **Email Later** at the top of the *Create Invoices* window.

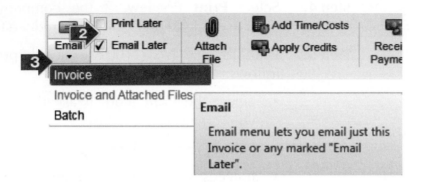

Step 3: To email the invoice later, you would select **Email > Invoice**. Since this is a sample company file, you will not be able to email the invoice and this is for demonstration purposes only.

Step 4: To close the *Create Invoices* window, click **Save & Close**.

If your company signs up for Online Bill Paying services, your customers can pay you online after receiving your email invoices.

CREDIT SALES: CREATE REMINDER STATEMENTS

Reminder statements are sent to remind customers to pay their bills. A reminder statement summarizes invoice charges and provides an account history for the customer. It does not provide the detailed information that an invoice provides.

If a company wants to provide a customer with detailed information about charges, a copy of the invoice should be sent instead of a reminder statement.

Reminder statements summarize:

- The customer's previous account balance.
- Charges for sales during the period.
- Payments received from the customer.
- The customer's ending account balance.

To print a QuickBooks reminder statement for the Whalen Exterior Door job:

Step 1: Click the **Statements** icon in the *Customers* section of the Home page to display the *Create Statements* window.

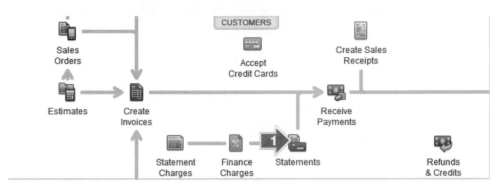

Step 2: Select Template: **Intuit Standard Statement**.

Step 3: Select Statement Date: **12/16/2019**.

Step 4: Select Statement Period From: **11/17/2019** To: **12/16/2019**.

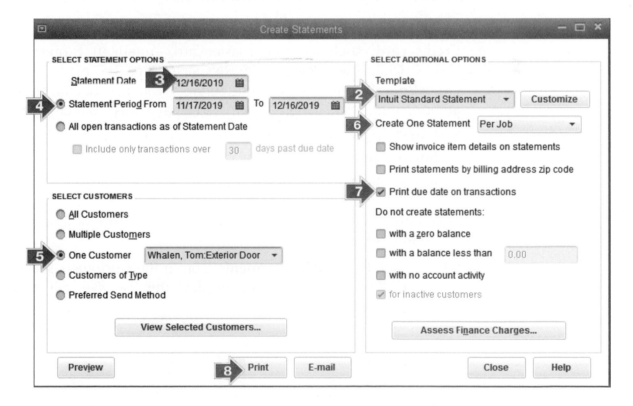

Step 5: In the *Select Customers* section, select **One Customer**. From the drop-down list, select **Whalen, Tom: Exterior Door**.

Step 6: In the *Select Additonal Options* section, select Create One Statement: **Per Job.**

Step 7: Check **Print due date on transactions**.

Step 8: Click **Print**, select the appropriate printer or PDF printer, then click **Print** to print the reminder statement.

Step 9: Click **Close**.

CREDIT SALES: RECORD CUSTOMER PAYMENTS

Recall that when recording credit sales in QuickBooks, you first create an invoice and then record the customer's payment. When a credit sale is recorded on an invoice, QuickBooks records (debits) an Account Receivable—an amount to be received from the customer in the future. When the customer's payment is received, the Account Receivable account is reduced (credited).

Customers may pay in the following ways:

1. **Credit card**, such as Visa, MasterCard, American Express, or Diners Club over the phone, in person, or by mail. Using QuickBooks' Merchant Account Service, you can obtain online authorization and then download payments directly into QuickBooks.

2. **Online** by credit card or bank account transfer.

3. **Customer check** delivered either in person or by mail.

To record the customer's payment by check for the Exterior Door job, complete the following steps:

Step 1: Click the **Receive Payments** icon in the *Customers* section of the Home page to display the *Receive Payments* window.

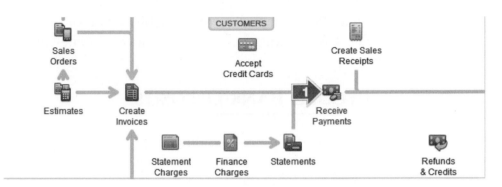

Step 2: Select Received From: **Whalen, Tom: Exterior Door**. Invoice No. 1100 for $304.30 should appear as an outstanding invoice.

Step 3: Select Date: **12/17/2019**.

+

If the full amount of the invoice is not received from the customer, then the amount received can be entered into the *Amount* field.

Step 4: Select Invoice Number **1100** when it appears. QuickBooks will automatically enter the selected invoice amount of $304.30 into the *Amount* field.

Step 5: Select: Pmt. Method: **Check**.

Step 6: Enter Check No. **1005**.

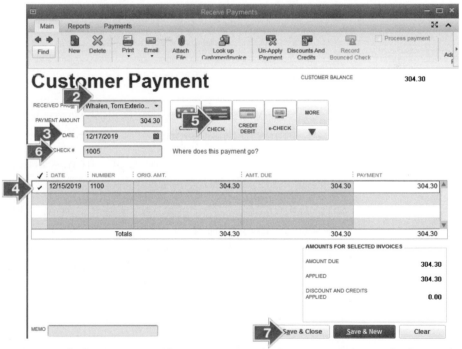

Step 7: Click **Save & Close** to record the payment and close the *Receive Payments* window.

QuickBooks will increase (debit) cash or undeposited funds and decrease (credit) the customer's account receivable.

RECORD BANK DEPOSITS

After recording a customer's payment in the *Receive Payments* window, the next step is to indicate which payments to deposit in which bank accounts.

To select customer payments to deposit:

Step 1: Click the **Record Deposits** icon in the *Banking* section of the Home page to display the *Payments to Deposit* window. The *Payments to Deposit* window lists undeposited funds that have been received but not yet deposited in the bank.

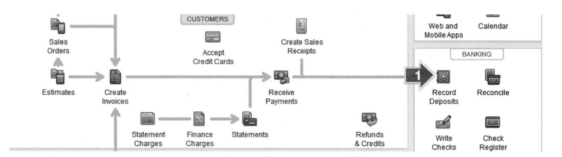

Step 2: **Select** the two payments that were added to undeposited funds in this chapter.

- $10.78 cash receipt from Ernesto Natiello on 12/15/2019

- $304.30 cash payment from Tom Whalen on 12/17/2019

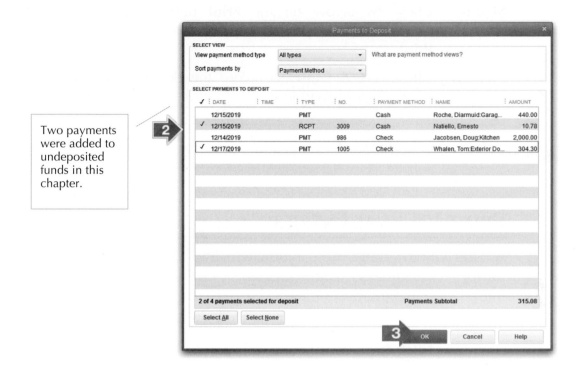

Two payments were added to undeposited funds in this chapter.

Step 3: Click **OK** to display the following *Make Deposits* window.

Step 4: Select Deposit To: **Checking**.

Step 5: Select Date: **12/17/2019**.

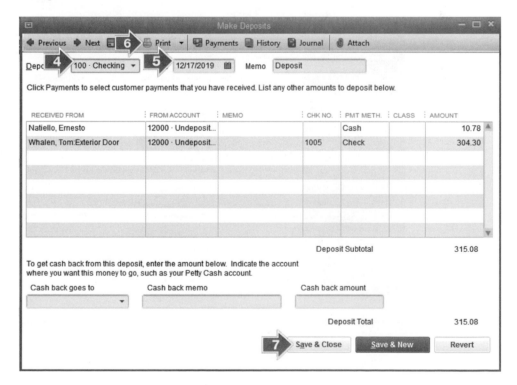

Step 6: Click the **arrow** on the **Print** button. Select: **Deposit Summary**. Select printer or PDF printer settings, then click **Print**.

Step 7: Click **Save & Close** to record the deposit and close the *Make Deposits* window.

> *Deposit Total is $315.08.*

PRINT JOURNAL ENTRIES

As you entered transaction information into QuickBooks' onscreen forms, QuickBooks automatically converted the transaction information into journal entries.

To print the journal entries for the transactions you entered:

Step 1: Click **Reports** in the Icon bar to display the *Report Center* window.

Step 2: Select the **List View** in the upper right corner of the window.

Step 3: Select: **Accountant & Taxes**.

Step 4:   Select: **Journal**.

Step 5:   Select Dates From: **12/15/2019** To: **12/17/2019**.

Step 6:   Select **Run**.

Step 7:   To filter for a specific customer, click **Customize Report > Filters**.

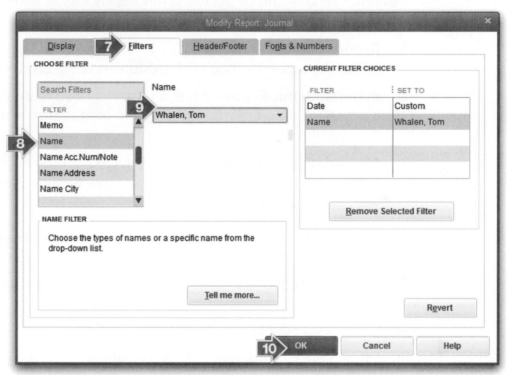

Step 8:   Select Filter: **Name**.

Step 9:   Select: **Whalen, Tom.**

Step 10:   Click **OK**.

Step 11:   Export to **Excel** or **print** the Journal.

Step 12:   **Highlight** the journal entry that corresponds to Invoice No. 1100. Notice that the journal entry records an increase (debit) to Accounts Receivable for $304.30, the net amount of the invoice.

CUSTOMER REPORTS

There are many different customer reports that a business may find useful. QuickBooks creates reports to answer the following questions:

- Which customers owe us money?
- Which customers have overdue balances?
- Which customers are profitable?
- Which jobs are profitable?

Customer reports can be accessed in QuickBooks in several different ways:

1. **Report Center.** Permits you to locate reports by type of report (Click Reports icon, then click Customers & Receivables.)

2. **Reports Menu.** Reports listed on the Reports menu are grouped by type of report. (From the Reports menu, click Customers & Receivables.)

3. **Memorized Customer Reports.** Selected customer reports are memorized for convenience. (From the Reports menu, select Memorized Reports, Customers.)

In this chapter, you will use the Report Center to access customer reports.

Step 1: To display the Report Center, click **Reports** on the Icon bar.

Step 2: Select the **List View** icon.

Step 3: Select: **Customers & Receivables** to display customer reports that can be accessed in QuickBooks.

Step 4: Notice that the customer reports are divided into three categories:

- Accounts Receivable Aging reports
- Customer Balance reports
- Lists reports

ACCOUNTS RECEIVABLE REPORTS:
WHICH CUSTOMERS OWE US MONEY?

Accounts Receivable reports provide information about which customers owe your business money. When Rock Castle Construction makes a credit sale, the company provides goods and services to a customer in exchange for a promise that the customer will pay later. Sometimes the customer breaks the promise and does not pay. Therefore, a business should have a credit policy to ensure that credit is extended only to customers who are likely to keep their promise and pay their bills.

After credit has been extended, a business needs to track accounts receivable to determine if accounts are being collected in a timely manner. The following reports provide information useful in tracking accounts receivable.

1. Accounts Receivable Aging Summary (age of amounts due you by customers).

2. Accounts Receivable Aging Detail.

3. Customers with Open Invoices (invoices not yet paid).

4. Collections Report (overdue customer accounts with contact information).

ACCOUNTS RECEIVABLE AGING SUMMARY REPORT

The Accounts Receivable Aging Summary report provides information about the age of customer accounts. This report lists the age of accounts receivable balances. In general, the older an account, the less likely the customer will pay the bill. Therefore, it is important to monitor the age of accounts receivable and take action to collect old accounts.

To print the Accounts Receivable Aging Summary:

Step 1: From the Report Center, select **Customers & Receivables**.

Step 2: Select **A/R Aging Summary**.

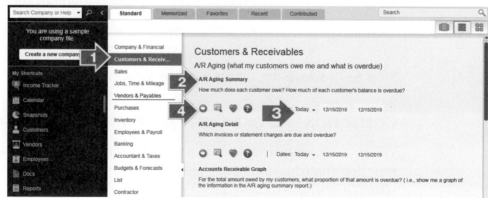

Step 3: Select Date: **Today**.

Step 4: Select **Run**.

Step 5: In the *A/R Aging Summary* window, select Sort By: **Total**.

Step 6: Sort in **Descending (Z to A)** order. If necessary, click and drag to adjust the column widths.

Step 7: Export the report to **Excel** or **print**.

Step 8: **Close** the *A/R Aging Summary* window.

CUSTOMERS WITH OPEN INVOICES REPORT

Customers with open invoices are those who have an unbilled or unpaid balance. It is important to track the status of open accounts to determine:

- Are these amounts unbilled? The sooner the balances are billed, the sooner your company receives cash to pay your bills.

- Are these amounts billed but not yet due?

- Are these amounts billed and overdue? These accounts should be monitored closely with an action plan for collecting the accounts.

The Open Invoices report lists all customers with open balances and can be printed as follows:

Step 1: From the *Customers & Receivables* section of the Report Center, click **Open Invoices**.

Step 2: Select Date: **Today**.

Step 3: Select **Run**.

Step 4: Export to **Excel** or **print** the Open Invoices report.

Step 5: Notice the *Aging* column in the report. This column indicates the age of overdue accounts.

Step 6: **Close** the *Open Invoices* window.

COLLECTIONS REPORT: CUSTOMERS WITH OVERDUE BALANCES

When reviewing the age of accounts receivable, a business should monitor overdue accounts closely and maintain ongoing collection efforts to collect its overdue accounts.

The Collections Report lists customers with overdue account balances. In addition, the Collections Report includes a contact phone number for convenience in contacting the customer.

To print the Collections Report summarizing information for all customers with overdue balances:

Step 1: From the *Customers & Receivables* section of the Report Center, select: **Collections Report**.

Step 2: Select: **Today**.

Step 3: Select **Run**. No customers have overdue balances so it appears that you are doing a good job collecting customer payments on accounts.

Step 4: Export to **Excel** or **print** the Collections Report.

Step 5: **Close** the *Collections Report* window.

The Collections Report provides the information necessary to monitor and contact overdue accounts and should be prepared and reviewed on a regular basis.

PROFIT AND LOSS REPORTS: WHICH CUSTOMERS AND JOBS ARE PROFITABLE?

To improve profitability in the future, a business should evaluate which customers and jobs have been profitable in the past. This information permits a business to improve profitability by:

- Increasing business in profitable areas

- Improving performance in unprofitable areas

- Discontinuing unprofitable areas

The following QuickBooks reports provide information about customer and job profitability:

1. Income by Customer Summary

2. Income by Customer Detail

3. Job Profitability Summary

4. Job Profitability Detail

INCOME BY CUSTOMER SUMMARY REPORT

To determine which customers are generating the most profit for your business, it is necessary to look at both the sales for the customer and associated costs. To print the Income by Customer Summary Report:

Step 1: From the Report Center, select **Company & Financial > Income by Customer Summary**.

Step 2: Select: **This Fiscal Year-to-date**.

Step 3: Select **Run**.

Step 4: In the *Income by Customer Summary* window, select Sort By: **Total**.

Step 5: Sort in **Descending (Z to A)** order. If necessary, click and drag to adjust the column widths.

Step 6: Export to **Excel** or **print** the report.

Step 7: **Highlight** Rock Castle Construction's most profitable customer.

Step 8: **Close** the *Income by Customer Summary* window.

QuickBooks offers other additional reports about customers that provide information useful to a business. These reports can be accessed from the Report Center.

SAVE CHAPTER 4

Save a backup of your Chapter 4 file using the file name: **YourName Chapter 4 Backup.QBB**. See *Appendix B: Back Up & Restore QuickBooks Files* for instructions.

WORKFLOW

If you are using the Workflow approach, leave your .QBW file open and proceed directly to Exercise 4.1.

RESTART & RESTORE

If you are using the Restart & Restore approach and are ending your computer session now, close your .QBW file and exit QuickBooks. When you restart, you will restore your backup file to complete Exercise 4.1.

www.My-QuickBooks.com

Go to www.My-QuickBooks.com to view additional QuickBooks resources including Excel Reports Templates, QuickBooks videos, and QuickBooks Hot Arrows and Hot Topics. The Hot Topics can be viewed on your computer or tablet and feature frequently used QuickBooks tasks. Bookmark www.My-QuickBooks.com for your future use.

Multiple-Choice Practice Test

Try the **Multiple-Choice Practice Test** for Chapter 4 on the *Computer Accounting with QuickBooks* Online Learning Center at www.mhhe.com/kay2015.

Go Digital!

Go Digital using Excel templates. See *Appendix D: Go Digital with QuickBooks* for instructions about how to save your QuickBooks reports electronically.

Learning Activities

Important: Ask your instructor whether you should complete the following assignments by printing reports or by exporting to Excel templates (see Appendix D: Go Digital with QuickBooks).

Exercise 4.1: Bill Customer

Scenario

"I just finished the Beneficio job, Mr. Castle." A workman tosses a job ticket over your cubicle wall into your inbox as he walks past. *"Mrs. Beneficio's pet dog, Wrecks, really did a number on that door. No wonder she wanted it replaced before her party tonight. Looks better than ever now!"*

You hear Mr. Castle reply, *"We want to keep Mrs. Beneficio happy. She will be a good customer."*

TASK 1: OPEN COMPANY FILE

WORKFLOW

If you are using the Workflow approach, you will use the same .QBW file. If your Chapter 4.QBW file is not already open, open it by selecting **File > Open Previous Company**. Select your **.QBW file**. Update Company Name to include **YourName Exercise 4.1**.

RESTART & RESTORE

If you are using the Restart and Restore approach, restore your backup file using the directions in *Appendix B: Back Up & Restore QuickBooks Files*. After restoring the file, update Company Name to include **YourName Exercise 4.1**.

TASK 2: ADD NEW CUSTOMER & JOB

Add a new customer from the *Customer Center* or from the *Create Invoices* window.	

Step 1: Add Mrs. Beneficio as a new customer.

Address Info:	
Customer Name	Beneficio, Katrina
Mr./Ms./…	Mrs
First Name	Katrina
M.I.	L
Last Name	Beneficio
Main Phone	415-555-1818
Mobile	415-555-3636
Address Details: **Bill To**	10 Pico Blvd Bayshore, CA 94326

Payment Settings:	
Account No.	12736
Payment Terms	Net 30
Preferred Payment Method	VISA
Credit Limit	10,000

Sales Tax Settings:	
Tax Code	Tax
Tax Item	San Tomas

Additional Info:	
Customer Type	Residential

Step 2: **Close** the *New Customer* window.

Step 3: Add a new job for Katrina Beneficio.

Job Name	Door Replacement
Job Description	Interior Door Replacement
Job Type	Repairs
Job Status	Closed
Start Date	12/17/2019
Projected End	12/17/2019
End Date	12/17/2019

Step 4: Sort the Customer List. (Hint: **Right-click > Re-sort List**.)

TASK 3: CREATE INVOICE

Step 1: Create an invoice for an interior door replacement using the following information:

Customer: Job	Beneficio, Katrina: Door Replacement
Customer Template	Rock Castle Invoice
Date	12/17/2019
Invoice No.	1101
Items	1 Wood Door: Interior @ $72.00 1 Hardware: Standard Doorknob @ 30.00 Installation Labor: 3 hours @ $35.00

Step 2: Select the appropriate printer or PDF printer, then **print** the invoice.

 The Invoice Total is $214.91.

TASK 4: SAVE EXERCISE 4.1

Save a backup of your Exercise 4.1 file using the file name: **YourName Exercise 4.1 Backup.QBB**. See *Appendix B: Back Up & Restore QuickBooks Files* for instructions.

WORKFLOW

If you are proceeding to Exercise 4.2 and using the same computer, you can leave your .QBW file open and use it for Exercise 4.2.

RESTART & RESTORE

If you are stopping your QuickBooks work session and changing computers, you will need to restore your .QBB file when you restart.

EXERCISE 4.2: RECORD CUSTOMER PAYMENT AND CUSTOMER CREDIT

SCENARIO

"It's time you learned how to record a credit to a customer's account." Mr. Castle groans, then rubbing his temples, he continues, *"Mrs. Beneficio called earlier today to tell us she was very pleased with her new bathroom door. However, she ordered locking hardware for the door, and standard hardware with no lock was installed instead. Although she appreciates our prompt service, she would like a lock on her bathroom door. We sent a workman over to her house, and when the hardware was replaced, she paid the bill.*

"We need to record a credit to her account for the standard hardware and then record a charge for the locking hardware set. And we won't charge her for the labor to change the hardware."

TASK 1: OPEN COMPANY FILE

WORKFLOW

If you are using the Workflow approach, you will use the same .QBW file. If your QBW file is not already open, open it by selecting **File > Open Previous Company**. Select your **.QBW file**. Update Company Name to include **YourName Exercise 4.2**.

RESTART & RESTORE

If you are using the Restart and Restore approach, restore your backup file using the directions in *Appendix B: Back Up & Restore QuickBooks Files*. After restoring the file, update Company Name to include **YourName Exercise 4.2**.

TASK 2: RECORD CUSTOMER CREDIT

Record a credit to Mrs. Beneficio's account for the $30.00 she was previously charged for standard door hardware by completing the following steps:

Step 1: Click the **Refunds and Credits** icon in the *Customers* section of the Home page.

Step 2: Select Customer and Job: **Beneficio, Katrina: Door Replacement.**

Step 3: Select Template: **Custom Credit Memo**. Credit No. 1102 should automatically appear.

Step 4: Select Date: **12/20/2019**.

Step 5: Select Item: **Hardware Standard Doorknobs**.

Step 6: Enter Quantity: **1**.

Step 7: Adjust the font size for the company name if needed. Select the appropriate printer or PDF printer, then **print** the Credit Memo.

Step 8: Select **Use credit to apply to invoice**.

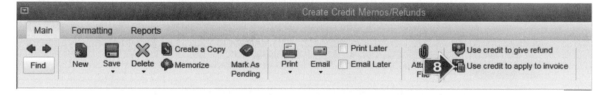

Step 9: Select **Yes** if asked if you want to record changes.

Step 10: When the following *Apply Credit to Invoices* window appears, select **Invoice No. 1101**. Click **Done**.

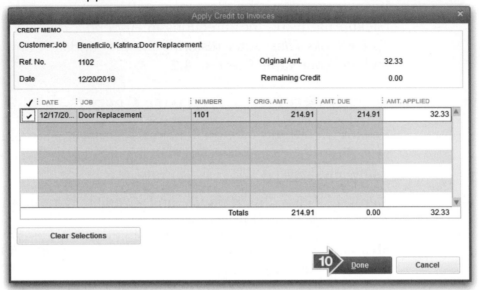

Step 11: Select **Save & Close** to close the *Create Credit Memos/Refunds* window.

 The Credit Memo No. 1102 totals $-32.33 ($30.00 plus $2.33 tax).

TASK 3: CREATE INVOICE

Step 1: Create a new invoice (Invoice No. 1103) for Katrina Beneficio: Door Replacement on 12/20/2019 to record the charges for the interior door locking hardware.

Step 2: Select the appropriate printer or PDF printer, then **print** the invoice.

 Invoice No. 1103 totals $40.95.

TASK 4: PRINT REMINDER STATEMENT

Using the appropriate printer or PDF printer, **print** a reminder statement for the Beneficio Door Replacement Job for 12/20/2019. Use Statement Period From: **12/02/2019** To: **12/20/2019**. Select **Show invoice item details on statements**. Select **Print due date on transactions**.

 The Reminder Statement shows a total amount due of $223.53.

TASK 5: RECEIVE PAYMENT

Record Mrs. Beneficio's payment for the door replacement by VISA credit card for $223.53 on 12/20/2019.

- Card No.: **4444-5555-6666-7777**

- Exp. Date: **07/2020**

- Print Payment Receipt.

- Click **Save & Close** to close the *Receive Payments* window.

TASK 6: RECORD BANK DEPOSIT

Step 1:   Record the deposit for $223.53 on 12/20/2019.

Step 2:   Select the appropriate printer or PDF printer, then **print** a deposit summary.

TASK 7: SAVE EXERCISE 4.2

Save a backup of your Exercise 4.2 file using the file name: **YourName Exercise 4.2 Backup.QBB**. See *Appendix B: Back Up & Restore QuickBooks Files* for instructions.

WORKFLOW

If you are using the Workflow approach, you can leave your .QBW file open and use it for Exercise 4.3.

RESTART & RESTORE

If you are stopping your QuickBooks work session and changing computers, you will need to restore your .QBB file when you restart.

EXERCISE 4.3:
CUSTOMER REPORTS & COLLECTION LETTERS

In this exercise, you will create additional customer reports that a business might find useful.

TASK 1: OPEN COMPANY FILE

WORKFLOW

If you are using the Workflow approach, you will use the same .QBW file. If your QBW file is not already open, open it by selecting **File > Open Previous Company**. Select your **.QBW file**. Update Company Name to include **YourName Exercise 4.3**.

RESTART & RESTORE

If you are using the Restart and Restore approach, restore your backup file using the directions in *Appendix B: Back Up & Restore QuickBooks Files*. After restoring the file, update Company Name to include **YourName Exercise 4.3**.

TASK 2: EDIT CUSTOMER LIST

Edit Ecker Designs' email address in the Customer List.

Step 1: Open the Customer Center.

Step 2: Select customer: **Ecker Designs**.

Step 3: Click the **Edit Customer** icon to display the *Edit Customer* window for Ecker Designs.

Step 4: Edit the email address for Ecker Designs: **decker@www.com**.

Step 5: Click **OK** to save the customer information and close the *Edit Customer* window.

TASK 3: PRINT CUSTOMER REPORT

Prepare a transactions report for Ecker Designs as follows.

Step 1: From the Customer List, select **Ecker Designs.**

Step 2: In the *Customer Information* section, transactions for Ecker Designs should appear. With your cursor over the *Customer Transactions* section of the *Customer Center* window, **right-click** to display the following pop-up menu. Select **View as a Report**.

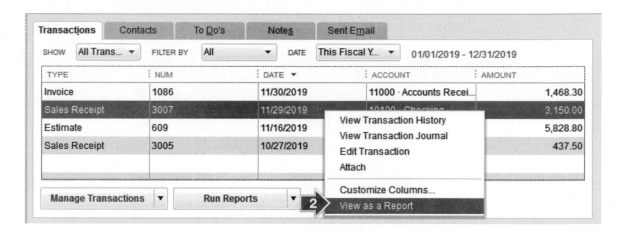

Step 3: Select Dates From: **11/01/2019** To: **12/31/2019**.

Step 4: Sort By: **Date** in **Ascending (A to Z)** order.

Step 5: Export to **Excel** or **print** the report for Ecker Designs.

> *The last amount charged to Ecker Designs' account was Invoice*
> *No. 1086 for $1,468.30 on November 30, 2019.*

Step 6: **Close** the *Report* window and the *Customer Center* window.

TASK 4: AVERAGE DAYS TO PAY SUMMARY REPORT

Prepare the Average Days to Pay Summary report for Rock Castle Construction as follows.

Step 1: From the Report Center, select **Customers & Receivables**.

Step 2: Select **Average Days to Pay Summary** report.

Step 3: Select Dates: **All**.

Step 4: Export to **Excel** or **print** the Average Days to Pay Summary report.

Step 5: **Highlight** how many days on average it takes for a customer to pay Rock Castle Construction.

Task 5: Customer Letters

Prepare a letter of apology to Katrina Beneficio for installing door hardware without a lock.

Step 1: From the Customer Center, click **Katrina Beneficio** in the Customer List.

Step 2: From the Customer Center, select the **Word** button.

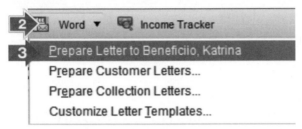

Step 3: Select **Prepare Letter to Beneficio, Katrina**. If a *Find Letter Templates* window appears, select **Copy** to install the templates.

Step 4: Select **Letter templates available for customers/jobs**.

Step 5: Select **Customer apology**.

Step 6: Click **Next**.

Step 7:   Enter Name: **Rock Castle**.

Step 8:   Enter Title: **President**.

Step 9:   Click **Next**.

Step 10:   If Word is installed, QuickBooks will automatically open Word and prepare the apology letter. Select the appropriate printer or PDF printer, then **print** the letter from Word.

Step 11:   Click **Cancel** when asked if you would like to print envelopes. **Close** the Customer Center.

TASK 6: PRINT TRIAL BALANCE

In this task, you will print a Trial Balance to double check that your accounting system is in balance and your account balances are correct.

To prepare the Trial Balance:

Step 1:   From the Report Center, select **Accountant and Taxes > Trial Balance**.

Step 2:   Select Dates From: **12/20/2019** To: **12/20/2019**.

Step 3:   Export to **Excel** or **print** the Trial Balance.

Step 4:   Compare your printout totals and account balances to the following printout. Correct any errors you find.

Your Name Exercise 4.3 Rock Castle Construction
Trial Balance
As of December 20, 2019

Accrual Basis

	Dec 20, 19	
	Debit	Credit
10100 · Checking	120,442.71	
10300 · Savings	17,910.19	
10400 · Petty Cash	500.00	
11000 · Accounts Receivable	93,007.93	
12000 · Undeposited Funds	2,440.00	
12100 · Inventory Asset	28,587.04	
12800 · Employee Advances	832.00	
13100 · Pre-paid Insurance	4,050.00	
13400 · Retainage Receivable	3,703.02	
15000 · Furniture and Equipment	34,326.00	
15100 · Vehicles	78,936.91	
15200 · Buildings and Improvements	325,000.00	
15300 · Construction Equipment	15,300.00	
16900 · Land	90,000.00	
17000 · Accumulated Depreciation		110,344.60
18700 · Security Deposits	1,720.00	
20000 · Accounts Payable		27,136.92
20500 · QuickBooks Credit Card		144.20
20600 · CalOil Credit Card		382.62
24000 · Payroll Liabilities:24010 · Federal Withholding		1,364.00
24000 · Payroll Liabilities:24020 · FICA Payable		2,118.82
24000 · Payroll Liabilities:24030 · AEIC Payable	0.00	
24000 · Payroll Liabilities:24040 · FUTA Payable		100.00
24000 · Payroll Liabilities:24050 · State Withholding		299.19
24000 · Payroll Liabilities:24060 · SUTA Payable		110.00
24000 · Payroll Liabilities:24070 · State Disability Payable		48.13
24000 · Payroll Liabilities:24080 · Worker's Compensation		1,214.31
24000 · Payroll Liabilities:24100 · Emp. Health Ins Payable		150.00
25500 · Sales Tax Payable		976.24
23000 · Loan - Vehicles (Van)		10,501.47
23100 · Loan - Vehicles (Utility Truck)		19,936.91
23200 · Loan - Vehicles (Pickup Truck)		22,641.00
28100 · Loan - Construction Equipment		13,911.32
28200 · Loan - Furniture/Office Equip		21,000.00
28700 · Note Payable - Bank of Anycity		2,693.21
28900 · Mortgage - Office Building		296,283.00
30000 · Opening Bal Equity		38,773.75
30100 · Capital Stock		73,500.00
32000 · Retained Earnings		61,756.76
40100 · Construction Income	0.00	
40100 · Construction Income:40110 · Design Income		36,729.25
40100 · Construction Income:40130 · Labor Income		208,505.42
40100 · Construction Income:40140 · Materials Income		120,160.67
40100 · Construction Income:40150 · Subcontracted Labor Income		82,710.35
40100 · Construction Income:40199 · Less Discounts given	48.35	
40500 · Reimbursement Income:40520 · Permit Reimbursement Income		1,223.75
40500 · Reimbursement Income:40530 · Reimbursed Freight & Delivery		896.05
50100 · Cost of Goods Sold	16,862.53	
54000 · Job Expenses:54200 · Equipment Rental	1,850.00	
54000 · Job Expenses:54300 · Job Materials	98,935.90	
54000 · Job Expenses:54400 · Permits and Licenses	700.00	
54000 · Job Expenses:54500 · Subcontractors	63,217.95	
54000 · Job Expenses:54520 · Freight & Delivery	842.10	
54000 · Job Expenses:54599 · Less Discounts Taken		201.81
60100 · Automobile:60110 · Fuel	1,588.70	
60100 · Automobile:60120 · Insurance	2,850.24	
60100 · Automobile:60130 · Repairs and Maintenance	2,406.00	
60400 · Selling Expenses:60410 · Advertising Expense	200.00	
60600 · Bank Service Charges	145.00	
62100 · Insurance:62110 · Disability Insurance	582.06	
62100 · Insurance:62120 · Liability Insurance	5,885.96	
62100 · Insurance:62130 · Work Comp	13,657.07	
62400 · Interest Expense:62420 · Loan Interest	1,995.65	
62700 · Payroll Expenses:62710 · Gross Wages	110,400.10	
62700 · Payroll Expenses:62720 · Payroll Taxes	8,445.61	
62700 · Payroll Expenses:62730 · FUTA Expense	268.00	
62700 · Payroll Expenses:62740 · SUTA Expense	1,233.50	
63000 · Office Supplies	50.00	
63100 · Postage	104.20	
63600 · Professional Fees:63610 · Accounting	250.00	
64200 · Repairs:64210 · Building Repairs	175.00	
64200 · Repairs:64220 · Computer Repairs	300.00	
64200 · Repairs:64230 · Equipment Repairs	1,350.00	
64800 · Tools and Machinery	2,820.68	
65100 · Utilities:65110 · Gas and Electric	1,164.16	
65100 · Utilities:65120 · Telephone	841.15	
65100 · Utilities:65130 · Water	264.00	
70100 · Other Income		146.80
70200 · Interest Income		229.16
TOTAL	**1,156,189.71**	**1,156,189.71**

> **!**
> Would you like more information about correcting errors in QuickBooks?
> See *Correcting Errors* in *Appendix C: QuickBooks Issue Resolution*.
> Or go to **www.My-QuickBooks.com**, select **QB Issue Resolution**.

TASK 7: PRINT JOURNAL

Prepare the Journal as follows.

Step 1: From the Report Center, select **Accountant and Taxes > Journal**.

Step 2: Select Dates From: **12/17/2019** To: **12/20/2019**.

Step 3: Export to **Excel** or **print** the Journal.

TASK 8: SAVE EXERCISE 4.3

 Save a backup of your Exercise 4.3 file using the file name: **YourName Exercise 4.3 Backup.QBB**. See *Appendix B: Back Up & Restore QuickBooks Files* for instructions.

 ### WORKFLOW

If you are using the Workflow approach, you can leave your .QBW file open and use it for the next chapter.

 ### RESTART & RESTORE

If you are stopping your QuickBooks work session and changing computers, you will need to restore your .QBB file when you restart.

EXERCISE 4.4: CORRECTING QUICKBOOKS ERRORS

Assume when reviewing your Trial Balance in Exercise 4.3, you find two errors.

A. The Checking account balance was understated by $304.30.
B. The Accounts Receivable account balance is overstated by $32.33.

Step 1: What do you think are the most likely causes of the two errors? Be specific regarding which transactions might be in error.

Step 2: How would you correct each of the errors? Specifically, what actions would you take so that your trial balance would show the correct balances?

EXERCISE 4.5: WEB QUEST

Rock Castle has heard that QuickBooks now offers a Point of Sale product to go with QuickBooks. He wants to know more about the product and whether it is a good choice for Rock Castle Construction.

Step 1: Using an Internet search engine, such as Google, research QuickBooks Point of Sale products.

Step 2: Prepare an email to Rock Castle summarizing the main features of the Point of Sale product. Include your recommendation whether this is a worthwhile product for Rock Castle Construction to use.

REFLECTION: A WISH AND A STAR

Reflection improves learning and retention. Reflect on what you have learned after completing Chapter 4 that you did not know before you started the chapter.

A Star:

What did you like best that you learned about QuickBooks in Chapter 4?

A Wish:

If you could pick one thing, what do you wish you knew more about when using QuickBooks?

CHAPTER 4 QUICK CHECK

NAME:

INSTRUCTIONS:

1. **CHECK OFF THE ITEMS YOU COMPLETED.**
2. **TURN IN THIS PAGE WITH YOUR PRINTOUTS.**

> **!**
> **Ask your instructor if you should Go Digital (Excel* or PDF) or use paper printouts.**

CHAPTER 4

- ☐ Cash Sales Receipt
- ☐ Invoice No. 1100
- ☐ Reminder Statement
- ☐ Deposit Summary
- ☐ * Journal
- ☐ * Accounts Receivable Aging Summary Report
- ☐ * Open Invoices Report
- ☐ * Collections Report
- ☐ * Income by Customer Summary Report

EXERCISE 4.1

- ☐ Task 3: Invoice No. 1101

EXERCISE 4.2

- ☐ Task 2: Credit Memo No. 1102
- ☐ Task 3: Invoice No. 1103
- ☐ Task 4: Statement
- ☐ Task 5: Payment Receipt
- ☐ Task 6: Deposit Summary

EXERCISE 4.3

- ☐ * Task 3: Customer Report
- ☐ * Task 4: Average Days to Pay Summary Report
- ☐ Task 5: Customer Letter
- ☐ * Task 6: Trial Balance
- ☐ * Task 7: Journal

EXERCISE 4.4

- ☐ Correcting QuickBooks Errors

EXERCISE 4.5

- ☐ QuickBooks Point of Sale

 Download Go Digital Excel templates at www.My-QuickBooks.com.

PROJECT 4 LARRY'S LANDSCAPING

To complete this project, download the Chapter 4 Go Digital Reports Excel template at www.My-QuickBooks.com. Follow the instructions provided in the Excel template.

Complete the following for Larry's Landscaping.

1. Use either your QuickBooks company file (.QBW file) or backup file (.QBB file) that you completed for Project 3. (If you have issues with your QuickBooks file, contact your instructor.) Update the Company Name to: **YourName Project 4 Larry's Landscaping**.

2. Download the Go Digital Reports Excel template for Chapter 4. Save the Excel file using the file name: **YourLastName FirstName CH4 REPORTS**.

3. Enter the following sales receipts for Larry's Landscaping. (Use Template: Sales Receipt - Retail.)

Date	Customer	Item	Quantity	Payment Method
12/19/2019	Bob Heldt	Pump (Fountain Pump)	1	Cash
12/20/2019	Tracy Stinson	Fertilizer (Lawn & Garden)	5	Cash
12/21/2019	Dave Perry	Rocks (Garden Rocks)	2	Check (No. 622)

4. Enter the following invoices.

Date	Customer	Item	Quantity	Price Each	Tax
12/19/2019	Anne Loomis	Pest Control Service	1	$60.00	Non
12/20/2019	Russell Chiropractic	Weekly Garden Service	1	$75.00	Non
12/20/2019	Gwen Price	Tree Removal	1	$80.00	Non

5. Record the following customer payments.

Date	Customer	Invoice No.	Amount	Payment Method
12/19/2019	Susie Rummens	No. 126	$135.00	Check (No. 321)
12/20/2019	Bob Heldt	No. 123	$1,825.92	Check (No. 823)
12/21/2019	Mike Balak	No. 116	$180.00	Check (No. 1281)

6. Record the following deposits (related to previous requirements 3 and 5) from Undeposited Funds to the Checking account.

Date	Customer	Amount
12/21/2019	Bob Heldt	$80.81
12/21/2019	Tracy Stinson	$10.06
12/21/2019	Susie Rummens	$135.00
12/21/2019	Bob Heldt	$1,825.92
12/21/2019	Dave Perry	$20.77
12/21/2019	Mike Balak	$180.00

7. Export to **Excel** the Open Invoices report for Larry's Landscaping for December 21, 2019.

8. Export to **Excel** the Deposit Detail report for December 19 - 21, 2019.

9. Export to **Excel** the Journal report for December 19 - 21, 2019.

10. Mark the reports completed on the 4 REPORTS sheet. Save your Excel file.

11. Save a .QBB backup of your work.

PROJECT 4 QUICK CHECK

NAME:

INSTRUCTIONS:

1. CHECK OFF THE ITEMS YOU COMPLETED.
2. ATTACH THIS PAGE TO YOUR PRINTOUTS.

!
Ask your instructor if you should Go Digital (Excel* or PDF) or use paper printouts.

PROJECT 4

☐ * Open Invoices
☐ * Deposit Detail
☐ * Journal

Download Go Digital Excel templates at www.My-QuickBooks.com.

NOTES:

CHAPTER 5
VENDORS, PURCHASES, AND INVENTORY

SCENARIO

As you work your way through stacks of paper in your desk's inbox, you hear Mr. Castle's rapid footsteps coming in your direction. He whips around the corner of your cubicle with another stack of papers in hand.

In his usual rapid-fire delivery, Mr. Castle begins, *"This is the way we do business."* He quickly sketches the following:

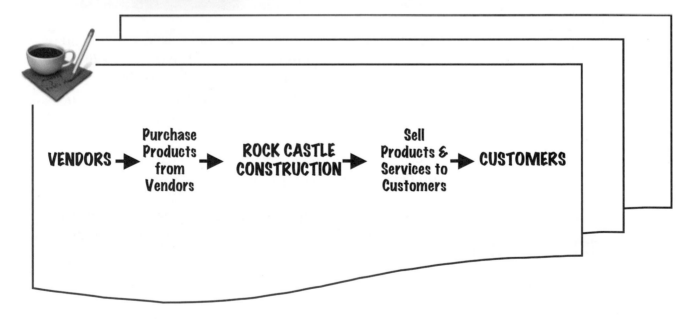

VENDORS → Purchase Products from Vendors → ROCK CASTLE CONSTRUCTION → Sell Products & Services to Customers → CUSTOMERS

"We purchase products from our vendors and suppliers, and then we sell those products and provide services to our customers. We use QuickBooks to track the quantity and cost of items we purchase and sell."

Mr. Castle tosses the papers into your inbox. *"Here are vendor and purchase transactions that need to be recorded."*

A few minutes later, Mr. Castle races past your cubicle engaged in an intense conversation on his mobile phone. Then the chime of your smartphone alerts you to an incoming text—from Mr. Castle!

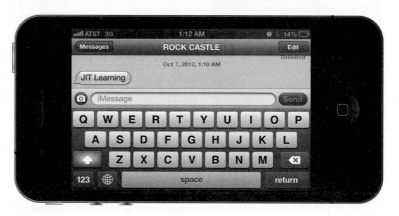

Clueless as to the meaning of Mr. Castle's text, you wait for him to circle back and explain. Within minutes, he circles past your cubicle and barks out, *"Check out the Quick Guide at the back of your book—it's the only way I managed until you arrived.*

"I call it JIT Learning—learn the QuickBooks feature you need—just in time to use it—"

JIT Learning

Before you can reply, Mr. Castle is gone. You turn to the Quick Guide to find one of Mr. Castle's sticky notes marking the page.

CHAPTER 5
LEARNING OBJECTIVES

In Chapter 5, you will learn about the following QuickBooks features:

INTRODUCTION

In Chapter 5 you will focus on using QuickBooks to record vendor transactions, including placing orders, receiving goods, and paying bills.

QuickBooks considers a vendor to be any individual or organization that provides products or services to your company. QuickBooks considers all of the following to be vendors:

- Suppliers from whom you buy inventory or supplies.

- Service companies that provide services to your company, such as cleaning services or landscaping services.

- Financial institutions, such as banks, that provide financial services including checking accounts and loans.

- Tax agencies such as the IRS. The IRS is considered a vendor because you pay taxes to the IRS.

- Utility and telephone companies.

If your company is a merchandising business that buys and resells goods, then you must maintain inventory records to account for the items you purchase from vendors and resell to customers.

The following diagram summarizes vendor and customer transactions.

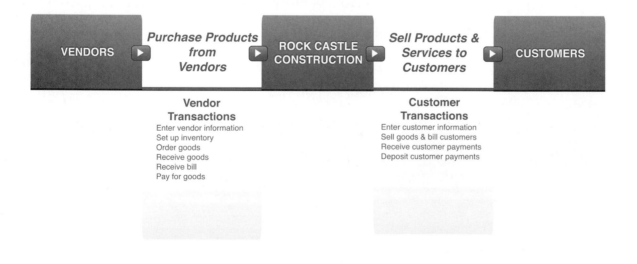

Vendor Transactions
Enter vendor information
Set up inventory
Order goods
Receive goods
Receive bill
Pay for goods

Customer Transactions
Enter customer information
Sell goods & bill customers
Receive customer payments
Deposit customer payments

The following table summarizes how to record Rock Castle Construction's business operations using QuickBooks.

	Activity	Record Using...
1.	Record vendor information.	*Vendor List*
2.	Record inventory information: Set up inventory records to track the quantity and cost of items purchased.	*Item List*
3.	Order goods: Use purchase orders (POs) to order goods from vendors.	*Purchase Orders*
4.	Receive goods: Record goods received as inventory.	*Receive Items*
5.	Receive bill: Record an obligation to pay a bill later (Account Payable).	*Enter Bills*
6.	Pay for goods: Pay bills for the goods received.	*Pay Bills*
7.	Record customer information.	*Customer List*
8.	Sell goods and bill customers: Record customer's promise to pay later (Account Receivable).	*Invoice*
9.	Receive customer payment: Record cash collected and reduce customer's Account Receivable.	*Receive Payments*
10.	Deposit customers' payments in bank account.	*Deposit*

Vendor Transactions bracket covers rows 1–6.
Customer Transactions bracket covers rows 7–10.

Start QuickBooks by clicking on the **QuickBooks desktop icon** or click **Start > Programs > QuickBooks > QuickBooks Premier Accountant Edition 2015**.

WORKFLOW

Use the Workflow approach if you are using the same computer and the same .QBW file from the prior chapter.

Step 1: If your .QBW file is not already open, open it by selecting **File > Open Previous Company**. Select your **.QBW file.**

Step 2: Add **YourName Chapter 5** to the company name.

RESTART & RESTORE

Use the Restart & Restore approach if you are moving your QuickBooks files between computers.

Step 1: Restore the **Backup.QBB** file using the directions in *Appendix B: Back Up & Restore QuickBooks Files.* You can restore using one of two different .QBB files.

1. Restore your own .QBB file from the last exercise completed in the previous chapter.

2. Restore the Chapter 5 DATA STARTER.QBB file that comes with *Computer Accounting with QuickBooks* (available on CD or download from the Online Learning Center).

   If the *QuickBooks Login* window appears:

   - Leave the *User Name* field as **Admin**.
   - Leave the *Password* field **blank**.
   - Click **OK**.

Step 2: After restoring the file, add **YourName Chapter 5** to the company name.

VENDOR NAVIGATION

After opening the company file for Rock Castle Construction, click the **Home** icon in the Icon bar.

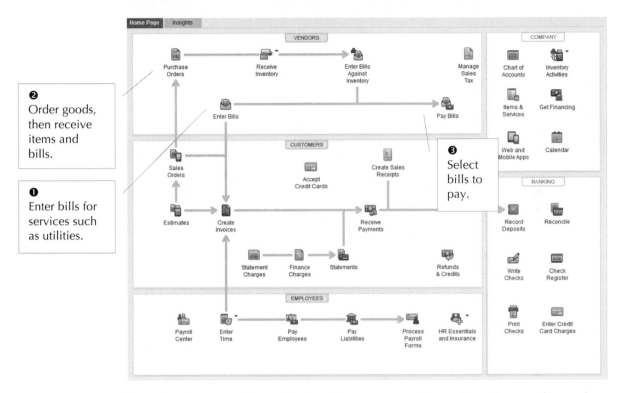

The *Vendors* section of the Home page is a flowchart of vendor transactions. As the flowchart indicates, Rock Castle Construction can record bills in QuickBooks as follows.

❶ **Record services received.** Use the *Enter Bills* window to record bills for services received. Examples include rent, utilities expense, insurance expense, and accounting and professional services. QuickBooks will record an obligation (accounts payable liability) to pay the bill later.

❷ **Record goods purchased.** Use the *Purchase Orders* window to record an order to purchase goods. Use the *Receive Items* window to record goods received. When the bill is received, use the *Enter Bills* window to record the bill. Again, when the bill is entered, QuickBooks records accounts payable to reflect the obligation to pay the bill later.

❸ **Select bills to pay.** Use the *Pay Bills* window to select the bills that are due and you are ready to pay.

Another QuickBooks feature available from the *Vendors* section of the Home page includes:

Manage Sales Tax: Sales taxes are charged on retail sales to customers. The sales tax collected from customers must be paid to the appropriate state agency.

VENDOR LIST

The first step in working with vendor transactions is to enter vendor information in the Vendor List.

The Vendor List contains information for each vendor, such as address, telephone number, and credit terms. Vendor information is entered in the Vendor List and then QuickBooks automatically transfers the vendor information to the appropriate forms, such as purchase orders and checks. This feature enables you to enter vendor information only once in QuickBooks instead of entering the vendor information each time a form is prepared.

VIEW VENDOR LIST

To view the Vendor List for Rock Castle Construction:

Step 1: Click **Vendors** in the Icon bar.

Step 2: Click the **Vendors** tab. The following Vendor List appears listing vendors with whom Rock Castle Construction does business. The Vendor List also displays the balance currently owed each vendor.

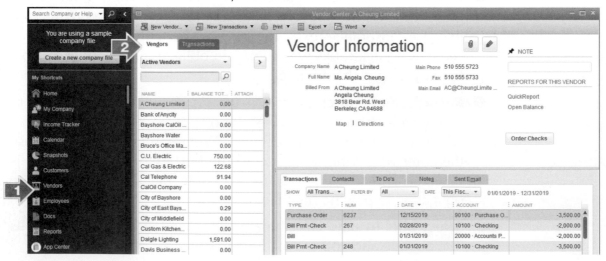

Step 3:   To view additional information about a vendor, click the vendor's name, and Vendor Information will appear on the right side of the Vendor Center.

ADD NEW VENDOR

Rock Castle Construction needs to add a new vendor, Kolbe Window & Door, to the Vendor List.

To add a new vendor to the Vendor List:

Step 1:   Click the **New Vendor** button at the top of the Vendor Center.

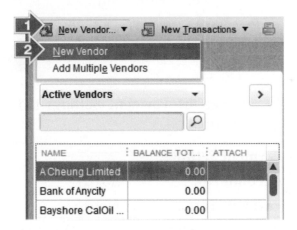

Step 2:   Select **New Vendor** from the drop-down menu.

Step 3:   Select the Address Info tab in the *New Vendor* window. Enter the following information.

Vendor Name	Kolbe Window & Door
Company Name	Kolbe Window & Door
Full Name	John Kolbe
Main Phone	415-555-1958
Mobile	415-555-1985
Main Email	Kolbe@windowdoor.com
Address	58 Charles Bayshore, CA 94326

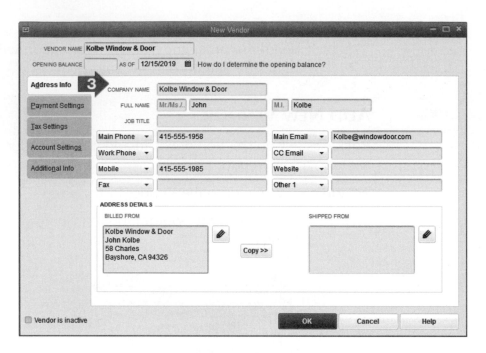

Step 4: Select the **Payment Settings** tab and enter the following information.

Payment Settings:	
Account No.	58101
Payment Terms	Net 15
Print on Check as	Kolbe Window & Door

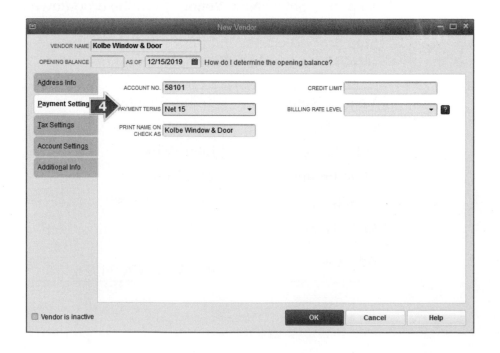

+

IRS Form 1099 must be completed for sole proprietorships and partnerships to which you paid $600 or more for services in a year. The vendor's Tax ID No. is required to complete the 1099.

Step 5:   Select the **Tax Settings** tab and enter the following information.

Tax Settings:	
Vendor Tax ID	37-1958101
Vendor eligible for 1099	Yes

Step 6:   Select the **Additional Info** tab and enter the following information.

Additional Info:	
Vendor Type	Materials

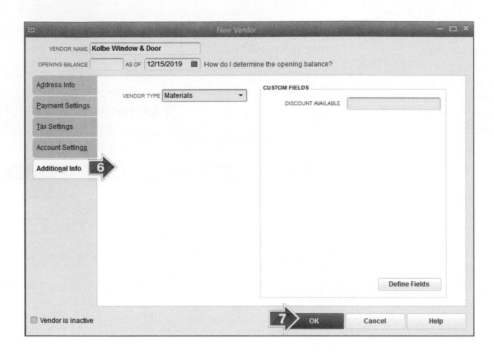

Step 7: Click **OK** to add the new vendor and close the *New Vendor* window.

> **+**
> The Vendor List can be imported from Excel into QuickBooks.

FYI: To edit vendor information later, simply click the vendor's name in the *Vendor List* window. The vendor information will appear on the right side of the Vendor Center. Click the Edit Vendor button, make the necessary changes in the *Edit Vendor* window that appears, and then click OK to close the *Edit Vendor* window.

PRINT VENDOR LIST

Print the Vendor List as follows:

Step 1: Click the **Excel** button at the top of the Vendor Center.

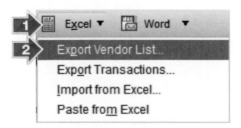

Step 2: Select **Export Vendor List** from the drop-down menu.

Step 3: Select **Replace an existing worksheet. Browse** for your **CH5 REPORTS Excel** workbook**.** Select the appropriate sheet. Select **Export.**

Step 4: **Close** the Vendor Center.

The Items and Services List, discussed next, is used to record information about goods and services purchased from vendors.

ITEMS: INVENTORY ITEMS, NON-INVENTORY ITEMS, AND SERVICES

Items provide supporting detail for accounts.

QuickBooks defines an item as anything that your company buys, sells, or resells including products, shipping charges, and sales taxes. QuickBooks classifies goods and services purchased and sold into three different categories of items:

+
QuickBooks tracks inventory costs using the weighted-average method. QuickBooks does not use FIFO (First-in, First-out) or LIFO (Last-in, First-out) inventory costing. The average cost of an inventory item is displayed in the *Edit Item* window.

1. **Service Items:** Service items can be services that are purchased *or* sold. For example, service items include:

   - Services you *buy* from vendors, such as cleaning services.

   - Services you *sell* to customers, such as installation labor.

2. **Inventory Items:** Inventory items are goods that a business purchases, holds as inventory, and then resells to customers. QuickBooks traces the quantity and cost of inventory items in stock.

   For consistency, the *same* inventory item is used when recording *sales* and *purchases*. QuickBooks has the capability to track both the cost and the sales price for inventory items. For example, in Chapter 4, you recorded the *sale* of an inventory item, an interior door. When the interior door was recorded on a sales invoice, QuickBooks automatically updated your inventory records by reducing the quantity of doors on hand. If you *purchased* an interior door, then you would record the door on the purchase order using the same inventory item number that you used on the invoice, except the purchase order uses the door cost while the invoice uses the door selling price.

+
QuickBooks does *not* track the **quantity** of non-inventory items. If it is important for your business to know the quantity of an item on hand, record the item as an inventory item.

3. **Non-Inventory Items:** QuickBooks does not track the quantity on hand for non-inventory items. Non-inventory items include:

- Items purchased for a specific customer job, such as a custom countertop.

- Items purchased and used by your company instead of resold to customers, such as office supplies or carpentry tools.

- Items purchased and resold (if the quantity on hand does not need to be tracked).

ITEMS AND SERVICES LIST

The Items and Services List (Item List) summarizes information about items (inventory items, non-inventory items, and service items) that a company purchases or sells.

To view the Item List in QuickBooks:

Step 1:   Click the **Items & Services** icon in the *Company* section of the Home page.

Step 2:   The following *Item List* window will appear.

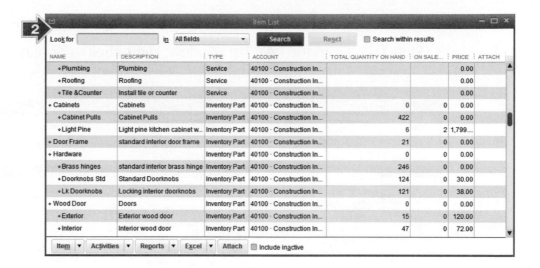

Notice the Item List contains the following information:

- Item name.

- Item description.

- Item type (service, inventory, non-inventory, other charge, discount, sales tax item).

- Account used.

- Quantity on hand.

- Price of the item.

Scroll down through the list to view the inventory and non-inventory items for Rock Castle Construction.

ADD NEW ITEM

Rock Castle Construction needs to add two new items to the Item List: bifold doors and bifold door hardware. Because Rock Castle Construction wants to track the quantity of each item, both will be inventory items.

To add an inventory item to the Item List:

Step 1: From the *Item List* window, **right-click** to display the following pop-up menu. Select **New**.

Step 2: In the *New Item* window that appears, enter information about the bifold door inventory item. From the Type drop-down list, select **Inventory Part**.

Then enter the following information in the *New Item* window.

Item Name/Number	Bifold Doors
Subitem of	Wood Door
Manufacturer's Part Number	BD42
Description on Purchase Transactions	Bifold interior door
Description on Sales Transactions	Bifold interior door
Cost	45.00
COGS Account	50100 – Cost of Goods Sold
Preferred Vendor	Kolbe Window & Door
Sales Price	70.00
Tax Code	Tax
Income Account	40140 Materials Income

Asset Account	12100 – Inventory Asset
Reorder Point	2
On Hand	0
Total Value	0.00
As of	12/15/2019

Use **Group** if the items are bought or sold as a package.

If spell checker starts, click **Add** to add Bifold to dictionary.

Step 3: Click **Next** to record this inventory item and clear the fields to record another inventory item.

Step 4: Enter bifold door knobs as an inventory part in the Item List using the following information:

Item Name/Number	Bifold Knobs
Subitem of	Hardware
Manufacturer's Part Number	BK36
Description on Purchase Transactions	Bifold door hardware

Description on Sales Transactions	Bifold door hardware
Cost	6.00
Sales Price	10.00
Tax Code	Tax
COGS Account	50100 – Cost of Goods Sold
Preferred Vendor	Patton Hardware Supplies
Income Account	40140 Materials Income
Asset Account	12100 – Inventory Asset
Reorder Point	2
On Hand	0
Total Value	0.00
As of	12/15/2019

Step 5: Click **OK** to record the item and close the *New Item* window.

PRINT ITEM LIST

Prepare the Item List as follows:

Step 1: Sort the Item List by selecting **Item** button > **Re-sort List**.

Step 2: Click the **Reports** button at the bottom of the *Item List* window. Select **Item Listing**.

Step 3: Export to **Excel** or **print** the Item List.

Step 4: **Close** the *Item List* window.

VENDOR TRANSACTIONS

After creating a Vendor List and an Item List, you are ready to enter vendor transactions. There are two basic ways to enter vendor transactions using QuickBooks.

1. **Enter Bills.** This is used to record services, such as utilities or accounting services. After the bill is entered, it is paid when it is due.

2. **Enter Purchase Order, Receive Inventory, Enter Bill.** This approach is used to record the purchase of inventory items. The purchase order provides a record of the items ordered.

PURCHASE INVENTORY

Display the Home page to view the flowchart of vendor transactions. Recording the purchase of inventory using QuickBooks involves the following steps:

1. **Purchase Orders.** Create a purchase order to order items from vendors.

2. **Receive Inventory.** Record inventory items received.

3. **Enter Bills Against Inventory.** Record bill received and the obligation to pay the vendor later (accounts payable).

4. **Pay Bills.** Select bills to pay.

5. **Print Checks.** Print checks to vendors. Since the obligation is fulfilled, accounts payable is reduced.

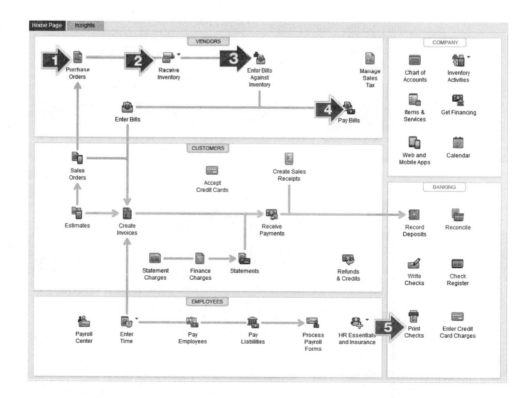

CREATE PURCHASE ORDERS

A purchase order is a record of an order to purchase inventory from a vendor.

Rock Castle Construction wants to order 6 bifold interior doors and 6 sets of bifold door hardware to stock in inventory.

To create a purchase order:

Step 1: Click the **Purchase Orders** icon in the *Vendors* section of the Home page.

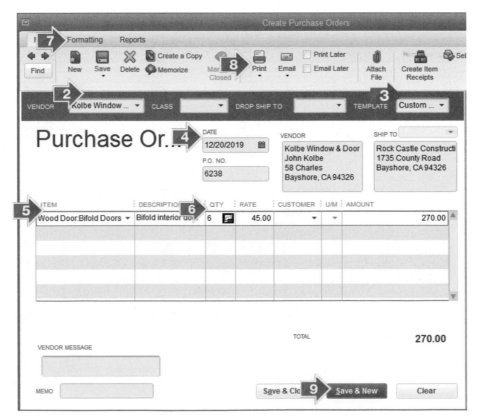

Step 2: From the drop-down Vendor List, select the vendor name: **Kolbe Window & Door**.

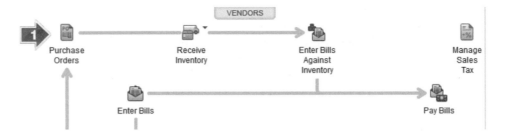

Step 3: Select Template: **Custom Purchase Order**.

Step 4: Enter the Purchase Order Date: **12/20/2019**.

Step 5: Select item ordered: **Wood Door: Bifold Doors**. ($45.00 now appears in the *Rate* column.)

Step 6: Enter Quantity: **6**. ($270.00 should now appear in the *Amount* column.)

Step 7: Format the font for the company name. **Formatting > Customize Data Layout > Basic Customization > Company Name > Change Font > 10**. Close the *Customization* windows.

Step 8: **Print** the purchase order as follows:

- Click **Print**.

- Select Print on: **Blank paper**.

- If necessary, uncheck **Do not print lines around each field**.

- Select printer or appropriate PDF printer, and then click **Print**.

Step 9: Click **Save & New**.

Step 10: Create and **print** a purchase order for bifold door hardware using the following information.

Vendor	Patton Hardware Supplies
Template	Custom Purchase Order
Date	12/20/2019
Item	Hardware: Bifold Knobs
Qty	6

 The purchase order total for bifold door hardware is $36.

Step 11: Click **Save & Close** to close the *Create Purchase Orders* window.

RECEIVE INVENTORY

To record inventory items received on 12/22/2019 ordered from the vendor, Kolbe Window & Door, complete the following steps:

Step 1: Click the **Receive Inventory** icon in the *Vendors* section of the Home page.

Step 2: Select: **Receive Inventory without Bill.**

Step 3: In the *Create Item Receipts* window, select vendor: **Kolbe Window & Door**.

Step 4:   If a purchase order for the item exists, QuickBooks will display the following *Open POs Exist* window. Click **Yes**.

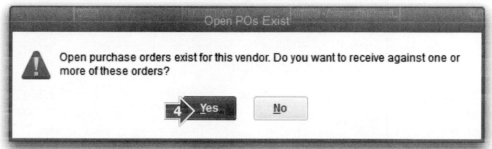

Step 5:   When the following *Open Purchase Orders* window appears, select the purchase order for the items received.

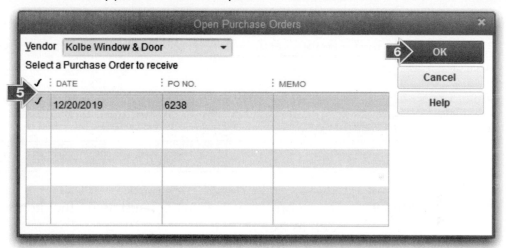

Step 6:   Click **OK**.

Step 7:   The *Create Item Receipts* window will appear with a total of $270. If necessary, change the Date to: **12/22/2019**.

Step 8:   Although Rock Castle Construction ordered 6 bifold doors, only 5 were received. Change the quantity from 6 to **5**.

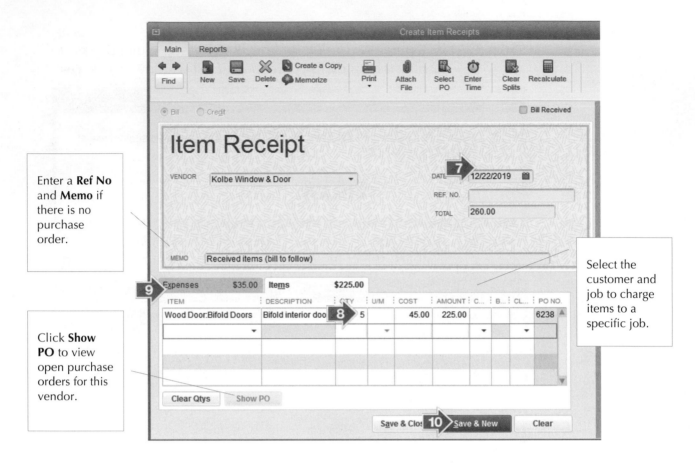

Enter a **Ref No** and **Memo** if there is no purchase order.

Select the customer and job to charge items to a specific job.

Click **Show PO** to view open purchase orders for this vendor.

Step 9: To record expenses associated with the items received, such as freight charges:

- Click the **Expenses** tab in the *Create Item Receipts* window.

- To record $35.00 in freight charges on the bifold doors received, select Account: **54520 Freight & Delivery**.

- Enter Amount: $**35.00**.

- Click the **Recalculate** button.

 The Total on the Create Item Receipts window is now $260.00.

Step 10: Click **Save & New** to record the bifold doors received and clear the window.

Step 11: Record the receipt of the bifold door hardware using the following information:

Vendor	Patton Hardware Supplies
Date	12/22/2019
PO No.	6239
Item	Bifold door hardware
Qty	6

Step 12:   Click **Save & Close** to record the items received and close the *Create Item Receipts* window.

RECEIVE BILLS

You may receive bills at three different times:

	Receive Bill...	Record Using...
1	You receive a bill for services and no inventory items will be received, as for example, if the bill is for security services.	*Enter Bills*
2	You receive a bill at the same time you receive inventory items.	*Receive Inventory with Bill*
3	You receive inventory without a bill, and you receive the bill later.	a. *Receive Inventory without Bill* b. *Enter Bills Against Inventory*

Later, you will learn how to record bills for situations 1 and 2 above. Next, you will record the bill received for the bifold doors ordered from Kolbe Window & Door (situation 3 above).

ENTER BILLS AGAINST INVENTORY

To enter a bill received after inventory items are received:

Step 1: Click the **Enter Bills Against Inventory** icon on the *Vendors* section of the Home page.

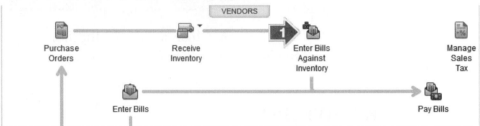

Step 2: When the *Select Item Receipt* window appears, select Vendor: **Kolbe Window & Door**. If necessary, press **Tab**.

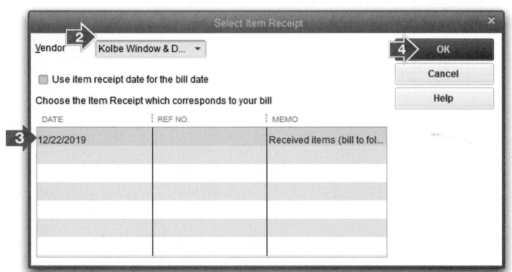

Step 3: Select the Item Receipt that corresponds to the bill.

Step 4: Click **OK**.

Step 5: The following *Enter Bills* window will appear. Notice that the *Enter Bills* window is the same as the *Create Item Receipts* window except:

- Bill Received in the upper right corner is checked.

- The title of the form changes from Item Receipt to Bill.

- The window name changes from *Create Item Receipts* to *Enter Bills*.

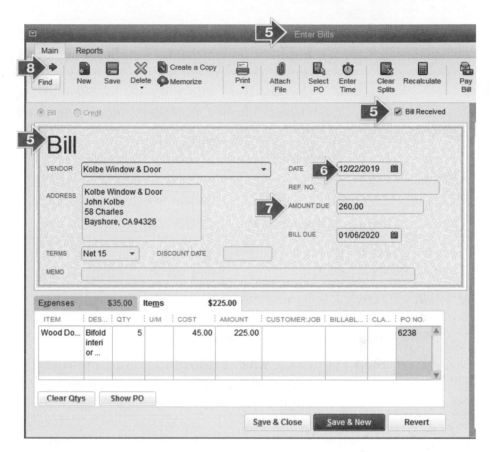

Step 6: At this point, you can make any changes necessary, such as:

- Change the date if the bill is received on a date different from the date the item was received. In this instance, the item and bill are both received on **12/22/2019**.

- Terms

- Ref. No.

- Memo

- Expenses, such as freight charges

Step 7: The Amount Due of **$260.00** should agree with the amount shown on the vendor's bill.

Step 8: Click **Next** to advance to the Item Receipt for the bifold door hardware purchased from Patton Hardware Supplies. If asked if you want to record changes, click **Yes**.

Step 9: To record the bill received for the bifold door hardware from Patton Hardware Supplies, check **Bill Received** in the upper right corner of the window. Notice that the *Item Receipt* form title changes to *Bill* and the window name changed from *Create Item Receipts* to *Enter Bills*.

Step 10: Use the following information to record the bill for the bifold door hardware.

Vendor	Patton Hardware Supplies
Date Bill Received	12/22/2019
PO No.	6239
Terms	Net 30
Item	Bifold door hardware
Qty	6

Step 11: Click **Save & Close** to record the bill and close the *Enter Bills* window. If asked if you want to change the terms, click **Yes**.

When you enter a bill, QuickBooks automatically adds the bill amount to your Accounts Payable account balance.

PAY BILLS

After receiving the items and entering the bill, the next step is to pay the bill.

To select the bills to pay:

Step 1: Click the **Pay Bills** icon in the *Vendors* section of the Home page.

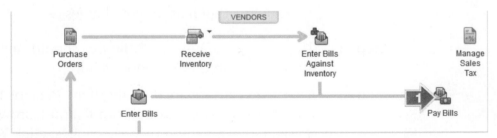

Step 2:   Select Show bills: **Show all bills**.

Step 3:   Select the bills you want to pay. Typically, you would select the bills that are due first. In this case, however, select **bills that you just recorded for:**

- **Kolbe Window and Door for $260.00**

- **Patton Hardware Supplies for $36.00**

If necessary, scroll down to view these two bills.

Step 4:   In the *Payment* section, select: Date: **12/23/2019**.

Step 5:   Select Method: **Check**.

Step 6:   Select: **To be printed**.

Step 7:   Select Account: **Checking**.

Step 8:   Click **Pay Selected Bills**.

   Bills selected for payment total $296.00

> To pay by debit card, select Method: **Check > Assign check number**. Then use **DC** (for debit card) as the check number.

To print the checks, when the *Payment Summary* window appears:

Step 1: Review the information to verify it is correct. Click **Print Checks**.

If you need to make a change, click *How do I find and change a bill payment?*

To print the checks later, click **Done**. Later, select **File menu > Print Forms > Checks**.

QuickBooks prints one check for each vendor, combining all amounts due to the same vendor.

If you use Intuit's preprinted check forms, you would now insert the check forms in your printer.

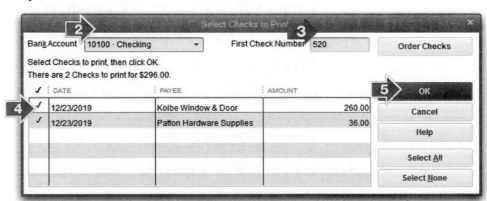

Step 2: When the *Select Checks to Print* window appears, select Bank Account: **Checking**.

Step 3: Select First Check Number: **520**.

Step 4: Select the two checks shown above:

- **12/23/2019 Kolbe Window & Door for $260.00**
- **12/23/2019 Patton Hardware Supplies for $36.00**

Step 5:   Click **OK**.

Step 6:   Select Check Style: **Standard**. Select: **Print company name and address**.

Step 7:   Select the printer or appropriate PDF printer, and click **Print**.

RECEIVE INVENTORY WITH BILL

If you receive the inventory item and the bill at the same time (situation 2 mentioned earlier), record both receiving the items and the related bill by completing the following steps:

Step 1:   Click the **Receive Inventory** icon in the *Vendors* section of the Home page.

Step 2:   Select: **Receive Inventory with Bill**.

Step 3:   In the following *Enter Bills* window, enter Vendor: **Wheeler's Tile Etc.**

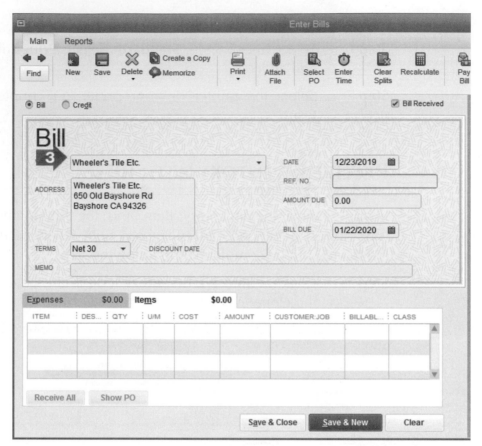

Step 4: If the *Open POs Exist* window appears, select **Yes**.

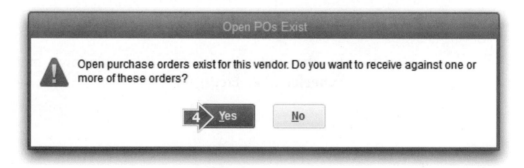

Step 5: Select the open purchase order that corresponds to the bill received: **PO No. 6234**.

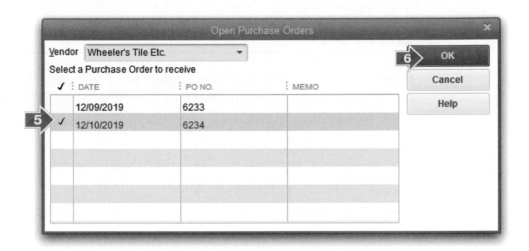

Step 6:   Click **OK**.

Step 7:   If necessary change the date to: **12/23/2019**.

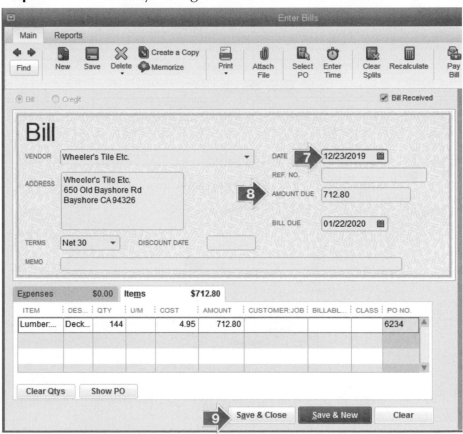

Step 8:   Verify the Amount Due: **712.80**.

Step 9:   Click **Save & Close** to close the *Enter Bills* window.

ENTER BILLS

When you received inventory items from vendors, you recorded those items using either the *Receive Inventory with Bill* option or the *Receive Inventory without Bill* option, entering the bill later.

To record services instead of inventory received, use the Enter Bills icon. Expenses that can be recorded using the *Enter Bills* window include utilities, insurance, and rent.

Recording bills for services, such as utilities, in QuickBooks requires two steps:

1. **Enter Bills.** Record bills received for services.

2. **Pay Bills.** Select bills to pay.

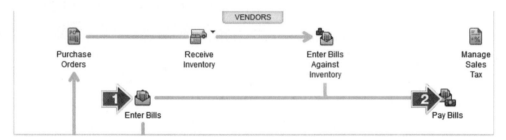

To enter bills for expenses:

Step 1:   Click the **Enter Bills** icon in the *Vendors* section of the Home page.

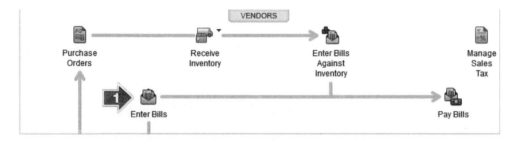

Step 2:   When the following *Enter Bills* window appears, click the **Expenses** tab.

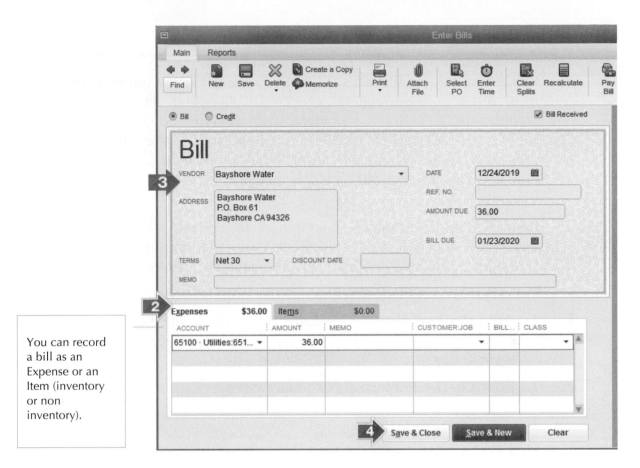

You can record a bill as an Expense or an Item (inventory or non-inventory).

Step 3: Enter the following information for Rock Castle's water bill in the *Enter Bills* window.

Vendor	Bayshore Water
Date	12/24/2019
Amount Due	$36.00
Terms	Net 30
Account	65130: Water

Step 4: Click **Save & Close** to close the *Enter Bills* window.

The next time you pay bills in QuickBooks, the water bill will appear on the list of bills to pay.

PAY SALES TAX

QuickBooks tracks the sales tax that you collect from customers and must remit to governmental agencies. When you set up a new company in QuickBooks, you identify which items and customers are subject to sales tax. In addition, you must specify the appropriate sales tax rate. Then whenever you prepare sales invoices, QuickBooks automatically calculates and adds sales tax to the invoices.

Rock Castle Construction is required to collect sales tax from customers on certain items sold. Rock Castle then must pay the sales tax collected to the appropriate governmental tax agency.

QuickBooks uses a two-step process to remit sales tax:

1. **Pay Sales Tax.** The *Manage Sales Tax* window lists the sales taxes owed and allows you to select the individual sales tax items you want to pay.

2. **Print Checks.** Print the check to pay the sales tax.

To select the sales tax to pay:

Step 1: Click the **Manage Sales Tax** icon in the *Vendors* section of the Home page.

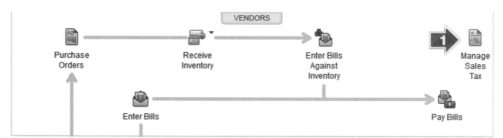

Step 2: When the *Manage Sales Tax* window appears, in the *Pay Sales Tax* section of the window, click the **Pay Sales Tax** button.

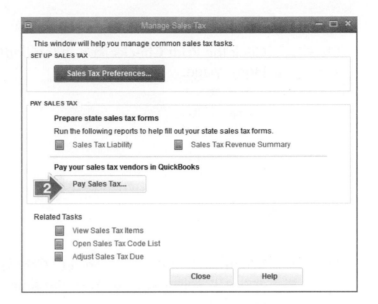

Step 3:   When the following *Pay Sales Tax* window appears, select Pay From Account: **Checking**.

Step 4:   Select Check Date: **12/31/2019**.

Step 5:   Show sales tax due through: **12/31/2019**.

Step 6:   ✓ Check **To be printed**.

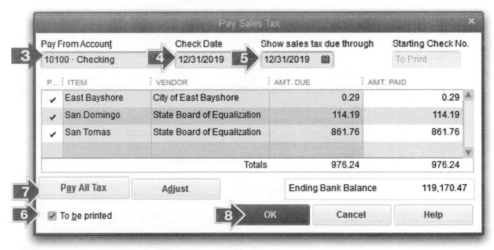

Step 7:   Select: **Pay All Tax**.

Step 8:   Click **OK**.

Step 9:   Click **Close** to close the *Manage Sales Tax* window.

To print the check to pay sales tax to a governmental agency:

Step 1: Click the **Print Checks** icon in the *Banking* section of the Home page.

Step 2: When the following *Select Checks to Print* window appears, select **City of East Bayshore** and **State Board of Equalization**.

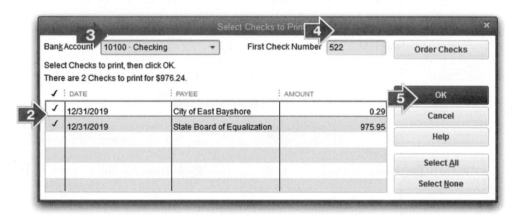

Step 3: Select Bank Account: **Checking**.

Step 4: Select First Check Number: **522**.

Step 5: Click **OK**.

Step 6: Select print settings and printer or PDF printer, then click **Print**.

VENDOR REPORTS

QuickBooks provides vendor reports to answer the following questions:

- How much do we owe? (Accounts Payable reports)
- How much have we purchased? (Purchase reports)
- How much inventory do we have? (Inventory reports)

QuickBooks offers several different ways to access vendor reports:

1. **Vendor Center.** Summarizes vendor information in one location (Access the Vendor Center by clicking the Vendors icon on the Icon bar.)

2. **Report Center.** Permits you to locate reports by type of report (Click the Reports icon on the Icon bar, then see Vendors & Payables, Purchases, and Inventory reports).

3. **Reports Menu.** Reports are grouped by type of report (See Vendors & Payables, Purchases, and Inventory reports).

VENDOR CENTER

The Vendor Center summarizes vendor information in one convenient location. Display the Vendor Center as follows:

Step 1:   From the Icon bar, select **Vendors**.

Step 2:   Select Vendor: **Kolbe Window & Door**.

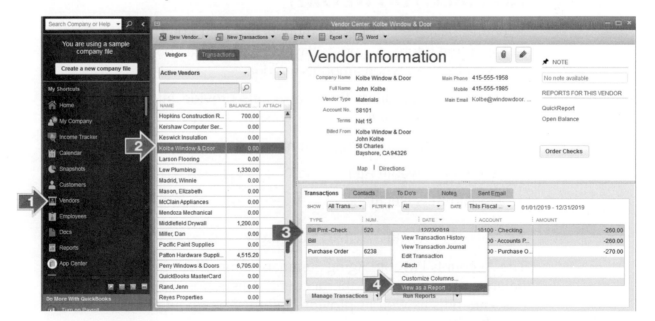

The *Vendor Information* section summarizes information about the vendor selected, including a list of the transactions for the specific vendor. In this case, you recorded three transactions for Kolbe Window & Door:

- Purchase order on 12/20/2019

- Bill received on 12/22/2019

- Bill paid on 12/23/2019

Step 3: Double-click **Bill Pymt – Check** on **12/23/2019** to drill-down and view the check to pay Kolbe Window & Door. After viewing, close the window.

Step 4: With the cursor over the *Vendor Transactions* section of the window, **right-click** to display the pop-up menu. Select **View as a Report**.

Step 5: Export to **Excel** or **print** the report of all transactions for Kolbe Window & Door for this fiscal year.

Step 6: **Close** the report window.

ACCOUNTS PAYABLE REPORTS: HOW MUCH DO WE OWE?

Accounts payable consists of amounts that your company is obligated to pay in the future. Accounts Payable reports tell you how much you owe vendors and when amounts are due.

The following Accounts Payable reports provide information useful when tracking amounts owed vendors:

1. Accounts Payable Aging Summary

2. Accounts Payable Aging Detail

3. Unpaid Bills Detail

ACCOUNTS PAYABLE AGING SUMMARY

The Accounts Payable Aging Summary summarizes accounts payable balances by the age of the account. This report helps to track any past due bills as well as provides information about bills that will be due shortly.

Although you can access the vendor reports in several different ways, we will access this report from the Report Center.

To prepare the A/P Aging Summary report:

Step 1:   Select **Reports** in the Icon bar.

Step 2:   Select: **Vendors & Payables**.

Step 3:   Select: **A/P Aging Summary**.

Step 4:   Select Date: **12/22/2019**.

Step 5:   Select **Run**.

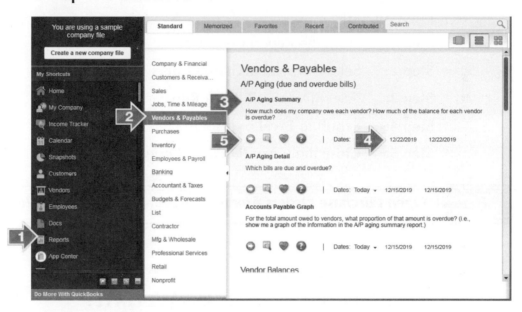

Step 6:   Export to **Excel** or **print** the report.

Step 7:   **Highlight** the vendors and amounts of any past due accounts payable.

Step 8:   **Close** the *A/P Aging Summary* window.

> ✓ ***$3,459.20 is 1-30 days past due.***

PURCHASE REPORTS: HOW MUCH HAVE WE PURCHASED?

Purchase reports provide information about purchases by item, by vendor, or by open purchase orders. Purchase reports include:

1. Open Purchase Orders (Outstanding Purchase Orders)

2. Purchases by Vendor Summary

3. Purchases by Item Summary

OPEN PURCHASE ORDERS REPORT

Open purchase orders are purchase orders for items ordered but not yet received. QuickBooks permits you to view all open purchase orders or just those for a specific vendor.

To prepare the Open Purchase Orders report that lists all open purchase orders:

Step 1: From the Report Center, select: **Purchases**.

Step 2: Select: **Open Purchase Orders**.

Step 3: Select Dates: **All**. Click **Run**.

Step 4: Export to **Excel** or **print** the report.

Step 5: **Close** the *Open Purchase Orders* window.

> *Open Purchase Orders Amount column equals $19,286.25.*

INVENTORY REPORTS: HOW MUCH INVENTORY DO WE HAVE?

Inventory reports list the amount and status of inventory. Inventory reports include:

1. Inventory Stock Status by Item

2. Physical Inventory Worksheet

INVENTORY STOCK STATUS BY ITEM

This report lists the quantity of inventory items on hand and on order. This information is useful for planning when and how many units to order.

To print the Inventory Stock Status by Item report:

Step 1: From the Report Center, select: **Inventory**.

Step 2: Select: **Inventory Stock Status by Item**.

Step 3:   Enter Date: From: **12/22/2019** To: **12/22/2019**. Click **Run**.

Step 4:   Export to **Excel** or **print** the report.

Step 5:   **Close** the *Inventory Stock Status by Item* window.

> *On 12/22/2019, 5 bifold wood doors are on hand and 1 more is on order.*

PHYSICAL INVENTORY WORKSHEET

The Physical Inventory Worksheet is used when taking a physical count of inventory on hand. The worksheet lists the quantity of inventory items on hand and provides a blank column in which to enter the quantity counted during a physical inventory count. This worksheet permits you to compare your physical inventory count with your QuickBooks records.

To prepare the Physical Inventory Worksheet:

Step 1:   From the Report Center, select: **Inventory**.

Step 2:   Select: **Physical Inventory Worksheet**. Use Date: **12/31/2019**. Select **Run**.

Step 3:   Export to **Excel** or **print** the worksheet.

Step 4:   **Close** the *Physical Inventory Worksheet* window.

QuickBooks offers other additional vendor reports that provide useful information to a business. These reports can also be accessed from the Reports menu or from the Report Center.

SAVE CHAPTER 5

Save a backup of your Chapter 5 file using the file name: **YourName Chapter 5 Backup.QBB**. See *Appendix B: Back Up & Restore QuickBooks Files* for instructions.

WORKFLOW

If you are using the Workflow approach, leave your .QBW file open and proceed directly to Exercise 5.1.

RESTART & RESTORE

If you are using the Restart & Restore approach and are ending your computer session now, close your .QBW file and exit QuickBooks. When you restart, you will restore your backup file to complete Exercise 5.1.

WWW.MY-QUICKBOOKS.COM

Go to www.My-QuickBooks.com to view additional QuickBooks resources including Excel Reports Templates, QuickBooks videos, and QuickBooks Hot Arrows and Hot Topics. The Hot Topics can be viewed on your computer or tablet and feature frequently used QuickBooks tasks. Bookmark www.My-QuickBooks.com for your future use.

MULTIPLE-CHOICE PRACTICE TEST

Try the **Multiple-Choice Practice Test** for Chapter 5 on the *Computer Accounting with QuickBooks* Online Learning Center at www.mhhe.com/kay2015.

GO DIGITAL!

Go Digital using Excel templates. See *Appendix D: Go Digital with QuickBooks* for instructions about how to save your QuickBooks reports electronically.

LEARNING ACTIVITIES

Important: Ask your instructor whether you should complete the following assignments by printing reports or by exporting to Excel templates (see Appendix D: Go Digital with QuickBooks).

EXERCISE 5.1: PURCHASE INVENTORY

SCENARIO

Mr. Castle tosses you a document as he charges past your cubicle, shouting over his shoulder, *"That's info about our new supplier. From now on, Rock Castle will install closet shelving instead of waiting on unreliable subcontractors. We do a better job and we get it done on time!"*

Vendor:	Joseph's Closets
Address:	13 Rheims Road
	Bayshore, CA 94326
Main Phone:	415-555-5813
Email:	joseph@closet.com
Account:	58127
Payment Terms:	Net 30
Vendor 1099:	No
Vendor Type:	Materials

<u>**New Inventory Item:**</u>	Closet Materials	Income Acct 40140
New Subitems:		
6' Closet Shelving	Cost: $11.00	Sales Price: $15.00
12' Closet Shelving	Cost: $18.00	Sales Price: $25.00
Closet Installation Kit	Cost: $ 5.00	Sales Price: $ 8.00

TASK 1: OPEN COMPANY FILE

WORKFLOW

If you are using the Workflow approach, you will use the same .QBW file.

- If your QBW file is not already open, open it by selecting **File > Open Previous Company**. Select your **.QBW file.**

- Add **YourName Exercise 5.1** to the company name.

RESTART & RESTORE

If you are not using the same computer, you must use the Restart and Restore approach.

- Restore your **Chapter 5 Backup.QBB** file using the directions in *Appendix B: Back Up & Restore QuickBooks Files*.

- After restoring the file, add **YourName Exercise 5.1** to the company name.

TASK 2: ADD NEW VENDOR

> Add a new vendor from the *Vendor Center.*

Add Joseph's Closets as a new vendor.

TASK 3: ADD NEW INVENTORY ITEM

Step 1: Add the new inventory item, Closet Materials, to the Item List for Rock Castle Construction.

Item Name/Number	Closet Materials
Item Type	Inventory Part
Item Description	Closet Materials
COGS Account	50100 – Cost of Goods Sold
Income Account	40140 – Materials Income
Asset Account	12100 – Inventory Asset
Tax Code	Tax

Step 2: Add the following three new inventory parts as **subitems** to Closet Materials. Use **Joseph's Closets** as the preferred vendor.

Item Name	6' Closet Shelving
Item Description	6' Closet Shelving
Cost	$11.00
Sales Price	$15.00

Item Name	12' Closet Shelving
Item Description	12' Closet Shelving
Cost	$18.00
Sales Price	$25.00

Item Name	Closet Install Kit
Item Description	Closet Installation Kit
Cost	$5.00
Sales Price	$8.00

Step 3: Sort the Item List by selecting **Item** button > **Re-sort List**.

TASK 4: CREATE PURCHASE ORDER

Step 1: Create a purchase order to order **6** each of the new inventory items from **Joseph's Closets** on **12/23/2019**.

Step 2: **Print** the purchase order.

 The total amount of the purchase order is $204.00.

TASK 5: RECEIVE INVENTORY

On **12/24/2019**, record the receipt of the closet inventory items ordered on **12/23/2019**. There are no freight charges.

TASK 6: RECEIVE BILL

Record the receipt of the bill for the closet items on **12/27/2019**. Use the **Enter Bills Against Inventory** icon in the *Vendors* section of the Home page.

TASK 7: PAY BILLS

Pay the bill for the closet materials ordered from Joseph's Closets on **12/28/2019** with Check No. **524**. **Print** the check.

TASK 8: PRINT TRANSACTION LIST BY VENDOR

To review the transactions you entered, print a Transaction List by Vendor report as follows.

Step 1: From the Report Center, select **Vendors & Payables > Transaction List by Vendor**.

Step 2: Select Date From: **12/23/2019** To: **12/28/2019**.

Step 3: Export to **Excel** or **print** the report.

Step 4: **Highlight** the transactions with Joseph's Closets that you entered in this exercise.

Step 5: **Close** the *Transaction List by Vendor* window.

TASK 9: SAVE EXERCISE 5.1

Save a backup of your Exercise 5.1 file using the file name: **YourName Exercise 5.1 Backup.QBB**. See *Appendix B: Back Up & Restore QuickBooks Files* for instructions.

WORKFLOW

If you are proceeding to Exercise 5.2 and using the same computer, you can leave your .QBW file open and use it for Exercise 5.2.

RESTART & RESTORE

If you are stopping your QuickBooks work session and changing computers, you will need to restore your .QBB file when you restart.

EXERCISE 5.2: RECORD SALE (CHAPTER 4 REVIEW)

SCENARIO

"I told you replacing Mrs. Beneficio's door hardware would pay off. She is going to become one of our best customers. Just wait and see." Mr. Castle appears to be in a much better mood today. "Katrina Beneficio just had us install new closet shelving in her huge walk-in closet. She said she wanted us to do it because we stand by our work."

TASK 1: OPEN COMPANY FILE

WORKFLOW

If you are using the Workflow approach, you will use the same .QBW file. If your QBW file is not already open, open it by selecting **File > Open Previous Company**. Select your **.QBW file.** Add **YourName Exercise 5.2** to the company name.

RESTART & RESTORE

If you are using the Restart and Restore approach, restore your backup file using the directions in *Appendix B: Back Up & Restore QuickBooks Files*. After restoring the file, add **YourName Exercise 5.2** to the company name.

TASK 2: ADD CUSTOMER JOB

Add the Closet Shelving job for Katrina Beneficio to the Customer & Job List. (Hint: From the Customer Center, select **Beneficio**, then **right-click** to display menu, and select **Add Job**.)

Job Name	Closet Shelving
Job Description	Replace Closet Shelving
Job Type	Repairs
Job Status	Closed
Start Date	12/27/2019
Projected End Date	12/27/2019
End Date	12/27/2019

TASK 3: CREATE INVOICE

Step 1: Create an invoice for the Beneficio closet shelving job using the following information.

Customer: Job	Beneficio, Katrina: Closet Shelving	
Custom Template	Rock Castle Invoice	
Date	12/27/2019	
Invoice No.	1104	
Items	(2) 12′ Closet Shelving	$25.00 each
	(1) 6′ Closet Shelving	$15.00 each
	(1) Closet Installation Kit	$ 8.00 each
	Installation Labor	3 hours

Step 2: **Print** the invoice.

> *The invoice for the Closet Shelving job totals $183.66.*

TASK 4: RECEIVE CUSTOMER PAYMENT

Record Katrina Beneficio's payment for the Closet Shelving job (Check No. 625) for the full amount on **12/29/2019**.

TASK 5: RECORD BANK DEPOSIT

Step 1: Record the bank deposit for Katrina Beneficio's payment on **12/29/2019**.

Step 2: **Print** a deposit summary.

TASK 6: PRINT TRANSACTION LIST BY CUSTOMER

To review the transactions you entered, print a Transaction List by Customer report as follows.

Step 1: From the Report Center, select **Customers & Receivables > Transaction List by Customer**.

Step 2: Select Date From: **12/27/2019** To: **12/29/2019**.

Step 3: Export to **Excel** or **print** the report.

Step 4: **Highlight** the transactions with Katrina Beneficio that you entered in this exercise.

Step 5: **Close** the *Transaction List by Customer* window.

TASK 7: SAVE EXERCISE 5.2

Save a backup of your Exercise 5.2 file using the file name: **YourName Exercise 5.2 Backup.QBB**. See *Appendix B: Back Up & Restore QuickBooks Files* for instructions.

WORKFLOW

If you are using the Workflow approach, you can leave your .QBW file open and use it for Exercise 5.3.

RESTART & RESTORE

If you are stopping your QuickBooks work session and changing computers, you will need to restore your .QBB file when you restart.

EXERCISE 5.3: ENTER BILLS

SCENARIO

When you arrive at work, you decide to sort through the papers stacked in the corner of your cubicle. You discover two unpaid utility bills amid the clutter.

TASK 1: OPEN COMPANY FILE

WORKFLOW

If you are using the Workflow approach, you will use the same .QBW file. If your QBW file is not already open, open it by selecting **File > Open Previous Company.** Select your **.QBW file.** Add **YourName Exercise 5.3** to the company name.

RESTART & RESTORE

If you are using the Restart and Restore approach, restore your backup file using the directions in *Appendix B: Back Up & Restore QuickBooks Files*. After restoring the file, add **YourName Exercise 5.3** to the company name.

TASK 2: ENTER BILLS

Using the **Enter Bills** icon in the *Vendors* section of the Home page, enter the following two utility bills for Rock Castle Construction.

Vendor	Cal Gas & Electric
Date	12/24/2019
Amount	$87.00
Account	65110: Gas and Electric

Vendor	Cal Telephone
Date	12/24/2019
Amount	$54.00
Account	65120: Telephone

TASK 3: PAY BILLS

On **12/28/2019**, pay the two utility bills that you entered in Task 2. (Hint: Select **Show all bills**.) **Print** the checks (Nos. 525 and 526).

The Amt. To Pay on the Pay Bills window totals $141.00.

TASK 4: PRINT CHECK DETAIL

To review the transactions you entered, print a Check Detail report as follows.

Step 1: From the Report Center, select **Banking > Check Detail**.

Step 2: Select Date From: **12/24/2019** To: **12/28/2019**.

Step 3: Export to **Excel** or **print** the report.

Step 4:   **Highlight** the transactions you entered in this exercise.

Step 5:   **Close** the *Check Detail* window.

TASK 5: SAVE EXERCISE 5.3

Save a backup of your Exercise 5.3 file using the file name: **YourName Exercise 5.3 Backup.QBB**. See *Appendix B: Back Up & Restore QuickBooks Files* for instructions.

WORKFLOW

If you are using the Workflow approach, you can leave your .QBW file open and use it for Exercise 5.4.

RESTART & RESTORE

If you are stopping your QuickBooks work session and changing computers, you will need to restore your .QBB file when you restart.

EXERCISE 5.4: VENDOR REPORTS

In this exercise, you will print a stock status report for the closet materials inventory and a Trial Balance to verify that your account balances are correct.

TASK 1: OPEN COMPANY FILE

WORKFLOW

If you are using the Workflow approach, you will use the same .QBW file. If your QBW file is not already open, open it by selecting **File > Open Previous Company**. Select your **.QBW file.** Add **YourName Exercise 5.4** to the company name.

RESTART & RESTORE

If you are using the Restart and Restore approach, restore your backup file using the directions in *Appendix B: Back Up & Restore QuickBooks Files*. After restoring the file, add **YourName Exercise 5.4** to the company name.

TASK 2: PRINT STOCK STATUS REPORT

Prepare the stock status report for closet materials inventory.

Step 1: Export to **Excel** or **print** an Inventory Stock Status by Item report to check the status of the closet inventory items as of **12/31/2019**.

Step 2: **Highlight** the closet inventory items on the Inventory Stock Status printout.

Step 3: **Close** the report window.

TASK 3: PRINT TRIAL BALANCE

Next, print a Trial Balance to double check that your accounting system is in balance and that your account balances are correct.

Prepare the Trial Balance as follows.

Step 1: From the Report Center, select **Accountant and Taxes > Trial Balance**.

Step 2: Select Date From: **12/31/2019** To: **12/31/2019**.

Step 3: Export to **Excel** or **print** the Trial Balance.

Step 4: Compare your printout totals and account balances to the following printout. Correct any errors you find.

Step 5: **Close** the *Trial Balance* report window.

Your Name Exercise 5.4 Rock Castle Construction
Trial Balance

Accrual Basis

As of December 31, 2019

	Dec 31, 19	
	Debit	Credit
10100 · Checking	119,009.13	
10300 · Savings	17,910.19	
10400 · Petty Cash	500.00	
11000 · Accounts Receivable	93,007.93	
12000 · Undeposited Funds	2,440.00	
12100 · Inventory Asset	29,000.04	
12800 · Employee Advances	832.00	
13100 · Pre-paid Insurance	4,050.00	
13400 · Retainage Receivable	3,703.02	
15000 · Furniture and Equipment	34,326.00	
15100 · Vehicles	78,936.91	
15200 · Buildings and Improvements	325,000.00	
15300 · Construction Equipment	15,300.00	
16900 · Land	90,000.00	
17000 · Accumulated Depreciation		110,344.60
18700 · Security Deposits	1,720.00	
20000 · Accounts Payable		27,885.72
20500 · QuickBooks Credit Card		144.20
20600 · CalOil Credit Card		382.62
24000 · Payroll Liabilities:24010 · Federal Withholding		1,364.00
24000 · Payroll Liabilities:24020 · FICA Payable		2,118.82
24000 · Payroll Liabilities:24030 · AEIC Payable	0.00	
24000 · Payroll Liabilities:24040 · FUTA Payable		100.00
24000 · Payroll Liabilities:24050 · State Withholding		299.19
24000 · Payroll Liabilities:24060 · SUTA Payable		110.00
24000 · Payroll Liabilities:24070 · State Disability Payable		48.13
24000 · Payroll Liabilities:24080 · Worker's Compensation		1,214.31
24000 · Payroll Liabilities:24100 · Emp. Health Ins Payable		150.00
25500 · Sales Tax Payable		5.66
23000 · Loan - Vehicles (Van)		10,501.47
23100 · Loan - Vehicles (Utility Truck)		19,936.91
23200 · Loan - Vehicles (Pickup Truck)		22,641.00
28100 · Loan - Construction Equipment		13,911.32
28200 · Loan Furniture/Office Equip		21,000.00
28700 · Note Payable - Bank of Anycity		2,693.21
28900 · Mortgage - Office Building		296,283.00
30000 · Opening Bal Equity		38,773.75
30100 · Capital Stock		73,500.00
32000 · Retained Earnings		61,756.76
40100 · Construction Income	0.00	
40100 · Construction Income:40110 · Design Income		36,729.25
40100 · Construction Income:40130 · Labor Income		208,610.42
40100 · Construction Income:40140 · Materials Income		120,233.67
40100 · Construction Income:40150 · Subcontracted Labor Income		82,710.35
40100 · Construction Income:40199 · Less Discounts given	48.35	
40500 · Reimbursement Income:40520 · Permit Reimbursement Inco...		1,223.75
40500 · Reimbursement Income:40530 · Reimbursed Freight & Delive..		896.05
50100 · Cost of Goods Sold	16,914.53	
54000 · Job Expenses:54200 · Equipment Rental	1,850.00	
54000 · Job Expenses:54300 · Job Materials	99,648.70	
54000 · Job Expenses:54400 · Permits and Licenses	700.00	
54000 · Job Expenses:54500 · Subcontractors	63,217.95	
54000 · Job Expenses:54520 · Freight & Delivery	877.10	
54000 · Job Expenses:54599 · Less Discounts Taken		201.81
60100 · Automobile:60110 · Fuel	1,588.70	
60100 · Automobile:60120 · Insurance	2,850.24	
60100 · Automobile:60130 · Repairs and Maintenance	2,406.00	
60400 · Selling Expenses:60410 · Advertising Expense	200.00	
60600 · Bank Service Charges	145.00	
62100 · Insurance:62110 · Disability Insurance	582.06	
62100 · Insurance:62120 · Liability Insurance	5,885.96	
62100 · Insurance:62130 · Work Comp	13,657.07	
62400 · Interest Expense:62420 · Loan Interest	1,995.85	
62700 · Payroll Expenses:62710 · Gross Wages	110,400.10	
62700 · Payroll Expenses:62720 · Payroll Taxes	8,445.61	
62700 · Payroll Expenses:62730 · FUTA Expense	268.00	
62700 · Payroll Expenses:62740 · SUTA Expense	1,233.50	
63000 · Office Supplies	50.00	
63100 · Postage	104.20	
63600 · Professional Fees:63610 · Accounting	250.00	
64200 · Repairs:64210 · Building Repairs	175.00	
64200 · Repairs:64220 · Computer Repairs	300.00	
64200 · Repairs:64230 · Equipment Repairs	1,350.00	
64800 · Tools and Machinery	2,820.68	
65100 · Utilities:65110 · Gas and Electric	1,251.16	
65100 · Utilities:65120 · Telephone	895.15	
65100 · Utilities:65130 · Water	300.00	
70100 · Other Income		146.80
70200 · Interest Income		229.16
TOTAL	**1,156,145.93**	**1,156,145.93**

TASK 4: PRINT JOURNAL

Prepare the Journal as follows.

Step 1: From the Report Center, select **Accountant and Taxes > Journal**.

Step 2: Select Dates From: **12/20/2019** To: **12/29/2019**.

Step 3: Export to **Excel** or **print** the Journal.

TASK 5: SAVE EXERCISE 5.4

 Save a backup of your Exercise 5.4 file using the file name: **YourName Exercise 5.4 Backup.QBB**. See *Appendix B: Back Up & Restore QuickBooks Files* for instructions.

 ### WORKFLOW

If you are using the Workflow approach, you can leave your .QBW file open and use it for the next chapter.

 ### RESTART & RESTORE

If you are stopping your QuickBooks work session and changing computers, you will need to restore your .QBB file when you restart.

 # EXERCISE 5.5: WEB QUEST

Increasingly, small businesses are targets for fraud.

Step 1: Search the QuickBooks website, quickbooks.intuit.com, to learn more about QuickBooks security features for checks and bill paying.

Step 2: Using word processing or email software, write an email to Mr. Castle summarizing your recommendations regarding security features that Rock Castle Construction should use when paying bills.

CHAPTER 5 QUICK CHECK

NAME:

INSTRUCTIONS:

1. CHECK OFF THE ITEMS YOU COMPLETED.

2. TURN IN THIS PAGE WITH YOUR PRINTOUTS.

Download Go Digital Excel templates at www.My-QuickBooks.com.

> **!**
> Ask your instructor if you should Go Digital (Excel* or PDF) or use paper printouts.

CHAPTER 5

- ☐ * Vendor List
- ☐ * Item List
- ☐   Purchase Order Nos. 6238 & 6239
- ☐   Check Nos. 520-521
- ☐   Check Nos. 522-523 for Sales Tax
- ☐ * Vendor Transaction Report
- ☐ * A/P Aging Summary Report
- ☐ * Open Purchase Orders Report
- ☐ * Inventory Stock Status by Item Report
- ☐ * Physical Inventory Worksheet

EXERCISE 5.1

- ☐   Task 4: Purchase Order 6240
- ☐   Task 7: Check No. 524
- ☐ * Task 8: Transaction List by Vendor

EXERCISE 5.2

- ☐   Task 3: Customer Invoice No. 1104
- ☐   Task 5: Bank Deposit Summary
- ☐ * Task 6: Transaction List by Customer

EXERCISE 5.3

- ☐   Task 3: Check Nos. 525-526
- ☐ * Task 4: Check Detail

EXERCISE 5.4

- ☐ * Task 2: Inventory Stock Status By Item Report
- ☐ * Task 3: Trial Balance
- ☐ * Task 4: Journal

EXERCISE 5.5

- ☐   Bill Pay Security

REFLECTION: A WISH AND A STAR

Reflection improves learning and retention. Reflect on what you have learned after completing Chapter 5 that you did not know before you started the chapter.

A Star:

What did you like best that you learned about QuickBooks in Chapter 5?

A Wish:

If you could pick one thing, what do you wish you knew more about when using QuickBooks?

PROJECT 5 LARRY'S LANDSCAPING

To complete this project, download the Chapter 5 Go Digital Reports Excel template at www.My-QuickBooks.com. Follow the instructions provided in the Excel template.

Complete the following for Larry's Landscaping.

1. Use either your QuickBooks company file (.QBW file) or backup file (.QBB file) that you completed for Project 4. (If you have issues with your QuickBooks file, contact your instructor.) Update the Company Name to: **YourName Project 5 Larry's Landscaping**.

2. Download the Chapter 5 Go Digital Reports Excel template. Save the Excel file using the file name: **YourLastName FirstName CH5 REPORTS**.

3. Enter the following purchase orders for Larry's Landscaping.

Date	Vendor	Item	Quantity
12/22/2019	Conner Garden Supplies	½" Vinyl Irrigation Line	100
12/23/2019	Nolan Hardware and Supplies	Plastic Sprinkler Piping	50
12/23/2019	Willis Orchards	Soil (2 cubic foot bag)	10

4. Record the following items received by Larry's Landscaping.

Date	Vendor	PO No.	Item	Quantity
12/22/2019	Nolan Hardware and Supplies	7	Sprinkler Head	36
12/22/2019	Gussman's Nursery	11	Lemon Tree	1
12/22/2019	Gussman's Nursery	11	Citrus Tree – Arizona Sweet	1
12/22/2019	Gussman's Nursery	11	Fruit Tree - Plum	1
12/23/2019	Conner Garden Supplies	12	½" Vinyl Irrigation Line	100

5. Use the Enter Bills Against Inventory icon to enter the following bills for Larry's Landscaping.

Date	Vendor	PO No.	Terms	Amount Due
12/22/2019	Gussman's Nursery	11	Net 15	$147.00
12/23/2019	Conner Garden Supplies	12	Net 30	$12.00

Use the Enter Bills icon to enter the following bill received by Larry's.

Date	Vendor	Account	Terms	Amount Due
12/23/2019	Sult Advertising	6000 Advertising Expense	Net 30	$100.00

6. Pay the following bills for Larry's on 12/23/2019.

Date	Vendor	Amount Due
12/23/2019	Gussman's Nursery	$147.00
12/23/2019	Conner Garden Supplies	$12.00
12/23/2019	Townley Insurance Agency	$427.62
12/23/2019	Great Statewide Bank	$699.12

7. Using your saved Excel template for Chapter 5, export to **Excel** the Open Purchase Orders report for Larry's Landscaping for this fiscal quarter (October 1 - December 31, 2019).

8. Export to **Excel** the Check Detail report for Larry's for December 22 - 23, 2019.

9. Export to **Excel** the Accounts Payable Aging Detail report as of December 23, 2019.

10. Export to **Excel** the Journal report for December 22 - 23, 2019.

11. Mark the reports completed on the 5 REPORTS sheet. Save your Excel file.

12. Save a .QBB backup of your work.

PROJECT 5 QUICK CHECK

NAME:

INSTRUCTIONS:

1. **CHECK OFF THE ITEMS YOU COMPLETED.**
2. **ATTACH THIS PAGE TO YOUR PRINTOUTS.**

!
Ask your instructor if you should Go Digital (Excel* or PDF) or use paper printouts.

PROJECT 5

☐   *   Open Purchase Orders
☐   *   Check Detail
☐   *   A/P Aging Detail
☐   *   Journal

Download Go Digital Excel templates at www.My-QuickBooks.com.

CHAPTER 6
EMPLOYEES AND PAYROLL

SCENARIO

The next morning on your way to your cubicle, two employees ask you if their paychecks are ready yet. Apparently, Rock Castle employees expect their paychecks today?! Then your smartphone chimes repeatedly with incoming texts from the construction crews asking about their paychecks.

Deciding that you do not want all the employees upset with you if paychecks are not ready on time, you take the initiative and ask Mr. Castle about the paychecks.

His reply: *"Oops! I was so busy I almost forgot about paychecks."* He hands you another stack of documents. *"Here—you will need these. I'm sure you won't have any trouble using QuickBooks to print the paychecks. And don't forget to pay yourself!"* he adds with a chuckle as he rushes out the door.

CHAPTER 6
LEARNING OBJECTIVES

In Chapter 6, you will learn about the following QuickBooks features:

INTRODUCTION

+

Employees
complete Form
W-4 when hired.
Form W-2
summarizes
annual wages
and tax
withholdings.

In Chapter 6 you will focus on recording employee and payroll transactions. Payroll involves preparing employee paychecks, withholding the appropriate amount in taxes, and paying the company's share of payroll taxes.

To assist in processing payroll, QuickBooks offers a time-tracking feature that permits you to track the amount of time worked. QuickBooks uses time tracked to:

1. Calculate employee paychecks.

2. Transfer time to sales invoices to bill customers for work performed.

+

No tax
withholdings are
necessary for
independent
contractors. Tax
Form 1099-MISC
summarizes
payments.

Although this chapter focuses on time worked by employees, work can be performed by employees, subcontractors, or owners. The time-tracking feature can be used to track time worked by any of the three. How you record the payment, however, depends upon who performs the work: employee, subcontractor, or business owner.

Status	Pay Using QB Window	Home Page Section
Employee	*Pay Employees* window	Employees
Subcontractor (Vendor)	*Enter Bills* window *Pay Bills* window	Vendors
Owner	*Write Checks* window	Banking

+

If a stockholder
is also an
employee, wages
are recorded as
payroll. If not
wages, then
payment to the
stockholder is a
dividend.

It is important that you determine the status of the individual performing the work. The status determines whether you record payments to the individual as an employee paycheck, vendor payment, or owner withdrawal.

Start QuickBooks by clicking on the **QuickBooks desktop icon** or click **Start > Programs > QuickBooks > QuickBooks Premier Accountant Edition 2015**.

WORKFLOW

Use the Workflow approach if you are using the same computer and the same .QBW file from the prior chapter.

Step 1: If your .QBW file is not already open, open it by selecting **File > Open Previous Company**. Select your **.QBW file.**

Step 2: Update the Company Name to include **YourName Chapter 6**.

RESTART & RESTORE

Use the Restart & Restore approach if you are moving your QuickBooks files between computers.

Step 1: Restore the **Backup.QBB** file using the directions in *Appendix B: Back Up & Restore QuickBooks Files*. You can restore using one of two different .QBB files.

1. Restore your own .QBB file from the last exercise completed in the previous chapter.

2. Restore the Chapter 6 .QBB data file that comes with *Computer Accounting with QuickBooks* (available on CD or download from the Online Learning Center).

   If the *QuickBooks Login* window appears:

   - Leave the *User Name* field as **Admin**.
   - Leave the *Password* field **blank**.
   - Click **OK**.

Step 2: After restoring the file, update the Company Name to include **YourName Chapter 6**.

PAYROLL SETUP

Payroll setup in QuickBooks is accessed from the Employees menu. (From the Employees menu, click Payroll Setup). The following *QuickBooks Payroll Setup* window summarizes the steps to set up QuickBooks payroll and time tracking. Click Finish Later.

Payroll accounts for Rock Castle Construction have already been established. To learn more about payroll setup, see Chapter 11.

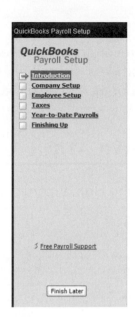

The following table summarizes the steps to set preferences and customize the payroll feature of QuickBooks.

QuickBooks automatically creates a Chart of Accounts with payroll liability and payroll expense accounts. Payroll Items track supporting detail for the payroll accounts.

QuickBooks Time Tracking and Payroll Roadmap	
Action	**Using QuickBooks...**
1. Set up payroll.	Employees menu, Payroll Setup
2. Turn on time tracking.	Edit menu, Preferences, Time & Expenses
3. Turn on payroll, enter Payroll and Employee Preferences.	Edit menu, Preferences, Payroll & Employees
4. Enter customer and jobs on which time is worked.	Customer & Job List
5. Record labor as a service item.	Item List
6. Enter individuals whose time will be tracked: ▶ Employee information ▶ Subcontractors ▶ Owners	 Employee List Vendor List Other Names List

In this chapter, we will focus on customizing payroll using preferences and recording employee and payroll transactions. To track time and process payroll in QuickBooks, you will use the *Employees* section of the Home page.

EMPLOYEE NAVIGATION

If necessary, click the **Home** icon to view the *Employees* section.

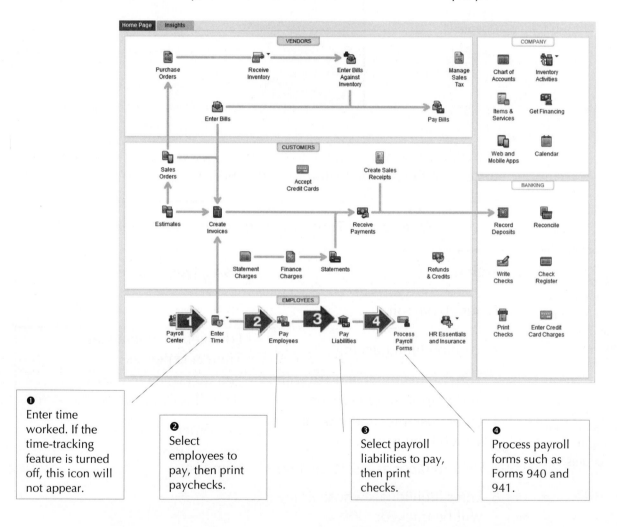

❶ Enter time worked. If the time-tracking feature is turned off, this icon will not appear.

❷ Select employees to pay, then print paychecks.

❸ Select payroll liabilities to pay, then print checks.

❹ Process payroll forms such as Forms 940 and 941.

The *Employees* section of the Home page is a flowchart of payroll transactions. As the flowchart indicates, there are four main steps to processing payroll using QuickBooks:

❶ **Enter Time**. QuickBooks permits you to track employee time worked to use in processing payroll and billing customers.

❷ **Pay Employees**. Select employees to pay and create their paychecks.

❸ **Pay Payroll Liabilities**. Pay payroll tax liabilities due governmental agencies such as the IRS. Payroll tax liabilities include federal income taxes withheld, state income taxes withheld, FICA (Social Security and Medicare), and unemployment taxes.

❹ **Process Payroll Forms**. Process payroll forms including Forms 940, 941, W-2, and W-3 that must be submitted to governmental agencies.

QuickBooks also has an Employee Center and a Payroll Center to help you manage employee and payroll information.

▪ **Employee Center**. This center can be accessed from the Icon bar and contains the Employee List with employee information, such as address and Social Security number.

▪ **Payroll Center**. This center is part of the Employee Center and is used to manage payroll and tax information, including information about wages, benefits, and withholding. The Payroll Center can be accessed by clicking the Payroll Center icon in the *Employees* section of the Home page.

CUSTOMIZE QUICKBOOKS PAYROLL

Use QuickBooks Preferences to customize time tracking and payroll to suit your company's specific needs. There are two types of preferences that affect payroll:

1. Time-tracking preferences.

2. Payroll and employees preferences.

TIME-TRACKING PREFERENCES

To turn on the QuickBooks time-tracking feature, complete the following steps:

Step 1:   From the Menu bar, select **Edit**.

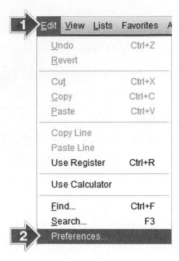

Step 2: Select **Preferences**.

Step 3: When the *Preferences* window appears, select **Time & Expenses** from the left scrollbar.

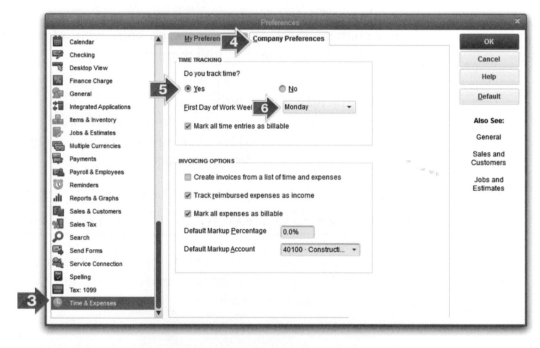

Step 4: Select the **Company Preferences** tab.

Step 5: Select Do you track time?: **Yes**.

Step 6: Select First Day of Work Week: **Monday**.

Step 7: Leave the *Preferences* window open.

PAYROLL AND EMPLOYEES PREFERENCES

Next, select QuickBooks payroll and employees preferences for your company.

With the *Preferences* window open:

Step 1:   From the left scrollbar of the *Preferences* window, click on the **Payroll & Employees** icon.

Step 2:   Select the **Company Preferences** tab.

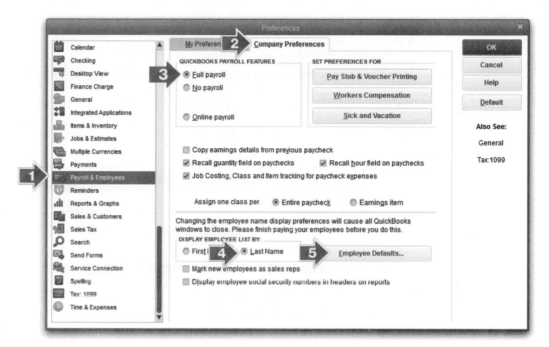

Step 3:   Select QuickBooks Payroll Features: **Full payroll**.

Step 4:   Select Display Employee List by: **Last Name**.

Step 5:   Click the **Employee Defaults** button to select payroll defaults.

Step 6:   Select the checkbox: **Use time data to create paychecks**. Now QuickBooks will automatically use tracked time to calculate payroll.

+

To save time, enter information common to most employees (such as a deduction for health insurance) as an employee default. QuickBooks then records the information for all employees. Later, you can customize the information as needed for a specific employee.

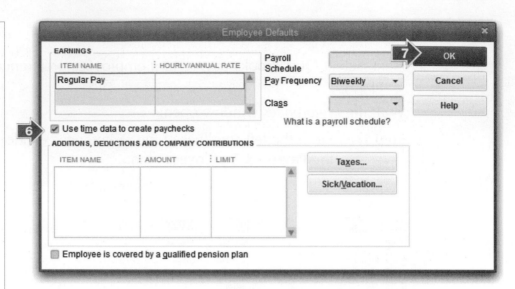

Step 7: Click **OK** to close the *Employee Defaults* window.

Step 8: Click **OK** again to close the *Preferences* window. When the following warning message appears, click **OK**.

Now that the time-tracking and payroll preferences are set, you will edit and print the Employee List.

EMPLOYEE LIST

The Employee List contains employee information such as address, telephone, salary or wage rate, and Social Security number.

To view the Employee List for Rock Castle Construction:

Step 1: Click **Employees** on the Icon bar or click the **Employees** button on the Home page to display the Employee Center.

Step 2: Click the **Employees** tab to display a list of employees.

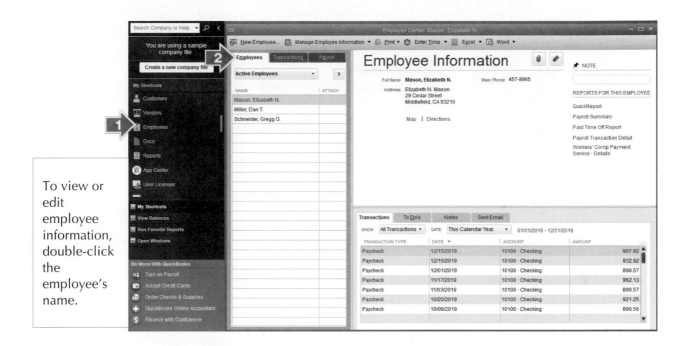

To view or edit employee information, double-click the employee's name.

ADD NEW EMPLOYEE

To enter your name as a new employee in the Employee List:

Step 1: Click the **New Employee** button in the Employee Center.

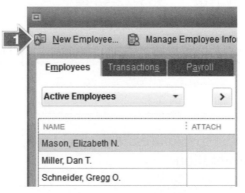

Step 2: When the following blank *New Employee* window appears, select **Personal** tab. Enter the following information.

Personal:	
First Name	[Enter your first name]
Last Name	[Enter your last name]
Social Security No.	333-22-4444
Gender	[Enter gender]
Date of Birth	[Enter a fictitious date of birth]
Marital Status	Single
U.S. Citizen	Yes

Step 3:   Select the **Address & Contact** tab, then enter the following information.

Address & Contact:	
Address	555 Lakeview Lane Bayshore, CA 94326
Main Phone	415-555-6677
Main Email	[Enter your email address]

Step 4:   Select the **Additional Info** tab, then enter the following information.

Additional Info:	
Employee ID	333-22-4444
B-Day	[Enter a fictitious birth date]

Step 5: Select the **Payroll Info** tab, then enter the following payroll information.

Payroll Info:	
Earnings Name	Regular Pay
Hourly/Annual Rate	10.00
Use time data to create paychecks	Yes
Pay Frequency	Biweekly
Deductions	Health Insurance
Amount	-25.00
Limit	-1200.00

+
If you receive a message that you must update QuickBooks before you can use payroll, update QuickBooks, then proceed.

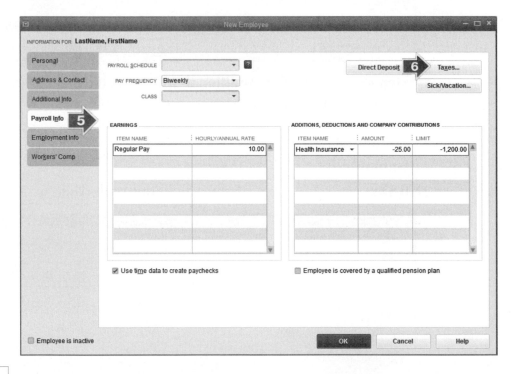

+
New employees complete Form W-4 to indicate filing status and allowances.

Step 6: Select the **Taxes** button to view federal, state, and other tax information related to your employment, such as filing status and allowances. Enter the following:

- Filing Status: **Single**.

- Allowances for **Federal: 1**.

- Allowances for **State: 1**.

- Click **OK** to close the *Taxes* window.

Step 7:   Click **OK** again to close the *New Employee* window and add your name to Rock Castle Construction's Employee List.

Step 8:   When asked if you want to set up payroll information for sick leave and vacation, click **Leave As Is** to use the employee default information for these items.

Step 9:   Leave the *Employee Center* window open.

PRINT EMPLOYEE LIST

Print the Employee List as follows:

Step 1:   Click the **Name** bar to sort employee names in alphabetical order.

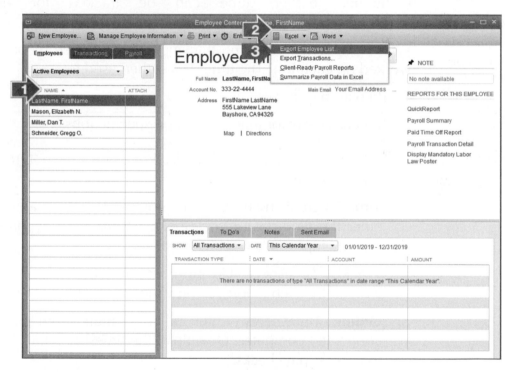

Step 2:   At the top of the Employee Center, select **Excel**.

Step 3:   Select **Export Employee List**.

Step 4:   When the *Export* window appears, select **Replace an existing worksheet**. Browse and select your **CH6 REPORTS** Excel template. Select the appropriate worksheet.

Step 5:   Click **Export**.

Step 6: **Highlight** your name and information on the Employee List.

Step 7: If your instructor requests, print the report from Excel.

Step 8: **Close** the *Employee Center* window.

For more information about payroll setup, see Chapter 11. The remainder of this chapter will cover time tracking, payroll processing, and payroll reports.

TIME TRACKING

> **+**
> If you start using QuickBooks midyear, enter year-to-date amounts for payroll *before* you start using QuickBooks to process paychecks.

QuickBooks permits you to track time worked on various jobs. As mentioned earlier, time can be tracked for employees, subcontractors, or owners.

When employees use time tracking, the employee records the time worked on each job. The time data is then used to:

1. Prepare paychecks.

2. Bill customers for time worked on specific jobs.

QuickBooks Pro and QuickBooks Premier provide three different ways to track time.

1. **Time Single Activity**. Use the Stopwatch to time an activity and enter the time data. QuickBooks automatically records the time on the employee's weekly timesheet.

2. **Weekly Timesheet**. Use the weekly timesheet to enter time worked by each employee on various jobs during the week.

3. **Online Timesheets**. Enter billable hours from any Internet-connected computer. Download the timesheets into QuickBooks to process paychecks.

TIME SINGLE ACTIVITY

You will use the QuickBooks Stopwatch feature to time how long it takes you to complete payroll activities in this chapter.

To start the Stopwatch:

Step 1: From the *Employees* section of the Home page, select the **Enter Time** icon.

Step 2: Select **Time/Enter Single Activity**.

Step 3: When the following *Time/Enter Single Activity* window appears, select Date: **12/15/2019**.

You can use the Stopwatch to time activities for today's date only. However, for this activity, use the programmed date for the sample company: 12/15/2019.

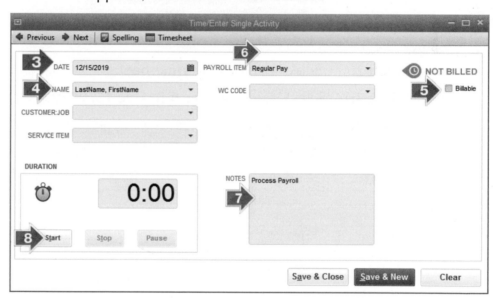

Step 4: Select Name: **Your FirstName, FirstName**.

Step 5: If the work was for a particular job or customer, you would enter the job or customer name and the service item, then click Billable. In this case, your time is not billable to a particular customer's job, so **uncheck Billable**.

Step 6: Select Payroll Item: **Regular Pay**.

Step 7: Enter Notes: **Process payroll**.

Step 8: Click the **Start** button to start the stopwatch.

Step 9: Leave the window open while you complete the following payroll activities.

TIMESHEET

Rock Castle Construction pays employees biweekly. Checks are issued on Friday for the biweekly pay period ending that day.

Use the timesheet to enter the hours you worked for Rock Castle Construction during the last pay period.

To use QuickBooks timesheet feature:

Step 1: In the *Employees* section of the Home page, select **Enter Time**.

Step 2: Select **Use Weekly Timesheet**.

Step 3: Select Week Of: **Dec 9 to Dec 15, 2019**.

If your time was billable to a specific customer or job, then select Customer: Job name and the Service Item.

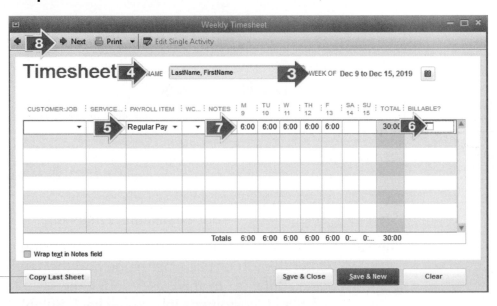

+

Use Copy Last Sheet if the timesheet does not change much from week to week.

Step 4: Select Name: **LastName, First Name**.

Step 5: From the Payroll Item drop-down list, select **Regular Pay**.

Step 6: Because your time is not billable to a specific customer or job, **uncheck** the **Billable?** field in the last column to indicate these charges will not be transferred to an invoice.

Step 7:   Enter **6** hours for each of the following dates for a total of 30 hours for the week:

- **Monday (December 9)**
- **Tuesday (December 10)**
- **Wednesday (December 11)**
- **Thursday (December 12)**
- **Friday (December 13)**

Step 8:   Click the **Next** button in the upper left corner of the *Weekly Timesheet* window to advance to the timesheet for the week of **Dec 16 to Dec 22, 2019.**

Remember to enter **Regular Pay** and uncheck **Billable?** to mark your hours as nonbillable.

Step 9:   Select **Copy Last Sheet.** Your timesheet should now show **6** hours of **nonbillable Regular Pay** on the following dates for a total of 30 hours:

- **Monday (December 16)**
- **Tuesday (December 17)**
- **Wednesday (December 18)**
- **Thursday (December 19)**
- **Friday (December 20)**

Step 10:   Click **Save & New** to record your hours and display a new timesheet.

If time is billable to a specific customer or job, this is indicated on the weekly timesheet. For example, Elizabeth Mason, a Rock Castle Construction employee, worked on the Teschner sun room; therefore, her hours are billable to the Teschner sun room job.

To enter billable hours on Elizabeth Mason's weekly timesheet:

!

Elizabeth Mason's name appears twice in the list, once as a vendor, and again as an employee. For the timesheet, be certain to select the employee, Elizabeth N. Mason.

Step 1:   On the new timesheet, select Employee Name: **Elizabeth N. Mason.**

Step 2:   Click the **Previous** button in the upper left corner of the *Weekly Timesheet* window to change the timesheet dates to **Dec 9 to Dec 15, 2019.**

Step 3:   To record time billable to a specific customer:

- Select Customer: Job: **Teschner, Anton: Sun Room.**
- Select Service Item: **Framing.**

Step 4: Complete Elizabeth's weekly timesheet for framing the sunroom as follows.

Monday, December 9	8 hours
Tuesday, December 10	8 hours
Wednesday, December 11	8 hours
Thursday, December 12	6 hours

Notice that if the Customer: Job or Service Item changes, the time is entered on a new line in the timesheet.

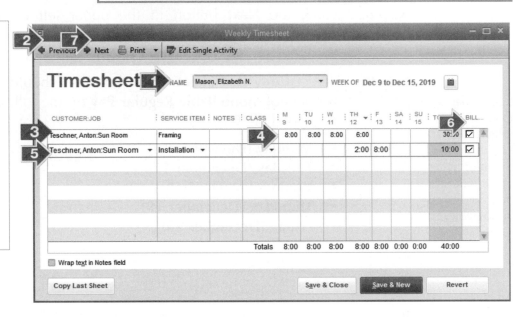

Step 5: Move to the next line in the timesheet to enter the installation work that Elizabeth performed on the Teschner sun room.

- Select Customer: Job: **Teschner, Anton: Sun Room**.

- Select Service Item: **Installation**.

- Enter hours worked:

Thursday, December 12	2 hours
Friday, December 13	8 hours

Step 6: ✓ Check: **Billable?**

Step 7: Click the **Next** button to record Elizabeth N. Mason's hours and display a new timesheet.

Step 8: Record **8** hours for each of the following dates that

Elizabeth worked on **installing** the Teschner sun room:

- **Monday (December 16)**
- **Tuesday (December 17)**
- **Wednesday (December 18)**
- **Thursday (December 19)**
- **Friday (December 20)**

Step 9:   ✓ Check: **Billable?**

Step 10:   Leave the *Weekly Timesheet* window open.

To print the weekly timesheets for yourself and Elizabeth N. Mason, complete the following steps:

Step 1:   From the *Weekly Timesheet* window, click the **Print** button.

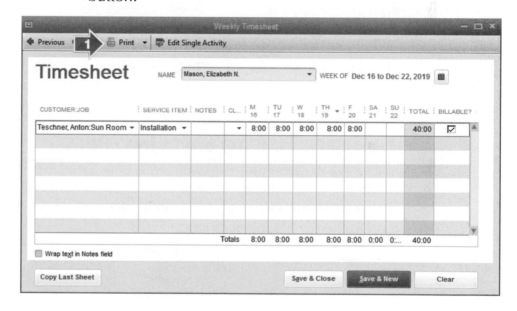

Step 2:   When the following *Select Timesheets to Print* window appears, select Dated: **12/09/2019** thru **12/15/2019**. If necessary, press **Tab**.

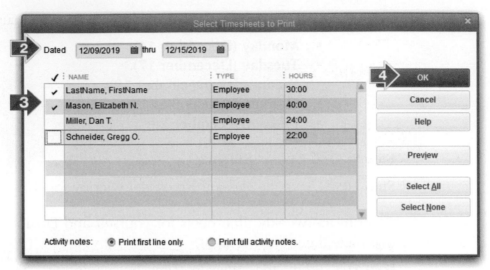

Step 3:   Select **YourName** and **Elizabeth N. Mason**.

Step 4:   Click **OK**.

Step 5:   **Print** and sign the timesheets.

Step 6:   Click **Save & Close** to close the *Weekly Timesheet* window.

TRANSFER TIME TO SALES INVOICES

Billable time can be transferred to a specific customer's invoice. This is shown in the Home page by an arrow going from the Enter Time icon to the Create Invoices icon.

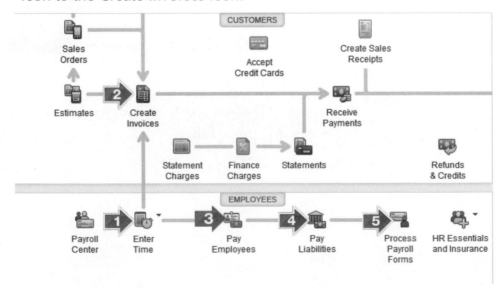

First, you must enter time worked, then open the *Create Invoices* window for the customer, and select the time billable to that customer. For the Teschner sun room job, you have already entered Elizabeth Mason's time. To transfer billable time to the Teschner invoice:

Step 1:   Open the *Create Invoices* window by clicking the **Create Invoices** icon in the *Customers* section of the Home page.

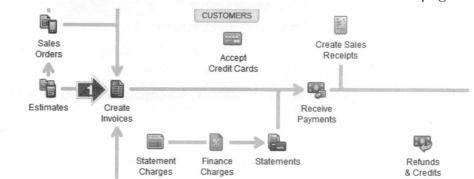

Step 2:   From the *Create Invoices* window, select the customer job to be billed. In this instance, select Customer: Job: **Teschner, Anton: Sun Room**.

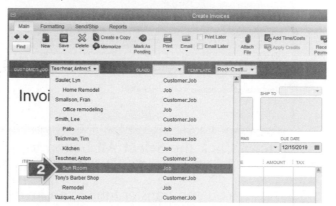

Step 3:   If the following *Billable Time/Costs* window appears, select: **Select the outstanding billable time and costs to add to this invoice?**

Step 4:   Click **OK**.

Step 5: When the *Choose Billable Time and Costs* window appears, click the **Time** tab.

Notice that items, expenses, and mileage can also be tracked and billed to specific customer jobs.

Step 6: Click the **Select All** button to select all the billable times listed for the Teschner sun room job.

You can transfer time to an invoice in three different ways:

1. Combine all the selected times and costs into *one* entry on the invoice.

2. List a *subtotal* for each *service* item on the invoice.

3. List a separate invoice line item for each *activity* you check.

Step 7:   In this instance, you will list a separate invoice line item for each activity you check, so ***uncheck* Print selected time and costs as one invoice item** in the lower left corner of the *Choose Billable Time and Costs* window.

Step 8:   Click the **Options** button.

Step 9:   Select **Enter a separate line on the invoice for each activity** on the *Options for Transferring Billable Time* window.

Step 10:   Select **Transfer item descriptions**.

Step 11:   Click **OK** to close the *Options for Transferring Billable Time* window.

Step 12:   Click **OK** to close the *Choose Billable Time and Costs* window and add the labor cost to the Teschner invoice.

If you had not entered the billable time when you opened the invoice, you can click the **Add Time/Costs** button to add billable time later.

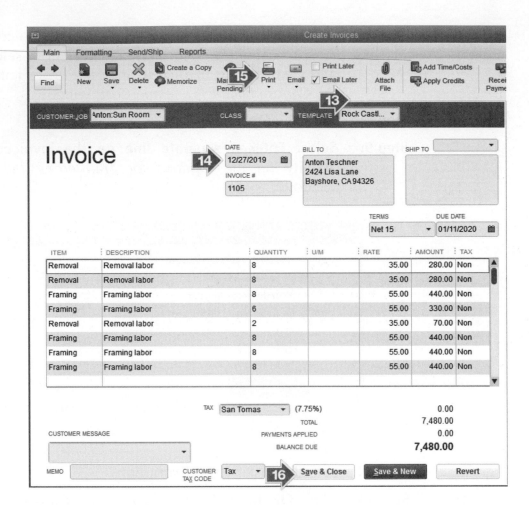

Step 13: Select Template: **Rock Castle Invoice**.

Step 14: Select Invoice Date: **12/27/2019**.

Step 15: **Print** the invoice.

Step 16: Click **Save & Close** to record the invoice and close the *Create Invoices* window.

 Total billable time is $7,480.

 Stop the Stopwatch now by clicking the **Stop** button and then clicking **Clear. Close** the *Stopwatch* window.

QUICKBOOKS PAYROLL

After entering time worked, the next step is to create employee paychecks. There are two ways that a company can perform payroll calculations.

1. Use QuickBooks payroll services:
    *   Basic Payroll
    *   Enhanced Payroll
    *   Full Service Payroll
2. Manually calculate payroll taxes.

QUICKBOOKS PAYROLL SERVICES

QuickBooks offers three levels of payroll services for the entrepreneur to use with QuickBooks software: QuickBooks Basic, Enhanced, or Full Service Payroll. When you subscribe to a payroll service, QuickBooks requires that you have an Internet connection. Then QuickBooks automatically calculates payroll tax deductions.

Features of the three levels of payroll services for entrepreneurs are summarized as follows.

Basic Payroll	• Create paychecks using automatic calculation of payroll tax deductions. • Tax forms are not automatically prepared. Entrepreneur must complete the tax forms or work with an accountant on payroll tax filings.
Enhanced Payroll	• Create paychecks using automatic calculation of payroll tax deductions. • Generate payroll tax forms for filings automatically. • File and pay taxes electronically.
Full Service Payroll	• Entrepreneur enter hours and Intuit does the rest. • Intuit runs and files payroll for entrepreneur. • Intuit processes payroll taxes and filings.

If a message appears about updating QuickBooks before using payroll, update QuickBooks and then proceed. If you are not able to use QuickBooks payroll tax tables, then enter amounts shown on the following pages manually in the *Create Paychecks* window.

If using a QuickBooks payroll service for a business, turn on the payroll auto update feature of QuickBooks to ensure you have the latest tax tables. If you update payroll when using this text, your answers may not be the same as the check figures so ask your instructor if you should update payroll.

CALCULATE PAYROLL TAXES MANUALLY

Chapter 6 covers payroll using QuickBooks *payroll service*. Chapter 11 covers QuickBooks *manual payroll* option.

If you do not use a QuickBooks payroll service, you must calculate tax withholdings and payroll taxes manually using IRS Publication 15 (Circular E), Employer's Tax Guide. Then enter the amounts in QuickBooks to process payroll.

CREATE AND PRINT PAYCHECKS

The QuickBooks payroll service is active for the sample company file, Rock Castle Construction.

To create paychecks for Rock Castle Construction using the QuickBooks payroll service:

Step 1: From the *Employees* section of the Home page, click the **Pay Employees** icon to display the *Employee Center: Payroll Center* window.

Notice that the following three sections on the right side of the Payroll Center correspond to icons in the *Employee* section of the Home page:

- Pay Employees.
- Pay Liabilities.
- Process (File) Payroll Forms.

You can also access the Payroll Center by selecting **Employees** (Icon bar) > **Payroll** tab.

You can schedule payroll to run at regular times, such as every week.

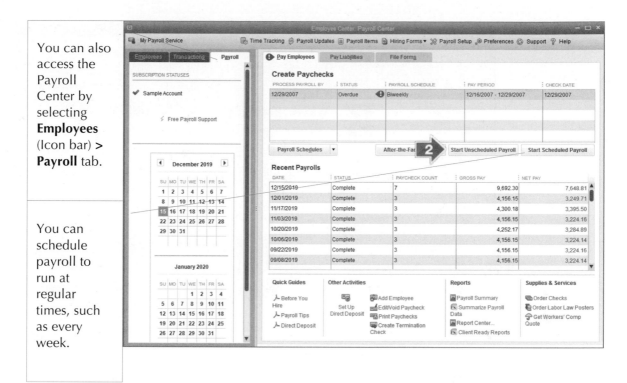

Step 2: In the *Pay Employees* section, select: **Start Unscheduled Payroll**.

Step 3: When the *Enter Payroll Information* window appears, notice there are three steps listed at the top of the window: *Enter Payroll Information -> Review & Create Paychecks -> Print & Distribute Paychecks*.

Select Pay Period Ends: **12/22/2019**. This is the last day of this pay period. If the *Pay Period Change* window appears, click **No** to change the date without updating the hours worked.

Step 4: Select Check Date: **12/22/2019**. This date will print on each check.

Step 5: Select Employee: **Elizabeth N. Mason**.

Step 6: Click **Continue**.

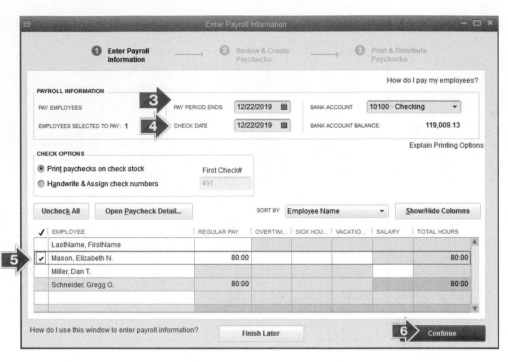

Step 7: When the following *Review and Create Paychecks* window appears, select **Print paychecks from QuickBooks**.

If you use a QuickBooks payroll service, payroll taxes and deductions would be calculated automatically and appear in the *Review and Create Paychecks* window.

If you planned to handwrite payroll checks instead, select Handwrite & Assign check numbers.

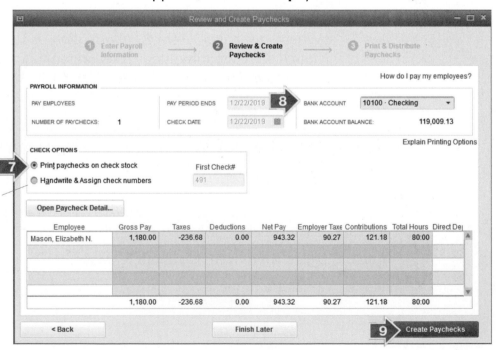

Step 8: Select Bank Account: **Checking**.

Notice that the tax withholding amounts appear automatically because Rock Castle uses a payroll service. If you are calculating payroll taxes manually, you must enter the withholding amounts manually.

+

Some businesses use a separate Payroll Checking account instead of using the regular Checking account.

+

Subcontractors are considered vendors, not employees. Subcontractor payments are entered using the *Enter Bills* window.

Step 9:   Select **Create Paychecks**.

Step 10: When the following *Confirmation and Next Steps* window appears, click **Print Paychecks**.

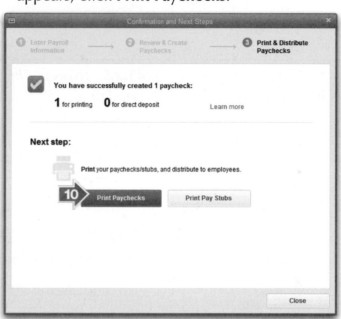

Step 11: In the *Select Paychecks to Print* window shown below, select: **Elizabeth N. Mason (12/22/2019)**.

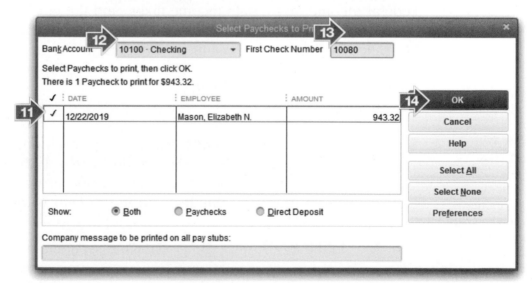

+

Rock Castle Construction uses a different series of check numbers for its payroll checks than it does for all other checks.

Step 12:   Select Bank Account: **Checking**.

Step 13:   Select First Check Number: **10080**.

Step 14:   Click **OK**.

Step 15:   Select Check Style: **Voucher**. Check **Print company name and address**.

Step 13:   Click **Print**.

Step 14:   **Close** the *Print Checks - Confirmation* window.

   Mason's net pay is $943.32. (Note: This amount may vary depending on your payroll update.)

PAY PAYROLL LIABILITIES

+

To help keep track of filing dates, see the IRS Tax Calendar at www.irs.gov.

Payroll liabilities include amounts for:

- Federal income taxes withheld from employee paychecks.

- State income taxes withheld from employee paychecks.

- FICA (Social Security and Medicare, including both the employee and the employer portions).

- Unemployment taxes.

Federal income taxes, state income taxes, and the employee portion of FICA are withheld from the employee, and the company has an obligation (liability) to remit these amounts to the appropriate tax agency. The employer share of FICA and unemployment taxes are payroll taxes the employer owes.

To pay the payroll tax liability:

You will process payroll liability payments in the exercises for Chapter 6.

Step 1:   If the *Employee Center: Payroll Center* window is already displayed, select the **Pay Liabilities** tab. (If the *Employee Center: Payroll Center* window is not already displayed, select the **Pay Liabilities** icon in the *Employees* section of the Home page.)

Step 2:   In the *Pay Taxes & Other Liabilities* section of the *Employee Center: Payroll Center* window, you can view the upcoming scheduled payments for payroll liabilities. If any payments were due, you would select the payroll liabilities to pay, then click View/Pay. In the Due Date column, you can see that no payments are currently due for Rock Castle Construction.

Step 3: Leave open the *Employee Center: Payroll Center* window.

FILE PAYROLL TAX FORMS

Notice that the third section of the Payroll Center is File Forms. Basically, payroll forms summarize the amount of payroll withholdings that have been collected and remitted.

Payroll tax forms include:

You will process payroll tax forms in the exercises for Chapter 6.

- **Federal Form 940: Employer's Annual Federal Unemployment (FUTA) Tax Return.** This form summarizes the amount of unemployment tax paid and due by the employer.

- **Federal Form 941: Employer's Quarterly Federal Tax Return.** Filed with the IRS, this form summarizes the amount of federal income tax, Social Security, and Medicare withheld from employee paychecks for the quarter.

- **Federal Form 944: Employer's Annual Federal Tax Return.** Filed with the IRS, this form summarizes the amount of federal income tax, Social Security, and Medicare withheld from employee paychecks for the year. Form 944 is used by very small employers instead of filing Form 941 each quarter.

- **Form W-2: Wage and Tax Statement.** Before the end of January, an employer must provide W-2s to employees that summarize amounts paid for salaries, wages, and withholdings for the year.

- **Form W-3: Transmittal of Wage and Tax Statements.** Filed with the Social Security Administration, this form is a summary of all an employer's W-2 forms.

Close the *Employee Center: Payroll Center* window.

PAYROLL REPORTS

In addition to providing assistance with filing payroll tax forms with federal, state, and local governmental agencies, QuickBooks also provides payroll reports for owners and managers to use to answer the following questions:

- How much did we pay our employees and pay in payroll taxes? (Payroll reports)

- How much time did we spend classified by employee and job? (Project reports)

Payroll reports can be accessed in the following ways:

1. **Reports menu.** (Select **Reports** menu > **Employees & Payroll**.)

2. **Report Center.** (Select **Reports** (Icon bar) > **Employees & Payroll**.)

3. **Employee Center.** (Select **Employees** (Icon bar) > **Reports for this Employee**.)

PAYROLL REPORTS: HOW MUCH DID WE PAY FOR PAYROLL?

The payroll reports list the amounts paid to employees and the amounts paid in payroll taxes.

To print the Payroll Summary report:

Step 1:   Select **Reports** in the Icon bar.

©McGraw-Hill Education, 2016

> !
> If you receive a message that you must enable Excel macros, select the Enable Macros button.

Step 2: In Grid View, select **Employees & Payroll**.

Step 3: Select **Payroll Summary**.

Step 4: Select Dates: **This Month** From: **12/01/2019** To: **12/31/2019**.

Step 5: Select **Run**.

Step 6: Export to **Excel** or **print**.

Step 7: Close the *Payroll Summary Report* window.

 Net pay for Dan Miller for December was $3,974.90.

PROJECT REPORTS: HOW MUCH TIME DID WE USE?

To create a report detailing time spent on a specific job:
1. Report Center
2. Jobs, Time & Mileage
3. Time by Job Detail
4. Filter for Customer & Job

Four different project reports are available in QuickBooks:

1. **Time by Job Summary Report**. Lists time spent on each job.

2. **Time by Job Detail Report**. Lists time by category spent on each job.

3. **Time by Name Report**. Lists amount of time worked by each employee.

4. **Time by Item Report**. Lists time worked on a particular job by service category.

Project reports are accessed as follows:

Step 1: From the Report Center, select: **Jobs, Time & Mileage > Time by Job Summary**.

Step 2: Export to **Excel** or **print** the Time by Job Summary report for **This Month** From: **12/01/2019** To: **12/31/2019**.

Step 3: **Highlight** the job requiring the most time for December 2019.

SAVE CHAPTER 6

Save a backup of your Chapter 6 file using the file name: **YourName Chapter 6 Backup.QBB**. See *Appendix B: Back Up & Restore QuickBooks Files* for instructions.

WORKFLOW

If you are using the Workflow approach, leave your .QBW file open and proceed directly to Exercise 6.1.

RESTART & RESTORE

If you are using the Restart & Restore approach and are ending your computer session now, close your .QBW file and exit QuickBooks.

WWW.MY-QUICKBOOKS.COM

Go to www.My-QuickBooks.com to view additional QuickBooks resources including Excel Reports Templates, QuickBooks videos, and QuickBooks Hot Arrows and Hot Topics. The Hot Topics can be viewed on your computer or tablet and feature frequently used QuickBooks tasks.

MULTIPLE-CHOICE PRACTICE TEST

Try the **Multiple-Choice Practice Test** for Chapter 6 on the *Computer Accounting with QuickBooks* Online Learning Center at www.mhhe.com/kay2015.

GO DIGITAL!

Go Digital using Excel templates. See *Appendix D: Go Digital with QuickBooks* for instructions about how to save your QuickBooks reports electronically.

LEARNING ACTIVITIES

Important: Ask your instructor whether you should complete the following assignments by printing reports or by exporting to Excel templates (see Appendix D: Go Digital with QuickBooks).

EXERCISE 6.1: TRACK TIME AND PRINT PAYCHECKS

SCENARIO

When sorting through the payroll documents that Mr. Castle gave you, you find the following timesheets for Dan Miller and Gregg Schneider.

Timesheet						
Dan Miller	**Salary**	**Dec 9**	**Dec 10**	**Dec 11**	**Dec 12**	**Dec 13**
Cook: 2nd Story	Installation	8				4
Pretell: 75 Sunset	Framing		8	8	7	4
Dan Miller	**Salary**	**Dec 16**	**Dec 17**	**Dec 18**	**Dec 19**	**Dec 20**
Pretell: 75 Sunset	Framing	8	8	8	8	3
Pretell: 75 Sunset	Installation					5

Timesheet						
Gregg Schneider	**Regular Pay**	**Dec 9**	**Dec 10**	**Dec 11**	**Dec 12**	**Dec 13**
Jacobsen: Kitchen	Installation	6	6		2	
Pretell: 75 Sunset	Framing		2	8	6	8
Gregg Schneider	**Regular Pay**	**Dec 16**	**Dec 17**	**Dec 18**	**Dec 19**	**Dec 20**
Pretell: 75 Sunset	Framing	8	8	8	8	
Pretell: 75 Sunset	Installation					8

TASK 1: OPEN COMPANY FILE

WORKFLOW

If you are using the Workflow approach, you will use the same .QBW file.

- If your QBW file is not already open, open it by selecting **File > Open Previous Company**. Select your **.QBW file.**

- Update the Company Name to include **YourName Exercise 6.1**.

RESTART & RESTORE

If you are not using the same computer, you must use the Restart and Restore approach.

- Restore your **Chapter 6 Backup.QBB** file using the directions in *Appendix B: Back Up & Restore QuickBooks Files*.

- After restoring the file, update the Company Name to include **YourName Exercise 6.1**.

TASK 2: TIMESHEET

> See the previous scenario for information to complete Tasks 2 and 3.

Step 1: Enter the hours employee **Dan T. Miller** worked using QuickBooks weekly timesheet.

Step 2: Enter the hours **Gregg O. Schneider** worked using QuickBooks weekly timesheet.

Step 3: **Print** and sign the timesheets for Dan Miller and Gregg Schneider.

TASK 3: PRINT PAYCHECKS

> **+**
> Rock Castle Construction uses a different series of check numbers for its payroll checks than for all other checks.

Print and sign paychecks using voucher checks for **Dan Miller** and **Gregg Schneider** dated **12/22/2019** for pay period ending **12/22/2019** (Checks No. 10081 and 10082).

TASK 4: PAYROLL TRANSACTION DETAIL

Export to **Excel** or **print** the Payroll Transaction Detail report dated From: **12/22/2019** To: **12/22/2019**.

TASK 5: SAVE EXERCISE 6.1

Save a backup of your Exercise 6.1 file using the file name: **YourName Exercise 6.1 Backup.QBB**. See *Appendix B: Back Up & Restore QuickBooks Files* for instructions.

WORKFLOW

If you are proceeding to Exercise 6.2 and using the same computer, you can leave your .QBW file open and use it for Exercise 6.2.

RESTART & RESTORE

If you are stopping your QuickBooks work session and changing computers, you will need to restore your .QBB file when you restart.

EXERCISE 6.2: TRANSFER TIME TO SALES INVOICE

SCENARIO

"By the way, did I mention that I need a current sales invoice for the Jacobsen Kitchen job? Make sure all labor charges have been posted to the invoice," Mr. Castle shouts over the top of your cubicle as he rushes past.

TASK 1: OPEN COMPANY FILE

WORKFLOW

If you are using the Workflow approach, you will use the same .QBW file. If your QBW file is not already open, open it by selecting **File > Open Previous Company**. Select your **.QBW file.** Update the Company Name to include **YourName Exercise 6.2**.

RESTART & RESTORE

If you are using the Restart and Restore approach, restore your backup file using the directions in *Appendix B: Back Up & Restore QuickBooks Files*. After restoring the file, update the Company Name to include **YourName Exercise 6.2**.

TASK 2: TRANSFER TIME TO SALES INVOICE

Step 1: From the *Customers* section of the Home page, click the **Create Invoices** icon.

Step 2: Transfer billable time and items to a sales invoice dated **12/22/2019** for the Jacobsen Kitchen job.

Step 3: From the *Choose Billable Time and Costs* window, click the **Time** tab, then click the **Select All** button to transfer employee time worked to the invoice. Select **Options** button > **Combine activities with the same service item and rate**.

Step 4: **Print** the invoice.

 Billable time totals $1,540.00.

TASK 3: TIME BY JOB DETAIL

Step 1: Export to **Excel** or **print** the Time by Job Detail report for the month of December 2019.

Step 2: **Highlight** any items on the report that are billable to specific jobs, yet still unbilled.

TASK 4: SAVE EXERCISE 6.2

 Save a backup of your Exercise 6.2 file using the file name: **YourName Exercise 6.2 Backup.QBB**. See *Appendix B: Back Up & Restore QuickBooks Files* for instructions.

 ## WORKFLOW

If you are using the Workflow approach, you can leave your .QBW file open and use it for Exercise 6.3.

 ## RESTART & RESTORE

If you are stopping your QuickBooks work session and changing computers, you will need to restore your .QBB file when you restart.

EXERCISE 6.3: PAYROLL LIABILITIES AND FORMS

SCENARIO

"Payroll tax forms always give me a headache," Mr. Castle rubs his temples, muttering as he rushes past your cubicle. *"You can take care of those this year, can't you?"* he shouts over your cubicle wall.

You nod and reply confidently, *"No problem, Mr. Castle,"* to the back of his head as he rushes to his next appointment.

TASK 1: OPEN COMPANY FILE

WORKFLOW

If you are using the Workflow approach, you will use the same .QBW file. If your QBW file is not already open, open it by selecting **File > Open Previous Company**. Select your **.QBW file.** Update Company Name to include **YourName Exercise 6.3**.

RESTART & RESTORE

If you are using the Restart and Restore approach, restore your backup file using the directions in *Appendix B: Back Up & Restore QuickBooks Files*. After restoring the file, update the Company Name to include **YourName Exercise 6.3**.

TASK 2: PAY PAYROLL LIABILITIES

To pay the payroll tax liability related to federal Forms 941/944:

Step 1: Select the **Pay Liabilities** icon in the *Employees* section of the Home page.

Step 2: In the *Employee Center: Payroll Center* window, select the **Pay Liabilities** tab.

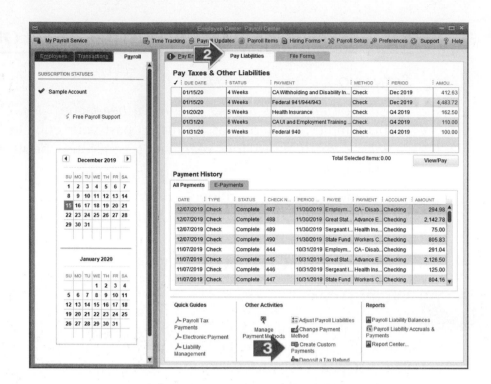

Step 3: In the *Other Activities* section, select **Create Custom Payments**.

Step 4: Select Dates: **12/01/2019** Through: **12/31/2019**.

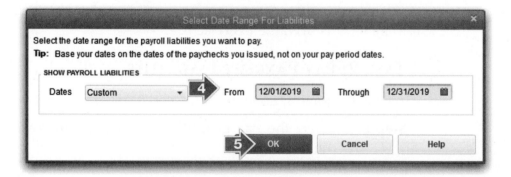

Step 5: Select **OK**.

Step 6: In the Pay Liabilities window, select **To be printed**.

Step 7: Select Bank Account: **Checking**.

Step 8: Select Check Date: **12/15/2019**.

Step 9: Select: **Review liability check to enter expenses/penalties**.

Step 10: Select: **Payroll Items** as shown.

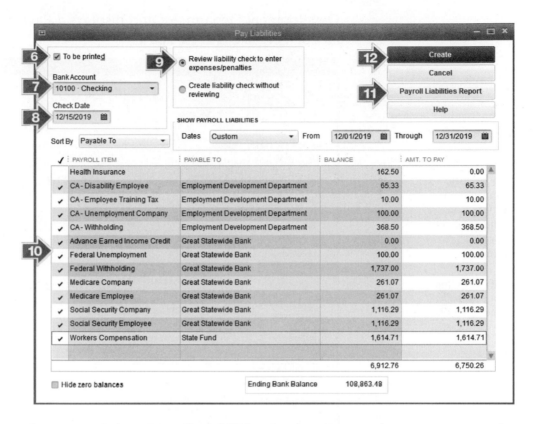

Step 11: Select **Payroll Liabilities Report**. **Export** the report to Excel.

Step 12: Select **Create**.

Step 13: Since you are going to be out of the office you are paying before the due date, so click **Continue**.

Step 14: When the following check appears on your screen, confirm that the check is payable to Employment

Development Department and displays a Payroll Liabilities tab. Select Date: **12/15/2019**.

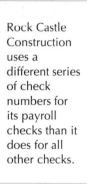

Rock Castle Construction uses a different series of check numbers for its payroll checks than it does for all other checks.

Step 15: Select **Save**.

Step 16: Select **Next**.

Step 17: **Save** the check to Great Statewide Bank for federal payroll liabilities.

Payroll liabilities paid for federal withholdings to Great Statewide Bank total $4,591.72. (Note: This amount may vary slightly depending upon your payroll update.)

Step 18: Select **Next**.

Step 19: **Save** the check to State Fund for Workers Compensation.

Step 20: **Print** this batch of three checks for payroll liabilities. Use **First Check Number 10083**. Print using **voucher checks**.

Step 21: If the checks printed correctly, select **OK** to close the *Print Checks Confirmation* window.

Step 22:   Select **Save & Close** to close the *Liability Check Checking* window. **Close** the *Employee Center: Payroll Center* window.

TASK 3: PAYROLL TRANSACTIONS BY PAYEE

From the Report Center, export to **Excel** or **print** the Payroll Transactions by Payee report for This Calendar Year From: **01/01/2019** To: **12/31/2019**.

TASK 4: SAVE EXERCISE 6.3

Save a backup of your Exercise 6.3 file using the file name: **YourName Exercise 6.3 Backup.QBB**. See *Appendix B: Back Up & Restore QuickBooks Files* for instructions.

WORKFLOW

If you are using the Workflow approach, you can leave your .QBW file open and use it for the next chapter.

RESTART & RESTORE

If you are stopping your QuickBooks work session and changing computers, you will need to restore your .QBB file when you restart.

EXERCISE 6.4: QUICKBOOKS PAYROLL SERVICES

To learn more about the payroll services offered by QuickBooks:

Step 1:   Go to www.payroll.intuit.com. Read about QuickBooks payroll options and print the differences between QuickBooks Basic Payroll, Enhanced Payroll, and Full Service Payroll Services.

Step 2:   Using word processing or email software, prepare and **print** a short email to Mr. Castle with your recommendation regarding which payroll service Rock Castle Construction should use.

EXERCISE 6.5: WEB QUEST

The IRS prepares Publication 15 (Circular E), Employer's Tax Guide, as well as other information about payroll taxes.

To view a copy of Forms 940 and 941 and instructions:

Step 1:   Go to the www.irs.gov website.

Step 2:   Search the IRS site to find information about Form 940 and Form 941.

Step 3:   **Print** blank Forms 940 and 941.

EXERCISE 6.6: WEB QUEST

When hiring individuals to perform work for a business, it is important to identify the status of the individual as either an employee or independent contractor. For an employee, your business must withhold taxes and provide a W-2. For an independent contractor, your business does not have to withhold taxes. Instead of a W-2, you provide a contractor with a Form 1099-MISC. To learn more about whether a worker is classified for tax purposes as an employee or independent contractor, visit the IRS website.

Step 1:   Go to the www.irs.gov website and locate Publication 1779 that provides information about requirements to determine employee or independent contractor status.

Step 2:   **Print** your search results.

CHAPTER 6 QUICK CHECK

NAME:

INSTRUCTIONS:

1. CHECK OFF THE ITEMS YOU COMPLETED.
2. TURN IN THIS PAGE WITH YOUR PRINTOUTS.

> **!**
> Ask your instructor if you should Go Digital (Excel* or PDF) or use paper printouts.

CHAPTER 6

- ☐ * Employee List
- ☐ Timesheets
- ☐ Invoice No. 1105
- ☐ Paycheck (Voucher Check) No. 10080
- ☐ * Payroll Summary
- ☐ * Time by Job Summary

EXERCISE 6.1

- ☐ Task 2: Timesheets
- ☐ Task 3: Paychecks (Voucher Checks) Nos. 10081 and 10082
- ☐ * Task 4: Payroll Transaction Detail

EXERCISE 6.2

- ☐ Task 2: Customer Invoice No. 1106
- ☐ * Task 3: Time by Job Detail

EXERCISE 6.3

- ☐ * Task 2: Payroll Liability Balances
- ☐ Task 2: Payroll Liabilities Check Nos. 10083-10085
- ☐ * Task 3: Payroll Transactions by Payee

EXERCISE 6.4

- ☐ QuickBooks Payroll Service Printouts
- ☐ QuickBooks Payroll Recommendation

EXERCISE 6.5

- ☐ IRS Forms 940 and 941

EXERCISE 6.6

- ☐ IRS Employee Status and Independent Contractor

Download Go Digital Excel templates at www.My-QuickBooks.com.

PROJECT 6 LARRY'S LANDSCAPING

To complete this project, download the Chapter 6 Go Digital Reports Excel template at www.My-QuickBooks.com. Follow the instructions provided in the Excel template.

Complete the following for Larry's Landscaping.

1. Use either your QuickBooks company file (.QBW file) or backup file (.QBB file) that you completed for Project 5. (If you have issues with your QuickBooks file, contact your instructor.) Update the Company Name to include: **YourName Project 6**.

2. Download the Chapter 6 Go Digital Reports Excel template. Save the Excel file using the file name: **YourLastName FirstName CH6 REPORTS**.

3. Prepare (but do not print) the following paychecks for Larry's Landscaping. (Select the **Pay Employees** icon > **Start Unscheduled Payroll**.)

Pay Period Ends	Employee	Check Date	Paycheck Amount
12/29/2019	Duncan Fisher	12/29/2019	$1,154.75
12/29/2019	Jenny Miller	12/29/2019	$1,275.02
12/29/2019	Shane Hamby	12/29/2019	$1,664.10

Paycheck amounts may vary slightly depending upon your payroll update.

4. Using your saved Excel template for Chapter 6, export to **Excel** the Payroll Summary report for Larry's Landscaping for December 16 - 29, 2019.

5. Export to **Excel** the Journal report for December 29, 2019.

6. Mark the reports completed on the 6 REPORTS sheet. Save your Excel file.

7. Save a .QBB backup of your work.

PROJECT 6 QUICK CHECK

NAME:

INSTRUCTIONS:

1. CHECK OFF THE ITEMS YOU COMPLETED.
2. ATTACH THIS PAGE TO YOUR PRINTOUTS.

> **!**
> Ask your instructor if you should **Go Digital** (Excel* or PDF) or use paper printouts.

PROJECT 6

☐   *   Payroll Summary

☐   *   Journal

Download Go Digital Excel templates at www.My-QuickBooks.com.

 # REFLECTION: A WISH AND A STAR

Reflection improves learning and retention. Reflect on what you have learned after completing Chapter 6 that you did not know before you started the chapter.

A Star:

What did you like best that you learned about QuickBooks in Chapter 6?

A Wish:

If you could pick one thing, what do you wish you knew more about when using QuickBooks?

NOTES:

CHAPTER 7
REPORTS AND GRAPHS

SCENARIO

"I need an income tax summary report ASAP—" Mr. Castle barks as he races past your cubicle. In a few seconds he charges past your cubicle again. *"Don't forget to adjust the accounts first. You'll need to use those confounded debits and credits!*

"Also, I need a P&L, balance sheet, and cash flow statement for my meeting with the bankers this afternoon. Throw in a graph or two if it'll make us look good."

Smiling, you push the *Send* button on your smartphone to send Mr. Castle the links to the financials. Then you send him a text message.

CHAPTER 7
LEARNING OBJECTIVES

In Chapter 7, you will learn about the following QuickBooks features:

THE ACCOUNTING CYCLE

The accounting cycle is a series of activities that a business performs each accounting period.

Financial reports are the end result of the accounting cycle. The accounting cycle usually consists of the following steps:

Chart of Accounts

The Chart of Accounts is a list of all accounts used to accumulate information about assets, liabilities, owners' equity, revenues, and expenses. Create a Chart of Accounts when the business is established and modify the Chart of Accounts as needed over time.

Transactions

During the accounting period, record transactions with customers, vendors, employees, and owners.

Trial Balance

A Trial Balance lists each account and the account balance at the end of the accounting period. Prepare a Trial Balance to verify that the accounting system is in balance—total debits should equal total credits. An unadjusted Trial Balance is a Trial Balance prepared *before* adjustments.

An accounting period can be one month, one quarter, or one year.

Adjustments

At the end of the accounting period before preparing financial statements, make any adjustments necessary to bring the accounts up to date. Adjustments are entered in the Journal using debits and credits.

Adjusted Trial Balance

Prepare an Adjusted Trial Balance (a Trial Balance *after* adjustments) to verify that the accounting system still balances. If additional account detail is required, print the general ledger (the collection of all the accounts listing the transactions that affected the accounts).

Financial Reports

Prepare financial statements for external users (Profit & Loss, Balance Sheet, and Statement of Cash Flows). Prepare income tax summary reports and reports for managers.

Three types of reports that a business prepares are:

> The objective of financial reporting is to provide information to external users for decision making.

1. **Financial statements**. Financial statements are reports used by investors, owners, and creditors to make decisions. A banker might use the financial statements to decide whether to make a loan to a company. A prospective investor might use the financial statements to decide whether to invest in a company.

   The three financial statements most frequently used by external users are:

   - The Profit & Loss (also called the Income Statement) that lists income and expenses.

   - The Balance Sheet listing assets, liabilities, and owners' equity.

   - The Statement of Cash Flows that lists cash flows from operating, investing, and financing activities.

> Financial statements can be prepared monthly, quarterly, or annually. Always make adjustments *before* preparing financial statements.

2. **Tax forms**. The objective of the tax form is to provide information to federal and state tax authorities. When preparing tax returns, a company uses different rules from those used to prepare financial statements. When preparing a federal tax return, use the Internal Revenue Code.

   Tax forms include the following:

   - Federal income tax return.

   - State tax return.

   - Forms 940, 941/944, W-2, W-3, 1099.

3. **Management reports**. Management reports are used by internal users (managers) to make decisions regarding company operations. These reports are created to satisfy a manager's information needs.

   Examples of reports that managers use include:

   - Cash forecast.

   - Cash budget.

   - Accounts receivable aging summary.

In this chapter, you will prepare several of these reports for Rock Castle Construction. First, you will prepare a Trial Balance and adjustments.

Start QuickBooks by clicking on the **QuickBooks desktop icon** or click **Start > Programs > QuickBooks > QuickBooks Premier Accountant Edition 2015**.

WORKFLOW

Use the Workflow approach if you are using the same computer and the same .QBW file from the prior chapter.

Step 1: If your .QBW file is not already open, open it by selecting **File > Open Previous Company**. Select your **.QBW file.**

Step 2: Update the Company Name to include **YourName Chapter 7**.

RESTART & RESTORE

Use the Restart & Restore approach if you are switching computers.

Step 1: Restore the **Backup.QBB** file using the directions in *Appendix B: Back Up & Restore QuickBooks Files*. You can restore using one of two different .QBB files.

1. Restore your own .QBB file from the last exercise completed in the previous chapter.

2. Restore the Chapter 7 .QBB data file that comes with *Computer Accounting with QuickBooks* (available on CD or download from the Online Learning Center). If the *QuickBooks Login* window appears:

   ▪ Leave the *User Name* field as **Admin.**

   ▪ Leave the *Password* field **blank.**

   ▪ Click **OK**.

Step 2: After restoring the file, update Company Name to include **YourName Chapter 7**.

TRIAL BALANCE

A Trial Balance is a listing of all of a company's accounts and the ending account balances. A Trial Balance is often printed both before and after making adjustments. The purpose of the Trial Balance is to verify that the accounting system balances. On a Trial Balance, all debit ending account balances are listed in the *debit* column and credit ending balances are listed in the *credit* column. If the accounting system balances, total debits equal total credits.

To print the Trial Balance for Rock Castle Construction:

Step 1: Click **Reports** in the Icon bar.

Step 2: Select: **Accountant & Taxes**.

Step 3: Select: **Trial Balance**.

Step 4: Select Date Range: **This Fiscal Quarter** From: **10/01/2019** To: **12/31/2019**.

Step 5: Select **Run**.

Step 6: Export to **Excel** or **print** the report. Compare your answers to the amounts shown on the following page.

Step 7: To memorize the report, click the **Memorize** button. In the *Name* field, enter: **Trial Balance**, then click **OK**.

Step 8: **Close** the *Trial Balance* window.

If necessary, display account numbers by selecting **Edit** menu **> Preferences > Accounting > Company Preferences > Use Account Numbers**.

	Dec 31, 19	
	Debit	Credit
10100 · Checking	108,863.48	
10300 · Savings	17,919.19	
10400 · Petty Cash	500.00	
11000 · Accounts Receivable	102,027.93	
12000 · Undeposited Funds	2,440.00	
12100 · Inventory Asset	30,680.14	
12800 · Employee Advances	832.00	
13100 · Pre-paid Insurance	4,050.00	
13400 · Retainage Receivable	3,703.02	
15000 · Furniture and Equipment	34,326.00	
15100 · Vehicles	78,936.91	
15200 · Buildings and Improvements	325,000.00	
15300 · Construction Equipment	15,300.00	
16900 · Land	90,000.00	
17000 · Accumulated Depreciation		110,344.60
18700 · Security Deposits	1,720.00	
20000 · Accounts Payable		27,685.72
20500 · QuickBooks Credit Card		144.20
20600 · CalOil Credit Card		382.62
24000 · Payroll Liabilities	0.00	
24000 · Payroll Liabilities:24010 · Federal Withholding	8.00	
24000 · Payroll Liabilities:24020 · FICA Payable	0.00	
24000 · Payroll Liabilities:24030 · AEIC Payable	0.00	
24000 · Payroll Liabilities:24040 · FUTA Payable	0.00	
24000 · Payroll Liabilities:24050 · State Withholding	4.00	
24000 · Payroll Liabilities:24060 · SUTA Payable	0.00	
24000 · Payroll Liabilities:24070 · State Disability Payable	17.20	
24000 · Payroll Liabilities:24080 · Worker's Compensation	0.00	
24000 · Payroll Liabilities:24100 · Emp. Health Ins Payable		162.50
25500 · Sales Tax Payable		5.66
23000 · Loan - Vehicles (Van)		10,501.47
23100 · Loan - Vehicles (Utility Truck)		19,936.91
23200 · Loan - Vehicles (Pickup Truck)		22,641.00
28100 · Loan - Construction Equipment		13,911.32
28200 · Loan - Furniture/Office Equip		21,000.00
28700 · Note Payable - Bank of Anycity		2,693.21
28900 · Mortgage - Office Building		296,283.00
30000 · Opening Bal Equity		38,773.75
30100 · Capital Stock		73,500.00
32000 · Retained Earnings		61,756.76
40100 · Construction Income	0.00	
40100 · Construction Income:40110 · Design Income		36,729.25
40100 · Construction Income:40130 · Labor Income		217,630.42
40100 · Construction Income:40140 · Materials Income		120,233.67
40100 · Construction Income:40150 · Subcontracted Labor Income		82,710.35
40100 · Construction Income:40199 · Less Discounts given	48.35	
40500 · Reimbursement Income:40520 · Permit Reimbursement Income		1,223.75
40500 · Reimbursement Income:40530 · Reimbursed Freight & Delivery		896.05
50100 · Cost of Goods Sold	15,234.43	
54000 · Job Expenses:54200 · Equipment Rental	1,850.00	
54000 · Job Expenses:54300 · Job Materials	93,646.70	
54000 · Job Expenses:54400 · Permits and Licenses	700.00	
54000 · Job Expenses:54500 · Subcontractors	63,217.66	
54000 · Job Expenses:54520 · Freight & Delivery	877.10	
54000 · Job Expenses:54599 · Less Discounts Taken		201.61
60100 · Automobile:60110 · Fuel	1,588.70	
60100 · Automobile:60120 · Insurance	2,860.24	
60100 · Automobile:60130 · Repairs and Maintenance	2,406.00	
60400 · Selling Expense:60410 · Advertising Expense	200.00	
60600 · Bank Service Charges	145.00	
62100 · Insurance:62110 · Disability Insurance	582.06	
62100 · Insurance:62120 · Liability Insurance	5,885.96	
62100 · Insurance:62130 · Work Comp	14,057.47	
62400 · Interest Expense:62420 · Loan Interest	1,995.65	
62700 · Payroll Expenses:62710 · Gross Wages	114,556.25	
62700 · Payroll Expenses:62720 · Payroll Taxes	8,763.86	
62700 · Payroll Expenses:62730 · FUTA Expense	268.00	
62700 · Payroll Expenses:62740 · SUTA Expense	1,233.50	
63000 · Office Supplies	50.00	
63100 · Postage	104.20	
63600 · Professional Fees:63610 · Accounting	250.00	
64200 · Repairs:64210 · Building Repairs	175.00	
64200 · Repairs:64220 · Computer Repairs	300.00	
64200 · Repairs:64230 · Equipment Repairs	1,350.00	
64800 · Tools and Machinery	2,820.68	
65100 · Utilities:65110 · Gas and Electric	1,251.16	
65100 · Utilities:65120 · Telephone	895.15	
65100 · Utilities:65130 · Water	300.00	
70100 · Other Income		146.60
70200 · Interest Income		229.16
TOTAL	**1,159,923.58**	**1,159,923.98**

If your payroll amounts in Chapter 6 differed due to payroll tax updates, your Trial Balance amounts may also differ.

ADJUSTING ENTRIES

In QuickBooks, the Journal is used to record adjustments (and corrections). Adjustments are often necessary to bring the accounts up to date at the end of the accounting period.

If you are using the accrual basis to measure profit, the following five types of adjusting entries may be necessary.

See your accountant for more information about calculating depreciation for tax purposes or see IRS Publication 946.

1. **Depreciation**. Depreciation has several different definitions. When conversing with an accountant, it is important to know which definition of depreciation is being used. See the table on the following page for more information about depreciation.

2. **Prepaid items**. Items that are prepaid, such as prepaid insurance or prepaid rent. An adjustment may be needed to record the amount of the prepaid item that has not expired at the end of the accounting period. For example, an adjustment may be needed to record the amount of insurance that has not expired as Prepaid Insurance (an asset with future benefit).

3. **Unearned revenue**. If a customer pays in advance of receiving a service, such as when a customer makes a deposit, your business has an obligation (liability) to either provide the service in the future or return the customer's money. An adjustment may be necessary to bring the revenue account and unearned revenue (liability) account up to date.

4. **Accrued expenses**. Expenses that are incurred but not yet paid or recorded. Examples of accrued expenses include accrued interest expense (interest expense that you have incurred but have not yet paid).

5. **Accrued revenues**. Revenues that have been earned but not yet collected or recorded. Examples of accrued revenues include interest revenue that has been earned but not yet collected or recorded.

Depreciation

The accounting definitions of depreciation differ from the popular definition of depreciation as a decline in value.

Depreciation Listed on….	Report Objective	Reporting Rules	Definition of Depreciation	Depreciation Calculation
Financial statements: Profit & Loss, Balance Sheet, Statement of Cash Flows	Provide information to external users (bankers and investors)	GAAP (Generally Accepted Accounting Principles)	*Financial Accounting Definition:* Allocation of asset's cost to periods used	Straight-line depreciation = (Cost − Salvage)/ Useful life
Income tax returns	Provide information to the Internal Revenue Service	Internal Revenue Code	*Tax Definition:* Recovery of asset's cost through depreciation deductions on return	MACRS (See IRS Publication 946 on depreciation)

RECORD ADJUSTING JOURNAL ENTRIES

> **+**
>
> QuickBooks Accountant 2015 features a Fixed Asset Manager (**Accountant** menu > **Manage Fixed Assets**) that can be used to record depreciation entries for fixed assets.

Adjusting entries are dated the last day of the accounting period. Some enterprises maintain accounting records using QuickBooks and then hire an outside accountant to prepare adjusting entries at year-end. You can create a copy of your QuickBooks company file for your accountant to use when making adjustments. For more information about creating an Accountant's Copy, see Chapter 12.

At December 31, Rock Castle Construction needs to make an adjustment to record $3,000 of depreciation expense on its truck.

To make the adjusting journal entry in QuickBooks:

Step 1: Select the **Accountant** menu.

> QuickBooks uses onscreen forms to record transactions, and the Journal is used to record adjustments and corrections.

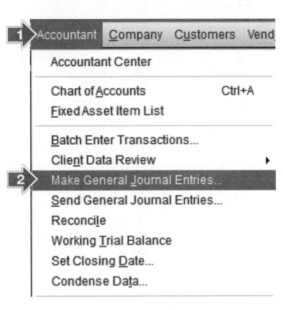

Step 2: Select **Make General Journal Entries**.

Step 3: When the following *Make General Journal Entries* window appears, select Date: **12/31/2019**.

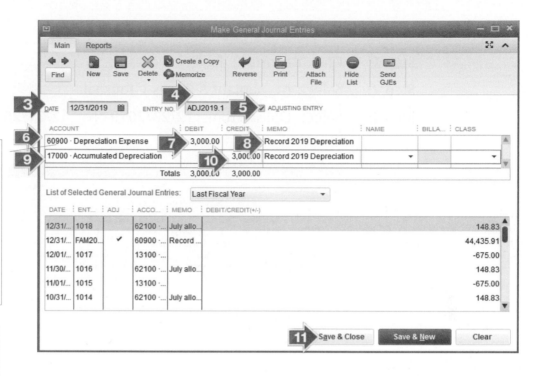

Type the Account No. **60900** and QuickBooks will automatically complete the account title.

+

Memorize the journal entry to reuse each accounting period:
1. With the Journal Entry displayed, click **Edit** menu.
2. Select **Memorize General Journal**.
To use the memorized transaction, select **Lists** menu > **Memorized Transaction List**.

Step 4: Enter Entry No: **ADJ2019.1**.

Step 5: **Check** the **Adjusting Entry** box.

Step 6: Select Account to Debit: **60900 Depreciation Expense**.

Step 7: Enter Debit amount: **3000.00**.

Step 8: Enter Memo: **Record 2019 Depreciation**.

Step 9: Select Account to Credit: **17000 Accumulated Depreciation**.

Step 10: If it does not appear automatically, enter Credit amount: **3000.00**. If it does not appear automatically, enter Memo: **Record 2019 Depreciation**.

Step 11: Click **Save & Close** to record the journal entry and close the *Make General Journal Entries* window.

PRINT JOURNAL ENTRIES

To view the journal entry you just recorded, display the Journal. The Journal also contains journal entries for all transactions recorded using onscreen forms, such as sales invoices. QuickBooks automatically converts transactions recorded in onscreen forms into journal entries with debits and credits.

To display and print the Journal:

Step 1: Click **Reports** in the Icon bar.

Step 2: Select: **Accountant & Taxes > Journal**.

Step 3: Select Dates From: **12/23/2019** To: **12/31/2019**. Click **Run**.

If you wanted to view only adjusting entries, select Accountant & Taxes > Adjusting Journal Entries.

Notice the adjusting entry for depreciation.

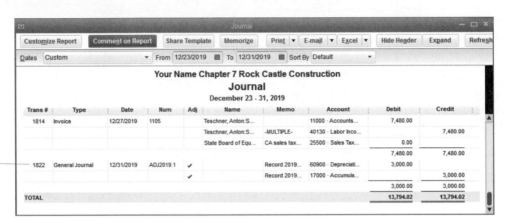

Step 4: Export to **Excel** or **print** the Journal.

Step 5: **Close** the *Journal* window.

ADJUSTED TRIAL BALANCE

The Adjusted Trial Balance is prepared to verify that the accounting system still balances after adjusting entries are made.

If you are not using QuickBooks Accountant, you would simply print another trial balance after adjustments are entered.

To print an Adjusted Trial Balance:

Step 1: From the Report Center, select **Accountant & Taxes > Adjusted Trial Balance**.

Step 2: Select Date: **12/31/2019**. Select **Run**.

Step 3: Export to **Excel** or **print** the Adjusted Trial Balance.

Step 4: **Highlight** the adjustments and any adjusted trial balance account balances that changed as a result of adjustments.

 Adjusted Trial Balance total debits and total credits equal $1,162,923.98.

GENERAL LEDGER

The general ledger is a collection of all of the company's accounts and account activity. While the Trial Balance lists only the ending balance for each account, the general ledger provides detail about all transactions affecting the account during a given period.

Each account in the general ledger lists:

- Beginning balance.

- Transactions that affected the account for the selected period.

- Ending balance.

Normally, the general ledger is not provided to external users, such as bankers. However, the general ledger can provide managers with supporting detail needed to answer questions bankers might ask about the financial statements.

To print the general ledger:

Step 1: If the Report Center is not open, click **Reports** in the Icon bar.

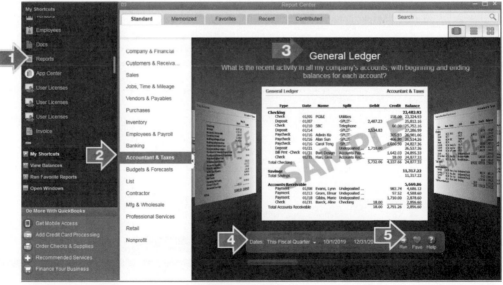

Step 2: Select: **Accountant & Taxes**.

Step 3: Select: **General Ledger**.

Step 4: Select Date Range: **This Fiscal Quarter**.

Step 5: Click **Run**.

The General Ledger report lists each account and all the transactions affecting the account. **Double-click on a transaction listed in the Checking account** to drill down to the original source document, such as a check or an invoice. **Close** the source document window.

Step 6: Use a filter to view only selected accounts in the general ledger. For example, to view only bank accounts, select **Customize Report**.

Step 7: Select: **Filters**.

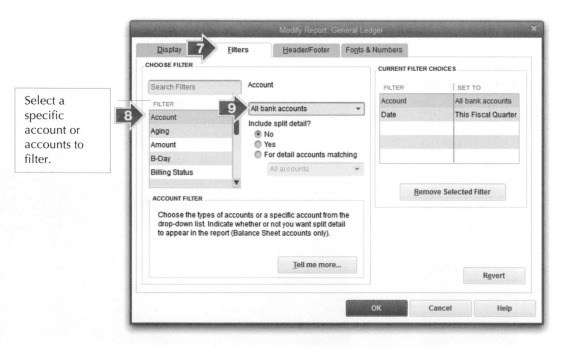

Select a specific account or accounts to filter.

Step 8: Select Filter: **Account**.

Step 9: Select Account: **All bank accounts**.

Step 10: To omit accounts with zero balances in the General Ledger report, from the *Modify Report* window, click the **Display** tab.

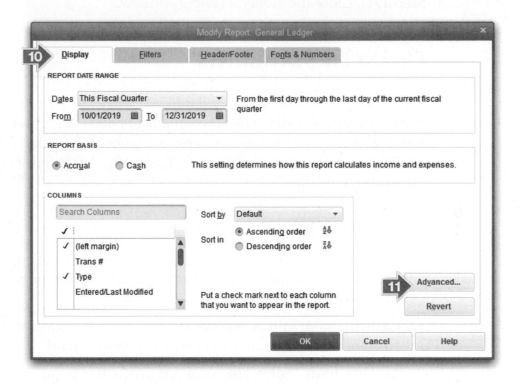

Step 11: Select **Advanced** button.

Step 12: Select Include: **In Use**.

Step 13: Select **Current (faster)**.

Step 14: Click **OK**.

Note: all accounts appearing on your General Ledger report should now have balances.

Step 15: Click **OK** to close the *Modify Report* window.

Step 16: Export to **Excel** or **print** the filtered General Ledger report.

Step 17: **Close** the *General Ledger* window.

FINANCIAL STATEMENTS

Financial statements are standardized financial reports given to bankers and investors. The three main financial statements are the Profit & Loss, Balance Sheet, and Statement of Cash Flows. The statements are prepared following Generally Accepted Accounting Principles (GAAP).

PROFIT AND LOSS

The Profit and Loss Statement is also called P&L or Income Statement.

GAAP requires the accrual basis for the Profit and Loss Statement because it provides a better matching of income and expenses.

The Profit and Loss Statement lists sales (sometimes called revenues) and expenses for a specified accounting period. Profit, or net income, can be measured two different ways:

1. **Cash basis**. A sale is recorded when cash is collected from the customer. Expenses are recorded when cash is paid.

2. **Accrual basis**. Sales are recorded when the good or service is provided regardless of when the cash is collected from the customer. Expenses are recorded when the cost is incurred or expires, even if the expense has not been paid.

QuickBooks permits you to prepare the Profit and Loss Statement using either the accrual or the cash basis. QuickBooks also permits you to prepare Profit and Loss Statements monthly, quarterly, or annually.

To prepare a quarterly Profit and Loss Statement for Rock Castle Construction using the accrual basis:

Step 1: From the Report Center, select **Company & Financial > Profit & Loss Standard**.

Step 2: Select Dates: **This Fiscal Quarter**. Click **Run**.

Step 3: Click the **Customize Report** button. Click the **Display** tab, and then select Report Basis: **Accrual**. Click **OK**.

Step 4: Export to **Excel** or **print** the Profit and Loss Statement.

Step 5: **Close** the *Profit & Loss* window.

 Net Income equals $40,326.40.

INCOME AND EXPENSE GRAPH

QuickBooks provides you with the ability to easily graph profit and loss information. A graph is simply another means to communicate financial information.

To create an Income and Expense Graph for Rock Castle Construction:

Step 1: From the Report Center, select: **Company & Financial > Income & Expense Graph**.

Step 2: Select Dates: **This Fiscal Quarter**. Click **Run** to display the following *QuickInsight: Income and Expense Graph* window.

Step 3: Click the **By Account** button. The income and expense graph depicts a bar chart of income and expense for the three months in the fiscal quarter. The pie chart in the lower section of the window displays the relative proportion of each expense as a percentage of total expenses.

Click the Income button to view the pie chart for income items.

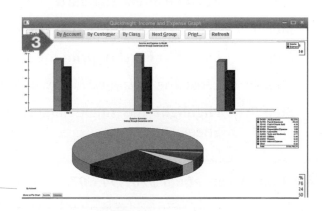

Step 4:   **Print** the income and expense graph.

Step 5:   **Close** the *QuickInsight: Income and Expense Graph* window.

BALANCE SHEET

The Balance Sheet presents a company's financial position on a particular date. The Balance Sheet can be prepared at the end of a month, quarter, or year. The Balance Sheet lists:

1.   **Assets**. What a company owns. On the Balance Sheet, assets are recorded at their historical cost, the amount you paid for the asset when you purchased it. Note that historical cost can be different from the market value of the asset, which is the amount the asset is worth now.

2.   **Liabilities**. What a company owes. Liabilities are obligations that include amounts owed vendors (accounts payable) and bank loans (notes payable).

3.   **Owners' equity**. The residual that is left after liabilities are satisfied. Also called net worth, owners' equity is increased by owners' contributions and net income. Owners' equity is decreased by owners' withdrawals (or dividends) and net losses.

To prepare a Balance Sheet for Rock Castle Construction at 12/31/2019:

Step 1:   From the Report Center, select **Company & Financial > Balance Sheet Standard**.

Step 2:   Select Dates: **This Fiscal Quarter**. Click **Run**.

Step 3:   Export to **Excel** or **print** the Balance Sheet.

Step 4:   **Close** the *Balance Sheet* window.

Step 5:   **Highlight** the single largest asset listed on the Balance Sheet.

 Total Assets equal $702,945.07.

STATEMENT OF CASH FLOWS

The Statement of Cash Flows summarizes cash inflows and cash outflows for a business over a period of time. Cash flows are grouped into three categories:

1. **Cash flows from operating activities**. Cash inflows and outflows related to the company's primary business, such as cash flows from sales and operating expenses.

2. **Cash flows from investing activities**. Cash inflows and outflows related to acquisition and disposal of long-term assets.

3. **Cash flows from financing activities**. Cash inflows and outflows to and from investors and creditors (except for interest payments). Examples include: loan principal repayments and investments by owners.

To print the Statement of Cash Flows for Rock Castle Construction:

Step 1: From the Report Center, select **Company & Financial > Statement of Cash Flows**.

Step 2: Select Date: **This Fiscal Quarter**. Click **Run**.

Step 3: Export to **Excel** or **print** the Statement of Cash Flows.

Step 4: **Close** the *Statement of Cash Flows* window.

Step 5: **Highlight** any items on the Statement of Cash Flows that you might classify differently than shown on the statement.

Net cash increase for period equals $53,100.45.

TAX REPORTS

QuickBooks provides two different approaches that you can use when preparing your tax return.

1. Print QuickBooks income tax reports and then manually enter the tax information on your income tax return.

2. Export your QuickBooks accounting data to tax software, such as TurboTax software, and then use TurboTax to complete your income tax return.

Three different income tax reports are provided by QuickBooks:

1. **Income Tax Preparation report**. Lists the assigned tax line for each account.

2. **Income Tax Summary report**. Summarizes income and expenses that should be listed on a business income tax return.

3. **Income Tax Detail report**. Provides more detailed information about the income or expense amount appearing on each tax line of the Income Tax Summary report.

INCOME TAX PREPARATION REPORT

Before printing the Income Tax Summary report, check your QuickBooks accounts to see that the correct Tax Line is selected for each account. An easy way to check the Tax Line specified for each account is to print the Income Tax Preparation report as follows.

Step 1: From the Report Center, select: **Accountant & Taxes > Income Tax Preparation**.

Step 2: Select Date: **This Tax Quarter**. Click **Run**.

If you are using QuickBooks Pro, your Income Tax Preparation report may appear and function differently than shown here.

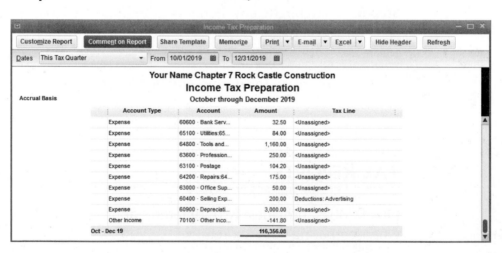

Step 3: Export to **Excel** or **print** the Income Tax Preparation report.

Step 4: **Close** the *Income Tax Preparation* window.

To determine if the correct tax line has been entered for each account, compare the tax lines listed on the Income Tax Preparation report with your business income tax return.

For example, if you wanted to change the Tax Line for the Postage account from Unassigned to the appropriate Tax Line:

Step 1: From the Home page, select *Chart of Accounts*.

Step 2: From the *Chart of Accounts* window, right-click on the account: **63100 Postage**.

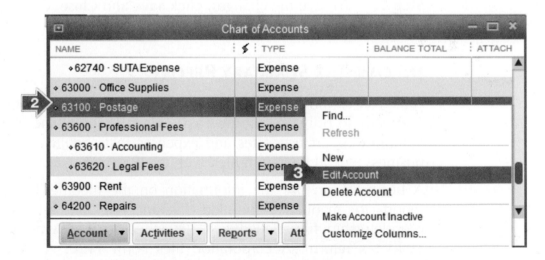

Step 3: Select **Edit Account**.

Step 4: When the following *Edit Account* window appears, change the Tax-Line Mapping to: **Other Deductions: Postage & delivery**.

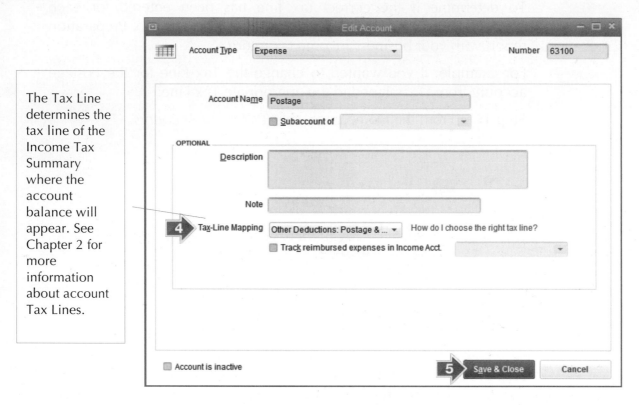

The Tax Line determines the tax line of the Income Tax Summary where the account balance will appear. See Chapter 2 for more information about account Tax Lines.

Step 5: To save the changes, click **Save and Close**. Close the *Chart of Accounts* window.

INCOME TAX SUMMARY REPORT

After you confirm that the Tax Line for each account is correct, you are ready to print an Income Tax Summary report. The Income Tax Summary report lists sales and expenses that should appear on the business federal tax return filed with the IRS.

A business can use the information on the Income Tax Summary report to manually complete its income tax return. A sole proprietorship files Schedule C (attached to the owner's personal 1040 tax return). A corporation files Form 1120. A subchapter S corporation files Form 1120S.

INCOME TAX DETAIL REPORT

If you want to view detail for the line items shown on the Income Tax Summary report, you could display the Income Tax Detail report.

EXPORT TO TURBOTAX

Another approach to preparing a tax return is to export the account information from QuickBooks into TurboTax software. TurboTax for Home and Business is used for a sole proprietorship Schedule C.

TurboTax for Business is for corporations, S corporations, and partnerships.

To import your QuickBooks tax data into TurboTax software:

Step 1:   Make a copy of your QuickBooks company data file.

Step 2:   Start TurboTax software.

Step 3:   Import your QuickBooks company file into TurboTax. In TurboTax, from the File menu, click Import.

MANAGEMENT REPORTS

Reports used by management do not have to follow a specified set of rules such as GAAP or the Internal Revenue Code. Instead, management reports are prepared as needed to provide management with information for making operating and business decisions.

Management reports include:

1. Cash flow forecast.

2. Budgets (See Chapter 12).

3. Accounts receivable aging (See Chapter 4).

4. Accounts payable aging (See Chapter 5).

5. Inventory reports (See Chapter 5).

CASH FLOW FORECAST

QuickBooks permits you to forecast cash flows. This enables you to project whether you will have enough cash to pay bills when they are due. If it appears that you will need additional cash, then you can arrange for a loan or line of credit to pay your bills. The Cash Flow Forecast report lists projected cash inflows and cash outflows.

To prepare a Cash Flow Forecast report for Rock Castle Construction:

Step 1: From the Report Center, select: **Company & Financial > Cash Flow Forecast**.

Step 2: Select Date: **Next 4 Weeks**. Click **Run**.

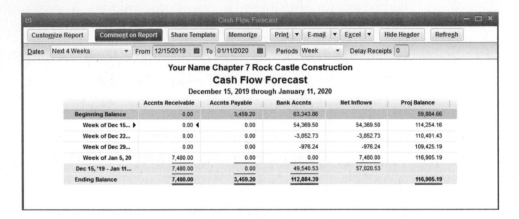

Step 3: Export to **Excel** or **print** the Cash Flow Forecast report.

Step 4: **Close** the *Cash Flow Forecast* window.

SAVE REPORTS TO ELECTRONIC FILES

QuickBooks also permits you to save a report to an electronic file. You can select from the following file formats:

- ASCII text file. After saving as a text file, the file can be used with word processing software.

- Comma delimited file. Comma delimited files can be imported into word processing, spreadsheet, or database software. Commas identify where columns begin and end.

- Tab delimited file. Tab delimited files can be used with word processing or database software. Tabs identify where columns begin and end.

- Adobe PDF file. This is a portable document file. See Appendix D for more information about using QuickBooks with PDF files.

FINANCIAL INSIGHTS

The accounting cycle addresses the logistics of making certain the accounting system balances with the trial balance, making necessary adjustments to bring accounts up to date, and preparing financial reports. However, entrepreneurs often need more than this from a financial software. They are often looking for financial insights as to how they can improve their business. QuickBooks now offers an Insights digital dashboard to assist entrepreneurs in this endeavor.

To use QuickBooks Insights:

Step 1: From the Home page, select: **Insights**.

Step 2: Select the **arrow** to the right of the screen to advance to the next insight. Notice in the yearly comparison how Rock Castle's income has increased in 2019.

Step 3: Select the right **arrow** again. This insight shows the top customers by sales, listing Brian Cook as the top customer. Although sales by customers are important, profitability by customer might be even more important for business success.

SAVE CHAPTER 7

 Save a backup of your Chapter 7 file using the file name: **YourName Chapter 7 Backup.QBB**. See *Appendix B: Back Up & Restore QuickBooks Files* for instructions.

WORKFLOW

 If you are using the Workflow approach, leave your .QBW file open and proceed directly to Exercise 7.1.

RESTART & RESTORE

 If you are using the Restart & Restore approach and are ending your computer session now, close your .QBW file and exit QuickBooks.

www.My-QuickBooks.com

Go to www.My-QuickBooks.com to view additional QuickBooks resources including Excel Reports Templates, QuickBooks videos, and QuickBooks Hot Arrows and Hot Topics. The Hot Topics can be viewed on your computer or tablet and feature frequently used QuickBooks tasks.

MULTIPLE-CHOICE PRACTICE TEST

Try the **Multiple-Choice Practice Test** for Chapter 7 on the *Computer Accounting with QuickBooks* Online Learning Center at www.mhhe.com/kay2015.

GO DIGITAL!

Go Digital using Excel templates. See *Appendix D: Go Digital with QuickBooks* for more information.

LEARNING ACTIVITIES

Important: Ask your instructor whether you should complete the following assignments by printing reports or by exporting to Excel templates (see Appendix D: Go Digital with QuickBooks).

EXERCISE 7.1: PROFIT & LOSS: VERTICAL ANALYSIS

SCENARIO

You vaguely recall from your college accounting course that performing financial statement analysis can reveal additional useful information. Since Mr. Castle asked for whatever additional information he might need, you decide to print a vertical analysis of the Profit and Loss Statement using QuickBooks.

TASK 1: OPEN COMPANY FILE

WORKFLOW

If you are using the Workflow approach, you will use the same .QBW file.

- If your QBW file is not already open, open it by selecting **File > Open Previous Company**. Select your **.QBW file.**

- Update the Company Name to include **YourName Exercise 7.1**.

RESTART & RESTORE

If you are moving between computers, you must use the Restart and Restore approach.

- Restore your **Chapter 7 Backup.QBB** file using the directions in *Appendix B: Back Up & Restore QuickBooks Files*.

- After restoring the file, update the Company Name to include **YourName Exercise 7.1**.

TASK 2: PROFIT & LOSS: VERTICAL ANALYSIS

Prepare a customized Profit and Loss Statement that shows each item on the statement as a percentage of sales (income):

Step 1: From the Report Center, select **Company & Financial > Profit & Loss Standard**.

Step 2: Select Dates: **This Fiscal Quarter**. Click **Run**.

Step 3: To customize the report, click the **Customize Report** button.

Step 4: When the following *Modify Report* window appears, select **Display** tab.

Step 5: Select: **% of Income**.

Step 6: Click **OK**.

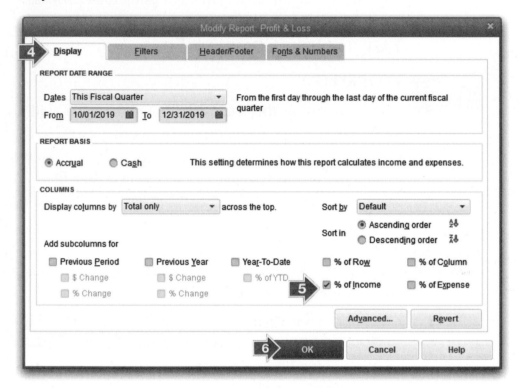

Step 7: Export to **Excel** or **print** the report.

Step 8: **Highlight** the single largest expense as a percentage of income.

Step 9: **Highlight** the profit margin (net income as a percentage of sales).

TASK 3: WORKFLOW

Leave your QuickBooks company file open to complete the next exercise.

EXERCISE 7.2:
BALANCE SHEET: VERTICAL ANALYSIS

SCENARIO

You decide to also prepare a customized Balance Sheet that displays each account on the Balance Sheet as a percentage of total assets. This vertical analysis indicates the proportion of total assets that each asset represents. For example, inventory might be 30 percent of total assets. Vertical analysis also helps to assess the percentage of assets financed by debt versus owners' equity.

TASK 1: CHANGE COMPANY NAME

Update the Company Name to: **YourName Exercise 7.2 Rock Castle Construction**.

TASK 2: BALANCE SHEET: VERTICAL ANALYSIS

Prepare a customized Balance Sheet that shows each account as a percentage of total assets.

Step 1:   From the Report Center, select: **Company & Financial > Balance Sheet Standard**.

Step 2:   Select Dates: **This Fiscal Quarter**. Click **Run**.

Step 3:   Click the **Customize Report** button and select: **% of Column**.

Step 4:   Export to **Excel** or **print** the customized Balance Sheet.

Step 5:   **Highlight** the asset that represents the largest percentage of total assets.

Step 6:   **Highlight** the percentage of assets financed with debt. (Hint: What is the percentage of total liabilities?)

TASK 3: WORKFLOW

Leave your QuickBooks company file open to complete the next exercise.

EXERCISE 7.3: ANALYSIS

SCENARIO

"Last year, the bank told us we had money in the bank, but QuickBooks told us we were broke and had no money in our Checking account to pay bills." Mr. Castle casts you a look as he rushes past your cubicle—a look that warns you to be ready to answer a QuickBooks question.

"We had to hire an accountant last year to find the missing cash in QuickBooks." Rock Castle now pauses as you anticipated the upcoming question. *"Will we need to hire an accountant this year to find the missing cash or can you show me the money?"*

Rapidly, you reply, *"No problem, Mr. Castle. This year we know where all our cash is."* When you look up to show him some QuickBooks reports, Mr. Castle is already back in his office on the phone.

TASK 1: CHANGE COMPANY NAME

Update the Company Name to: **YourName Exercise 7.3 Rock Castle Construction**.

TASK 2: GENERAL LEDGER: SHOW ME THE MONEY

To show Mr. Castle the money, complete the following steps.

Step 1: Display a General Ledger report for Rock Castle Construction for December 15 to December 31, 2019, listing all **asset** accounts in use with a balance.

Step 2: Export to **Excel** or **print** the General Ledger report using the filter.

Step 3: **Highlight** the account on your General Ledger report where the accountant found the missing cash last year.

TASK 3: RATIOS

In addition to the QuickBooks reports you will be providing Mr. Castle, you decide that preparing ratio analysis for him will provide additional insight into Rock Castle Construction operations.

Using your QuickBooks reports from this chapter, calculate the following ratios.

Step 1: The Current Ratio is used as a measure of how well current assets cover the current liabilities that will be due within the next year. If an enterprise has $2 in current assets for each $1 in current liabilities, the current ratio is stated as 2:1.

Calculate the Current Ratio (Current Assets/Current Liabilities) for Rock Castle Construction. _____:_____

Step 2: The debt ratio focuses on the percentage of company assets financed with debt as opposed to equity. For example, a debt ratio of 40% indicates that 40 percent of the enterprise's assets are financed with debt. Too high a debt ratio can indicate increased risk of default on the debt.

Calculate the Debt Ratio (Total Liabilities/Total Assets) for Rock Castle Construction. _____%

Step 3: The profit margin shows the percentage of each sales dollar that is left in profit. For example, a profit margin of 10% indicates that on average, 10 cents of each dollar of sales is profit. Profit margin varies greatly by industry with some industries, such as discount stores, having low profit margins.

Calculate the Profit Margin (Net Income or Net Profit/Total Sales) for Rock Castle Construction for this fiscal quarter. _____%

Step 4: Prepare a brief email to Rock Castle summarizing the results of your ratio analysis and outlining your conclusions, comments, or recommendations based on your analysis.

TASK 4: SAVE EXERCISE 7.3

Save a backup of your Exercise 7.3 file using the file name: **YourName Exercise 7.3 Backup.QBB**. See *Appendix B: Back Up & Restore QuickBooks Files* for instructions.

EXERCISE 7.4: YEAR-END GUIDE

QuickBooks provides a Year-End Guide to assist in organizing the tasks that a business must complete at the end of its accounting period.

Print the Year-End Guide as follows:

Step 1: Select **Help** menu **> Year-End Guide**.

Step 2: ✓ **Check** the items that you have already completed for Rock Castle Construction.

Step 3: **Print** the Year-End Guide by clicking the **Print** icon at the top of the window.

EXERCISE 7.5: WEB QUEST

To learn more information about TurboTax software, visit Intuit's TurboTax website.

Step 1: Go to www.turbotax.com website.

Step 2: Prepare a short email to Mr. Castle summarizing the difference between TurboTax Home & Business and TurboTax Business. Which TurboTax product would you recommend for Rock Castle Construction?

EXERCISE 7.6: WEB QUEST

Publicly traded companies (companies that sell stock to the public) are required to provide an annual report to stockholders. The annual report contains financial statements including an Income Statement, Balance Sheet, and Statement of Cash Flows. Many publicly traded companies now post their financial statements on their websites. Print financial statements for Intuit, the company that sells QuickBooks software.

Step 1: Go to www.intuit.com website. Select **Company > Investor Relations > Financial Information > Annual Reports.**

Step 2: Select **2013 Annual Report on Form 10-K**.

Step 3: In the Consolidated Financial Statements, find and **print** Intuit's Consolidated Statements of Operations, which shows results for three years.

Step 4: **Highlight** net income for the year Intuit was most profitable.

CHAPTER 7 QUICK CHECK

NAME:

INSTRUCTIONS:

1. CHECK OFF THE ITEMS YOU COMPLETED.

2. TURN IN THIS PAGE WITH YOUR PRINTOUTS.

> **!**
> Ask your instructor if you should Go Digital (Excel* or PDF) or use paper printouts.

CHAPTER 7

☐ * Trial Balance

☐ * Journal

☐ * Adjusted Trial Balance

☐ * General Ledger

☐ * Profit & Loss

☐ Income and Expense Graph

☐ * Balance Sheet

☐ * Statement of Cash Flows

☐ * Income Tax Preparation Report

☐ * Cash Flow Forecast

EXERCISE 7.1

☐ * Task 2: Profit & Loss Vertical Analysis

EXERCISE 7.2

☐ * Task 2: Balance Sheet Vertical Analysis

EXERCISE 7.3

☐ * Task 2: General Ledger Account

☐ Task 3: Ratios

EXERCISE 7.4

☐ Year-End Guide

EXERCISE 7.5

☐ TurboTax Recommendation

EXERCISE 7.6

☐ Statements of Operations for Intuit, Inc.

Download Go Digital Excel templates at www.My-QuickBooks.com.

PROJECT 7 LARRY'S LANDSCAPING

To complete this project, download the Chapter 7 Go Digital Reports Excel template at www.My-QuickBooks.com. Follow the instructions provided in the Excel template.

Complete the following for Larry's Landscaping.

1. Use either your QuickBooks company file (.QBW file) or backup file (.QBB file) that you completed for Project 6. (If you have issues with your QuickBooks file, contact your instructor.) Update the Company Name to include: **YourName Project 7**.

2. Download the Chapter 7 Go Digital Reports Excel template. Save the Excel file using the file name: **YourLastName FirstName CH7 REPORTS**.

3. Complete the following instructions to ensure that your accounts are in the proper order in the Chart of Accounts. Open the *Chart of Accounts* window. Click **Account > Re-sort List**. When asked: Are you sure you want to return this list to its original order?, click **OK**.

    Using your saved Excel template for Chapter 7, export to **Excel** the Trial Balance report for Larry's Landscaping for the fiscal quarter October 1 to December 31, 2019.

4. Enter the following adjusting entries for Larry's Landscaping.

Date	Entry Number	Account to Debit	Account to Credit	Amount
12/31/2019	A108	6700 Depreciation (Expense)	1520 Accumulated Depreciation – Truck	$575.00
12/31/2019	A109	6900 Insurance (Expense)	Prepaid Insurance	$100.00

5. Export to **Excel** the Adjusting Journal Entries report for December 31, 2019. (Select: Report Center > Accountant & Taxes > Adjusting Journal Entries.)

6. Export to **Excel** the Adjusted Trial Balance for Larry's Landscaping at December 31, 2019. **Highlight** the adjustments and any adjusted trial balance account balances that changed as a result of adjustments.

7. Export to **Excel** the Profit and Loss Standard report for the fiscal quarter October 1 to December 31, 2019.

8. Export to **Excel** the Profit and Loss Detail report for the fiscal quarter October 1 to December 31, 2019.

9. Export to **Excel** the Balance Sheet Standard report as of December 31, 2019.

10. Export to **Excel** the Balance Sheet Standard report with a vertical analysis showing each account as a percentage of total assets as of December 31, 2019. **Highlight** the asset that represents the largest percentage of total assets.

11. Export to **Excel** the General Ledger report using only the **accounts in use** for December 15 through December 31, 2019.

12. Mark the reports completed on the 7 REPORTS sheet. Save your Excel file.

13. Save a .QBB backup of your work.

 PROJECT 7 QUICK CHECK

NAME:

INSTRUCTIONS:
1. CHECK OFF THE ITEMS YOU COMPLETED.
2. ATTACH THIS PAGE TO YOUR PRINTOUTS.

!
Ask your instructor if you should Go Digital (Excel* or PDF) or use paper printouts.

PROJECT 7

- ☐ * Trial Balance
- ☐ * Adjusting Journal Entries
- ☐ * Adjusted Trial Balance
- ☐ * Profit & Loss
- ☐ * Profit & Loss Detail
- ☐ * Balance Sheet
- ☐ * Balance Sheet Vertical Analysis
- ☐ * General Ledger

 Download Go Digital Excel templates at www.My-QuickBooks.com.

REFLECTION: A WISH AND A STAR

Reflection improves learning and retention. Reflect on what you have learned after completing Chapter 7 that you did not know before you started the chapter.

A Star:

What did you like best that you learned about QuickBooks in Chapter 7?

A Wish:

If you could pick one thing, what do you wish you knew more about when using QuickBooks?

NOTES:

SECTION 2
QUICKBOOKS
ACCOUNTING FOR ENTREPRENEURS

CHAPTER 8
NEW COMPANY SETUP

SCENARIO

Lately, you've considered starting your own business and becoming an entrepreneur. You have been looking for a business opportunity that would use your talents to make money.

While working at Rock Castle Construction, you have overheard conversations that some of the customers have been dissatisfied with the quality of the paint jobs. In addition, you believe there is a demand for custom painting. You know that Rock Castle Construction lost more than one job because it could not find a subcontractor to do custom painting.

One morning when you arrive at work, you hear Mr. Castle's voice booming throughout the office. *"That's the second time this month!"* he roars into the telephone. *"How are we supposed to finish our jobs on time when the painting subcontractor doesn't show up?!"* Mr. Castle slams down the phone.

That morning you begin to seriously consider the advantages and disadvantages of starting your own painting service business. Perhaps you could pick up some work from Rock Castle Construction. You could do interior and exterior painting for homes and businesses including custom-painted murals while continuing to work part-time for Rock Castle Construction maintaining its accounting records. Now that you have learned QuickBooks, you can quickly enter transactions and create the reports Mr. Castle needs, leaving you time to operate your own painting service business.

When you return from lunch, you notice Katrina Beneficio in Mr. Castle's office. Then you overhear Mr. Castle telling her, *"We would like to help you, Mrs. Beneficio, but we don't have anyone who can do a custom-painted landscape on your dining room wall. If I hear of anyone who does that type of work, I will call you."*

You watch as the two of them shake hands and Mrs. Beneficio walks out the front door. Sensing a window of opportunity, you turn to Mr. Castle and ask, *"Would you mind if I help out Mrs. Beneficio with the mural?"*

Mr. Castle nods his approval. *"If it keeps one of our customers happy, then I'm happy."*

You swiftly pursue Mrs. Beneficio into the parking lot. *"Mrs. Beneficio—"*

She stops and turns to look at you. *"Mrs. Beneficio—I understand that you are looking for someone to paint a landscape mural in your home. I would like to bid on the job."*

With a sparkle in her eye, Mrs. Beneficio asks, *"How soon can you start?"*

"As soon as I get off work this afternoon!" you reply as the two of you shake hands. *"Would you like a bid on the job?"*

Without hesitation, Mrs. Beneficio replies, *"I trust you will be fair to your first customer."*

When you reenter the office building, Mr. Castle is waiting for you. Finally, Mr. Castle speaks. *"Congratulations. Give Tom Whalen a call. He would like you to do marble faux painting in his home's foyer."*

"Thanks, Mr. Castle. I'll do that right away," you reply as you head toward your cubicle.

Walking back to your cubicle, you quickly make start-up decisions:
1. To use the sole proprietorship form of business.
2. To name your business Paint Palette.
3. To use environmentally friendly paints and European painting techniques (faux and murals) for competitive advantage.
4. To invest in a computer so that you can use QuickBooks to maintain the accounting records for your business.

Now you will have two sources of income:
- Wages from Rock Castle Construction reported on your W-2 and attached to your 1040 tax return.
- Income from your painting business reported on a Schedule C attached to your 1040 tax return.

So you decide to treat yourself to a reward—a new iPad—and use social media marketing to reach new customers for your new business endeavor.

CHAPTER 8
LEARNING OBJECTIVES

In Chapter 8, you will learn about the following QuickBooks features:

INTRODUCTION

In this chapter, you will set up a new service company in QuickBooks by completing the following steps:

---

1. EasyStep Interview

Use the EasyStep Interview to enter information and preferences for the new company. Based on the information entered, QuickBooks automatically creates a Chart of Accounts.

2. Customize the Chart of Accounts

Modify the Chart of Accounts to customize it for your business.

3. Customer List

In the Customer List, enter information about customers to whom you sell products and services.

4. Vendor List

In the Vendor List, enter information about vendors from whom you buy products, supplies, and services.

5. Item List

In the Item List, enter information about (1) products and services you *sell to customers* and (2) products and services you *buy from vendors*.

If you hired employees, you would also enter information into the Employee List. In this case, Paint Palette has no employees.

To begin Chapter 8, start QuickBooks software by clicking on the **QuickBooks** desktop icon or click **Start > Programs > QuickBooks > QuickBooks Premier Accountant Edition 2015**.

EASYSTEP INTERVIEW

To create a new company data file in QuickBooks, use the EasyStep Interview. The EasyStep Interview asks you a series of questions about your business. Then QuickBooks uses the information to customize QuickBooks to fit your business needs.

Open the EasyStep Interview as follows:

Step 1: Select **Create a new company**.

On the **File** menu, notice the **New Company from Existing Company File** option. This choice permits you to create quickly a new company file by copying the preferences and key lists from an existing company.

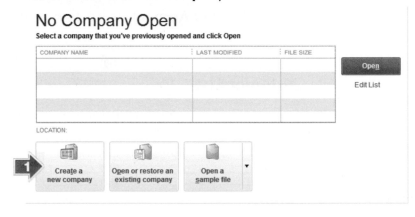

When the following *QuickBooks Setup* window appears, you will see four options for how to set up a new company:

- Express Start: Recommended for new QuickBooks users, this option will ask you a few basic questions and do the rest for you.

- Detailed Start: This option lets you control the setup and fine-tune the company file to meet your specific needs.

- Create: This choice permits you to create quickly a new company file by copying the preferences and key lists from an existing company.

- Other Options: This option lets you convert data from Quicken or other accounting software to create a new QuickBooks company file.

Let's get your business set up quickly!

> Answer some basic questions and we'll do the rest. You can always make changes later. (Recommended for new users)
>
> **Express Start**
>
> Control the setup and fine-tune the company file.
>
> **2** Detailed Start
>
> Create a new company file based on an existing one.
>
> Create
>
> Convert data from Quicken or other accounting software.
>
> Other Options ▼

Need help? Give us a call

Step 2: Select **Detailed Start**.

Step 3: When the following *EasyStep Interview Enter Your Company Information* window appears:

- Enter Company Name: **YourName Paint Palette**.

- Press the **Tab** key, and QuickBooks will automatically enter the company name in the *Legal name* field. Since your company will do business under its legal name, the *Company name* and *Legal name* fields are the same.

> Your DBA (Doing Business As) name is used to identify your company for sales, advertising, and marketing.

Step 4: Enter the following company information.

> Your company's Legal Name is used on all legal documents, such as contracts, tax returns, licenses, and patents.

Tax ID	333-22-4444
Address	127 Ashuer Boulevard
City	Bayshore
State	CA
Zip	94326
Phone	800-555-1358
Email	<Enter your email address>

For a Federal Tax ID number:
1. A sole proprietorship uses the owner's Social Security number.
2. A corporation uses an EIN (Employer Identification Number).

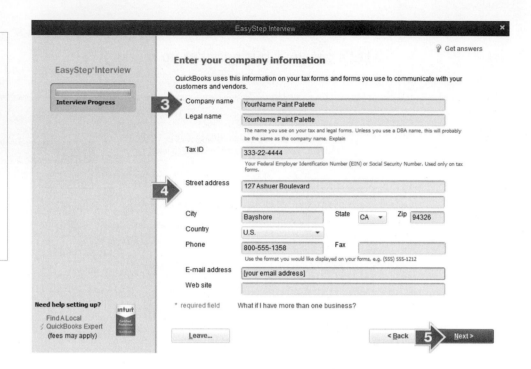

Step 5: Select **Next**.

Step 6: In the *Select Your Industry* window, select **General Service-based Business**.

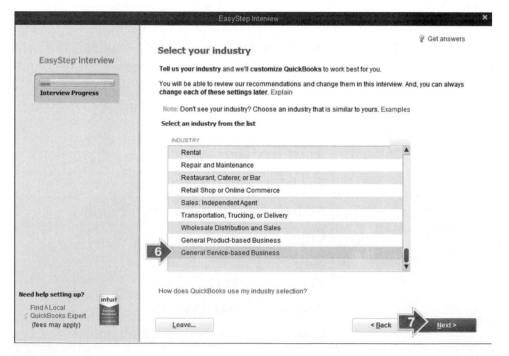

Step 7: Select **Next**.

Step 8:   When the *How Is Your Company Organized?* window appears, select **Sole Proprietorship**.

How your business entity is organized (Sole Proprietorship, Partnership, Limited Liability Partnership (LLP), Limited Liability Company (LLC), C Corporation, S Corporation, or Non-Profit) determines which tax form and tax lines you use.

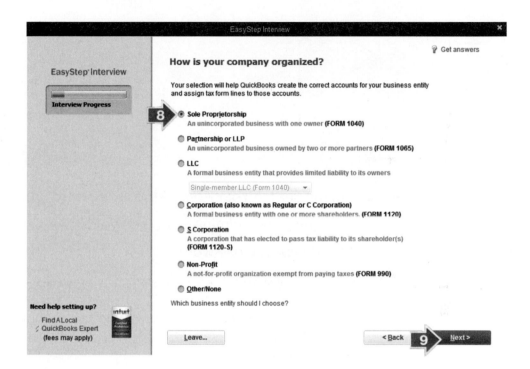

Step 9:   Select **Next**.

Step 10:   Select the first month of your fiscal year: **January**.

Step 11:   Select **Next**.

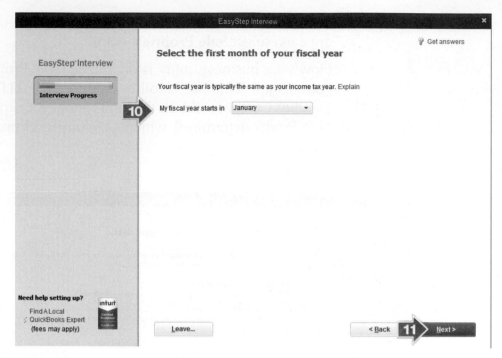

Step 12: In the *Set Up Your Administrator Password* window:

- Enter your administrator password.

- Retype the password.

- Click **Next.**

> **!** Write your password on the inside front cover of your text.

Step 13: When the *Create Your Company File* window appears, click **Next** to choose a file name and location to save your company file.

Step 14: When the *Filename for New Company* window appears, select Save in: **Desktop**.

Step 15: Enter File name: **YourName Chapter 8.**

Step 16: Click **Save**.

If you are using removable media such as a USB drive or external hard drive to save the .QBW file, check if there is enough disk space on the drive and then specify that drive for the location to save the .QBW file.

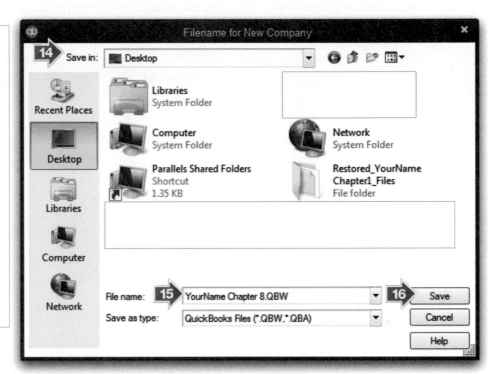

The *My Shortcuts* window should appear on the left side of your QuickBooks company screen. The next section of the EasyStep Interview is to customize QuickBooks by turning on features to fit your business needs.

Step 1: When the *Customizing QuickBooks For Your Business* window appears, click **Next**

Step 2: When the *What Do You Sell?* window appears:

- Select: **Services only**.

- Click **Next**.

Step 3: When asked "Do you charge sales tax?"

- Select: **No**.

- Click **Next**.

Step 4: When asked "Do you want to create estimates in QuickBooks?"

- Select **Yes**.

- Click **Next**.

Step 5: When the *Using Statements in QuickBooks* window appears:

  - "Do you want to use billing statements in QuickBooks?" Select: **Yes**.
  - Click **Next**.

Step 6: When the *Using Progress Invoicing* window appears:

  - "Do you want to use progress invoicing?" Select: **No**.
  - Click **Next**.

Step 7: When the *Managing Bills You Owe* window appears:

  - "Do you want to keep track of bills you owe?" Select: **Yes**.
  - Click **Next**.

Step 8: When the *Tracking Time in QuickBooks* window appears:

  - "Do you want to track time in QuickBooks?" Select: **Yes**.
  - Click **Next**.

Step 9: When the *Do You Have Employees?* window appears:

  - Select: **No**.
  - Click **Next**.

Step 10: Read the *Using Accounts in QuickBooks* window. Click **Next**.

Step 11: When the *Select a Date to Start Tracking Your Finances* window appears:

  - Select: **Use today's date or the first day of the quarter or month**.
  - Enter Date: **01/01/2020**.
  - Click **Next**.

Step 12: When the *Review Income and Expense Accounts* window appears, click **Next**.

Step 13:   When the following *Congratulations!* window appears, click **Go to Setup**.

If a *Set Up an External Accountant User* window appears, select **No**.

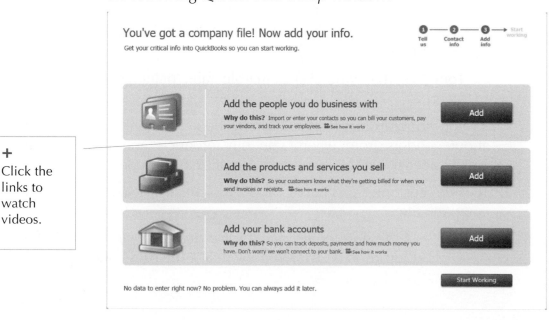

QUICKBOOKS COMPANY SETUP

After the EasyStep Interview is finished, you can start using the QuickBooks company file or you can finish the company setup using the following *QuickBooks Setup* window.

+
Click the links to watch videos.

As shown in the *QuickBooks Setup* window, you can:

1. **Add the people you do business with**:
   - Customer List
   - Vendor List
   - Employee List (Omit since you have no employees.)

2. **Add the products and services you sell**
   - Item List

3. **Add your bank accounts**

After completing these steps, you can customize your QuickBooks company file by completing the following:

1. **Complete the company information**
2. **Customize preferences**
3. **Customize your Chart of Accounts**

ADD THE PEOPLE YOU DO BUSINESS WITH

As you know from Chapter 4, the Customer List contains information about the customers to whom you sell services. In addition, the Customer List also contains information about jobs or projects for each customer. Paint Palette has two customers:

1. Katrina Beneficio, who wants a custom landscape mural painted on her dining room wall.

2. Tom Whalen, who wants marble faux painting in his home's foyer.

As you know from Chapter 5, the Vendor List contains information about vendors from whom you buy products and services. Paint Palette needs to add Brewer Paint Supplies as a vendor.

To add customers, vendors, and employees to your QuickBooks company file:

Step 1: In the *Add the People You Do Business With* section of the *QuickBooks Setup* window, click the **Add** button.

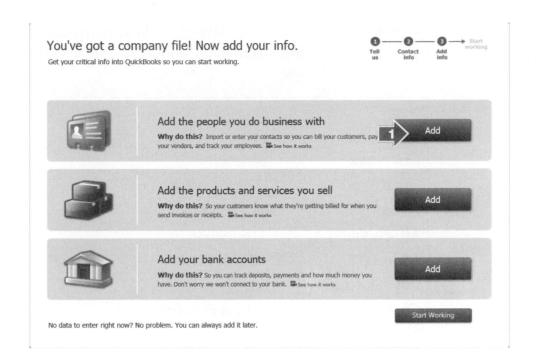

Step 2: You have several options for how to add information about people you do business with as shown in the following *Add the People You Do Business With* window. Select **Paste from Excel or enter manually**.

+
You can import list information using Excel. See QuickBooks Help for more information.

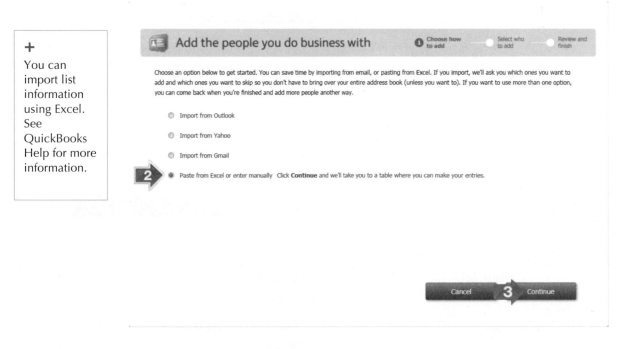

Step 3: Select **Continue**.

Step 4: When the *Select Who to Add* window appears, enter the following information about your first customer, Katrina Beneficio.

Name	Beneficio, Katrina
First Name	Katrina
Last Name	Beneficio
Email	kbeneficio@ch8.com
Phone	415-555-0013
Alt. Phone	415-555-3636
Address	10 Pico Blvd
City, State, Zip	Bayshore, CA 94326
Contact Name	Katrina Beneficio

Step 5: Select **Customer** radio button for Katrina Beneficio.

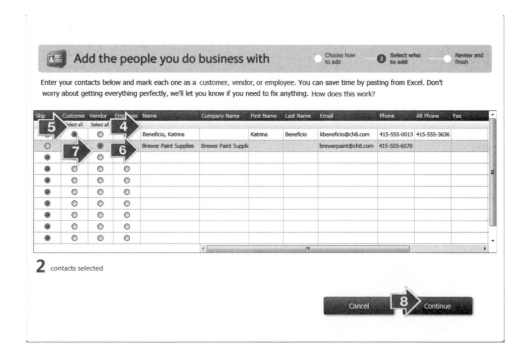

Step 6: Move to the next line and enter the following information about Brewer Paint Supplies.

Name	Brewer Paint Supplies
Company Name	Brewer Paint Supplies
Email	brewerpaint@ch8.com
Phone	415-555-6070
Address	200 Spring Street
City, State, Zip	Bayshore, CA 94326
Contact Name	Ella Brewer

Step 7: Select **Vendor** radio button for Brewer Paint Supplies.

Step 8: Click **Continue**.

Step 9: If you had opening balances, you could enter those now. Instead, click **Continue**.

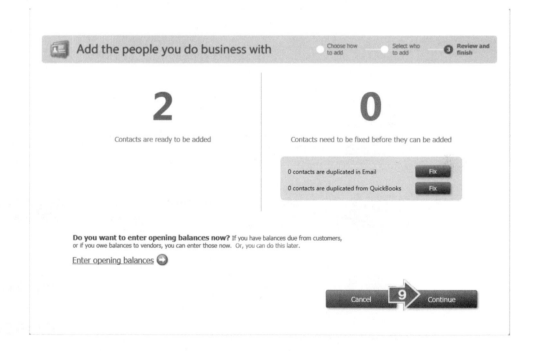

ADD THE PRODUCTS AND SERVICES YOU SELL

The products and services you sell are entered into an Item List. As you know from Chapter 5, the Item List contains information about service items, inventory items, and non-inventory items. Paint Palette plans to sell four different service items to customers:

1. Labor: mural painting

2. Labor: faux painting

3. Labor: interior painting

4. Labor: exterior painting

To add a service item to the Item List for Paint Palette:

Step 1: In the *Add the Products and Services You Sell* section of the *QuickBooks Setup* window, select the **Add** button.

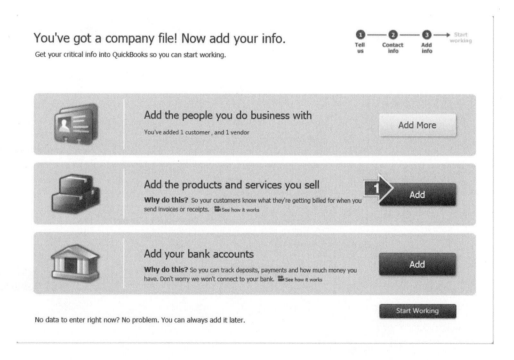

Step 2: Select Item type: **Service**.

Step 3: Select **Continue**.

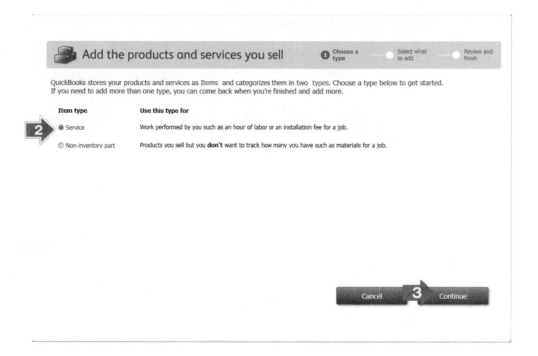

Step 4: Enter the following information about the new service item:

Name	Labor
Description	Painting Labor
Price	0.00

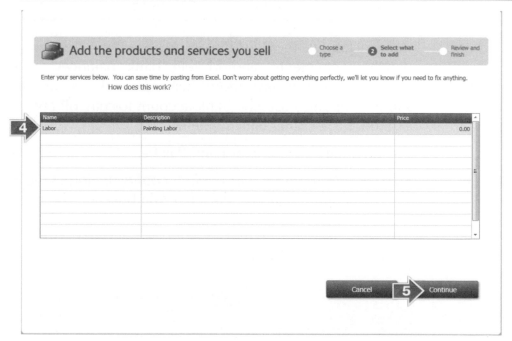

Step 5:   Click **Continue**.

Step 6:   Click **Continue** again to return to the *QuickBooks Setup* window.

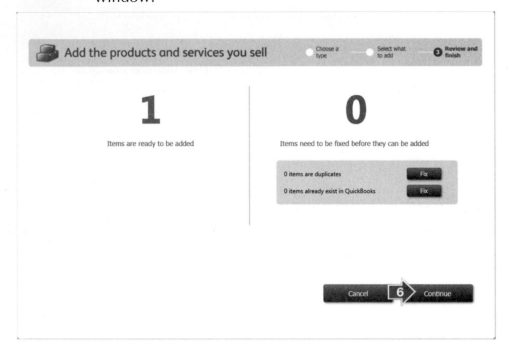

ADD YOUR BANK ACCOUNTS

Bank accounts in QuickBooks are used to track your company's deposits, payments, and current bank balances. A QuickBooks company file can have more than one bank account. For example, some companies use one bank account for payroll and another bank account for all other banking items.

To add a bank account for Paint Palette:

Step 1:   In the *Add Your Bank Accounts* section of the *QuickBooks Setup* window, click the **Add** button.

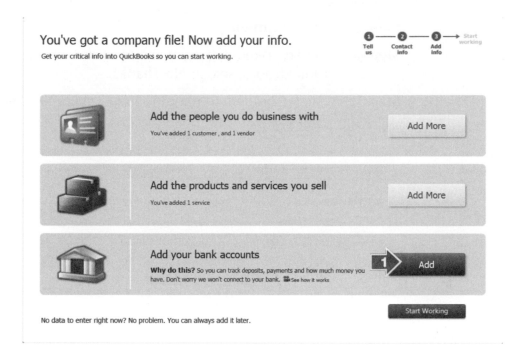

Step 2: Enter the following information about Paint Palette's bank account.

Account Name	Checking
Account Number	0123456789
Opening Balance	0.00
Opening Balance Date	01/01/2020

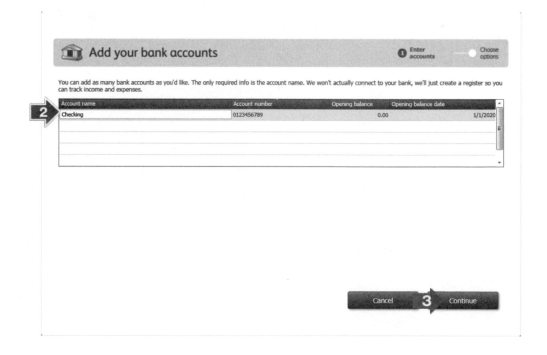

Step 3:   Click **Continue**.

Step 4:   When asked if you want to order checks designed for QuickBooks, select: **No Thanks**.

Step 5:   Click **Continue** to return to the *QuickBooks Setup* window.

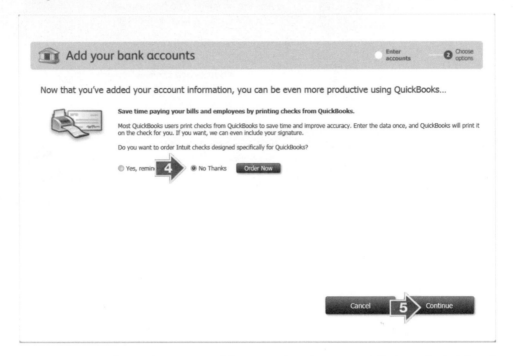

Step 6:   Select **Start Working** at the bottom of the *QuickBooks Setup* window.

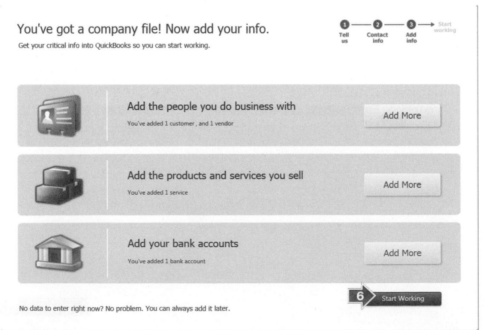

Step 7:   When the following *Quick Start Center* window appears, view the videos about *Charge customers for money they owe you* and *Track bills that are due and those you paid.*

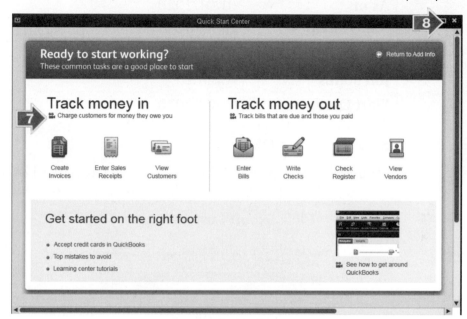

Step 8:   **Close** the *Quick Start Center* window by clicking the ☒ in the upper right corner of the window.

PRINT CUSTOMER, VENDOR, AND ITEM LISTS

Before printing the Customer List, let's add a new job for Katrina Beneficio.

Step 1:   To add a new job, first display the Customer Center by selecting **Customers** on the Icon bar.

Step 2:   Select Katrina Beneficio in the Customers & Jobs List, then **right-click** to display the pop-up menu. Select **Add Job**.

Step 3:   Enter the following information into the *New Job* window.

Job Name	Dining Room
Opening Balance	0.00
As of	01/01/2020
Job Description	Dining Room Landscape Mural
Job Type	Mural
Job Status	Awarded
Start Date	01/03/2020

Select **Add New**.

Step 4: Click **OK** to save.

Step 5: To export to Excel or print the Customer List, click the **Excel** button at the top of the Customer Center.

Step 6: Click **Export Customer List**.

Step 7: Select **Replace an existing worksheet.**

Step 8: **Browse** for **YourName CH8 REPORTS** template.

Step 9: Select worksheet: **CH8 CUST**.

Step 10: Select **Advanced.**

- *Uncheck* **Space between columns**.

- *Uncheck* **Include QuickBooks Export Guide worksheet with helpful advice**.

- Select **On printed report and screen**.

- Click **OK**.

Step 11: Select **Export**.

Step 12: If an *Export Report Alert* window appears asking if you want to continue, select **Yes**.

Step 13: **Close** the Customer Center.

To print the Vendor List for Paint Palette:

Step 1: Display the Vendor Center by selecting **Vendors** on the Icon bar.

Step 2: Select the Excel button at the top of the Vendor Center.

Step 3: Select **Export Vendor List**.

Step 4: Export the Vendor List to Excel.

Step 5: **Close** the Vendor Center.

To print the Item List for Paint Palette:

Step 1: Display the Report Center by selecting **Reports** on the Icon bar.

Step 2: Select **List**.

Step 3: Select **Item Listing**.

Step 4: Select Date: **01/01/2020**.

Step 5: Select **Run**.

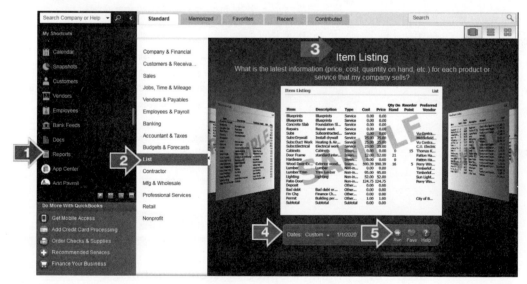

Step 6: With the Item Listing report displayed on your screen, select **Excel**.

Step 7: Select **Create New Worksheet**.

Step 8: When the following *Send Report to Excel* window appears, select **Replace an existing worksheet**.

Step 9: If not already selected, click the **Browse** button and select your **CH8 REPORTS** Excel file.

Step 10: From the drop-down list, select the sheet: **CH8 ITEM**.

Step 11: Click the **Advanced** button.

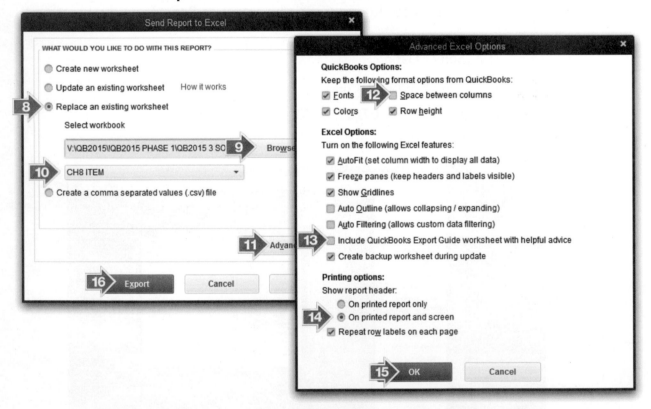

Step 12: Uncheck **Space between columns**.

Step 13: Uncheck **Include QuickBooks Export Guide worksheet with helpful advice**.

Step 14: Select Show report header: **On printed report and screen**.

Step 15: Click **OK.**

Step 16: Click **Export**.

Step 17: If an Export Report Alert message appears, select: **Do not display this message in the future**. Then select **Yes.**

Step 18: In Excel, select the **8 REPORTS** sheet tab. Mark the report sheet(s) you completed by inserting an "**X**".

Step 19: Save your **CH8 REPORTS** Excel workbook.

Step 20: Close the *Item Listing* window and the *Report Center* window.

CUSTOMIZE QUICKBOOKS

Notice that the Home page for Paint Palette differs from the Home page for Rock Castle Construction in the following ways:

1. The *Vendors* section of the Home page for Paint Palette does not include Purchase Orders, Receive Inventory, and Enter Bills Against Inventory icons. During the company setup, you indicated that Paint Palette was a service company. Since you will not be selling a product, you will not be tracking inventory for resale.

2. Also notice that the *Employees* section does not include the Pay Employees, Pay Liabilities, and Process Payroll Forms icons. During the company setup, you indicated that there were no employees so these icons are not needed for Paint Palette.

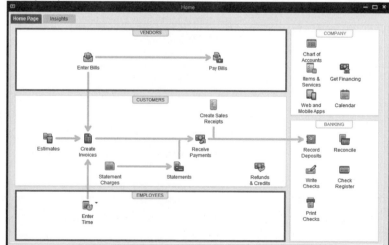

Next, you will customize QuickBooks for Paint Palette by entering company information, customizing preferences, and customizing the Chart of Accounts.

ENTER COMPANY INFORMATION

To enter additional company information:

Step 1: Select **My Company** on the Icon bar.

Business tax returns:
1. Sole proprietorships file Schedule C attached to owner's Form 1040.
2. Corporations file Form 1120.
3. S corporations file Form 1120S.
4. Partnerships file Form 1065.

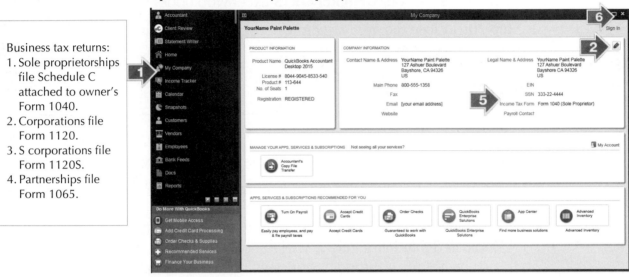

Step 2: Select **Edit**.

Step 3: Update the Company Name: **YourName Chapter 8 Paint Palette**.

Step 4: Click **OK**.

Step 5: Verify Income Tax Form: **Form 1040 (Sole Proprietor)**.

Step 6: **Close** the *My Company* window.

CUSTOMIZE QUICKBOOKS PREFERENCES

To customize your QuickBooks preferences:

Step 1: Select **Edit** menu **> Preferences > General > My Preferences**.

Step 2: Select Default Date to Use for New Transactions: **Use the last entered date as default**.

Step 3: Select **Desktop View > My Preferences > Show Home page when opening a company file**.

Step 4: To customize the appearance of your QuickBooks, select **Company File Color Scheme**.

Step 5: Click **OK** to close the *Preferences* window.

CUSTOMIZE CHART OF ACCOUNTS

The Chart of Accounts is a list of all the accounts Paint Palette will use when maintaining its accounting records. The Chart of Accounts is like a table of contents for accounting records.

In the EasyStep Interview, when you selected General Service-based Business as the type of industry, QuickBooks automatically created a Chart of Accounts for Paint Palette. Then QuickBooks permits you to customize the Chart of Accounts to fit your accounting needs.

DISPLAY CHART OF ACCOUNTS

To display the following *Chart of Accounts* window, click **Chart of Accounts** in the *Company* section of the Home page.

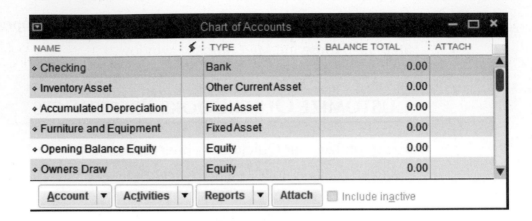

DISPLAY ACCOUNT NUMBERS

Notice that the Chart of Accounts does not list the account numbers. Display account numbers in the Chart of Accounts by completing the following steps:

Step 1: Select **Edit** menu.

Step 2: Select **Preferences**.

Step 3: When the *Preferences* window appears, select the **Accounting** icon on the left scrollbar.

Step 4: Select the **Company Preferences** tab.

Step 5: Select **Use account numbers**.

Step 6: *Uncheck* **Warn if transactions are 30 day(s) in the future.**

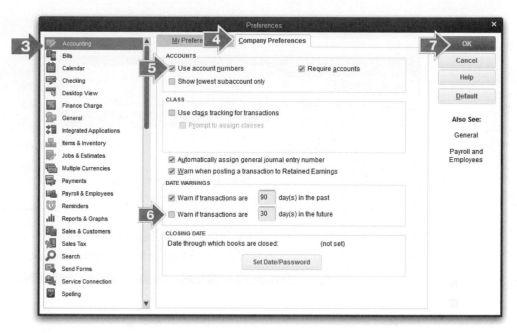

Step 7: Click **OK** to close the *Preferences* window.

Your Chart of Accounts should now display account numbers.

ADD NEW ACCOUNTS

Paint Palette will be purchasing a new computer. To account for the computer, you will need to add the following three accounts to the Chart of Accounts:

Account	Computer
Subaccount	Computer Cost
Subaccount	Accumulated Depreciation Computer

The Computer Cost subaccount contains the original cost of the computer. The Accumulated Depreciation subaccount for the computer accumulates all depreciation recorded for the computer over its useful life. The parent account, Computer, will show the net book value of the computer (cost minus accumulated depreciation).

To add new accounts to the Chart of Accounts for Paint Palette:

Step 1: From the following *Chart of Accounts* window:

- **Right-click** to display the pop-up menu.
- Select **New**.

+
If your business has a large number of fixed asset accounts, you can use the Fixed Asset Item List to track fixed asset information.

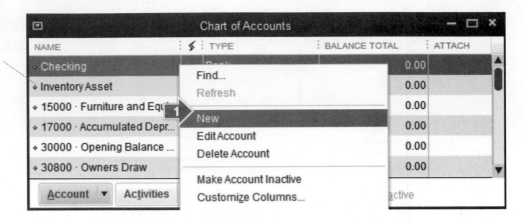

The Chart of Accounts now lists account numbers.

Step 2: From the *Add New Account: Choose Account Type* window, select **Fixed Asset (major purchases)**.

Step 3: Click **Continue**.

Step 4: When the following *Add New Account* window appears, select Account Type: **Fixed Asset**.

Step 5: Enter Account Number: **14100**.

Step 6: Enter Account Name: **Computer**.

Step 7: Enter Description: **Computer**.

Step 8: Select Tax Line: **<Unassigned>**.

Step 9: Click **Save & New** to enter another account.

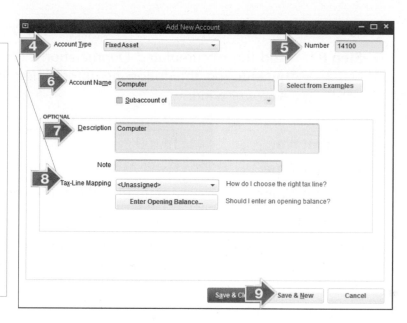

> **!**
> The Tax Line determines where QuickBooks lists the account balance on the Income Tax Summary report. Because only income and expense accounts are listed on Schedule C of the tax return, an Unassigned Tax Line is used for other accounts not appearing on the tax return.

When a blank *Add New Account* window appears, add a Computer Cost subaccount as follows:

Step 1:   Select Account Type: **Fixed Asset**.

Step 2:   Enter Account Number: **14200**.

Step 3:   Enter Account Name: **Computer Cost**.

Step 4:   Check ✔ Subaccount of: **14100 – Computer**.

Step 5:   Enter Description: **Computer Cost**.

Step 6:   Select Tax Line: **<Unassigned>**.

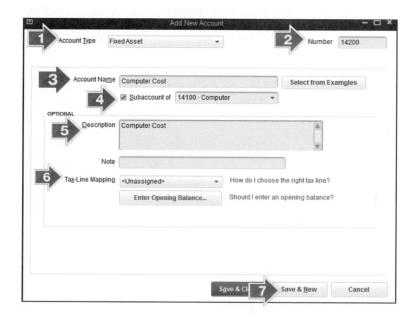

Step 7: Click **Save & New** to add another subaccount.

Step 8: Add the Accumulated Depreciation Computer subaccount by entering the following information in the *Add New Account* window:

Account No.	14300
Account Type	Fixed Asset
Account Name	Accumulated Depr Computer
Subaccount of	14100 Computer
Account Description	Accumulated Depreciation Computer
Tax Line	Unassigned

Step 9: Click **Save & Close** to close the *Add New Account* window.

PRINT THE CHART OF ACCOUNTS

To create the Chart of Accounts (Account Listing) report, complete the following steps:

Step 1: From the *Report Center:*

- Select: **List (or Accountant & Taxes) > Account Listing**.
- Select Date: **01/01/2020**. Click **Run**.
- Export to **Excel** or **print** the Chart of Accounts.
- **Close** the *Account Listing* and *Report Center* windows.

Step 2: **Close** the *Chart of Accounts* window.

SAVE CHAPTER 8

Save a backup of your Chapter 8 file using the file name: **YourName Chapter 8 Backup.QBB**. See *Appendix B: Back Up & Restore QuickBooks Files* for instructions.

WORKFLOW

If you are using the Workflow approach, leave your .QBW file open and proceed directly to Exercise 8.1.

RESTART & RESTORE

If you are using the Restart & Restore approach and are ending your computer session now, close your .QBW file and exit QuickBooks.

www.My-QuickBooks.com

Go to www.My-QuickBooks.com to view additional QuickBooks resources including Excel Reports Templates, QuickBooks videos, and QuickBooks Hot Arrows and Hot Topics. The Hot Topics can be viewed on your computer or tablet and feature frequently used QuickBooks tasks.

MULTIPLE-CHOICE PRACTICE TEST

Try the **Multiple-Choice Practice Test** for Chapter 8 on the *Computer Accounting with QuickBooks* Online Learning Center at www.mhhe.com/kay2015.

GO DIGITAL!

Go Digital using Excel templates. See *Appendix D: Go Digital with QuickBooks* for instructions about how to save your QuickBooks reports electronically.

LEARNING ACTIVITIES

Important: Ask your instructor whether you should complete the following assignments by printing reports or by exporting to Excel templates (see Appendix D: Go Digital with QuickBooks).

EXERCISE 8.1: CHART OF ACCOUNTS

In this exercise, you will add new accounts and subaccounts to Paint Palette's Chart of Accounts.

TASK 1: OPEN COMPANY FILE

WORKFLOW

If you are using the Workflow approach, you will use the same .QBW file.

- If your QBW file is not already open, open it by selecting **File > Open Previous Company**. Select your **.QBW file.**

- Update Company Name to include **YourName Exercise 8.1**.

RESTART & RESTORE

If you are not using the same computer, you must use the Restart and Restore approach.

- Restore your **Chapter 8 Backup.QBB** file using the directions in *Appendix B: Back Up & Restore QuickBooks Files*.

- After restoring the file, update Company Name to include **YourName Exercise 8.1**.

TASK 2: ADD ACCOUNTS

Step 1: Add the following new accounts and subaccounts to the Chart of Accounts for Paint Palette. Click **Save & New** after entering each account.

Account No.	11000
Account Type	Accounts Receivable
Account Name	Accounts Receivable
Account Description	Accounts Receivable
Tax Line	Unassigned

Account No.	13000
Account Type	Other Current Asset

Account Name	Paint Supplies
Account Description	Paint Supplies
Tax Line	Unassigned

Account No.	14400
Account Type	Fixed Asset
Account Name	Equipment
Account Description	Equipment
Tax Line	Unassigned

Account No.	14500
Account Type	Fixed Asset
Account Name	Equipment Cost
Account Description	Equipment Cost
Subaccount of	14400 Equipment
Tax Line	Unassigned

Account No.	14600
Account Type	Fixed Asset
Account Name	Acc Depr Equipment
Account Description	Acc Depr Equipment
Subaccount of	14400 Equipment
Tax Line	Unassigned

Account No.	21000
Account Type	Accounts Payable
Account Name	Accounts Payable
Account Description	Accounts Payable
Tax Line	Unassigned

Account No.	65300
Account Type	Expense

Since the Tax-Line drop-down list does not include Schedule C: Depreciation and section 179 expense deduction as a tax line option, we will leave the tax line for these two Depreciation Expense accounts as Unassigned.

Account Name	Depr Expense Computer
Account Description	Depr Expense Computer
Tax Line	Unassigned

Account No.	65600
Account Type	Expense
Account Name	Depr Expense Equipment
Account Description	Depr Expense Equipment
Tax Line	Unassigned

Account No.	64800
Account Type	Expense
Account Name	Paint Supplies Expense
Account Description	Paint Supplies Expense
Tax Line	Sch C: Supplies (not from COGS)

Step 2: Export to **Excel** or **print** the Chart of Accounts (Hint: Report Center > List > Account Listing > January 1, 2020.)

TASK 3: SAVE EXERCISE 8.1

Save a backup of your Exercise 8.1 file using the file name: **YourName Exercise 8.1 Backup.QBB**. See *Appendix B: Back Up & Restore QuickBooks Files* for instructions.

WORKFLOW

Use the Workflow approach and leave your .QBW file open to use for the following exercise.

EXERCISE 8.2: CUSTOMER LIST

In this exercise, you will add to Paint Palette's customers list.

TASK 1: OPEN COMPANY FILE

WORKFLOW

Use the Workflow approach to use the same .QBW file as for the previous exercise.

- If your QBW file is not already open, open it by selecting **File > Open Previous Company**. Select your **.QBW file.**

- Update Company Name to include **YourName Exercise 8.2**.

TASK 2: ADD CUSTOMERS

Step 1: Add Tom Whalen to Paint Palette's Customer List.

Customer	Whalen, Tom
Opening Balance	0.00
As of	01/01/2020
Address Info:	
Mr./Ms./...	Mr.
First Name	Tom
M.I.	M
Last Name	Whalen
Main Phone	415-555-1234
Mobile	415-555-5678
Address	100 Sunset Drive Bayshore, CA 94326

Payment Settings:	
Account No.	1002
Payment Terms	Net 30
Preferred Payment Method	Check

Additional Info:	
Customer Type	Referral

Step 2: Click **OK** to close the *New Customer* window.

TASK 3 ADD JOB

Step 1: To add a new job, select: **Tom Whalen**.

Step 2: **Right-click** to display pop-up menu. Select **Add Job**.

Step 3: After entering the following job information, **close** the *New Job* window.

Job Info:	
Job Name	Foyer
Opening Balance	0.00
As of	01/01/2020
Job Description	Foyer Marbled Faux Painting
Job Type	Faux Painting
Job Status	Pending

Step 4: From the Customer Center, export the Customer List to **Excel**. (Print from Excel if your instructor requires printouts.)

Step 5: **Close** the Customer Center.

TASK 4: SAVE EXERCISE 8.2

Save a backup of your Exercise 8.2 file using the file name: **YourName Exercise 8.2 Backup.QBB**. See *Appendix B: Back Up & Restore QuickBooks Files* for instructions.

WORKFLOW

Use the Workflow approach and leave your .QBW file open to use for the following exercise.

EXERCISE 8.3: VENDOR LIST

In this exercise, you will add Paint Palette vendors.

TASK 1: OPEN COMPANY FILE

WORKFLOW

If you are using the Workflow approach, you will use the same .QBW file.

- If your QBW file is not already open, open it by selecting **File > Open Previous Company**. Select your **.QBW file.**

- Update Company Name to include **YourName Exercise 8.3**.

TASK 2: ADD VENDORS

Step 1:   Add the following vendors to the Vendor List for Paint Palette.

Use the Vendor Center to add new vendors.

Vendor	Cornell Technologies
Opening balance	0.00
As of	01/01/2020
Address Info:	
Company Name	Cornell Technologies
Full Name	Becky Cornell
Main Phone	415-555-7507
Address	72 Business Parkway Bayshore, CA 94326

Payment Settings:	
Account No.	2002
Payment Terms	Net 30
Credit Limit	3000.00
Tax Settings:	
Vendor Tax ID	37-4356712
Additional Info:	
Vendor Type	Supplies

Step 2: Add another vendor.

Vendor	Hartzheim Leasing
Opening balance	0.00
As of	01/01/2020
Address Info:	
Company Name	Hartzheim Leasing
Full Name	Joseph Hartzheim
Main Phone	415-555-0412
Address	13 Appleton Drive Bayshore, CA 94326
Payment Settings:	
Account No.	2003
Payment Terms	Net 30
Tax Settings:	
Vendor Tax ID	37-1726354
Additional Info:	
Vendor Type	Leasing

Step 3: From the Vendor Center, export the Vendor List to **Excel**.

TASK 3: SAVE EXERCISE 8.3

Save a backup of your Exercise 8.3 file using the file name: **YourName Exercise 8.3 Backup.QBB**. See *Appendix B: Back Up & Restore QuickBooks Files* for instructions.

WORKFLOW

Use the Workflow approach and leave your .QBW file open to use for the following exercise.

EXERCISE 8.4: ITEM LIST

In this exercise, you will add to Paint Palette's item list.

TASK 1: OPEN COMPANY FILE

WORKFLOW

If you are using the Workflow approach, you will use the same .QBW file.

- If your QBW file is not already open, open it by selecting **File > Open Previous Company**. Select your **.QBW file.**

- Update Company Name to include **YourName Exercise 8.4**.

TASK 2: ADD ITEMS

Step 1:   Add the following items to Paint Palette's Item List. Click **Next** after entering each item.

Item Type	Service
Item Name	Labor Mural
Subitem of	Labor
Description	Labor: Mural Painting
Rate	40.00
Account	47900 – Sales

Item Type	Service
Item Name	Labor Faux
Subitem of	Labor
Description	Labor: Faux Painting
Rate	40.00
Account	47900 – Sales

Item Type	Service
Item Name	Labor Interior
Subitem of	Labor
Description	Labor: Interior Painting

Rate	20.00
Account	47900 – Sales

Item Type	Service
Item Name	Labor Exterior
Subitem of	Labor
Description	Labor: Exterior Painting
Rate	30.00
Account	47900 - Sales

Step 2: Export the Item List to **Excel**. (Hint: From the *Item List* window, select Reports button > Item Listing.)

TASK 3: SAVE EXERCISE 8.4

 Save a backup of your Exercise 8.4 file using the file name: **YourName Exercise 8.4 Backup.QBB**. See *Appendix B: Back Up & Restore QuickBooks Files* for instructions.

WORKFLOW

 If you are using the Workflow approach, you can leave your .QBW file open and use it for the following chapter which is a continuation of this exercise.

RESTART & RESTORE

 If you are stopping your QuickBooks work session and changing computers, you will need to restore your .QBB file when you restart Chapter 9.

EXERCISE 8.5: WEB QUEST

The Small Business Administration (SBA) summarizes government resources to assist the small business owner. When starting a new business, an entrepreneur is faced with numerous decisions. As a result, planning becomes crucial for business success. The SBA website provides information about how to write a successful business plan.

Step 1:   Go to www.sba.gov website.

Step 2:   Find and print information on the sba.gov site that you think is the most useful to an entrepreneur starting a new business.

> The websites used in the Web Quests are subject to change due to website updates.

CHAPTER 8 QUICK CHECK

NAME:

INSTRUCTIONS:

1. CHECK OFF THE ITEMS YOU COMPLETED.

2. TURN IN THIS PAGE WITH YOUR PRINTOUTS.

> **!**
> Ask your instructor if you should Go Digital (Excel* or PDF) or use paper printouts.

CHAPTER 8

☐ * Customer List

☐ * Vendor List

☐ * Item List

☐ * Chart of Accounts (Account Listing)

EXERCISE 8.1

☐ * Task 2: Chart of Accounts (Account Listing)

EXERCISE 8.2

☐ * Task 3: Customer List

EXERCISE 8.3

☐ * Task 2: Vendor List

EXERCISE 8.4

☐ * Task 2: Item List

EXERCISE 8.5

☐ sba.gov Printout

Download Go Digital Excel templates at www.My-QuickBooks.com.

REFLECTION: A WISH AND A STAR

Reflection improves learning and retention. Reflect on what you have learned after completing Chapter 8.

A Star:

What did you like best that you learned about QuickBooks in Chapter 8?

A Wish:

If you could pick one thing, what do you wish you knew more about when using QuickBooks?

PROJECT 8 DOMINIC CONSULTING

To complete this project, download the Chapter 8 Go Digital Reports Excel template at www.My-QuickBooks.com. Follow the instructions provided in the Excel template.

Dominic Leonardo founded a new business, Dominic Consulting, a firm that provides consulting and design services to companies using social networking for marketing purposes. The firm advises companies regarding how to use internet marketing and social networking tools, such as Facebook, Twitter, and blogs, to market and promote their companies, products, and brands. Social networking tools are revolutionizing marketing to promote dating services, spas, grocery stores, and even emergency rooms. Dominic Consulting is poised to provide the expertise to assist firms in capitalizing upon social networking to gain a competitive advantage.

You plan to maintain the accounting records using QuickBooks software.

1. If necessary, download the Chapter 8 Go Digital Reports Excel template. Save the Excel file using the file name: **YourLastName FirstName CH8 REPORTS**.

2. Set up a new company file for Dominic Consulting using the EasyStep Interview and QuickBooks Setup.

Company:	YourName Project 8 Dominic Consulting
Tax ID:	123-45-6789
Address:	23 Ashley Avenue
	Bayshore, CA 94326
Phone:	415-555-1122
Email:	[your email address]
Industry:	General Service-based Business
Type of Organization:	Sole Proprietorship
First Month of Fiscal Year:	January
File Name:	YourName Project 8
What do you sell?	Services Only
Sales Tax?	No
Estimates?	Yes
Billing Statements?	Yes
Progress Invoicing?	No
Track Bills?	Yes
Track Time?	Yes

Employees?	No
Start Date	01/01/2020
Use Recommended Accts?	Yes
Bank Account Name	Checking
Bank Account Number	2345678901
Bank Account Balance	0.00 as of 01/01/2020

3. Display account numbers. Using your saved Chapter 8 Reports Excel template and the Report Center, export to **Excel** the Chart of Accounts (Account Listing using the appropriate report settings specified in the template instructions).

4. Use the following information to create a Customer List.

Customer/ Company Name	Address/Phone	Full Name	Customer Type	Terms	Account No.	Preferred Payment Method
Holcomb Health Foods	15 Stanford Dr Bayshore, CA 94326 415-555-6213	Ann Holcomb	Commercial	Net 15	1001	Check
Redeker Bed & Breakfast	42 Saluki Way Bayshore, CA 94326 415-555-5769	Kari Redeker	Commercial	Net 15	1002	Check
Etzkin Realty	98 Cleveland St Bayshore, CA 94326 415-555-5521	Brian Etzkin	Commercial	Net 15	1003	Check

5. From the Customer Center, export to **Excel** the Customer List.

6. Use the following information to create a Vendor List.

Vendor/ Company Name	Address/Phone	Full Name	Print on Check As	Account No.	Vendor Type	Payment Terms
Jackson Computer Services	723 Stellar Ave Bayshore, CA 94326 415-555-6312	Keith Jackson	Jackson Computer Services	2001	Service Providers	Net 30
Pitts Leasing	18 Selvan Lane Bayshore, CA 94326 415-555-9498	Amy Pitts	Pitts Leasing	2002	Service Providers	Net 30

7. From the Vendor Center, export to **Excel** the Vendor List.

8. Use the following information to create an Item List.

Type	Item Name	Description	Rate	Account
Service	Internet Marketing	Internet Marketing Consulting	$50.00	Sales
Service	Social Network Marketing	Social Network Marketing Consulting	$60.00	Sales

9. Export to **Excel** the Item List. (Report Center > List > Item Listing.)

10. Mark the reports completed on the **8 REPORTS** sheet. Save your Excel file.

11. Save a .QBB backup of your work.

PROJECT 8 QUICK CHECK
NAME:
INSTRUCTIONS:
1. CHECK OFF THE ITEMS YOU COMPLETED.
2. ATTACH THIS PAGE TO YOUR PRINTOUTS.

> **!**
> **Ask your instructor if you should Go Digital (Excel* or PDF) or use paper printouts.**

PROJECT 8

- ☐ *   Chart of Accounts
- ☐ *   Customer List
- ☐ *   Vendor List
- ☐ *   Item List

Download Go Digital Excel templates at www.My-QuickBooks.com.

NOTES:

CHAPTER 9
ACCOUNTING FOR A SERVICE COMPANY

SCENARIO

Preferring to use your savings rather than take out a bank loan, you invest $6,000 of your savings to launch Paint Palette.

You prepare the following list of items your business will need.

My Business Needs

ITEM		ESTIMATED COST
Computer & printer	$	1,500
Paint equipment (ladder, drop clothes, etc)	$	500
Paint supplies (paint brushes, rollers, etc)	$	300
Van lease	$	200 per month

CHAPTER 9
LEARNING OBJECTIVES

In Chapter 9, you will learn about the following QuickBooks features:

INTRODUCTION

In this chapter, you will enter business transactions for Paint Palette's first year of operations. These include transactions with the owner, customers, and vendors.

To begin Chapter 9, first start QuickBooks by clicking on the **QuickBooks desktop icon** or click **Start > Programs > QuickBooks > QuickBooks Premier Accountant Edition 2015**.

WORKFLOW

Use the Workflow approach if you are using the same .QBW file from the prior chapter.

- If your QBW file is not already open, open it by selecting **File > Open Previous Company**. Select your previous **Paint Palette .QBW file.**

- Update Company Name to include **YourName Chapter 9**.

RESTART & RESTORE

Use the Restart & Restore approach if you are restarting your work session.

- Restore your **Backup.QBB** file using the directions in *Appendix B: Back Up & Restore QuickBooks Files*.

- After restoring the file, update Company Name to include **YourName Chapter 9**.

> **!**
> If a login appears, use Admin for User ID and leave the password field blank.

RECORD OWNER'S INVESTMENT

To launch your new business, you invest $6,000 in Paint Palette. In order to keep business records and your personal records separate, you open a business Checking account at the local bank for Paint Palette. You then deposit your personal check for $6,000 in the business Checking account.

In Chapters 3 and 4 you recorded deposits using the Record Deposits icon in the *Banking* section of the Home page. You can also record deposits directly in the Check Register. QuickBooks then transfers the information to the *Make Deposits* window.

To record the deposit to Paint Palette's Checking account using the *Make Deposits* window, complete the following steps:

Step 1: Click the **Record Deposits** icon in the *Banking* section of the Home page.

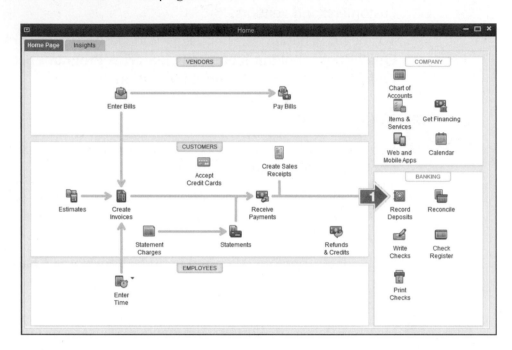

Step 2: In the *Make Deposits* window, select Deposit To: **Checking**.

Step 3: Select Date: **01/01/2020**.

Step 4: On *the Received From* drop-down list, select **<Add New>**. Select **Other**, then click **OK**. Enter Name: **YourName**. Click **OK**.

Step 5: Account: **30000: Opening Balance Equity**. Press the **Tab** key.

Step 6: Memo: **Invested $6,000 in business**.

Step 7: Check No.: **1001**.

Step 8: Payment Method: **Check**.

Step 9: Amount: **6000.00**.

Step 10: To **print** the deposit slip, select **Print** arrow **> Deposit Summary**. Select **Portrait** orientation **> Print**.

Step 11: Click **Save & Close** to close the *Make Deposits* window.

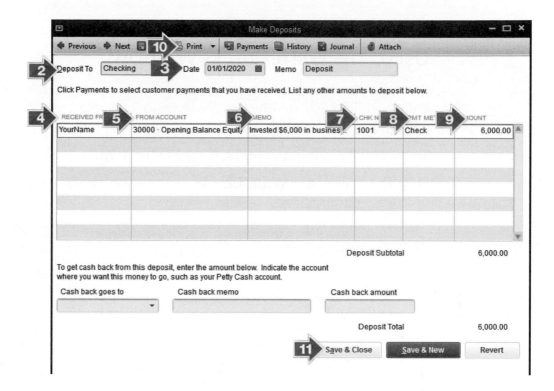

RECORD PURCHASE TRANSACTIONS

Purchases can be either cash purchases or credit purchases on account.

Transaction	Description	Record Using...
Cash purchase	Pay cash at the time of purchase.	*Write Checks* window
Credit purchase	Pay for purchase at a later time with a check, credit card, or debit card.	1. *Enter Bills* window 2. *Pay Bills* window

Paint Palette purchased a computer, painting equipment, and paint supplies. To record these purchases, complete the following steps.

RECORD CASH PURCHASES
USING THE WRITE CHECKS WINDOW

Paint Palette purchased a computer for $1,500 cash. Because Paint Palette paid cash for the purchase, you can use the *Write Checks* window to record the purchase.

To record the computer purchase using the *Write Checks* window:

Step 1: Click the **Write Checks** icon in the *Banking* section of the Home page.

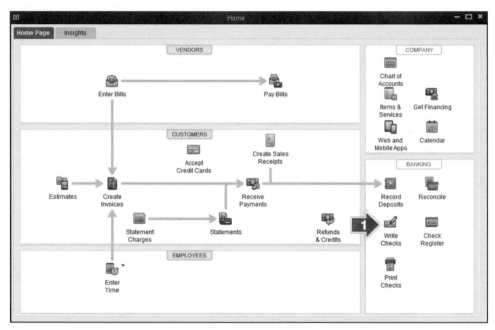

Step 2: In the following *Write Checks* window, select Bank Account: **Checking**.

Step 3: Date: **01/01/2020**.

Step 4: Pay to the Order of: **Cornell Technologies**.

Step 5: Amount: **1500.00**.

Step 6: Account: **14200 Computer Cost**.

Step 7: Check: **Print Later**.

Step 8: To print the check, click the **Print** icon.

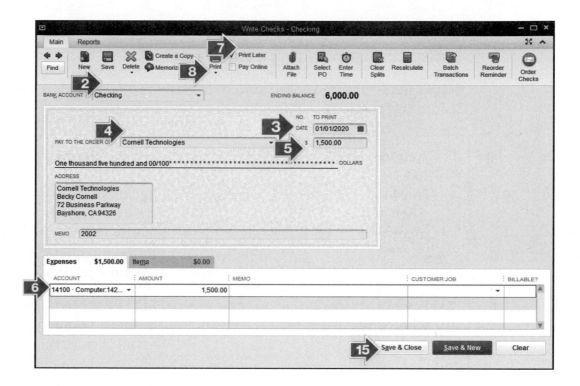

Step 9:   When the *Print Check* window appears, enter Check No. **501**.

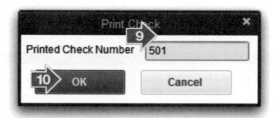

Step 10:   Click **OK**.

Step 11:   Select **Print company name and address**.

Step 12:   Select Check Style: **Standard**

Step 13:   Click **Print**.

Step 14:   When asked if the check(s) printed OK, select **OK**.

Step 15:   Click **Save & Close** to record Check No. 501 and close the *Write Checks* window.

RECORD CREDIT PURCHASES USING THE ENTER BILLS WINDOW

When items are purchased on credit, a two-step process is used to record the purchase in QuickBooks.

	Action	Record Using...	Result
1	**Enter bill when received**	*Enter Bills* window	QuickBooks records an expense (or asset) and records an obligation to pay the bill later (accounts payable).
2	**Pay bill when due**	*Pay Bills* window	QuickBooks reduces accounts payable when the bill is paid. Bills can be paid using a check, credit card, or debit card.

Next, you will enter bills for items Paint Palette purchased on credit. The first bill is for paint and supplies that Paint Palette purchased for the Beneficio job.

Step 1: Click the **Enter Bills** icon in the *Vendors* section of the Home page.

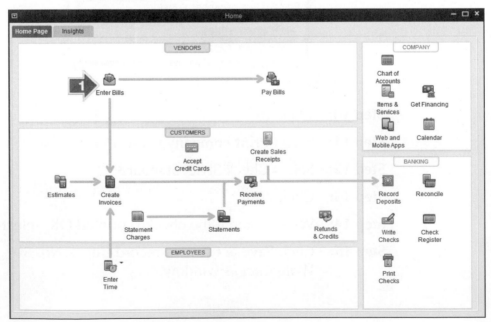

Step 2:   Enter the following information in the *Enter Bills* window, select **Bill**.

Step 3:   Enter Date: **01/03/2020**.

Step 4:   Select Vendor: **Brewer Paint Supplies**.

Step 5:   Enter Amount Due: **300.00**.

Step 6:   Select Terms: **Net 30**.

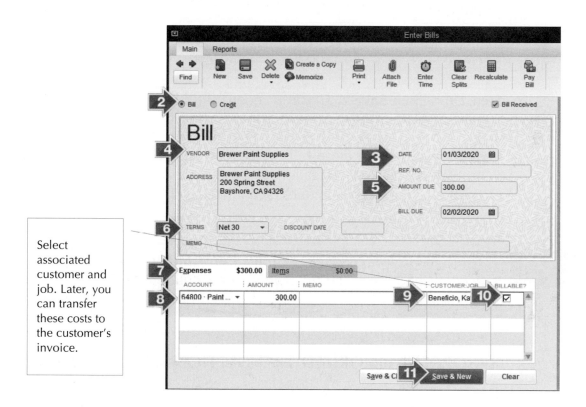

Step 7:   Click the **Expenses** tab.

Step 8:   Select Account: **64800 Paint Supplies Expense**.

Step 9:   Select Customer & Job: **Beneficio, Katrina: Dining Room**.

Step 10:   Verify that **Billable** is ✓ checked.

Step 11:   Click **Save & New** to enter another bill. If an *Information Changed* window appears asking if you want the new terms to appear next time, select **Yes**.

Step 12:   Paint Palette made a credit purchase of painting equipment including ladders and drop cloths. The painting equipment is recorded as an asset because it will benefit more than one accounting period. The painting equipment will be depreciated over the useful life of the equipment.

Enter the following bill for paint equipment purchased on account.

Date	01/04/2020
Vendor	Brewer Paint Supplies
Amount Due	500.00
Terms	Net 30
Account	14500 Equipment Cost

Step 13: Click **Save & Close** to record the bill and close the *Enter Bills* window.

QuickBooks records these bills as accounts payable, indicating that Paint Palette has an obligation to pay these amounts to vendors. QuickBooks increases liabilities (accounts payable) on the company's Balance Sheet.

> ***Total fixed assets equal $2,000 (consisting of the Computer account of $1,500 and the Equipment account of $500).***

RECORD A MEMORIZED TRANSACTION

Often a transaction is recurring, such as monthly rent or utility payments. QuickBooks' memorized transaction feature permits you to memorize or save recurring transactions.

Paint Palette leases a van for a monthly lease payment of $200. You will use a memorized transaction to reuse each month to record the lease payment.

To create a memorized transaction:

Step 1: First, enter the transaction in QuickBooks. To enter the bill for the van lease payment for Paint Palette, click the **Enter Bills** icon in the *Vendors* section of the Home page.

Step 2: Enter the following information about the van lease bill.

Date	01/04/2020
Vendor	Hartzheim Leasing
Amount Due	200.00
Terms	Net 30
Account	67100 Rent Expense
Memo	Van lease

Step 3:   Select **Memorize** icon at the top of the *Enter Bills* window.

Step 4:   When the following *Memorize Transaction* window appears, select **Add to my Reminders List**.

Step 5:   Select How Often: **Monthly**.

Step 6:   Enter Next Date: **02/01/2020**.

Step 7:   Click **OK** to record the memorized transaction.

Step 8: Click **Save & Close** to close the *Enter Bills* window and record the van lease.

To use the memorized transaction at a later time:

Step 1: Select **Lists** menu **> Memorized Transaction List**.

Step 2: When the following *Memorized Transaction List* window appears, **double-click** the memorized transaction you want to use.

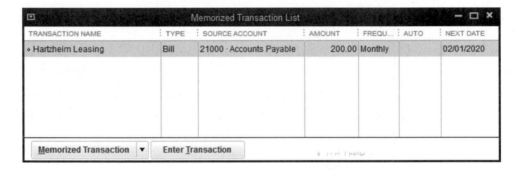

Step 3: QuickBooks displays the *Enter Bills* window with the memorized transaction data already entered. You can make any necessary changes on the form, such as changing the date. To record the bill in QuickBooks, you would click Save & Close.

At this time, **close the *Enter Bills* window without saving**. Then **close** the *Memorized Transaction List* window. Later, you will use the memorized transaction in **Exercise 9.1** at the end of the chapter.

PAY BILLS

To pay bills already entered:

Step 1:   Click the **Pay Bills** icon in the *Vendors* section of the Home page.

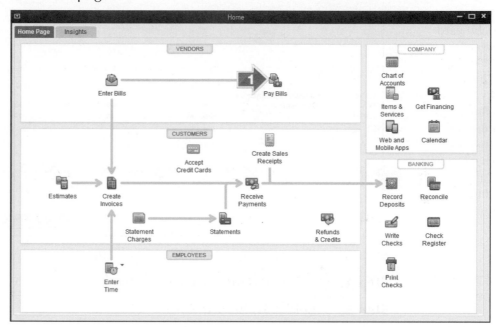

Step 2:   When the following *Pay Bills* window appears, select Show Bills: **Due on or before 02/04/2020**, then press the **Tab** key. (If a *Warning* window appears, click OK, and then select All Vendors from the Filter By drop-down list.)

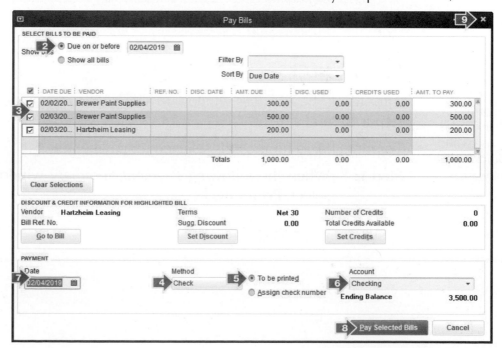

To pay by credit card, select Method: **Credit Card**.

To pay by debit card, select Method: **Check > Assign check number**. Then use DC (Debit Card) as check number.

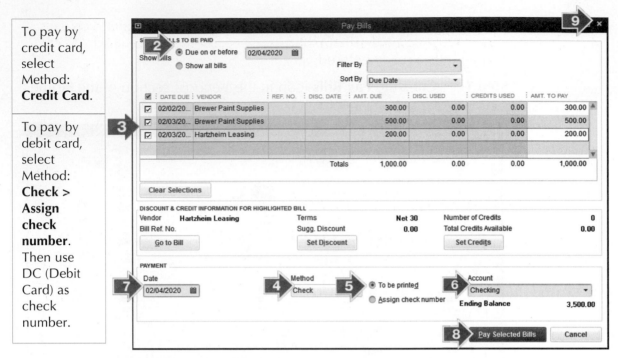

Step 3: Select to pay the three bills listed.

Step 4: Select Payment Method: **Check**.

Step 5: Select **To be printed**.

Step 6: Select Payment Account: **Checking**.

Step 7: Enter Payment Date: **02/04/2020**.

Step 8: Click **Pay Selected Bills** to record the bills selected for payment.

Step 9: If necessary, close the *Pay Bills* window.

PRINT CHECKS

You can buy preprinted check forms to use with QuickBooks software.

After using the *Pay Bills* window to select bills for payment, the next step is to print checks.

To print checks for the bills selected for payment:

Step 1: When the following *Payment Summary* window appears, select: **Print Checks**.

You can also print checks by selecting **File** menu > **Print Forms** > **Checks** or clicking the **Print Checks** icon in the *Banking* section of the Home page.

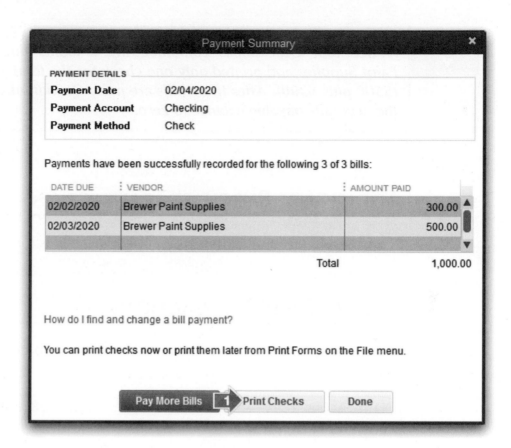

Step 2:   When the *Select Checks to Print* window appears, select Bank Account: **Checking**.

Step 3:   First Check No.: **502**.

Step 4:   Click the **Select All** button.

Step 5:   Click **OK**.

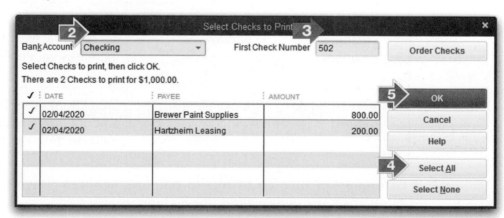

Step 6:   Select print settings and standard checks, then click **Print**.

Notice that QuickBooks combined the amounts due Brewer Paint Supplies and printed only one check for the total $800 due ($500 plus $300). After these bills are paid, QuickBooks reduces the accounts payable balance to zero.

ADDITIONAL PURCHASE TRANSACTIONS

See **Exercise 9.1** for additional purchase transactions for Paint Palette.

RECORD SALES TRANSACTIONS

When using QuickBooks, sales transactions are recorded using three steps.

	Action	Record Using…	Result
1	**Prepare invoice to record charges for services provided customer**	*Create Invoices* window	The invoice is used to bill the customer for services. QuickBooks records the services provided on credit as an account receivable (an amount to be received in the future).
2	**Receive customer payment**	*Receive Payments* window	QuickBooks reduces accounts receivable and increases undeposited funds.
3	**Record bank deposit**	*Make Deposits* window	QuickBooks transfers the amount from undeposited funds to the bank account.

To create an invoice to record painting services provided by Paint Palette to Katrina Beneficio during January:

Step 1: Click the **Create Invoices** icon in the *Customers* section of the Home page.

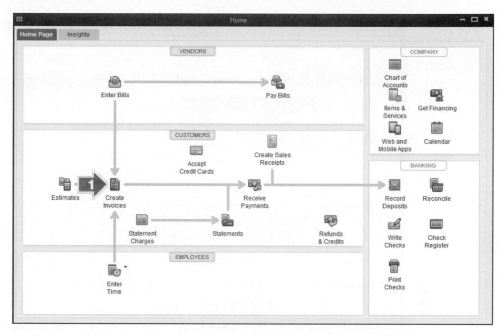

Step 2: Select Customer & Job: **Beneficio, Katrina: Dining Room**.

Step 3: When the *Billable Time/Costs* window appears to remind you the job has outstanding billable time, click **Select the outstanding billable time and costs to add to this invoice?**

Step 4: Click **OK.**

Step 5: To select billable costs to apply to the Beneficio invoice, from the *Choose Billable Time and Costs* window select the **Expenses** tab.

> Be sure to enter %, otherwise $40 will be the markup.

Step 6: Enter Markup Amount or %: **40.0%**.

Step 7: Select Markup Account: **47900 – Sales**.

Step 8: Check ✓ to select: **Brewer Paint Supplies**.

Step 9: Click **OK** to bill the Paint Supplies cost.

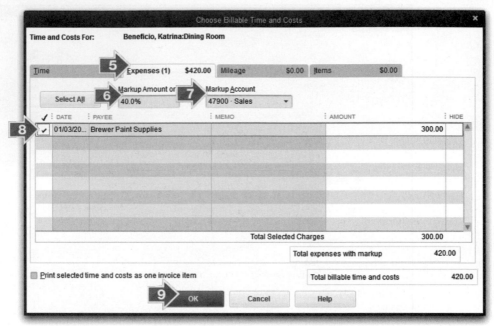

Step 10: Select Template: **Intuit Service Invoice**.

Step 11: Enter Date: **01/31/2020**.

Step 12: The Beneficio invoice will list Total Reimbursable Expenses of $420.00. Next, enter the service provided in the *Create Invoices* window. Select Item: **Labor Mural**.

Step 13: Enter Quantity: **82** (hours).

Step 14: Select **Print Later**.

Step 15: Click the **Print** icon and print the invoice.

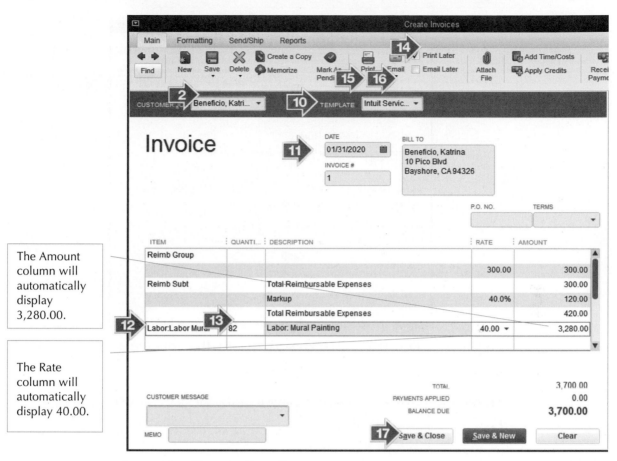

The Amount column will automatically display 3,280.00.

The Rate column will automatically display 40.00.

Step 16:   To email an invoice:

- Click the **Email** icon at the top of the *Create Invoices* window. Select **Invoice**.

- If asked if you want to record your changes to the transaction, select **Yes**.

- If an *Information Missing or Invalid* window appears, enter your email address.

- When the *Send Invoice* window appears, select Send by: **Email**. Select **Send Later**.

For purposes of this exercise, email the invoice to yourself.

If Outlook is installed on your computer, an *Outlook Profile Does Not Exist* window may appear.

Step 17: Click **Save & Close** to record the invoice and close the *Create Invoices* window.

To record Katrina Beneficio's payment for the $3,700.00 invoice:

Step 1: From the *Customers* section of the Home page, click the **Receive Payments** icon.

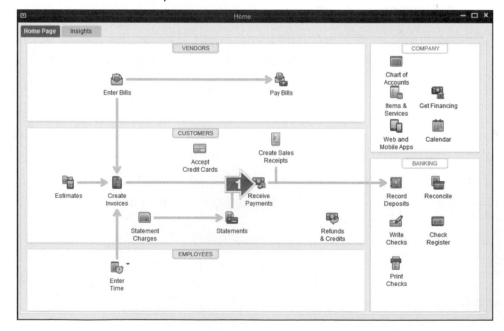

Step 2:   Select Received From: **Beneficio, Katrina: Dining Room**.

Step 3:   Enter Amount: **3700.00**.

Step 4:   Select Date: **02/04/2020**.

Step 5:   Select Payment Method: **Check**.

Step 6:   Enter Check No. **555**.

If a message appears regarding payment methods, select No.

Verify that QuickBooks has selected the outstanding invoice.

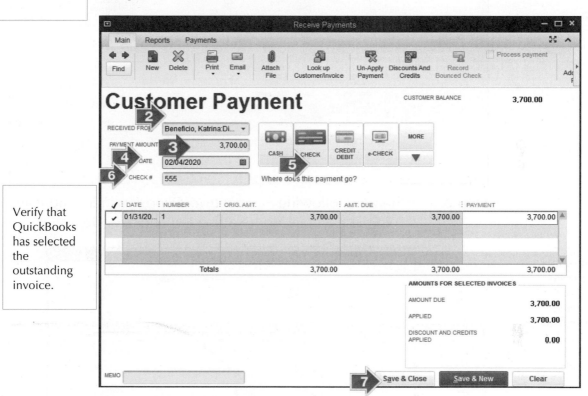

Step 7:   Click **Save & Close** to record the payment and close the *Receive Payments* window.

When a customer makes a payment, the customer's account receivable is reduced by the amount of the payment. In this case, Beneficio's account receivable is reduced by $3,700.

To record the deposit of the customer's payment in the bank:

Step 1:   From the *Banking* section of the Home page, click the **Record Deposits** icon.

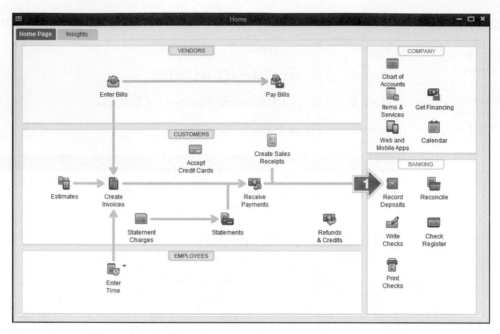

Step 2: When the following *Payments to Deposit* window appears, select the payment from Katrina Beneficio for deposit.

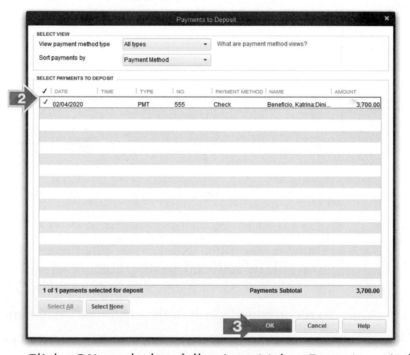

Step 3: Click **OK** and the following *Make Deposits* window appears.

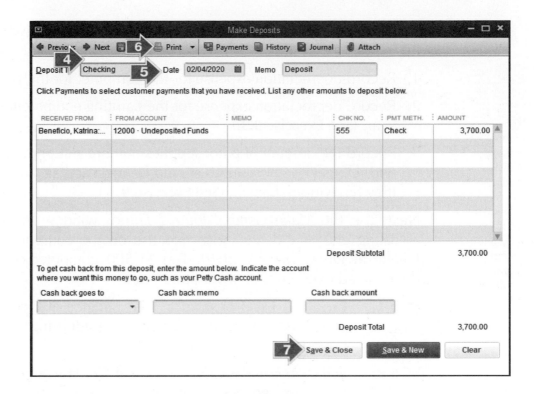

Step 4: Select Deposit To: **Checking**.

Step 5: Select Date: **02/04/2020**.

Step 6: Click the **Print** icon. When the *Print Deposit* window appears, select **Deposit summary only > OK**. Select printer settings, then click **Print**.

Step 7: Click **Save & Close** to record the deposit and close the *Make Deposits* window.

ADDITIONAL SALES TRANSACTIONS

See **Exercise 9.2** for additional sales transactions for Paint Palette.

MAKE ADJUSTING ENTRIES

At the end of Paint Palette's accounting period, December 31, 2020, it is necessary to record adjustments to bring the company's accounts up to date as of year-end.

The following adjustments are necessary for Paint Palette at December 31, 2020:

1. Record depreciation expense for the computer for the year.

2. Record depreciation expense for the painting equipment for the year. (See **Exercise 9.3**.)

3. Record the amount of paint supplies that are still on hand at year-end. Unused paint supplies should be recorded as assets because they have future benefit. (See **Exercise 9.3**.)

Next, use the *Make General Journal Entries* window to record the adjusting entry for depreciation expense on the computer for Paint Palette at December 31, 2020. The $1,500 computer cost will be depreciated over a useful life of three years.

+

Before making adjusting entries, prepare a trial balance to see if the accounting system is in balance (debits equal credits).

Step 1: Export to **Excel** or **print** a Trial Balance at December 31, 2020 prior to making the following adjusting entry. (Hint: Reports icon > Accountant & Taxes > Trial Balance.)

Step 2: Select **Accountant** menu **> Make General Journal Entries**. If a message about numbering journal entries appears, click **OK**.

Step 3: To record the entry for depreciation on the computer equipment in the General Journal, select Date: **12/31/2020**.

Step 4: Entry No.: **ADJ1**.

Step 5: Select **Adjusting Entry**.

Step 6: Enter Account: **65300**. Press the **Tab** key to advance the cursor to the *Debit* column.

Step 7: Next, use QuickMath calculator to calculate the amount of depreciation expense. With the cursor in the *Debit* column, press the **=** key to display the QuickMath calculator.

Step 8: Enter **1500.00**.

Step 9: Press /.

Step 10: Enter **3** to divide by the 3-year useful life.

Step 11: Press the **Enter** key. $500.00 should now appear in the *Debit* column.

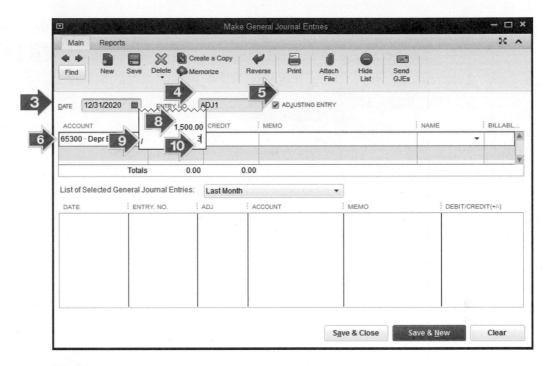

Step 12: Enter Account: **14300**.

Step 13: Enter Credit: **500.00**.

Step 14: Click the **Save** button at the top of the *Make General Journal Entries* window.

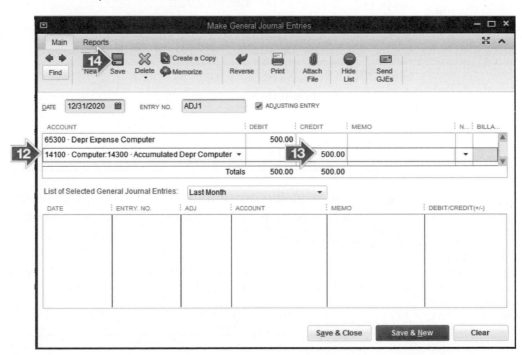

Step 15: To **print** the adjusting journal entry, click the **Reports** tab.

To print the entire Journal instead of just one entry, from Report Center select: **Accountant & Taxes > Journal**.

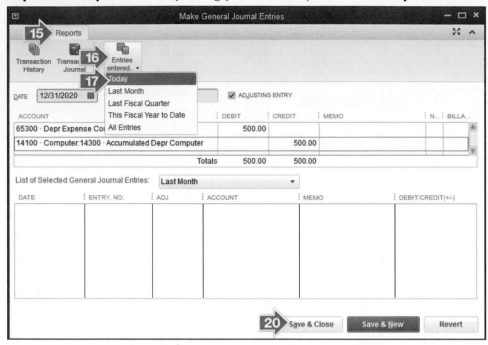

Step 16: Select **Entries entered**.

Step 17: Select **Today**.

Step 18: Select Date: **12/31/2020**.

Step 19: Export to **Excel** or **print** the Adjusting Journal Entries report. Close the *Adjusting Journal Entries* window.

Step 20: Click **Save & Close** to close the *Make General Journal Entries* window.

PRINT REPORTS

To print the General Ledger, from Report Center, select: **Accountant & Taxes > General Ledger**.

The next step in the accounting cycle is to print financial reports. Usually, a company prints the following financial reports for the year:

- General Ledger
- Profit & Loss (also known as the P & L or Income Statement)
- Balance Sheet
- Statement of Cash Flows

The General Ledger report lists each account with its opening balance, ending balance, and changes to the account during the period.

The Profit & Loss, the Balance Sheet, and the Statement of Cash Flows are financial statements typically given to external users, such as bankers and investors.

You will print financial statements for Paint Palette for the year 2020 in **Exercise 9.4**.

> To print financial statements, from Report Center, select: **Company & Financial**.

CLOSE THE ACCOUNTING PERIOD

When using a manual accounting system, closing entries are made in the General Journal to close the temporary accounts (revenues, expenses, and withdrawals or dividends). Closing entries are used in order to start the new year with a zero balance in the temporary accounts.

QuickBooks automatically closes temporary accounts to start each new year with $-0- balances in all temporary accounts (revenues, expenses, and dividends).

To prevent changes to prior periods, QuickBooks permits you to restrict access to the accounting records for past periods that have been closed. See **Exercise 9.5** for instructions on closing the accounting period in QuickBooks.

SAVE CHAPTER 9

Save a backup of your Chapter 9 file using the file name: **YourName Chapter 9 Backup.QBB**. See *Appendix B: Back Up & Restore QuickBooks Files* for instructions.

WORKFLOW

If you are using the Workflow approach, leave your .QBW file open and proceed directly to Exercise 9.1.

RESTART & RESTORE

If you are using the Restart & Restore approach and are ending your computer session now, close your .QBW file and exit QuickBooks.

When you restart, you will restore your backup file to complete Exercise 9.1.

www.My-QuickBooks.com

Go to www.My-QuickBooks.com to view additional QuickBooks resources including Excel Reports Templates, QuickBooks videos, and QuickBooks Hot Arrows and Hot Topics. The Hot Topics can be viewed on your computer or tablet and feature frequently used QuickBooks tasks.

MULTIPLE-CHOICE PRACTICE TEST

Try the **Multiple-Choice Practice Test** for Chapter 9 on the *Computer Accounting with QuickBooks* Online Learning Center at www.mhhe.com/kay2015.

GO DIGITAL!

Go Digital using Excel templates. See *Appendix D: Go Digital with QuickBooks* for instructions about how to save your QuickBooks reports electronically.

LEARNING ACTIVITIES

Important: Ask your instructor whether you should complete the following assignments by printing reports or by exporting to Excel templates (see Appendix D: Go Digital with QuickBooks).

EXERCISE 9.1: PURCHASE TRANSACTIONS

In this exercise, you will enter purchase transactions for Paint Palette.

TASK 1: OPEN COMPANY FILE

WORKFLOW

If you are using the Workflow approach, you will use the same .QBW file. If your QBW file is not already open, open it by selecting **File > Open Previous Company**. Select your **.QBW file.** Update Company Name to include **YourName Exercise 9.1**.

RESTART & RESTORE

If you are not using the same computer, you must use the Restart and Restore approach. Restore your **Chapter 9 Backup.QBB** file using the directions in *Appendix B: Back Up & Restore QuickBooks Files*. After restoring the file, update Company Name to include **YourName Exercise 9.1**.

TASK 2: RECORD PURCHASE TRANSACTIONS

Record the following purchase transactions for Paint Palette during the year 2020. Print checks as appropriate.

> **+**
> To streamline transaction entry, select: **View > Open Window List**.

> For memorized transactions select **Lists** menu **> Memorized Transaction List**.

> To view the van lease bill, select **Show All Bills** in the *Pay Bills* window.

Date	Purchase Transaction
02/01/2020	Use the memorized transaction to record the $200 bill for the February van lease to be paid later.
02/28/2020	Paid van lease for February.
03/01/2020	Received $200 bill for van lease for March.
03/30/2020	Paid van lease for March. (Due: 03/31/2020)
04/01/2020	Received $200 bill for van lease for April.
04/04/2020	Purchased $50 of paint supplies on account from Brewer Paint Supplies. Record as Paint Supplies Expense.
04/30/2020	Paid van lease for April. (Due: 05/01/2020) Paid for paint supplies purchased on April 4.
05/01/2020	Received $200 bill for van lease for May.
05/30/2020	Paid van lease for May. (Due: 05/31/2020)
06/01/2020	Received $200 bill for van lease for June.
06/30/2020	Paid van lease for June. (Due: 07/01/2020)

07/01/2020	Purchased $100 of paint supplies on account from Brewer Paint Supplies. Record as Paint Supplies Expense.
07/01/2020	Received $200 bill for van lease for July.
07/30/2020	Paid van lease for July. (Due: 07/31/2020)
	Paid for paint supplies purchased on July 1.
08/01/2020	Received $200 bill for van lease for August.
08/30/2020	Paid van lease for August. (Due: 08/31/2020)
09/01/2020	Received $200 bill for van lease for September.
09/02/2020	Purchased $75 of paint supplies on account from Brewer Paint Supplies. Record as Paint Supplies Expense.
09/30/2020	Paid September van lease. (Due: 10/01/2020).
	Paid for paint supplies purchased on 09/02/2020.
10/01/2020	Received $200 bill for van lease for October.
10/30/2020	Paid van lease for October. (Due: 10/31/2020)
11/01/2020	Received $200 bill for van lease for November.
11/30/2020	Paid van lease for November. (Due: 12/01/2020)
12/01/2020	Received $200 bill for van lease for December.
12/20/2020	Purchased $50 of paint supplies on account from Brewer Paint Supplies. Record as Paint Supplies Expense.
12/30/2020	Paid van lease for December. (Due: 12/31/2020)

TASK 3: PRINT CHECK DETAIL

Export to **Excel** or **print** the Check Detail report for 2020.

TASK 4: SAVE EXERCISE 9.1

Save a backup of your Exercise 9.1 file using the file name: **YourName Exercise 9.1 Backup.QBB**. See *Appendix B: Back Up & Restore QuickBooks Files* for instructions.

WORKFLOW

Use the Workflow approach and leave your .QBW file open to use for the following exercise.

EXERCISE 9.2: SALES TRANSACTIONS

In this exercise, you will record sales transactions for Paint Palette.

TASK 1: CHANGE COMPANY NAME

WORKFLOW

Since you are using the Workflow approach, you will use the same .QBW file. If your QBW file is not already open, open it by selecting **File > Open Previous Company**. Select your **.QBW file.** Update Company Name to include **YourName Exercise 9.2**.

TASK 2: SALES TRANSACTIONS AND DEPOSIT SUMMARIES

+
To streamline transaction entry, select: **View > Open Window List**.

Use the **Intuit Service Invoice** template.

Print invoices and deposit summaries for the following sales transactions for Paint Palette during the year 2020.

Date	02/28/2020
Customer	Katrina Beneficio
Job	Dining Room
Item	Labor: Mural
Hours	86
Payment Received & Deposited	03/15/2020
Check No.	675

Date	03/31/2020
Customer	Katrina Beneficio
Job	Dining Room

Item	Labor: Mural
Hours	84
Payment Received & Deposited	04/15/2020
Check No.	690

Date	04/30/2020
Customer	Tom Whalen
Job	Foyer
Item	Labor: Faux
Hours	80
Payment Received & Deposited	05/15/2020
Check No.	432

Date	05/31/2020
Customer	Tom Whalen
Job	Foyer
Item	Labor: Faux
Hours	75
Payment Received & Deposited	06/15/2020
Check No.	455

When necessary, add a new job. For more information about adding jobs, see Chapter 4.

Date	06/30/2020
Customer	Katrina Beneficio
Job	Vaulted Kitchen
Item	Labor: Mural
Hours	100
Payment Received & Deposited	07/15/2020
Check No.	733

Date	07/31/2020
Customer	Katrina Beneficio
Job	Vaulted Kitchen
Item	Labor: Mural

Hours	90
Payment Received & Deposited	08/15/2020
Check No.	750

Date	08/31/2020
Customer	Katrina Beneficio
Job	Vaulted Kitchen
Item	Labor: Mural
Hours	92
Payment Received & Deposited	09/15/2020
Check No.	782

Date	10/31/2020
Customer	Tom Whalen
Job	Screen Porch
Item	Labor: Mural
Hours	85
Payment Received & Deposited	11/15/2020
Check No.	685

Date	11/30/2020
Customer	Tom Whalen
Job	Screen Porch
Item	Labor: Mural
Hours	87
Payment Received & Deposited	12/15/2020
Check No.	725

TASK 3: PRINT DEPOSIT DETAIL

Export to **Excel** or **print** the Deposit Detail report for 2020.

TASK 4: SAVE EXERCISE 9.2

Save a backup of your Exercise 9.2 file using the file name: **YourName Exercise 9.2 Backup.QBB**. See *Appendix B: Back Up & Restore QuickBooks Files* for instructions.

WORKFLOW

Use the Workflow approach and leave your .QBW file open to use for the following exercise.

EXERCISE 9.3: YEAR-END ADJUSTMENTS

In this exercise, you will first print a Trial Balance and then record adjusting entries for Paint Palette.

TASK 1: CHANGE COMPANY NAME

WORKFLOW

Since you are using the Workflow approach, you will use the same .QBW file.

- If your QBW file is not already open, open it by selecting **File > Open Previous Company**. Select your **.QBW file.**

- Update Company Name to include **YourName Exercise 9.3**.

TASK 2: TRIAL BALANCE

+
The purpose of the Trial Balance is to determine whether the accounting system is in balance (debits equal credits).

Create a Trial Balance for Paint Palette at December 31, 2020.

Step 1: From the Report Center select **Accountant & Taxes > Trial Balance**.

Step 2: Select Dates From: **12/31/2020** To: **12/31/2020**.

Step 3: Export to **Excel** or **print** the Trial Balance for Paint Palette.

Step 4: **Close** the *Trial Balance* window.

 Total debits equal $41,110.

TASK 3: RECORD ADJUSTING ENTRIES

At the end of the accounting period, it is necessary to make adjusting entries to bring a company's accounts up to date as of year-end. Three adjusting entries are needed for Paint Palette as of December 31, 2020:

1. Record depreciation expense for the computer for the year.

2. Record depreciation expense for the painting equipment for the year. The $500 painting equipment cost is depreciated using straight-line depreciation over five years with no salvage value. (Use Account No. 65600 to record the depreciation expense.)

3. On December 31, 2020, you take an inventory of unused paint supplies on hand to learn that all the paint supplies had been used as of that date. Thus, no adjusting entry is needed since the supplies were recorded as supplies expense when originally purchased.

> This adjusting entry was recorded in Chapter 9.

>
> For convenience, entrepreneurs often record supplies as supplies expense when originally purchased. At year end, the supplies are often used up or what is left on hand is an immaterial amount.

Step 1: Enter the adjusting entry (ADJ2 above) at 12/31/2020 to record depreciation expense for the painting equipment for the year in the Adjusting Entries Journal. (**Accountant menu > Make General Journal Entries**.)

Step 2: Click **Save & Close** to save the adjusting journal entry.

TASK 4: PRINT ADJUSTING ENTRIES

Print the two adjusting entries (ADJ1 and ADJ2) recorded on December 31, 2020, for Paint Palette.

Step 1: From the Report Center, select **Accountant & Taxes > Adjusting Journal Entries**.

Step 2: Select Dates From: **12/31/2020** To: **12/31/2020**.

Step 3: Export to **Excel** or **print** the Adjusting Journal Entries report.

TASK 5: PRINT ADJUSTED TRIAL BALANCE

> An adjusted trial balance is simply a trial balance printed after adjusting entries are recorded.

Step 1: Export to **Excel** or **print** an Adjusted Trial Balance at December 31, 2020. (**Report Center > Accountant & Taxes > Adjusted Trial Balance**.)

Step 2: On the Adjusted Trial Balance, **highlight** amounts affected by the adjusting entries.

TASK 6: SAVE EXERCISE 9.3

Save a backup of your Exercise 9.3 file using the file name: **YourName Exercise 9.3 Backup.QBB**. See *Appendix B: Back Up & Restore QuickBooks Files* for instructions.

WORKFLOW

Use the Workflow approach and leave your .QBW file open to use for the following exercise.

EXERCISE 9.4: FINANCIAL REPORTS

In this exercise, you will print out financial statements for Paint Palette for the year 2020.

TASK 1: CHANGE COMPANY NAME

WORKFLOW

Since you are using the Workflow approach, you will use the same .QBW file.

- If your QBW file is not already open, open it by selecting **File > Open Previous Company**. Select your **.QBW file.**

- Update Company Name to include **YourName Exercise 9.4**.

TASK 2: GENERAL LEDGER

> +
> To eliminate accounts with zero balances from the *General Ledger* report, select **Customize Report > Display > Advanced > In Use**.

Export to **Excel** or **print** the General Ledger report for Paint Palette for the year 2020.

TASK 3: FINANCIAL STATEMENTS

Create the following financial statements for Paint Palette for the year 2020.

- Export to **Excel** or **print** the Profit & Loss, Standard.

- Export to **Excel** or **print** the Balance Sheet, Standard.

- Export to **Excel** or **print** the Statement of Cash Flows. **Highlight** any items that might be classified differently than the classifications used by QuickBooks software.

> ✔ *Net income for the year 2020 is $31,285.*

WORKFLOW

Use the Workflow approach and leave your .QBW file open to use for the following exercise.

> ! Complete Exercise 9.5 only after you have completed Exercise 9.4.

EXERCISE 9.5: CLOSE THE ACCOUNTING PERIOD

To prevent changes to prior periods, QuickBooks permits you to restrict access to the accounting records for past periods that have been closed.

The QuickBooks Administrator can restrict user access to closed periods either at the time a new user is set up or later.

WORKFLOW

Since you are using the Workflow approach, you will use the same .QBW file. If your QBW file is not already open, open it by selecting **File > Open Previous Company**. Select your **.QBW file.**

> The QuickBooks Administrator has access to all areas of QuickBooks and is established when a new company is set up. For more information about the QuickBooks Administrator, see Chapter 2.

TASK 1: CLOSE THE ACCOUNTING PERIOD

To enter the closing date in QuickBooks:

Step 1:   Select **Company** menu **> Set Up Users and Passwords > Set Up Users**.

Step 2:   If necessary, enter information for the QuickBooks Administrator, then click **OK**.

Step 3:   When the following *User List* window appears, click the **Closing Date** button.

> ! **Write your password on the inside of your text cover.**
> You will not be able to access your company file without your password.

Step 4:   Enter the closing date: **12/31/2020**.

Step 5:   Click **OK** to close the *Set Closing Date and Password* window.

TASK 2: SAVE EXERCISE 9.5

Save a backup of your Exercise 9.5 file using the file name: **YourName Exercise 9.5 Backup.QBB**. See *Appendix B: Back Up & Restore QuickBooks Files* for instructions.

WORKFLOW

Chapter 12 is a continuation of Exercise 9.5.

RESTART & RESTORE

If you use the restart and restore approach, you will restore your .QBB file when you restart in Chapter 12.

EXERCISE 9.6: ALEXANDRA LLC

SCENARIO

Alexandra LLC, a start-up business, provides custom hardwood floor cleaning and refinishing. In addition, the business provides specialized cleaning of fine oriental rugs.

First, set up a new QuickBooks company file for Alexandra using the EasyStep Interview. Then create the Customer List, Vendor List, and the Item List for the new company. Then you will enter transactions for the new company.

TASK 1: NEW COMPANY SETUP

Step 1:   Create a new company in QuickBooks for Alexandra LLC. Use the following information.

Company name	YourName Exercise 9.6 Alexandra LLC
Legal name	YourName Exercise 9.6 Alexandra LLC
Tax ID	130-13-3636
Address	1958 Rue Grand
City	Bayshore
State	CA
Zip	94326
Phone	415-555-1313
Email	[enter your email address]
Industry	General Service-based Business
Type of organization	LLC Single-member LLC (Form 1040)
First month of fiscal year	January
File name	YourName Exercise 9.6
What do you sell?	Services only
Sales tax	No
Estimates	No
Billing statements	Yes
Invoices	Yes
Progress invoicing	No
Track bills you owe	Yes
Track time	Yes
Employees	No
Start date	01/01/2020
Use recommended income and expense accounts	Yes

Step 2: Click **Go to Setup** to exit the EasyStep Interview.

Step 3: In the *Add Your Bank Accounts* section of the *QuickBooks Setup* window, select **Add**.

Step 4: Enter the following information about the bank account.

Account Name	Checking
Account Number	1234567890
Opening Balance	0.00
Opening Balance Date	01/01/2020

Step 5: When asked if you want to order checks designed for QuickBooks, select: **No Thanks**.

Step 6: Click **Continue** to return to the *QuickBooks Setup* window.

Step 7: Select **Start Working** at the bottom of the *QuickBooks Setup* window.

Step 8: **Close** the *Quick Start Center* window by clicking the ☒ in the upper right corner of the window.

TASK 2: ADD ACCOUNTS

Step 1: Display account numbers.

Step 2: Add the following new accounts and subaccounts to the Chart of Accounts for Alexandra. Click **Save & New** after entering each account.

Account No.	13000
Account Type	Other Current Asset
Account Name	Cleaning Supplies
Account Description	Cleaning Supplies
Tax Line	Unassigned

Account No.	14400
Account Type	Fixed Asset
Account Name	Cleaning Equipment
Account Description	Cleaning Equipment
Tax Line	Unassigned

Account No.	14500
Account Type	Fixed Asset
Account Name	Cleaning Equipment Cost
Account Description	Cleaning Equipment Cost
Subaccount of	14400 Cleaning Equipment
Tax Line	Unassigned

Account No.	14600
Account Type	Fixed Asset
Account Name	Acc Depr Cleaning Equipment
Account Description	Acc Depr Cleaning Equipment
Subaccount of	14400 Cleaning Equipment
Tax Line	Unassigned

Account No.	21000
Account Type	Accounts Payable
Account Name	Accounts Payable
Account Description	Accounts Payable
Tax Line	Unassigned

Account No.	64800
Account Type	Expense
Account Name	Supplies Expense
Account Description	Supplies Expense
Tax Line	Sch C: Supplies (not from COGS)

Step 3: Export to **Excel** (without spaces between columns) or **print** the Chart of Accounts on January 1, 2020. (Hint: Report Center > List > Account Listing.)

TASK 3: ADD CUSTOMER & JOB

Step 1: Add Thomas Dent to the Alexandra Customer List.

Use the Customer Center to add new customers.

Customer	Dent, Thomas
Address Info:	
First Name	Thomas
Last Name	Dent
Main Phone	415-555-4242
Address	36 Penny Lane Bayshore, CA 94326

Payment Settings:	
Account No.	1005
Payment Terms	Net 15
Preferred Payment Method	Check

Additional Info:	
Customer Type	Residential

Step 2: Click **OK** to close the *New Customer* window.

Step 3: To add a new job, select Thomas Dent in the Customer List, then **right-click** to display the pop-up menu. Select **Add Job**.

Job Info:	
Job Name	Oriental Rugs
Job Description	Oriental rug cleaning
Job Type	Residential
Job Status	Pending

Step 4: From the Customer Center, export to **Excel** or **print** the Customer List.

Step 5: **Close** the Customer Center.

TASK 4: ADD VENDORS

Step 1: Add the following vendor to the Vendor List for Alexandra.

Use the Vendor Center to add new vendors.

Vendor	Blumer Cleaning Supplies
Opening balance	0.00
As of	01/01/2020
Address Info:	
Company Name	Blumer Cleaning Supplies
Full Name	Charlie Blumer
Mobile	415-555-7272
Address	72 St. Charles Blvd Bayshore, CA 94326
Payment Settings:	
Account No.	2004
Payment Terms	Net 30
Tax Settings:	
Vendor Tax ID	37-6543219
Additional Info:	
Vendor Type	Supplies

Step 2: From the Vendor Center, export to **Excel** or **print** the Vendor List.

TASK 5: ADD ITEMS

Step 1: Add the following items for Alexandra. Click **Next** after entering each item.

Item Type	Service
Item Name	Rug Cleaning
Description	Oriental Rug Cleaning
Account	47900 – Sales

Item Type	Service
Item Name	3x5 Rug Cleaning
Subitem of	Rug Cleaning
Description	3x5 Oriental Rug Cleaning
Rate	50.00
Account	47900 – Sales

Item Type	Service
Item Name	5x7 Rug Cleaning
Subitem of	Rug Cleaning
Description	5x7 Oriental Rug Cleaning
Rate	100.00
Account	47900 – Sales

Item Type	Service
Item Name	8x10 Rug Cleaning
Subitem of	Rug Cleaning
Description	8x10 Oriental Rug Cleaning
Rate	150.00
Account	47900 - Sales

Step 2: Using the Report Center, export to **Excel** or **print** the Item Listing as of January 1, 2020.

<table>
<tr><td>

+

To streamline transaction entry, select: **View > Open Window List**.

</td></tr>
</table>

TASK 6: RECORD TRANSACTIONS

During January, Alexandra entered into the transactions listed below. Record the transactions. **Print** invoices (Intuit Service Invoice), checks, and deposit summaries as appropriate.

Use *Make Deposits* window and account 30000.

Use *Write Checks* window.

Use *Enter Bills* window to record Supplies Expense.

Date	Transaction
01/01/2020	Alexandra Simon invested $5,000 cash in the business. Print the deposit summary.
01/02/2020	Purchased cleaning equipment for $900 from Blumer Cleaning Supplies (Check No. 5001).
01/05/2020	Purchased $100 of cleaning supplies on account from Blumer Cleaning Supplies.
01/09/2020	Cleaned oriental rugs for Tom Dent on account: ▪ (2) 3 x 5 ▪ (3) 5 x 7 ▪ (4) 8 x 10
01/20/2020	Paid Blumer Cleaning Supply bill.
01/29/2020	Collected Tom Dent payment for cleaning services (Check No. 580). Print the deposit summary.

TASK 7: REPORTS

Create the following reports for Alexandra for January 2020.

- ▪ Export to **Excel** or **print** the Check Detail report.
- ▪ Export to **Excel** or **print** the Deposit Detail report.

TASK 8: ADJUSTING ENTRIES & JOURNAL

There were no cleaning supplies left on hand so no adjusting entry is needed.

Step 1:   Make an adjusting entry (ADJ1) for Alexandra at January 31, 2020, to record one month of depreciation for the cleaning equipment. The cleaning equipment cost $900 and has a three-year (36-month) life and no salvage value.

Step 2:   Export to **Excel** or **print** the Journal report for January 2020.

TASK 9: FINANCIAL REPORTS

Export to **Excel** or **print** the following reports for Alexandra for January 2020.

Eliminate unused accounts with zero balances in the General Ledger by selecting **Customize Report > Display > Advanced > In Use**.

- Adjusted Trial Balance at 01/31/2020. (Hint: Report Center > Accountant & Taxes > Adjusted Trial Balance.)

- General Ledger from **01/01/2020** to **01/31/2020**.

- Profit & Loss, Standard.

- Balance Sheet, Standard.

- Statement of Cash Flows. **Highlight** any items that might be classified differently than the classifications used by QuickBooks software.

TASK 10: SAVE EXERCISE 9.6

Save a backup of your Exercise 9.6 file using the file name: **YourName Exercise 9.6 Backup.QBB**. See *Appendix B: Back Up & Restore QuickBooks Files* for instructions.

EXERCISE 9.7 WEB QUEST

The Internal Revenue Service (IRS) provides tax information useful for the small business. A sole proprietorship must file Form 1040 Schedule C for the annual tax return. If a sole proprietorship meets certain criteria, it may file a simplified Schedule C-EZ.

Step 1: Go to the www.irs.gov website.

Step 2: Search for Schedule C-EZ on the IRS website. **Print** the Schedule C-EZ.

Step 3: **Highlight** the information about whether you may use Schedule C-EZ instead of Schedule C.

CHAPTER 9 QUICK CHECK

NAME:

INSTRUCTIONS:

1.   **CHECK OFF THE ITEMS YOU COMPLETED.**
2.   **TURN IN THIS PAGE WITH YOUR PRINTOUTS.**

> **!**
>
> **Ask your instructor if you should Go Digital (Excel* or PDF) or use paper printouts.**

CHAPTER 9

- ☐   Deposit Summary
- ☐   Check No. 501
- ☐   Check Nos. 502 & 503
- ☐   Invoice No. 1
- ☐   Deposit Summary
- ☐ * Trial Balance
- ☐ * Adjusting Entry

EXERCISE 9.1

- ☐   Task 2: Checks
- ☐ * Task 3: Check Detail

EXERCISE 9.2

- ☐   Task 2: Invoices and Deposit Summaries
- ☐ * Task 3: Deposit Detail

EXERCISE 9.3

- ☐ * Task 2: Trial Balance
- ☐ * Task 4: Adjusting Entries
- ☐ * Task 5: Adjusted Trial Balance

EXERCISE 9.4

- ☐ * Task 2: General Ledger
- ☐ * Task 3: Profit & Loss
- ☐ * Task 3: Balance Sheet
- ☐ * Task 3: Statement of Cash Flows

EXERCISE 9.6

- ☐ * Task 2: Chart of Accounts (Account Listing)
- ☐ * Task 3: Customer List
- ☐ * Task 4: Vendor List
- ☐ * Task 5: Item List

☐   Task 6: Invoices, Checks & Deposit Summaries

☐ * Task 7: Check Detail

☐ * Task 7: Deposit Detail

☐ * Task 8: Journal

☐ * Task 9: Adjusted Trial Balance

☐ * Task 9: General Ledger

☐ * Task 9: Profit & Loss

☐ * Task 9: Balance Sheet

☐ * Task 9: Statement of Cash Flows

     EXERCISE 9.7

☐   Schedule C-EZ

Download Go Digital Excel templates at www.My-QuickBooks.com.

REFLECTION: A WISH AND A STAR

Reflection improves learning and retention. Reflect on what you have learned after completing Chapter 9 that you did not know before you started the chapter.

A Star:

What did you like best that you learned about QuickBooks in Chapter 9?

A Wish:

If you could pick one thing, what do you wish you knew more about when using QuickBooks?

PROJECT 9 DOMINIC CONSULTING

To complete this project, use the Chapter 9 Go Digital Reports Excel template at www.My-QuickBooks.com. Save the Excel file using the file name: **YourLastName FirstName CH9 REPORTS**.

Using your company file from Project 8 for Dominic Consulting, enter the transactions for the month of January 2020. (If you have issues with your file, contact your instructor for the Project 9 data file.)

1. Update Company Name to include **YourName Project 9**. Select preferences to use account numbers.

2. Enter the following transactions for the month of January 2020. (Click **View > Open Window List** to streamline transaction entry.)

Date	Transaction
01/01/2020	Dominic Leonardo invested $5,000 in the business (Check No. 432).
01/01/2020	Paid $800 for rent expense to Pitts Leasing (Check No. 101). (Record with the two-step method using the *Enter Bills* and *Pay Bills* windows.)
01/02/2020	Purchased a computer for $2,100 on account from Jackson Computer Services (Account: Furniture & Equipment).
01/03/2020	Purchased copier/printer/fax machine for $550 on account from Jackson Computer Services (Account: Furniture & Equipment).
01/06/2020	Emailed invoice to Redeker Bed & Breakfast for 10 hours of Internet marketing consulting and 5 hours of social network marketing consulting. Use the Intuit Service Invoice template.
01/08/2020	Emailed invoice to Etzkin Realty for 7 hours of Internet marketing consulting and 5 hours of social network marketing consulting.
01/10/2020	Emailed invoice to Holcomb Health Foods for 10 hours of Internet marketing consulting.
01/15/2020	Emailed invoice to Etzkin Realty for 15 hours of social network marketing consulting.
01/20/2020	Paid $100 for office supplies from Jackson Computer Services (Check No. 102). (Record as Office Supplies Expense using the *Enter Bills* and *Pay Bills* windows.)
01/20/2020	Received $800 payment from Redeker Bed & Breakfast (Check No. 589) and recorded deposit.
01/22/2020	Emailed invoice to Redeker Bed & Breakfast for 12 hours of Internet marketing consulting.
01/22/2020	Received $650 payment from Etzkin Realty (Check No. 935) and recorded deposit.
01/23/2020	Received $500 payment from Holcomb Health Foods (Check No. 1245) and recorded deposit.
01/24/2020	Paid $200 for office supplies from Jackson Computer Services (Check No. 103). (Record as Office Supplies Expense using the *Enter Bills* and *Pay Bills* windows.)
01/27/2020	Emailed invoice to Holcomb Health Foods for 4 hours of Internet marketing consulting and 12 hours of social network marketing consulting.
01/28/2020	Received $900 payment from Etzkin Realty (Check No. 876) and recorded deposit.
01/31/2020	Paid Jackson Computer Services bill for $2,100 computer (Check No. 104).

3. Using your saved CH9 Reports Excel template, export to **Excel** the Deposit Detail report for January 1-31, 2020.

4. Export to **Excel** the Check Detail report for January 1-31, 2020.

5. Export to **Excel** the Trial Balance at January 31, 2020.

6. Enter adjusting entries at January 31, 2020, using the following information. Then from the Report Center, export to **Excel** the Adjusting Journal Entries report.

   ▪ Entry No. ADJ1: The $2,100 computer is depreciated over 24 months using straight-line depreciation and no salvage value. Use Account No. 62400 Depreciation Expense and Account No. 17000 Accumulated Depreciation.

   ▪ Entry No. ADJ2: The $550 copier/printer/fax is depreciated over 36 months using straight-line depreciation and no salvage value. Use Account No. 62400 Depreciation Expense and Account No. 17000 Accumulated Depreciation.

   ▪ Entry No. ADJ3: Office supplies on hand at January 31, 2020, totaled $60. Add a new current asset account, No. 13000, Office Supplies on Hand, to transfer $60 from Office Supplies Expense.

7. Export to **Excel** the Adjusted Trial Balance at January 31, 2020. **Highlight** amounts affected by the adjusting entries.

8. Export to **Excel** the General Ledger for accounts **in use** for the month of January 2020.

9. Export to **Excel** the Profit & Loss Standard report for the month of January 2020.

10. Export to **Excel** the Balance Sheet Standard at January 31, 2020.

11. Export to **Excel** the Statement of Cash Flows for January 2020. **Highlight** any items that might be classified differently than the classifications used by QuickBooks software.

12. Mark the reports completed on the 9 REPORTS sheet. Save your Excel file.

13. Save a .QBB backup of your work.

PROJECT 9 QUICK CHECK

NAME:

INSTRUCTIONS:

1. **CHECK OFF THE ITEMS YOU COMPLETED.**
2. **ATTACH THIS PAGE TO YOUR PRINTOUTS.**

> **!**
> **Ask your instructor if you should Go Digital (Excel* or PDF) or use paper printouts.**

PROJECT 9

- ☐ * Deposit Detail
- ☐ * Check Detail
- ☐ * Trial Balance
- ☐ * Adjusting Entries
- ☐ * Adjusted Trial Balance
- ☐ * General Ledger
- ☐ * Profit & Loss
- ☐ * Balance Sheet
- ☐ * Statement of Cash Flows

Download Go Digital Excel templates at www.My-QuickBooks.com.

QUICKBOOKS CASE 9 TUSCANY LANDSCAPES

SCENARIO

Your friend and entrepreneur, Tomaso Moltissimo, is starting a new landscape care business, Tuscany Landscapes, to help pay his college expenses. Consistent with consumer demand for more environmentally friendly lawn and landscape care, Tomaso decides to specialize in the maintenance and landscape care of native plantings.

You and Tomaso reach an agreement: you will help Tomaso with his accounting records and provide customer referrals, and he will help you with your painting business.

TASK 1: SET UP A NEW COMPANY

Step 1: Create a new company in QuickBooks for Tuscany Landscapes using the EasyStep Interview and QuickBooks Setup. Use the following information.

Company name	YourName QB Case 9 Tuscany Landscapes
Tax ID	314-14-7878
Address	2300 Olive Boulevard
City	Bayshore
State	CA
Zip	94326
Email	<enter your own email address>
Industry	Lawn Care or Landscaping
Type of organization	Sole Proprietorship
First month of fiscal year	January
File name	YourName QB Case 9
What do you sell?	Services only
Sales tax	No
Estimates	No
Billing statements	Yes
Invoices	Yes

Progress invoicing	No
Track bills you owe	Yes
Track time	Yes
Employees	No
Start date	01/01/2020
Use recommended accounts?	Yes
Bank account name	Checking
Bank account number	9876543210
Bank account balance	0.00 as of 01/01/2020

Step 2: Select Tax Form: Form 1040 (Sole Proprietor). (From the **Company** menu, select **My Company**. Select Income Tax Form: **Form 1040 (Sole Proprietor)**.

TASK 2: CUSTOMIZE THE CHART OF ACCOUNTS

Customize the Chart of Accounts for Tuscany Landscapes as follows:

Step 1: Display account numbers in the Chart of Accounts.

Step 2: Add the following accounts to the Chart of Accounts.

To display account numbers, select **Edit** menu > **Preferences > Accounting > Company Preferences > Use Account Numbers.**

Account No.	14000
Account Type	Fixed Asset
Account Name	Mower
Account Description	Mower
Tax Line	Unassigned

Account No.	14100
Account Type	Fixed Asset
Account Name	Mower Cost
Subaccount of	Mower
Account Description	Mower Cost
Tax Line	Unassigned

Account No.	14200
Account Type	Fixed Asset
Account Name	Accumulated Depreciation Mower
Subaccount of	Mower
Account Description	Accumulated Depreciation Mower
Tax Line	Unassigned

Account No.	18000
Account Type	Fixed Asset
Account Name	Trimmer Equipment
Account Description	Trimmer Equipment
Tax Line	Unassigned

Account No.	18100
Account Type	Fixed Asset
Account Name	Trimmer Equipment Cost
Subaccount of	Trimmer Equipment
Account Description	Trimmer Equipment Cost
Tax Line	Unassigned

Account No.	18200
Account Type	Fixed Asset
Account Name	Accumulated Depr Trimmer
Subaccount of	Trimmer Equipment
Account Description	Accumulated Depr Trimmer
Tax Line	Unassigned

Account No.	64800
Account Type	Expense
Account Name	Supplies Expense
Account Description	Supplies Expense
Tax Line	Sch C: Supplies (not from COGS)

Step 3: From the Report Center, export to **Excel** or **print** the Chart of Accounts (Account Listing) report for Tuscany Landscapes.

TASK 3: CUSTOMER LIST

Step 1: Create a Customer List for Tuscany Landscapes using the following information.

Customer	Beneficio, Katrina
Opening Balance	0 as of 01/01/2020
Address Info:	
First Name	Katrina
Last Name	Beneficio
Main Phone	415-555-1818
Mobile	415-555-3636
Address	10 Pico Blvd Bayshore, CA 94326

Payment Settings:	
Account No.	3001
Payment Terms	Net 30
Preferred Payment Method	Check

Select **Add New**.

Additional Info:	
Customer Type	Residential

Add jobs by selecting the customer in the Customer List, **right-click > Add Job**.

Step 2: Add a job for Katrina Beneficio with Job Name: Lawn.

Job Info:	
Job Status	Awarded
Job Description	Mow/Trim Lawn
Job Type	Lawn

Select **Add New**.

Step 3: Add another customer.

Customer	Whalen, Tom
Opening balance	0 as of 01/01/2020
Address Info:	
First Name	Tom
Last Name	Whalen
Main Phone	415-555-1234
Mobile	415-555-5678
Address	100 Sunset Drive Bayshore, CA 94326

Payment Settings:	
Account No.	3002
Payment Terms	Net 30
Preferred Payment Method	Check

Additional Info:	
Customer Type	Residential

Step 4: Add a job for Tom Whalen with Job Name: Lawn.

Job Info:	
Job Description	Mow/Trim Lawn
Job Type	Lawn
Job Status	Awarded

Step 5: Add a new customer.

Customer	Rock Castle Construction
Opening balance	0 as of 01/01/2020
Address Info:	
Company Name	Rock Castle Construction
First Name	Rock
Last Name	Castle

Main Phone	415-555-7878
Mobile	415-555-5679
Address	1735 County Road Bayshore, CA 94326

Payment Settings:	
Account No.	3003
Payment Terms	Net 30
Preferred Payment Method	Check

Additional Info:	
Customer Type	Commercial

Step 6:   Add a job for Rock Castle Construction with Job Name: Lawn & Shrubs.

Job Info:	
Job Description	Mow/Trim Lawn & Shrubs
Job Type	Lawn & Shrubs
Job Status	Awarded

Step 7:   From the Customer Center, export to **Excel** or **print** the Customer List.

TASK 4: VENDOR LIST

Step 1:   Create a Vendor List for Tuscany Landscapes using the following information.

Vendor	AB Gas Station
Opening Balance	0 as of 01/01/2020
Address Info:	
Company Name	AB Gas Station
First Name	Norm
Main Phone	415-555-7844

Address	100 Manchester Road Bayshore, CA 94326
Payment Settings:	
Account No.	4001
Payment Terms	Net 30
Credit Limit	500.00
Print on Check as	AB Gas Station
Tax Settings:	
Vendor Tax ID	37-8910541
Additional Info:	
Vendor Type	Fuel

Vendor	Mower Sales & Repair
Opening Balance	0 as of 01/01/2020
Address Info:	
Company Name	Mower Sales & Repair
First Name	Teresa
Main Phone	415-555-8222
Address	650 Manchester Road Bayshore, CA 94326
Payment Settings:	
Account No.	4002
Payment Terms	Net 30
Credit Limit	1000.00
Print on Check as	Mower Sales & Repair
Tax Settings:	
Vendor Tax ID	37-6510541
Additional Info:	
Vendor Type	Mower

Step 2: From the Vendor Center, export to **Excel** or **print** the Vendor List.

TASK 5: ITEM LIST

Step 1: Create an Item List for Tuscany Landscapes using the following information.

Item Type	Service
Item Name	Mowing
Description	Lawn Mowing
Rate	25.00
Account	45700 – Maintenance Services

Item Type	Service
Item Name	Trim Shrubs
Description	Trim Shrubs
Rate	30.00
Account	45700 – Maintenance Services

Step 2: From the Report Center, export to **Excel** or **print** the Item List.

TASK 6: CUSTOMIZE INVOICE TEMPLATE

Create a Custom Invoice Template with a *Service Date* column. This permits Tuscany Landscapes to bill customers once a month for all services provided during the month, listing each service date separately on the invoice.

To create a Custom Invoice Template, complete the following steps:

Step 1: Click the **Create Invoices** icon in the *Customers* section of the Home page.

Step 2: Click the **Formatting** tab in the upper portion of the *Create Invoices* window.

Step 3: Select **Manage Templates**.

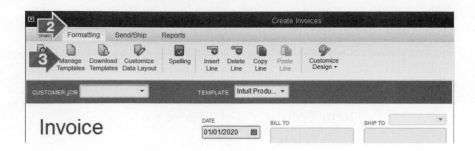

Step 4: In the *Manage Templates* window, select **Intuit Service Invoice**.

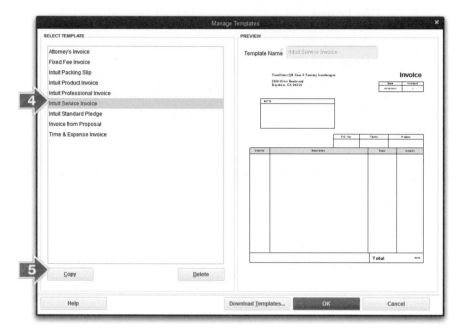

Step 5: Then click **Copy**.

Step 6: Change the invoice template name as follows:

- Select **Copy of: Intuit Service Invoice**.

- In the Template Name field, change the template name to: **Service Date Invoice**.

- Click **OK** to close the *Manage Templates* window.

Step 7: Verify the Selected Template is: **Service Date Invoice**.

Step 8: Click the **Additional Customization** button.

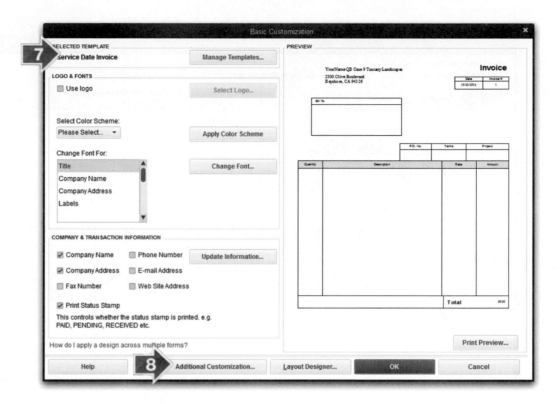

Step 9: To add a *Service Date* column to the custom template, when the *Additional Customization* window appears, click the **Columns** tab.

If an Overlapping Fields message appears, click **Continue**.

Step 10: ✓ Check **Service Date: Screen**. If the Layout Designer message appears, click OK.

Step 11: ✓ Check **Service Date: Print**.

Step 12: ✓ Check **Item: Print**.

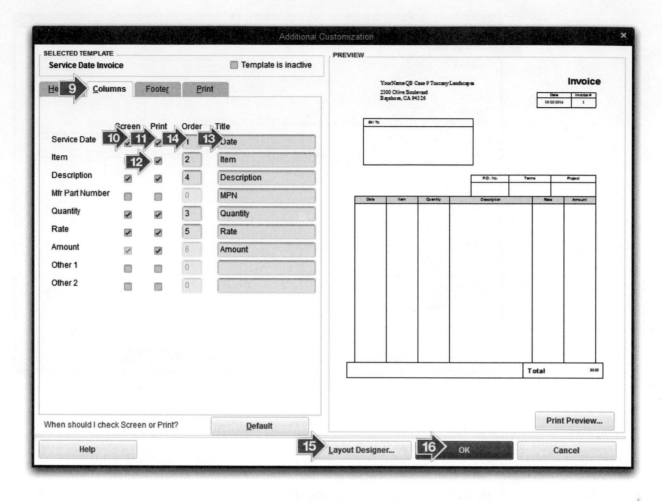

Step 13: Enter Title for Service Date: **Date**.

Step 14: Renumber the Order so they appear as shown above.

Step 15: Click the **Layout Designer** button and adjust the field sizes as needed.

Step 16: Click **OK** to close the *Layout Designer* window.

Step 17: Click **OK** again to close the *Customization* windows.

Step 18: To view the custom invoice:

- If necessary, from the *Create Invoices* window, select Template: **Service Date Invoice**.

- Notice that the first column of the invoice is now the *Date* column.

TASK 7: RECORD TRANSACTIONS

During the year, Tuscany Landscapes entered into the transactions listed below.

Step 1:   Record the following transactions for Tuscany Landscapes. Customers are billed monthly. **Print** invoices, checks, and deposit summaries as appropriate. Use memorized transactions for recurring transactions.

+
To streamline transaction entry, select: **View > Open Window List.**

Use *Make Deposits* window.

Use *Write Checks* window.

Use *Enter Bills* window.

Record Supplies Expense.

Select **Show All Bills** in the *Pay Bills* window.

Date	Transaction		
01/01/2020	Tomaso Moltissimo invested $1,500 cash in the business.		
02/01/2020	Purchased a mower for $800 by check from Mower Sales & Repair (Check No. 501).		
02/20/2020	Purchased trimming equipment from Mower Sales & Repair for $200 on account.		
03/01/2020	Purchased $100 of gasoline and supplies on account from AB Gas Station.		
03/20/2020	Paid $200 on the account with Mower Sales & Repair. Paid $100 on the account with AB Gas Station.		
04/30/2020	Printed and mailed invoices to customers for the following work performed in April. Use the Service Date Invoice to record all work performed for the same customer on **one** invoice, indicating the date of service in the *Date* column.		
	04/01/2020 04/15/2020	Mowed Katrina Beneficio's lawn Mowed Katrina Beneficio's lawn	6 hrs 6 hrs
	04/04/2020 04/19/2020	Mowed R.C. Construction's lawn Mowed R.C. Construction's lawn	8 hrs 8 hrs
	04/08/2020 04/22/2020	Mowed Tom Whalen's lawn Mowed Tom Whalen's lawn	4 hrs 4 hrs
05/01/2020	Purchased $100 of gasoline and supplies on account from AB Gas Station.		

05/15/2020	Received payments from Beneficio (Check No. 755), Whalen (Check No. 645), and Rock Castle Construction (Check No. 1068) for April invoices. Recorded deposits.		
05/30/2020	Paid AB Gas Station bill.		
05/30/2020	Mailed invoices to customers for the following services provided during May.		
	05/01/2020	Mowed Katrina Beneficio's lawn	6 hrs
	05/15/2020	Mowed Katrina Beneficio's lawn	6 hrs
	05/04/2020	Mowed R.C. Construction's lawn	8 hrs
	05/19/2020	Mowed R.C. Construction's lawn	8 hrs
	05/08/2020	Mowed Tom Whalen's lawn	4 hrs
	05/22/2020	Mowed Tom Whalen's lawn	4 hrs
06/01/2020	Purchased $100 of gasoline and supplies on account from AB Gas Station.		
06/15/2020	Received payments from Beneficio (Check No. 895), Whalen (Check No. 698), and Rock Castle Construction (Check No. 1100) for May services. Recorded deposits.		
06/30/2020	Paid AB Gas Station bill.		

06/30/2020	Mailed invoices to customers for the following services provided during June. (Edit job name to include Lawn & Shrubs for Beneficio and Whalen.)		
	06/01/2020	Mowed Katrina Beneficio's lawn	6 hrs
	06/02/2020	Trimmed Katrina Beneficio's shrubs	7 hrs
	06/15/2020	Mowed Katrina Beneficio's lawn	6 hrs
	06/04/2020	Mowed R. C. Construction's lawn	8 hrs
	06/05/2020	Trimmed R.C. Construction's shrubs	9 hrs
	06/19/2020	Mowed R. C. Construction's lawn	8 hrs
	06/08/2020	Mowed Tom Whalen's lawn	4 hrs
	06/09/2020	Trimmed Tom Whalen's shrubs	3 hrs
	06/22/2020	Mowed Tom Whalen's lawn	4 hrs
07/01/2020	Purchased $100 of gasoline and supplies on account from AB Gas Station.		
07/15/2020	Received payments from Beneficio (Check No. 910), Whalen (Check No. 715), and Rock Castle Construction (Check No. 1200) for June services. Recorded deposits.		
07/31/2020	Paid AB Gas Station bill.		
07/31/2020	Mailed invoices to customers for the following services provided during July.		
	07/01/2020	Mowed Katrina Beneficio's lawn	6 hrs
	07/15/2020	Mowed Katrina Beneficio's lawn	6 hrs
	07/04/2020	Mowed R.C. Construction's lawn	8 hrs
	07/19/2020	Mowed R.C. Construction's lawn	8 hrs
	07/08/2020	Mowed Tom Whalen's lawn	4 hrs
	07/22/2020	Mowed Tom Whalen's lawn	4 hrs
08/01/2020	Purchased $100 of gasoline and supplies on account from AB Gas Station.		
08/15/2020	Received payments from Beneficio (Check No. 935), Whalen (Check No. 742), and Rock Castle Construction (Check No. 1300) for July services. Recorded deposits.		
08/31/2020	Paid AB Gas Station bill.		

08/31/2020	Mailed invoices to customers for the following services provided during August.		
	08/01/2020	Mowed Katrina Beneficio's lawn	6 hrs
	08/15/2020	Mowed Katrina Beneficio's lawn	6 hrs
	08/04/2020	Mowed R.C. Construction's lawn	8 hrs
	08/19/2020	Mowed R.C. Construction's lawn	8 hrs
	08/08/2020	Mowed Tom Whalen's lawn	4 hrs
	08/22/2020	Mowed Tom Whalen's lawn	4 hrs
09/01/2020	Purchased $100 of gasoline and supplies on account from AB Gas Station.		
09/15/2020	Received payments from Beneficio (Check No. 934), Whalen (Check No. 746), and Rock Castle Construction (Check No. 1400) for August services. Recorded deposits.		
09/30/2020	Paid AB Gas Station bill.		
09/30/2020	Mailed invoices to customers for the following services provided during September.		
	09/01/2020	Mowed Katrina Beneficio's lawn	6 hrs
	09/15/2020	Mowed Katrina Beneficio's lawn	6 hrs
	09/04/2020	Mowed R.C. Construction's lawn	8 hrs
	09/19/2020	Mowed R.C. Construction's lawn	8 hrs
	09/08/2020	Mowed Tom Whalen's lawn	4 hrs
	09/22/2020	Mowed Tom Whalen's lawn	4 hrs
10/01/2020	Purchased $50 of gasoline on account from AB Gas Station.		
10/15/2020	Received payments from Beneficio (Check No. 956), Whalen (Check No. 755), and Rock Castle Construction (Check No. 1500) for September services. Recorded deposits.		
10/31/2020	Paid AB Gas Station bill.		

10/31/2020	Mailed invoices to customers for the following services provided during October.		
	10/01/2020	Mowed Katrina Beneficio's lawn	6 hrs
	10/02/2020	Trimmed Katrina Beneficio's shrubs	7 hrs
	10/15/2020	Mowed Katrina Beneficio's lawn	6 hrs
	10/04/2020	Mowed R. C. Construction's lawn	8 hrs
	10/05/2020	Trimmed R.C. Construction's shrubs	9 hrs
	10/19/2020	Mowed R. C. Construction's lawn	8 hrs
	10/08/2020	Mowed Tom Whalen's lawn	4 hrs
	10/09/2020	Trimmed Tom Whalen's shrubs	3 hrs
	10/22/2020	Mowed Tom Whalen's lawn	4 hrs
11/15/2020	Received payments from Beneficio (Check No. 967), Whalen (Check No. 765), and Rock Castle Construction (Check No. 1600) for October services. Recorded deposits.		

Step 2:   Export to **Excel** or **print** the Deposit Detail report for January 1, 2020, to December 31, 2020.

Step 3:   Export to **Excel** or **print** the Check Detail report for January 1, 2020, to December 31, 2020.

TASK 8: ADJUSTING ENTRIES

Step 1:   Make adjusting entries for Tuscany Landscapes at December 31, 2020, using the following information.

- ADJ1: The mowing equipment cost $800 and has a four-year life and no salvage value.

- ADJ2: The trimming equipment cost $200 and has a two-year life and no salvage value.

Step 2:   From the Report Center, export to **Excel** or **print** the Adjusting Journal Entries report for December 31, 2020.

Step 3:   Export to **Excel** or **print** the Adjusted Trial Balance. **Highlight** amounts affected by the adjusting entries.

TASK 9: FINANCIAL REPORTS

Export to **Excel** or **print** the following 2020 reports for Tuscany Landscapes.

- General Ledger. (Omit unused accounts with zero balances.)

- Profit & Loss, Standard.

- Balance Sheet, Standard.

- Statement of Cash Flows. **Highlight** any items that might be classified differently than the classifications used by QuickBooks software.

> ✓ *Net income is $6,490.00.*

TASK 10: SAVE QUICKBOOKS CASE 9

Save a backup of your QuickBooks Case 9 file using the file name: **YourName QB Case 9 Backup.QBB**. See *Appendix B: Back Up & Restore QuickBooks Files* for instructions.

WORKFLOW

If you are using the Workflow approach, leave your .QBW file open and proceed to QuickBooks Case 12.

RESTART & RESTORE

If you are using the Restart & Restore approach and are ending your computer session now, close your .QBW file and exit QuickBooks. When you restart, you will restore your backup file to complete QuickBooks Case 12.

QUICKBOOKS CASE 9 QUICK CHECK

NAME:

INSTRUCTIONS:

1. **CHECK OFF THE ITEMS YOU COMPLETED.**
2. **TURN IN THIS PAGE WITH YOUR PRINTOUTS.**

> **!**
> **Ask your instructor if you should Go Digital (Excel* or PDF) or use paper printouts.**

QB CASE 9

- ☐ * Chart of Accounts
- ☐ * Customer List
- ☐ * Vendor List
- ☐ * Item List
- ☐ Invoices
- ☐ Checks
- ☐ Deposit Summaries
- ☐ * Deposit Detail
- ☐ * Check Detail
- ☐ * Adjusting Entries
- ☐ * Adjusted Trial Balance
- ☐ * General Ledger
- ☐ * Profit & Loss
- ☐ * Balance Sheet
- ☐ * Statement of Cash Flows

> Download Go Digital Excel templates at www.My-QuickBooks.com.

BUILD YOUR DREAM ENTERPRISE

Do you have an interest in being an entrepreneur? Would you like to start your own business? *Build Your Dream Enterprise* QuickBooks cases give you that opportunity. Go to www.My-QuickBooks.com and download the *Build Your Dream Enterprise Case* for Chapter 9.

NOTES:

CHAPTER 10
MERCHANDISING CORPORATION:
SALES, PURCHASES AND INVENTORY

SCENARIO

After only one year of operation, your painting service is growing as more customers learn of your custom murals. Customers take photos of whatever they want for their wall murals (sunsets, waterfalls, the beach, and so on) and then text the photos to your iPad. Then you display the photo on your iPad while you paint the mural on their walls or ceilings. It saves you time, you no longer have to guess what the customer wants, and customer satisfaction couldn't be better. You created a digital gallery of your completed murals for your website. As a promotion, you hold an annual contest for best photos for murals with an iPad as the winning prize.

You buy paint from a small paint store owned and operated by Wil Miles. He provides excellent customer service, delivers paint to a job when you run short, and custom mixes paint colors you use for your murals. To your dismay, you discover that Wil Miles is planning to close the store and retire, taking his first vacation since he opened the store 15 years ago. After your initial disappointment, however, you see a business opportunity.

If you owned the paint store, you could make a profit on the markup from paint sales made to your Paint Palette customers. In addition, you are certain you could land three large commercial customers for whom you have worked: Cara Interiors, Decor Centre, and Rock Castle Construction. With your connections, you could sell paint to other customers, including paint contractors and homeowners.

Convinced there is a profitable market for custom-mixed paint, you approach Wil Miles about purchasing his store. Wil agrees to sell the business to you for $11,000 cash. In addition, you agree to assume a $1,000 bank loan as part of the purchase agreement. You have some extra cash you can invest, and you decide to seek other investors to finance the remainder.

Two of Rock Castle Construction's subcontractors, John of Kolbe Window & Door, and Joseph of Joseph's Closets are long-time customers of the paint store. When they learn of your plans to buy the paint store, both eagerly offer to invest.

John suggests that you investigate incorporating the new business to provide limited liability to the owners. You vaguely recall discussion of limited liability in your college accounting class and decide to email your college accounting professor, Pat Vollenger, for more information.

Professor Vollenger's email reply:

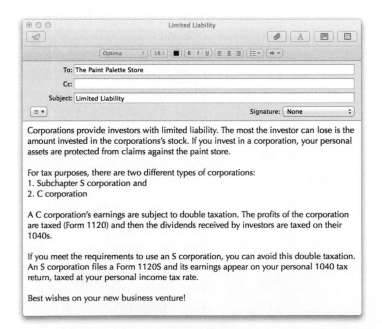

John, Joseph, and you form an S Corporation. John and Joseph each buy $3,000 of stock, and you buy $5,000 of stock. The stock proceeds are used to purchase the business from Wil Miles. Until you can hire a store manager, you will manage the store.

You prepare the following list of planned expenditures to launch the business:

Paint Palette Store opens for business on January 1, 2021.

CHAPTER 10
LEARNING OBJECTIVES

In Chapter 10, you will learn about the following QuickBooks activities:

INTRODUCTION

A company can sell customers either (1) a product or (2) a service. In Chapters 8 and 9, you maintained accounting records for a company that sells a service to customers. In this chapter, you will maintain an accounting system for a company that sells a product. In Chapter 10, you will complete the following:

---

1. Easy Step Interview

Use the EasyStep Interview to enter information and preferences for the new company. Based on the information entered, QuickBooks automatically creates a Chart of Accounts.

---

2. Create Lists

Enter information in the following lists:
- Customer List. Enter information about customers to whom you sell.
- Vendor List. Enter information about vendors from whom you buy.
- Item List. Enter information about products (inventory) you buy and resell to customers.
- Employee List. Enter information about employees.

---

3. Customize the Chart of Accounts

Customize the Chart of Accounts for your business. Enter beginning account balances. Make opening adjustments.

---

4. Record Transactions

Enter business transactions in QuickBooks using onscreen forms and the onscreen Journal.

---

5. Reports

After preparing adjusting entries, print financial reports.

To begin Chapter 10, start QuickBooks software by clicking on the QuickBooks desktop icon or click **Start > Programs > QuickBooks > QuickBooks Premier Accountant Edition 2015**.

Set Up a New Company

To create a new company data file in QuickBooks, use the EasyStep Interview. The EasyStep Interview will ask you a series of questions about your business. QuickBooks then uses the information to customize QuickBooks to fit your business needs.

Open the EasyStep Interview as follows:

Step 1:   Select **File** menu **> New Company**.

Step 2:   Click **Detailed Start.** Enter the following information for Paint Palette Store using the EasyStep Interview and QuickBooks Setup.

Company name	YourName Chapter 10 Paint Palette Store
Legal name	YourName Chapter 10 Paint Palette Store
Federal tax ID	37-9875602
Address	2301 Olive Boulevard
City	Bayshore
State	CA
Zip	94326
Email	<your email address>
Industry	Retail Shop or Online Commerce
Type of organization	S Corporation
First month of fiscal year	January
File name	YourName Chapter 10
What do you sell?	Products only
Enter sales	Record each sale individually
Sales tax	Yes
Estimates	No
Sales orders	No

!
Write your password on the inside front cover of your text.

Billing statements	No
Invoices	Yes
Progress invoicing	No
Track bills you owe	Yes
Track inventory in QuickBooks	Yes
Track time	Yes
Employees	No
Start date	01/01/2021
Use recommended accounts	Yes
Bank account name	Checking
Bank account number	4567891230
Bank account opened	0.00 on 01/01/2021

Step 3:   Click **Start Working** to exit QuickBooks Setup.

COMPLETE COMPANY SETUP

+
If you need to return to QuickBooks Setup, select **Help** menu **> Quick Start Center > Return to Add Info**.

Use the following checklist to complete the company setup:

- Customize QuickBooks.
- Add customers.
- Add vendors.
- Add products and services as items.
- Customize Chart of Accounts.
- Enter opening adjustments.

CUSTOMIZE QUICKBOOKS

You will customize QuickBooks for Paint Palette Store by customizing preferences and by customizing the Chart of Accounts. First, to customize preferences:

Step 1:   Select **Edit** menu **> Preferences > General > My Preferences**.

Step 2: Select Default Date to Use for New Transactions: **Use the last entered date as default**.

Step 3: Select **Accounting > Company Preferences**.

- Select **Use account numbers**.

- Uncheck **Use class tracking for transactions**.

- Uncheck **Warn if transactions are 30 day(s) in the future**.

Step 4: Select **Checking > My Preferences**. Select default accounts to use:

- Open the Write Checks form with **Checking** account.

- Open the Pay Bills form with **Checking** account.

- Open the Pay Sales Tax form with **Checking** account.

- Open the Make Deposits form with **Checking** account.

Step 5: Select **Desktop View > Company Preferences**. Verify the following preference settings. To change the settings for these preferences in the future, you would return to this screen.

- Estimates (off)

- Sales Tax (on)

- Sales Orders (off)

- Inventory (on)

- Payroll (off)

- Time Tracking (on)

Step 6: Select **Sales Tax > Company Preferences**. Select Your Most Common Sales Tax Item: **State Tax**.

Step 7: Click **OK** to save your customized preference settings.

In setting up QuickBooks for Paint Palette Store, the next steps are to enter information into lists for customers, vendors, and items.

CREATE A CUSTOMER LIST

Next, enter customer information in the Customer List. When using QuickBooks to account for a merchandising company that sells a product to customers, you must indicate whether the specific customer is charged sales tax.

Paint Palette Store will sell to:

1. Retail customers, such as homeowners who must pay sales tax.

2. Wholesale customers, such as Decor Centre, who resell the product and do not pay sales tax.

Step 1:   Create a Customer List for Paint Palette Store using the following information.

Customer	Beneficio, Katrina
Opening Balance	0.00 as of 01/01/2021
Address Info:	
Mr./Ms./…	Mrs.
First Name	Katrina
Last Name	Beneficio
Main Phone	415-555-1818
Mobile	415-555-3636
Address	10 Pico Blvd Bayshore, CA 94326
Payment Settings:	
Account No.	3001
Payment Terms	Net 30
Sales Tax Settings:	
Tax Code	Tax
Tax Item	State Tax
Additional Info:	
Customer Type	Residential
Special Interest	Italian

Select **Define Fields > Label**.
Enter Label: **Special Interest**.
Select: **Customer**.

Select **Add New**.

Right-click **Add Job**.

Select **Add New**.

Job Info:	
Job Description	Custom Paint
Job Type	Custom Paint
Job Status	Awarded

Customer	Decor Centre
Opening Balance	0.00 as of 01/01/2021
Address Info:	
Company Name	Decor Centre
First Name	Vicki
Main Phone	415-555-9898
Address	750 Clayton Road Bayshore, CA 94326
Payment Settings:	
Account No.	3005
Payment Terms	Net 30
Sales Tax Settings:	
Tax Code	Non
Additional Info:	
Customer Type	Commercial
Special Interest	Hi Tech
Job Info:	
Job Description	Custom & Stock Paint
Job Type	Custom & Stock Paint
Job Status	Awarded

Customer	Rock Castle Construction
Opening Balance	0.00 as of 01/01/2021
Address Info:	
Company Name	Rock Castle Construction
Mr./Ms./…	Mr.
First Name	Rock
Last Name	Castle

Main Phone	415-555-7878
Mobile	415-555-5679
Address	1735 County Road Bayshore, CA 94326
Payment Settings:	
Account No.	3003
Payment Terms	Net 30
Sales Tax Settings:	
Tax Code	Non
Additional Info:	
Customer Type	Commercial
Special Interest	Various
Job Info:	
Job Description	Custom Paint
Job Type	Custom Paint
Job Status	Awarded

Customer	Cara Interiors
Opening Balance	0.00 as of 01/01/2021
Address Info:	
Company Name	Cara Interiors
First Name	Cara
Main Phone	415-555-4356
Address	120 Ignatius Drive Bayshore, CA 94326
Payment Settings:	
Account No.	3004
Payment Terms	Net 30
Sales Tax Settings:	
Tax Code	Non
Additional Info:	
Customer Type	Commercial
Special Interest	Provence

Job Info:	
Job Description	Custom & Stock Paint
Job Type	Custom & Stock Paint
Job Status	Awarded

Customer	Whalen, Tom
Opening Balance	0.00 as of 01/01/2021
Address Info:	
Mr./Ms./…	Mr.
First Name	Tom
Last Name	Whalen
Main Phone	415-555-1234
Address	100 Sunset Drive Bayshore, CA 94326
Payment Settings:	
Account No.	3002
Payment Terms	Net 30
Sales Tax Settings:	
Tax Code	Tax
Tax Item	State Tax
Additional Info:	
Customer Type	Residential
Special Interest	Rustic
Job Info:	
Job Description	Custom Paint
Job Type	Custom Paint
Job Status	Awarded

Step 2: From the Customer Center, export to **Excel** or **print** Paint Palette Store Customer List.

CREATE A VENDOR LIST

Step 1: Create a Vendor List for Paint Palette Store using the following information.

Vendor	Brewer Paint Supplies
Opening Balance	0.00 as of 01/01/2021
Address Info:	
Company Name	Brewer Paint Supplies
Full Name	Ella Brewer
Main Phone	415-555-6070
Address	200 Spring Street Bayshore, CA 94326
Payment Settings:	
Account No.	4001
Payment Terms	Net 30
Print on Check as	Brewer Paint Supplies
Credit Limit	15,000.00
Tax Settings:	
Vendor Tax ID	37-7832541
Additional Info:	
Vendor Type	Paint

Select **Add New**.

Vendor	Hartzheim Leasing
Opening Balance	0.00 as of 01/01/2021
Address Info:	
Company Name	Hartzheim Leasing
First Name	Joseph
Main Phone	415-555-0412
Address	13 Appleton Drive Bayshore, CA 94326
Payment Settings:	
Account No.	4002
Payment Terms	Net 30

Tax Settings:	
Vendor Tax ID	37-1726354
Additional Info:	
Vendor Type	Leasing

Vendor	Shades of Santiago
Opening Balance	0.00 as of 01/01/2021
Address Info:	
Company Name	Shades of Santiago
First Name	Juan
Main Phone	415-555-0444
Address	650 Chile Avenue Bayshore, CA 94326
Payment Settings:	
Account No.	4003
Payment Terms	Net 30
Tax Settings:	
Vendor Tax ID	37-1726355
Additional Info:	
Vendor Type	Inventory

Step 2: From the Vendor Center, export to **Excel** or **print** Paint Palette Store Vendor List.

CREATE AN ITEM LIST

Each of the inventory items that Paint Palette Store sells is entered in the QuickBooks Item List. Paint Palette Store will stock and sell paint inventory to both retail and wholesale customers. The store will charge retail customers the full price and charge wholesale customers a discounted price. Because the sales price varies depending upon the type of customer, instead of entering the sales price in the Item List, you will enter the sales price on the invoice at the time of sale.

Step 1: Create an Item List for Paint Palette Store inventory using the following information.

Item Type	Inventory Part
Item Name	Paint Base
Description	Paint Base
COGS Account	50000 – Cost of Goods Sold
Income Account	46000 – Merchandise Sales
Asset Account	12100 – Inventory Asset
Qty on Hand	0.00 as of 01/01/2021

Item Type	Inventory Part
Item Name	IntBase 1 gal
Subitem of	Paint Base
Description	Interior Paint Base (1 gallon)
Cost	10.00
COGS Account	50000 – Cost of Goods Sold
Tax Code	Tax
Income Account	46000 – Merchandise Sales
Asset Account	12100 – Inventory Asset
Qty on Hand	0.00 as of 01/01/2021

Item Type	Inventory Part
Item Name	ExtBase 1 gal
Subitem of	Paint Base
Description	Exterior Paint Base (1 gallon)
Cost	10.00
COGS Account	50000 – Cost of Goods Sold
Tax Code	Tax
Income Account	46000 – Merchandise Sales
Asset Account	12100 – Inventory Asset
Qty on Hand	0.00 as of 01/01/2021

Item Type	Inventory Part
Item Name	Paint Color
Description	Paint Color

COGS Account	50000 – Cost of Goods Sold
Income Account	46000 – Merchandise Sales
Asset Account	12100 – Inventory Asset
Qty on Hand	0.00 as of 01/01/2021

Item Type	Inventory Part
Item Name	Stock Color
Subitem of	Paint Color
Description	Stock Paint Color
Cost	2.00
COGS Account	50000 – Cost of Goods Sold
Tax Code	Tax
Income Account	46000 – Merchandise Sales
Asset Account	12100 – Inventory Asset
Qty on Hand	0.00 as of 01/01/2021

Item Type	Inventory Part
Item Name	Custom Color
Subitem of	Paint Color
Description	Custom Paint Color
Cost	8.00
COGS Account	50000 – Cost of Goods Sold
Tax Code	Tax
Income Account	46000 – Merchandise Sales
Asset Account	12100 – Inventory Asset
Qty on Hand	0.00 as of 01/01/2021

Step 2: Export to **Excel** or **print** the Item List as of January 1, 2021. (Use **Report Center > List > Item Listing**. If necessary, *uncheck* **Space between columns** and use settings specified in the Excel template instructions.)

CREATE A SALES TAX ITEM

A merchandiser selling products to consumers must charge sales tax. A sales tax item is created in the Item List with the rate and tax agency information.

To enter a sales tax item:

Step 1: In the *Item List* window, **double-click** on **State Sales Tax**.

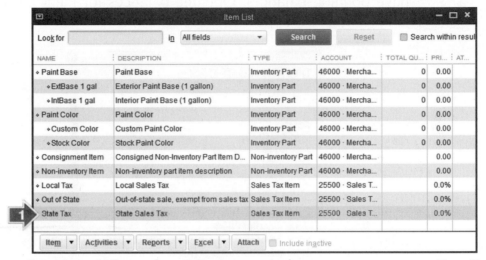

Step 2: When the *Edit Item* window appears, enter Tax Rate: **7.75%**.

Step 3: Enter Tax Agency: **California State Board of Equalization**.

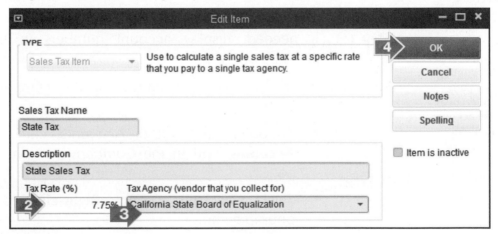

Step 4: Click **OK**.

Step 5: If a *Vendor Not Found* window appears, select: **Quick Add**. If necessary, click **OK** again to close the *Edit Item* window.

CUSTOMIZE CHART OF ACCOUNTS

Based on your answers in the EasyStep Interview, QuickBooks automatically creates a Chart of Accounts for Paint Palette Store. You can customize the Chart of Accounts to suit your specific business needs.

Because you are purchasing an existing business, some accounts have opening balances. Opening balances for Paint Palette Store at January 1, 2021, appear as follows.

> THE PAINT PALETTE STORE
> Balance Sheet
>
> Assets:
> Checking $2,400
> Supplies on hand $600
> Store fixtures $5,000
> Paint mixing equipment $4,000
> Total assets $12,000
>
> Liabilities & equity:
> Notes payable $1,000
> Capital stock (opening balance equity) $11,000
> Total liabilities & equity $12,000

You purchased $5,000 in stock and John and Joseph each purchased $3,000 in stock for a total of $11,000.

To display account numbers select **Edit** menu > **Preferences > Accounting > Company Preferences > Use account numbers**.

Customize the Chart of Accounts and enter opening balances as follows:

Step 1: If needed, display account numbers in the Chart of Accounts.

Step 2: Enter the opening balance for the company Checking account:

- To open the Chart of Accounts, click the **Chart of Accounts** icon in the *Company* section of the Home page.
- Select **Checking** account. **Right-click** to display the pop-up menu.
- Select **Edit Account**.
- When the *Edit Account* window for the Checking account appears, enter Account No.: **10100**.

Enter opening balances when you customize the Chart of Accounts.

- Select **Enter Opening Balance**. Enter Statement Ending Balance: **$2,400**. Statement Ending Date: **01/01/2021**. Click **OK**.

- Click **Save & Close** to close the *Edit Account* window.

Step 3: Add the following accounts and opening balances to the Chart of Accounts. Abbreviate account titles as shown.

Account No.	26000
Account Type	Other Current Liability
Account Name	Notes Payable
Account Description	Notes Payable
Tax Line	B/S-Liabs/Eq.: Other current liabilities
Opening Balance	$1,000 as of 01/01/2021

Account No.	12500
Account Type	Other Current Asset
Account Name	Supplies on Hand
Account Description	Supplies on Hand
Tax Line	B/S-Assets: Other current assets
Opening Balance	$600 as of 01/01/2021

Account No.	14000
Account Type	Fixed Asset
Account Name	Store Fixtures
Account Description	Store Fixtures
Tax Line	B/S-Assets: Buildings/oth. depr. assets
Opening Balance	$0 as of 01/01/2021

Account No.	14100
Account Type	Fixed Asset
Account Name	Store Fixtures Cost
Subaccount of	Store Fixtures
Account Description	Store Fixtures Cost
Tax Line	B/S-Assets: Buildings/oth. depr. assets
Opening Balance	$5,000 as of 01/01/2021

Account No.	14200
Account Type	Fixed Asset
Account Name	Accumulated Depr Store Fixtures
Subaccount of	Store Fixtures
Account Description	Accumulated Depr Store Fixtures
Tax Line	B/S-Assets: Buildings/oth. depr. assets
Opening Balance	$0 as of 01/01/2021

Account No.	14300
Account Type	Fixed Asset
Account Name	Paint Mixing Equipment
Account Description	Paint Mixing Equipment
Tax Line	B/S-Assets: Buildings/oth. depr. assets
Opening Balance	$0 as of 01/01/2021

Account No.	14400
Account Type	Fixed Asset
Account Name	Paint Mixing Equipment Cost
Subaccount of	Paint Mixing Equipment
Account Description	Paint Mixing Equipment Cost
Tax Line	B/S-Assets: Buildings/oth. depr. assets
Opening Balance	$4,000 as of 01/01/2021

Account No.	14500
Account Type	Fixed Asset
Account Name	Acc Depr Paint Mixing Equipment

Subaccount of	Paint Mixing Equipment
Account Description	Acc Depr Paint Mixing Equipment
Tax Line	B/S-Assets: Buildings/oth. depr. assets
Opening Balance	$0 as of 01/01/2021

Account No.	14600
Account Type	Fixed Asset
Account Name	Color Match Equipment
Account Description	Color Match Equipment
Tax Line	B/S-Assets: Buildings/oth. depr. assets
Opening Balance	$0 as of 01/01/2021

Account No.	14700
Account Type	Fixed Asset
Account Name	Color Match Equipment Cost
Subaccount of	Color Match Equipment
Account Description	Color Match Equipment Cost
Tax Line	B/S-Assets: Buildings/oth. depr. assets
Opening Balance	$0 as of 01/01/2021

Account No.	14800
Account Type	Fixed Asset
Account Name	Acc Depr Color Match Equipment
Subaccount of	Color Match Equipment
Account Description	Acc Depr Color Match Equipment
Tax Line	B/S-Assets: Buildings/oth. depr. assets
Opening Balance	$0 as of 01/01/2021

Account No.	64800
Account Type	Expense
Account Name	Supplies Expense
Account Description	Supplies Expense
Tax Line	Other Deductions: Supplies

PURCHASING TRANSACTION CYCLE

The purchasing transaction cycle for a merchandising company consists of the following transactions:

1. Create a purchase order to order inventory.

2. Receive the inventory items ordered and update inventory.

3. Enter the bill in QuickBooks when the bill is received.

4. Pay the bill.

5. Print the check.

Next, you will record each of the above transactions in the purchasing cycle for Paint Palette Store.

CREATE A PURCHASE ORDER

The first step in the purchasing cycle is to create a purchase order which is sent to the vendor to order inventory. The purchase order provides a record of the type and quantity of item ordered.

Paint Palette Store needs to order 50 gallons of Interior Base Paint. To order the paint, Paint Palette Store must create a purchase order indicating the item and quantity desired.

To create a purchase order in QuickBooks:

Step 1: Click the **Purchase Orders** icon in the *Vendors* section of the Home page.

Step 2: Select Vendor: **Brewer Paint Supplies**.

Step 3: Select Template: **Custom Purchase Order**.

Step 4: Enter Date: **01/03/2021**.

Step 5: Enter the item ordered, by selecting Item: **Interior Paint Base (1 gallon)**.

Step 6: Enter Quantity: **50**.

Step 7: Select: **Print Later**.

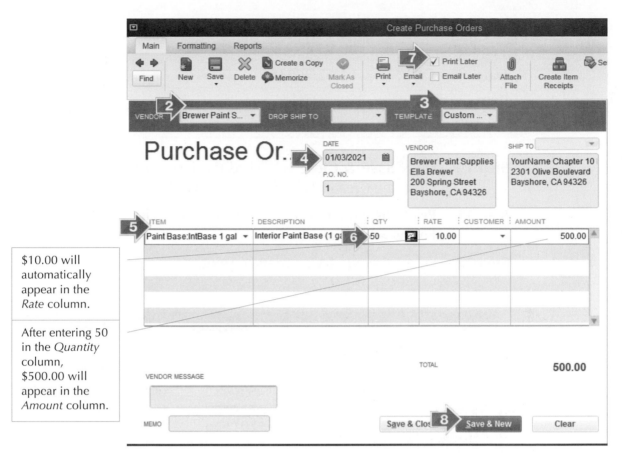

Step 8: Click **Save & New** to record the purchase order and advance to a blank purchase order.

Step 9: Create purchase orders for the following inventory items for Paint Palette Store.

Vendor	Brewer Paint Supplies
Date	01/05/2021
Item	Exterior Paint Base (1 gallon)
Quantity	40

Vendor	Shades of Santiago
Date	01/10/2021
Item	Custom Color
Quantity	25 (cartons)
Item	Stock Color
Quantity	5 (cartons)

Vendor	Brewer Paint Supplies
Date	01/12/2021
Item	Stock Color
Quantity	10 (cartons)

Step 10: Click **Save & Close** to record the last purchase order and close the *Create Purchase Orders* window.

Step 11: **Print** the purchase orders by selecting **File** menu **> Print Forms > Purchase Orders**.

Step 12: Select the purchase orders to print.

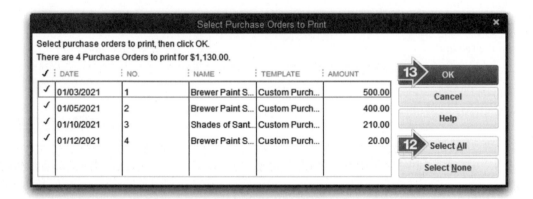

Step 13: Click **OK**.

Step 14: Select print settings: **Blank paper** and uncheck **Do not print lines around each field**.

Step 15: Click **Print**.

RECEIVE INVENTORY ITEMS

When the inventory items that have been ordered are received, record their receipt in QuickBooks. QuickBooks will then add the items received to the Inventory account.

On January 12, 2021, Paint Palette Store received 40 gallons of interior paint base from Brewer Paint Supplies.

To record the inventory items received from Brewer Paint Supplies:

Step 1: Click the **Receive Inventory** icon in the *Vendors* section of the Home page. Select **Receive Inventory without Bill**.

Step 2: When the *Create Item Receipts* window appears, select Vendor: **Brewer Paint Supplies**.

Step 3: If a purchase order for the vendor exists, QuickBooks displays the following *Open POs Exist* window. Click **Yes** to receive against an open purchase order for Brewer Paint Supplies.

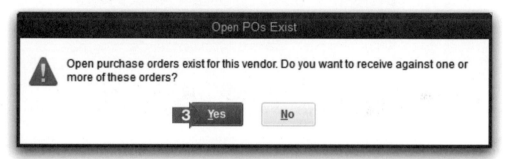

Step 4: When the following *Open Purchase Orders* window appears, select **Purchase Order No. 1** dated **01/03/2021**.

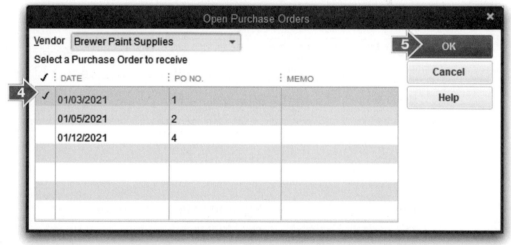

Step 5: Click **OK**.

Step 6: The following *Create Item Receipts* window will appear. Enter Date: **01/12/2021**.

Step 7: The quantity received (40 gallons) differs from the quantity ordered (50 gallons). Enter Quantity: **40**.

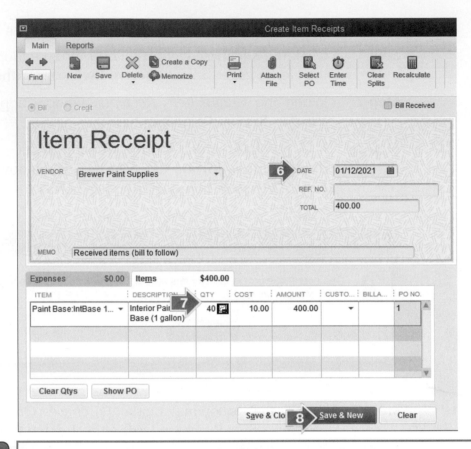

 Total for items received is $400.00.

Step 8: Click **Save & New** on the *Create Item Receipts* window to record the paint received and advance to a blank screen.

Step 9: Record the following inventory items received.

Vendor	Brewer Paint Supplies
Date	01/13/2021
PO No.	2
Item	1 gallon Exterior Paint Base
Quantity	40

Vendor	Brewer Paint Supplies
Date	01/14/2021
PO No.	4
Item	Stock Color
Quantity	10 (cartons)

Vendor	Shades of Santiago
Date	01/15/2021
PO No.	3
Item	Custom Color
Quantity	25 (cartons)
Item	Stock Color
Quantity	5 (cartons)

Step 10: Click **Save & Close** to record the items received and close the *Create Item Receipts* window.

Step 11: Export to **Excel** or **print** the Item Listing from the Report Center as of January 15, 2021, showing the quantity on hand for each item in inventory.

Enter Bills

Bills can be entered in QuickBooks when the bill is received or when the bill is paid. (For more information, see Chapter 5.)

Paint Palette Store will enter bills in QuickBooks when bills are received. At that time, QuickBooks records an obligation to pay the bill later (account payable). QuickBooks tracks bills due. If you use the reminder feature, QuickBooks will even remind you when it is time to pay bills.

Paint Palette Store previously received 40 1-gallon cans of interior paint base. To record the bill when it is received:

+
If the items and the bill were received at the same time, use the *Receive Item with Bill* window.

Step 1: Click the **Enter Bills Against Inventory** icon in the *Vendors* section of the Home page.

Step 2: When the following *Select Item Receipt* window appears, select Vendor: **Brewer Paint Supplies**.

Step 3: Select Item Receipt corresponding to the bill (**Date: 01/12/2021**).

Step 4: Click **OK**.

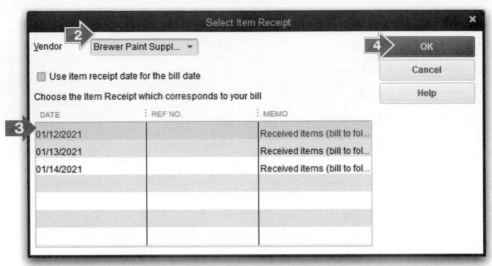

Step 5: When the following *Enter Bills* window appears, make any necessary changes. In this case, change the date to **01/15/2021** (the date the bill was received).

✚
The *Enter Bills* window is the same as the *Create Item Receipts* window except:
1. *Bill* stamp appears in the upper left instead of *Item Receipt* stamp.
2. *Bill Received* in the upper right corner is checked.

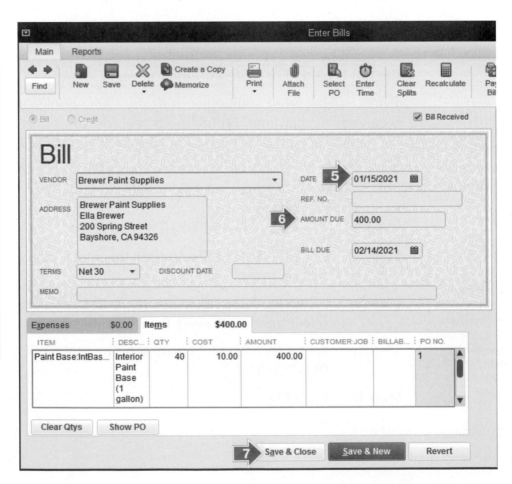

Step 6: The Amount Due of **$400.00** should agree with the amount shown on the vendor's bill received.

Step 7: Click **Save & Close**.

Step 8: Record the following bills against inventory that Paint Palette Store received.

Vendor	Brewer Paint Supplies
Date Bill Received	01/16/2021
Terms	Net 30
PO No.	2
Item	Exterior Paint Base (1 gallon)
Quantity	40

Vendor	Shades of Santiago
Date Bill Received	01/16/2021
Terms	Net 30
PO No.	3
Item	Custom Color
Quantity	25 cartons
Item	Stock Color
Quantity	5 cartons

Step 9: Click the **Enter Bills** icon to enter the Hartzheim Leasing bill for January rent.

Click the **Expenses** tab to record.

With the *Enter Bills* window still open, click the **Memorize** icon.

Vendor	Hartzheim Leasing
Date Bill Received	01/16/2021
Terms	Net 30
Amount Due	$1,000.00
Account	67100 Rent Expense

Step 10: Record the bill for rent as a memorized transaction.

Step 11: Click **Save & Close** to record the bill and close the *Enter Bills* window.

When you enter bills, QuickBooks automatically adds the amount of the bill to Accounts Payable, reflecting your obligation to pay the bills later.

PAY BILLS

After receiving an inventory item and entering the bill in QuickBooks, the next step is to pay the bill when due. To pay the bill, select bills to pay, then print the checks. Paint Palette Store will pay the bills for paint and paint color that have been received and recorded.

To pay bills in QuickBooks:

Step 1: Click the **Pay Bills** icon on the Home page.

Step 2: When the *Pay Bills* window appears:

- Select: **Show All Bills**.
- Select bills from **Brewer Paint Supplies** and **Shades of Santiago**.
- Select **Checking** account.
- Select Payment Method: **To be Printed**.
- Select Payment Date: **01/31/2021**.

Step 3: Click **Pay Selected Bills** to close the *Pay Bills* window.

PRINT CHECKS

After selecting bills to pay, you can prepare checks in two different ways:

1. Write the checks manually, or

2. Print the checks using QuickBooks. If you use QuickBooks to print checks, preprinted check forms are inserted in the printer before printing.

If the *Payment Summary* window does not appear automatically, to print checks:

QuickBooks prints one check for each vendor, combining all amounts due the same vendor.

Step 1: Select **File** menu **> Print Forms > Checks**.

Step 2: Select **Checking** account.

Step 3: First Check No.: **402**.

Step 4: Select checks to print: **Brewer Paint Supplies** and **Shades of Santiago**. Then click **OK**.

Step 5: Select printer settings, then click **Print**.

RECORD SALES TRANSACTIONS

The sales cycle for a merchandising company consists of the following transactions:

1. Create an invoice to record the sale and bill the customer.

2. Receive the customer payments.

3. Deposit the customer payments in the bank.

Next, you will record each of these transactions in QuickBooks for Paint Palette Store.

CREATE INVOICES

When inventory is sold to a customer, the sale is recorded on an invoice in QuickBooks. The invoice lists the items sold, the quantity, and the price. In addition, if the product is sold to a retail customer, sales tax is automatically added to the invoice.

To create an invoice:

Step 1: Click the **Create Invoices** icon on the Home page.

Step 2: Using the Intuit Product Invoice Template, create and **print** invoices for the following sales made by Paint Palette Store.

Sale of 3 gallons of custom color interior paint to Katrina Beneficio:

Date	01/20/2021
Customer	Katrina Beneficio: Custom Paint
Terms	Net 30
Quantity	3 gallons
Item Code	Interior Paint Base (1 gallon)
Price Each	25.00
Quantity	3

Item Code	Custom Color
Price Each	6.00
Print Later	Yes
Tax	State Tax

 The invoice total for Katrina Beneficio is $100.21.

Sale of 10 gallons of stock color interior paint to Decor Centre:

Date	01/22/2021
Customer	Decor Centre: Custom & Stock Paint
Terms	Net 30
Quantity	10 gallons
Item Code	Interior Paint Base (1 gallon)
Price Each	20.00
Quantity	10
Item Code	Stock Color
Price Each	3.50
Print Later	Yes
Tax Code	Non

Sale of 5 gallons stock color interior paint and 2 gallons customer color exterior paint to Cara Interiors:

Date	01/25/2021
Customer	Cara Interiors: Custom & Stock Paint
Terms	Net 30
Quantity	5 gallons
Item Code	Interior Paint Base (1 gallon)
Price Each	20.00
Quantity	5
Item Code	Stock Color

Price Each	3.50
Quantity	2 gallons
Item Code	Exterior Paint Base (1 gallon)
Price Each	22.00
Quantity	2
Item Code	Custom Color
Price Each	5.00
Print Later	Yes
Tax Code	Non

RECEIVE PAYMENTS

When a credit sale is recorded, QuickBooks records an account receivable at the time the invoice is created. The account receivable is the amount that Paint Palette Store expects to receive from the customer later.

If a customer pays cash at the time of sale, it can be recorded using the Sales Receipts window.

To record a payment received from a customer:

Step 1: Click the **Receive Payments** icon in the *Customers* section of the Home page.

Step 2: Record the following payments received by Paint Palette Store from customers.

Date Received	01/30/2021
Customer	Katrina Beneficio: Custom Paint
Amount Received	100.21
Payment Method	Check
Check No.	1001

Date Received	01/31/2021
Customer	Cara Interiors: Custom & Stock Paint
Amount Received	171.50
Payment Method	Check
Check No.	4567

MAKE DEPOSITS

When the customer's payment is deposited in Paint Palette Store's Checking account, record the bank deposit in QuickBooks.

To record a bank deposit:

Step 1: Click the **Record Deposits** icon in the *Banking* section of the Home page.

Step 2: On January 31, 2021, record the deposit of customer payments received from **Katrina Beneficio** and **Cara Interiors**. Select Deposit To: **Checking**.

Step 3: **Print** the deposit summary.

MAKE ADJUSTING ENTRIES

Before preparing financial statements for Paint Palette Store for January, print a Trial Balance and make adjusting entries to bring the accounts up to date.

Step 1: Export to **Excel** or **print** the Trial Balance for Paint Palette Store at January 31, 2021.

Step 2: Make adjusting entries for Paint Palette Store at January 31, 2021, using the following information.

- **ADJ1**: The store fixtures cost of $5,000 will be depreciated over a 10-year useful life with no salvage value. Depreciation expense is $42 per month.

- **ADJ2**: The paint mixing equipment cost of $4,000 will be depreciated over a 5-year useful life with no salvage value. Depreciation expense is $67 per month.

- **ADJ3**: The computer paint color match equipment cost of $1,000 will be depreciated over a four-year useful life with no salvage value. Depreciation expense is $21 per month.

- **ADJ4**: A count of supplies on hand at the end of January totaled $400. The Supplies on Hand account balance before adjustment is $600, so Supplies on Hand (Account 12500) should be decreased by $200. An adjusting entry is required to transfer $200 from the Supplies on Hand account to the Supplies Expense account. So the adjusting entry will increase (debit) Supplies Expense (Account 64800) by $200, and decrease (credit) Supplies on Hand (Account 12500) by $200.

- **ADJ5**: Interest on the notes payable balance is 1 percent per month. The adjusting entry to record interest expense for January 2021 and the liability for interest payable is $10. To record this adjustment, add Other Current Liability account: Account No. 21000 Interest Payable.

Step 3: From the Report Center, export to **Excel** or **print** the adjusting journal entries for Paint Palette Store for January 31, 2021.

Step 4: Export to **Excel** or **print** the Adjusted Trial Balance for Paint Palette Store at January 31, 2021.

Step 5: On the Adjusted Trial Balance, **highlight** any account balances affected by the adjusting entries.

 Total debits on the Adjusted Trial Balance equal $13,666.71.

PRINT REPORTS

 To eliminate the 0.00 appearing for accounts with zero balances, from the *General Ledger* report window, select **Customize Report** button **> Display > Advanced > In Use**.

Export to **Excel** or **print** the following reports for Paint Palette Store for the month of January 2021.

- General Ledger.
- Profit and Loss, Standard.
- Balance Sheet, Standard.
- Statement of Cash Flows. **Highlight** any amounts that you might classify differently than shown on the QuickBooks Statement of Cash Flows report.

After reviewing the financial statements for Paint Palette Store, what are your recommendations to improve financial performance?

SAVE CHAPTER 10

 Save a backup of your Chapter 10 file using the file name: **YourName Chapter 10 Backup.QBB**. See *Appendix B: Back Up & Restore QuickBooks Files* for instructions.

 ### WORKFLOW

If you are using the Workflow approach, leave your .QBW file open and proceed to Chapter 11.

 ### RESTART & RESTORE

If you are using the Restart & Restore approach and are ending your computer session now, close your .QBW file and exit QuickBooks. When you restart, you will restore your backup file to complete Chapter 11.

www.My-QuickBooks.com

Go to www.My-QuickBooks.com to view additional QuickBooks resources including Excel Reports Templates, QuickBooks videos, and QuickBooks Hot Arrows and Hot Topics. The Hot Topics can be viewed on your computer or tablet and feature frequently used QuickBooks tasks.

MULTIPLE-CHOICE PRACTICE TEST

Try the **Multiple-Choice Practice Test** for Chapter 10 on the *Computer Accounting with QuickBooks* Online Learning Center at www.mhhe.com/kay2015.

GO DIGITAL!

Go Digital using Excel templates. See *Appendix D: Go Digital with QuickBooks* for instructions about how to save your QuickBooks reports electronically.

LEARNING ACTIVITIES

Important: Ask your instructor whether you should complete the following assignments by printing reports or by exporting to Excel templates (see Appendix D: Go Digital with QuickBooks).

EXERCISE 10.1: BRITTANY'S YARNS

SCENARIO

Brittany, owner of Brittany's Yarns, has asked if you would be interested in maintaining the accounting records for her yarn shop. She would like to begin using QuickBooks software for her accounting records, converting from her current manual accounting system. After reaching agreement on your fee, Brittany gives you the following information to enter into QuickBooks.

TASK 1: NEW COMPANY SETUP

Step 1: Create a new company in QuickBooks for Brittany's Yarns using the following information.

Company name	YourName Exercise 10.1 Brittany's Yarns
Federal tax ID	37-1872613
Address	13 Isla Boulevard
City	Bayshore
State	CA
Zip	94326
Email	<enter your email address>
Industry	Retail Shop or Online Commerce
Type of organization	S Corporation
First month of fiscal year	January
File name	YourName Exercise 10.1
What do you sell?	Products only
Enter sales	Record each sale individually
Sales tax	Yes

Estimates	No
Sales orders	Yes
Billing statements	No
Progress invoicing	No
Track bills you owe	Yes
Track inventory in QuickBooks	Yes
Track time	Yes
Employees	No
Start date	01/01/2021
Use recommended income and expense accounts	Yes
Bank account name	Checking
Bank account number	3216549870
Bank account balance	0.00 as of 01/01/2021

Step 2: Click **Start Working** to exit QuickBooks Setup.

Step 3: Display account numbers in the Chart of Accounts.

TASK 2: ADD CUSTOMER & JOB

Step 1: Add Ella Brewer to Brittany's Yarns Customer List.

Customer	Brewer, Ella
Address Info:	
First Name	Ella
Last Name	Brewer
Main Phone	415-555-3600
Address	18 Spring Street Bayshore, CA 94326

Payment Settings:	
Account No.	10000
Payment Terms	Net 15
Preferred Payment Method	Check

Sales Tax Settings:	
Tax Code	Tax
Tax Item	State Tax

Step 2: Next add Suzanne Counte to Brittany's Yarns Customer List.

Customer	Counte, Suzanne
Address Info:	
First Name	Suzanne
Last Name	Counte
Main Phone	415-555-2160
Address	220 Johnson Avenue Bayshore, CA 94326

Payment Settings:	
Account No.	12000
Payment Terms	Net 15
Preferred Payment Method	Check

Sales Tax Settings:	
Tax Code	Tax
Tax Item	State Tax

Step 3: Click **OK**.

Step 4: From the Customer Center, export to **Excel** or **print** the Customer List.

Step 5: **Close** the Customer Center.

TASK 3: ADD VENDORS

Step 1: Add the following vendors to the Vendor List for Brittany's Yarns.

Vendor	Shahrzad Enterprises
Opening Balance	$0.00 as of 01/01/2021
Address Info:	
Company Name	Shahrzad Enterprises
First Name	Shahrzad
Main Phone	415-555-1270
Address	720 Yas Avenue Bayshore, CA 94326
Payment Settings:	
Account No.	2400
Payment Terms	Net 30
Tax Settings:	
Vendor Tax ID	37-3571595

Vendor	Hartzheim Leasing
Opening Balance	$0.00 as of 01/01/2021
Address Info:	
Company Name	Hartzheim Leasing
Full Name	Joe Hartzheim
Main Phone	415-555-0412
Address	13 Appleton Drive Bayshore, CA 94326
Payment Settings:	
Account No.	2500
Payment Terms	Net 30
Tax Settings:	
Vendor Tax ID	37-1726354
Additional Info:	
Vendor Type	Leasing

Vendor	Shufang's Supplies
Opening balance	$0.00 as of 01/01/2021
Address Info:	
Company Name	Shufang's Supplies
First Name	Shufang
Main Phone	415-555-1700
Address	5 Austin Drive Bayshore, CA 94326
Payment Settings:	
Account No.	2600
Payment Terms	Net 30
Tax Settings:	
Vendor Tax ID	37-1599515

Step 2: From the Vendor Center, export to **Excel** or **print** the Vendor List.

TASK 4: ADD ITEMS

Step 1: Add the following items for Brittany's Yarns.

Item Type	Inventory Part
Item Name	Alpaca Yarn
Description	Alpaca Yarn 3 ply
Income Account	46000 – Merchandise Sales

Item Type	Inventory Part
Item Name	Alpaca Yarn Creme
Subitem of	Alpaca Yarn
Description	Alpaca Yarn Creme
Sales Price	10.00 (per skein)
Income Account	46000 – Merchandise Sales

Item Type	Inventory Part
Item Name	Alpaca Yarn Earthen Tweed

Subitem of	Alpaca Yarn
Description	Alpaca Yarn Earthen Tweed
Sales Price	12.00 (per skein)
Income Account	46000 – Merchandise Sales

Item Type	Inventory Part
Item Name	Peruvian Wool
Description	Peruvian Wool Yarn 4 ply
Income Account	46000 – Merchandise Sales

Item Type	Inventory Part
Item Name	Peruvian Wool Yarn Charcoal
Subitem of	Peruvian Wool
Description	Peruvian Wool Yarn Charcoal
Sales Price	20.00 (per skein)
Income Account	46000 – Merchandise Sales

Item Type	Inventory Part
Item Name	Peruvian Wool Yarn Black
Subitem of	Peruvian Wool
Description	Peruvian Wool Yarn Black
Sales Price	25.00 (per skein)
Income Account	46000 – Merchandise Sales

Step 2: From the Item List, enter the 7.75% sales tax rate as follows:

- **Double-click** on **State Tax** in the Item List.
- Enter Tax Rate: **7.75%.**
- Enter Tax Agency: **California State Board of Equalization**.
- Click **OK**.

Step 3: Export to **Excel** (without spaces between columns) or **print** the Item List as of January 1, 2021. (Use **Report Center > List > Item Listing**.)

TASK 5: CUSTOMIZE CHART OF ACCOUNTS

Edit the Chart of Accounts and enter opening balances as follows:

Step 1: Enter the opening balance of $1,300 for the company Checking account:

- To open the Chart of Accounts, click the **Chart of Accounts** icon in the *Company* section of the Home page.

- Select **Checking** account. **Right-click** to display the pop-up menu.

- Select **Edit Account**.

- When the *Edit Account* window for the Checking account appears, enter Account No.: **10100**.

- Enter Opening Balance: **$1,300** as of **01/01/2021**.

- Click **OK**.

Step 2: Enter the opening balance of **$1,800** for the Inventory Asset account.

Step 3: Add the following Notes Payable account and opening balance of $800 to the Chart of Accounts.

Account No.	26000
Account Type	Other Current Liability
Account Name	Notes Payable
Account Description	Notes Payable
Tax Line	B/S-Liabs/Eq.: Other current liabilities
Opening Balance	$800 as of 01/01/2021

Step 4: From the Report Center, export to **Excel** or **print** the Chart of Accounts (Account Listing) report as of January 1, 2021, with opening balances for Brittany's Yarns.

Step 5: Export to **Excel** or **print** a Trial Balance report for Brittany's Yarns dated **01/01/2021**. Compare your Trial Balance to the following to verify your account balances are correct.

> *Checking equals $1,300.00 (debit balance).*
> *Inventory Asset equals $1,800.00 (debit balance).*
> *Notes Payable equals $800.00 (credit balance).*
> *Opening Balance Equity equals $2,300.00.*
> *Total debits and total credits equal $3,100.00.*

Step 6: Transfer the Opening Balance Equity account balance to the Capital Stock account using a journal entry. Use Entry No.: **Open ADJ1**.

Step 7: Export to **Excel** or **print** the Adjusted Trial Balance (after opening adjustments) to verify that the Opening Balance Equity account balance was transferred to the Capital Stock account.

TASK 6: ENTER TRANSACTIONS

Brittany's Yarns entered into the following transactions during January 2021.

Step 1: Record the transactions for Brittany's Yarns.

- Record all deposits to: **Checking**. If necessary, change the Make Deposits default to Checking (select **Edit** menu > **Preferences > Checking > My Preferences > Open the Make Deposits form with 10100 Checking account**).

- **Print** invoices, checks, purchase orders, and deposit summaries as appropriate. Use memorized transactions for recurring transactions.

Date	Transaction
01/01/2021	Brittany paid $600 store rent to Hartzheim Leasing (Check No. 1001).
01/02/2021	Purchased $300 of office supplies on account from Shufang's Supplies.
01/13/2021	Placed the following order with Shahrzad Enterprises. ■ 10 skeins of Alpaca creme yarn at a cost of $4 each ■ 20 skeins of Alpaca earthen tweed yarn at a cost of $4.80 each
01/15/2021	Received Alpaca yarn ordered on 01/13/2021.
01/19/2021	Sold to Suzanne Counte on account 6 skeins of Alpaca creme yarn and 8 skeins of Alpaca earthen tweed yarn.
01/19/2021	Received bill from Shahrzad Enterprises for Alpaca yarn received on 01/15/2021.
01/21/2021	Ordered the following yarn from Shahrzad Enterprises on account. ■ 20 skeins of Peruvian wool charcoal @ $8 each ■ 12 skeins of Peruvian wool black @ $10 each
01/23/2021	Received the Peruvian wool yarn ordered on 01/21/2021.
01/25/2021	Sold 13 skeins of Peruvian wool charcoal and 5 skeins of Peruvian wool black to Ella Brewer on account.
01/25/2021	Paid Shahrzad Enterprises for bill received on 01/19/2021 for Alpaca yarn (Check No. 1002).
01/25/2021	Received and deposited to the Checking account the customer payment from Suzanne Counte for sale of Alpaca yarn on 01/19/2021 (Check No. 1200).
01/27/2021	Paid $300 bill from Shufang's Supplies (Check No. 1003).

Use *Write Checks* window, then create a memorized transaction.

Use *Enter Bills* window to record Office Supplies Expense.

Click **Yes** if asked to update cost.

Use *Create Invoices* window.

Step 2: Export to **Excel** or **print** the Deposit Detail report for January 2021.

Step 3: Export to **Excel** or **print** the Check Detail report for January 2021.

TASK 7: ADJUSTING ENTRIES

Step 1: Export to **Excel** or **print** the Trial Balance report for Brittany's Yarns at January 31, 2021.

Step 2: Make adjusting entries for Brittany's Yarns at January 31, 2021, using the following information.

- **ADJ1**: A count of supplies revealed $180 of supplies on hand. Since $300 of supplies were recorded as Office Supplies Expense when purchased and $180 still remain on hand unused, it is necessary to transfer $180 into an asset account, Office Supplies on Hand. Add a new account: **12500 Office Supplies on Hand** as Account Type: **Other Current Asset**. Make the adjusting entry to transfer $180 from the Office Supplies Expense account to the Office Supplies on Hand account, an asset.

- **ADJ2**: Make an adjusting entry to record Interest Expense and Interest Payable for $7.00. Add a new account: **21000 Interest Payable** as Account Type: **Other Current Liability**.

Step 3: From the Report Center, export to **Excel** or **print** the Adjusting Journal Entries for January 31, 2021.

Step 4: Export to **Excel** or **print** the Adjusted Trial Balance report for Brittany's Yarns at January 31, 2021.

Step 5: On the Adjusted Trial Balance report, **highlight** the amounts affected by the adjusting entries.

TASK 8: FINANCIAL REPORTS

Export to **Excel** or **print** the following reports for Brittany's Yarns.

- General Ledger for the month of January 2021. (Remember to omit unused accounts with zero balances.)

- Profit & Loss, Standard for the month of January 2021.

- Balance Sheet, Standard at January 31, 2021.
- Statement of Cash Flows for the month of January 2021.

TASK 9: SAVE EXERCISE 10.1

Save a backup of your Exercise file using the file name: **YourName Exercise 10.1 Backup.QBB**. See *Appendix B: Back Up & Restore QuickBooks Files* for instructions.

WORKFLOW

Exercise 11.1 is a continuation of Exercise 10.1.

RESTART & RESTORE

If you use the restart and restore approach, you will restore your .QBB file when you restart Exercise 11.1.

EXERCISE 10.2 WHAT'S NEW

Explore an app that streamlines accounting data entry and integrates with QuickBooks software.

Step 1: In the *My Shortcuts* section, select **App Center**.

Step 2: **Print** the information about Concur, an expense management app that syncs with QuickBooks.

EXERCISE 10.3: WEB QUEST

When setting up a Chart of Accounts for a business, it is helpful to review the tax form that the business will use. Then accounts can be used to track information needed for the business tax return.

The tax form used by the type of organization is listed below.

Type of Organization	Tax Form
Sole Proprietorship	Schedule C (Form 1040)
Partnership	Form 1065
Corporation	Form 1120
S Corporation	Form 1120S

In this exercise, you will download the tax form for a Subchapter S corporation from the Internal Revenue Service website.

Step 1:   Go to the Internal Revenue Service website: www.irs.gov.

Step 2:   Using the IRS website, find and **print** Form 1120S: U.S. Income Tax Return for an S Corporation.

CHAPTER 10 QUICK CHECK
NAME:
INSTRUCTIONS:
1. **CHECK OFF THE ITEMS YOU COMPLETED.**
2. **TURN IN THIS PAGE WITH YOUR PRINTOUTS.**

<table>
<tr><td>!</td></tr>
<tr><td>Ask your instructor if you should Go Digital (Excel* or PDF) or use paper printouts.</td></tr>
</table>

CHAPTER 10
- ☐ * Customer List
- ☐ * Vendor List
- ☐ * Item List
- ☐ * Chart of Accounts (Account Listing)
- ☐ * Trial Balance
- ☐ * Opening Adjusted Trial Balance
- ☐ * Balance Sheet Beginning
- ☐ Check No. 401
- ☐ Purchase Orders
- ☐ * Item List: Quantity on Hand
- ☐ Check Nos. 402 and 403
- ☐ Invoices
- ☐ Deposit Summary
- ☐ * Trial Balance
- ☐ * Adjusting Journal Entries
- ☐ * Adjusted Trial Balance
- ☐ * General Ledger
- ☐ * Profit & Loss
- ☐ * Balance Sheet
- ☐ * Statement of Cash Flows
- ☐ Analysis and Recommendations

EXERCISE 10.1
- ☐ * Task 2: Customer List
- ☐ * Task 3: Vendor List
- ☐ * Task 4: Item List
- ☐ * Task 5: Chart of Accounts
- ☐ * Task 5: Trial Balance
- ☐ * Task 5: Opening Adjusted Trial Balance

☐   Task 6: Purchase Orders

☐   Task 6: Checks

☐   Task 6: Invoices

☐   Task 6: Deposit Summary

☐ * Task 6: Deposit Detail

☐ * Task 6: Check Detail

☐ * Task 7: Trial Balance

☐ * Task 7: Adjusting Journal Entries

☐ * Task 7: Adjusted Trial Balance

☐ * Task 8: General Ledger

☐ * Task 8: Profit & Loss

☐ * Task 8: Balance Sheet

☐ * Task 8: Statement of Cash Flows

EXERCISE 10.2

☐   What's New

EXERCISE 10.3

☐   Form 1120S: U.S. Income Tax Return S Corporation

Download Excel templates at www.My-QuickBooks.com.

REFLECTION: A WISH AND A STAR

Reflection improves learning and retention. Reflect on what you have learned after completing Chapter 10 that you did not know before you started the chapter.

A Star:

What did you like best that you learned about QuickBooks in Chapter 10?

A Wish:

If you could pick one thing, what do you wish you knew more about when using QuickBooks?

PROJECT 10 RONEN ENTERPRISES

To complete this project, download the Chapter 10 Excel Reports template at www.My-QuickBooks.com *and follow the template instructions.*

Ronen Enterprises sells smartphone accessories including earbuds, bluetooth earpieces, portable speakers, and cases. The company is converting from a manual accounting system to QuickBooks software beginning January 2021.

1. Download the Chapter 10 Excel Reports template. Save the Excel file using the file name: **YourLastName FirstName CH10 REPORTS**.

2. Set up a new company file for Ronen Enterprises.

Company:	YourName Project 10 Ronen Enterprises
Tax ID:	30-1958546
Address:	45 Seminole Way, Bayshore, CA 94326
Main Phone:	415-555-2223
Email:	<your email address>
Industry:	Retail Shop or Online Commerce
Type of Organization:	S Corporation
First Month of Fiscal Year:	January
File Name:	YourName Project 10
What do you sell?	Products only
Enter Sales?	Record each sale individually
Sales Tax?	Yes
Estimates?	No
Sales Orders?	No
Billing Statements?	No
Invoices?	Yes
Progress Invoicing?	No
Track Bills?	Yes
Track Inventory?	Yes
Track Time?	Yes
Employees?	No
Start Date?	01/01/2021
Use Recommended Accts?	Yes
Bank Account Name	Checking
Bank Account Number	7894561230
Bank Account Balance	0.00 as of 01/01/2021

3. Set preferences as follows:

    a. Sales tax preferences to Your Most Common Sales Tax Item: **Out of State**.

    b. Accounting preferences to display account numbers in the Chart of Accounts.

    c. Accounting preferences to uncheck Warn if transactions are 30 day(s) in the future.

    d. Checking preferences to Open the Make Deposits form with **10100 Checking** account.

4. Add the following information to the Chart of Accounts.

    a. Add the following account number and beginning balance for the company Checking account.

Account	Account No.	Statement Ending Balance	Statement Ending Date
Checking	10100	$10,000	01/01/2021

    b. Add the following accounts and opening balances to the Chart of Accounts.

Account No.	Account Title	Account Type	Subaccount of:	Account Description	Tax Line	Opening Balance
26000	Notes Payable	Other Current Liability		Notes Payable	B/S-Liabs/Eq: Other current liabilities	$2,500 as of 01/01/2021
12500	Office Supplies on Hand	Other Current Asset		Office Supplies on Hand	B/S-Assets: Other current assets	$250 as of 01/01/2021
64800	Office Supplies Expense	Expense		Office Supplies Expense	Other Deductions: Supplies	
14000	Store Fixtures	Fixed Asset		Store Fixtures	B/S-Assets: Buildings/oth depr assets	$0 as of 01/01/2021
14100	Store Fixtures Cost	Fixed Asset	Store Fixtures	Store Fixtures Cost	B/S-Assets: Buildings/oth depr assets	$4,000 as of 01/01/2021
14200	Acc Depr Store Fixtures	Fixed Asset	Store Fixtures	Acc Depr Store Fixtures	B/S-Assets: Buildings/oth depr assets	$0 as of 01/01/2021

    c. Using the Report Center and your saved Excel template and the template instructions, export to **Excel** (without spaces between columns) the Chart of Accounts (Account Listing) as of January 1, 2021.

5. Use the following information to create a Customer List.

Customer Company Name	Address/Phone	Full Name	Acct No.	Terms	Preferred Payment Method	Tax Code	Tax Item	Type
Hudson, Thea	12 Castle Dr Bayshore, CA 94326 415-555-5253	Thea Hudson	1001	Net 15	Check	Tax	State Tax	Residential
Holcomb Health Foods	15 Stanford Dr Bayshore, CA 94326 415-555-6213	Ann Holcomb	1002	Net 15	Check	Non		Commercial
Etzkin Realty	98 Cleveland St Bayshore, CA 94326 415-555-5521	Brian Etzkin	1003	Net 15	Check	Non		Commercial

6. From the Customer Center, export to **Excel** the Customer List.

7. Enter the Vendor List using the following information.

Vendor Company Name	Address/Phone	First Name	Acct No.	Terms	Print on Check as	Type
Jackson Computer Services	723 Normal Ave Bayshore, CA 94326 415-555-6312	Keith	2001	Net 30	Jackson Computer Services	Service Providers
Lehde Cell Phone Supplies	45 Tiffany Lane Bayshore, CA 94326 415-555-4445	Eric	2002	Net 30	Lehde Cell Phone Supplies	Suppliers
Pitts Leasing	18 Jane Lane Bayshore, CA 94326 415-555-9498	Meredith	2003	Net 30	Pitts Leasing	Service Providers

8. From the Vendor Center, export to **Excel** the Vendor List.

9. Using the following information create an Item List.

Type	Item Name/ Description	Cost	COGS Account	Sales Price	Tax	Income Account	Asset Account	Qty on Hand
Inventory Part	Bluetooth Earpiece	$5.00	50000 – Cost of Goods Sold	$15.00	Tax	46000 – Merchandise Sales	12100 – Inventory Asset	0 as of 01/01/2021
Inventory Part	Cell Phone Case	$2.00	50000 – Cost of Goods Sold	$10.00	Tax	46000 – Merchandise Sales	12100 – Inventory Asset	0 as of 01/01/2021
Inventory Part	Portable Speakers	$9.00	50000 – Cost of Goods Sold	$20.00	Tax	46000 – Merchandise Sales	12100 – Inventory Asset	0 as of 01/01/2021

10. Edit the sales tax item to add the following:

   a. Sales tax rate: 7.75%

   b. Tax agency: California State Board of Equalization

11. From the Report Center, export to **Excel** the Item Listing as of January 1, 2021.

12. On January 1, 2021, transfer the Opening Balance Equity account balance of $11,750 to the Capital Stock account using a journal entry: Open ADJ1.

13. Record the following transactions. Make deposits to the Checking account.

Date	Transaction
01/01/2021	Paid $850 for store rent to Pitts Leasing (Check No. 501). (Use *Write Checks* window.)
01/02/2021	Ordered 200 Bluetooth earpieces, 250 cell phone cases, and 100 portable speakers from Lehde Cell Phone Supplies.
01/04/2021	Received items ordered from Lehde Cell Phone Supplies on 01/02/2021.
01/05/2021	Sold 50 Bluetooth earpieces and 50 cell phone cases to Etzkin Realty on account.
01/06/2021	Received bill from Lehde Cell Phone Supplies.
01/08/2021	Sold 80 Bluetooth earpieces and 100 cell phone cases to Holcomb Health Foods on account.
01/11/2021	Sold 20 portable speakers and 10 Bluetooth earpieces to Thea Hudson on account.
01/15/2021	Paid $75 for office supplies from Jackson Computer Services (Check No. 502). (Use the Office Supplies on Hand account. Record using the *Enter Bills* and *Pay Bills* windows.)
01/20/2021	Received and deposited $1,250 payment from Etzkin Realty (Check No. 906).
01/22/2021	Received and deposited $2,200 payment from Holcomb Health Foods (Check No. 787).
01/24/2021	Sold 50 Bluetooth earpieces and 10 portable speakers to Etzkin Realty on account.
01/25/2021	Ordered 100 Bluetooth earpieces from Lehde Cell Phone Supplies.
01/26/2021	Received and deposited $592.63 payment from Thea Hudson (Check No. 321).
01/27/2021	Received items ordered from Lehde Cell Phone Supplies on 01/25/2021.
01/28/2021	Received bill from Lehde Cell Phone Supplies.
01/29/2021	Sold 58 portable speakers and 2 cell phone cases to Holcomb Health Foods on account.
01/31/2021	Paid Lehde Cell Phone Supplies bill due on 02/05/2021 (Check No. 503).

14. Export to **Excel** the Trial Balance report at January 31, 2021.

15. Enter the following adjusting entries at January 31, 2021.

   - **ADJ1:** A count of office supplies revealed $225 on hand. (Hint: Debit Account No. 64800: Office Supplies Expense.)

   - **ADJ2**: January depreciation expense for store fixtures was $50.

   - **ADJ3**: Interest expense and interest payable on the Notes Payable equaled $22.00. Add Account No. 21000 Interest Payable (Other Current Liability).

16. Export to **Excel** the Adjusting Journal Entries report at January 31, 2021.

17. Export to **Excel** the Adjusted Trial Balance at January 31, 2021. **Highlight** the amounts affected by the adjusting journal entries.

18. Export to **Excel** a Profit and Loss Standard report for the month of January 2021.

19. Export to **Excel** a Balance Sheet Standard report at January 31, 2021.

20. Export to **Excel** the Statement of Cash Flows report for January 2021. **Highlight** any items that might appear differently than shown on the QuickBooks Statement of Cash Flows.

21. Export to **Excel** the Customer Balance Detail report for January 1-31, 2021.

22. Export to **Excel** the Vendor Balance Detail report for January 1-31, 2021.

23. Mark the reports completed on the Excel 10 REPORTS sheet. Save your Excel file.

24. Save a .QBB backup of your work.

PROJECT 10 QUICK CHECK

NAME:

INSTRUCTIONS:
1. CHECK OFF THE ITEMS YOU COMPLETED.
2. ATTACH THIS PAGE TO YOUR PRINTOUTS.

> **!**
> Ask your instructor if you should Go Digital (Excel* or PDF) or use paper printouts.

PROJECT 10

- ☐ * Chart of Accounts
- ☐ * Customer List
- ☐ * Vendor List
- ☐ * Item List
- ☐ * Trial Balance
- ☐ * Adjusting Entries
- ☐ * Adjusted Trial Balance
- ☐ * Profit & Loss
- ☐ * Balance Sheet
- ☐ * Statement of Cash Flows
- ☐ * Customer Balance Detail
- ☐ * Vendor Balance Detail

 Download Go Digital Excel templates at www.My-QuickBooks.com.

QuickBooks Case 10 Tomaso's Mowers & More

Scenario

On March 1, 2021, your friend Tomaso Moltissimo approaches you with another investment opportunity. He asks if you would like to buy stock in a business that sells lawn mowers and equipment. Tomaso would like to buy the business but needs additional investors.

Tomaso plans to invest $10,000 and you agree to invest $5,000 in the business. You also enter into an arrangement with Tomaso whereby you agree to help Tomaso with the accounting records for his new business in exchange for lawn service for your paint store.

Task 1: Set Up a New Company

Step 1: Create a new company in QuickBooks for Tomaso's Mowers & More using the following information.

Company name	YourName QB Case 10 Tomaso's Mowers & More
Legal name	YourName QB Case 10 Tomaso's Mowers & More
Federal tax ID	37-7879146
Address	2300 Olive Boulevard
City	Bayshore
State	CA
Zip	94326
Email	<your email address>
Industry	Retail Shop or Online Commerce
Type of organization	S Corporation
First month of fiscal year	January
File name	YourName QB Case 10
What do you sell?	Products only
Enter sales	Record each sale individually
Sales tax	Yes

Estimates	No
Sales orders	No
Billing statements	No
Invoices	Yes
Progress invoicing	No
Track bills	Yes
Track inventory	Yes
Track time	Yes
Employees	No
Start date	03/01/2021
Use recommended income and expense accounts?	Yes
Bank account name	Checking
Bank account number	4564564561
Bank account balance	0.00 as of 03/01/2021

Step 2: Click **Start Working** to exit QuickBooks Setup.

TASK 2: CUSTOMER LIST

From the Customer Center, create and export to **Excel** the Customer List for Tomaso's Mowers & More. If requested by your instructor, print the list.

Customer	Fowler, Gerry
Opening Balance	$200.00 as of 03/01/2021
Address Info:	
First Name	Gerry
Last Name	Fowler
Main Phone	415-555-9797
Mobile Phone	415-555-0599
Address	500 Lindell Blvd Bayshore, CA 94326

Payment Settings:	
Account No.	3001
Payment Terms	Net 30
Sales Tax Settings:	
Tax Code	Tax
Tax Item	State Tax
Additional Info:	
Customer Type	Residential

Select **Add New**.

Customer	Stanton, Mike
Opening Balance	$0.00 as of 03/01/2021
Address Info:	
First Name	Mike
Last Name	Stanton
Main Phone	415-555-7979
Mobile Phone	415-555-0596
Address	1000 Grand Avenue Bayshore, CA 94326
Payment Settings:	
Account No.	3002
Payment Terms	Net 30
Sales Tax Settings:	
Tax Code	Tax
Tax Item	State Tax
Additional Info:	
Customer Type	Residential

Customer	Grady's Bindery
Opening Balance	$0.00 as of 03/01/2021
Address Info:	
Company Name	Grady's Bindery
First Name	Mike
Last Name	Grady

Main Phone	415-555-7777
Address	700 Laclede Avenue Bayshore, CA 94326
Payment Settings:	
Account No.	3003
Payment Terms	Net 30
Sales Tax Settings:	
Tax Code	Tax
Tax Item	State Tax
Additional Info:	
Customer Type	Commercial

TASK 3: VENDOR LIST

From the Vendor Center, create and export to **Excel** the Vendor List for Tomaso's Mowers & More. If requested by your instructor, print the list.

Vendor	Astarte Supply
Opening Balance	$0 as of 03/01/2021
Address Info:	
Company Name	Astarte Supply
First Name	Freyja
Main Phone	415-555-0500
Address	100 Salem Road Bayshore, CA 94326
Payment Settings:	
Account No.	4001
Payment Terms	Net 30
Print on Check as	Astarte Supply
Credit Limit	20,000.00
Tax Settings:	
Vendor Tax ID	37-4327651
Additional Info:	
Vendor Type	Mowers

Vendor	Marcus Mower Sales & Repairs
Opening Balance	$0 as of 03/01/2021
Address Info:	
Company Name	Marcus Mower Sales & Repairs
First Name	Marcus
Main Phone	415-555-8222
Address	650 Manchester Road Bayshore, CA 94326
Payment Settings:	
Account No.	4002
Payment Terms	Net 30
Print on Check as	Marcus Mower Sales & Repairs
Credit Limit	10,000.00
Tax Settings:	
Vendor Tax ID	37-6510541
Additional Info:	
Vendor Type	Mowers

Vendor	Hartzheim Leasing
Opening Balance	$0 as of 03/01/2021
Address Info:	
Company Name	Hartzheim Leasing
Full Name	Joseph Hartzheim
Main Phone	415-555-0412
Address	13 Appleton Drive Bayshore, CA 94326
Payment Settings:	
Account No.	4003
Payment Terms	Net 30
Print on Check as	Hartzheim Leasing
Tax Settings:	
Vendor Tax ID	37-1726354
Additional Info:	
Vendor Type	Leasing

Task 4: Item List

Step 1: From the Item List, enter the 7.75% sales tax rate as follows:

- **Double-click** on **State Tax** in the Item List.
- Enter Tax Rate: **7.75%.**
- Enter Tax Agency: **California State Board of Equalization**.
- Click **OK**.

Step 2: Enter the following items in the Item List for Tomaso's Mowers & More. If necessary, display account numbers.

Item Type	Inventory Part
Item Name	Mowers
Description	Lawn Mowers
COGS Account	50000 – Cost of Goods Sold
Tax Code	Tax
Income Account	46000 – Merchandise Sales
Asset Account	12100 – Inventory Asset
Quantity on Hand	0 as of 03/01/2021

Item Type	Inventory Part
Item Name	Riding Mower
Subitem of	Mowers
Description	48" Riding Mower
Cost	2,000.00
COGS Account	50000 – Cost of Goods Sold
Tax Code	Tax
Sales Price	3800.00
Income Account	46000 – Merchandise Sales
Asset Account	12100 – Inventory Asset
Quantity on Hand	0 as of 03/01/2021

Item Type	Inventory Part
Item Name	Push Mower
Subitem of	Mowers
Description	Push Mower
Cost	400.00
COGS Account	50000 – Cost of Goods Sold
Tax Code	Tax
Sales Price	780.00
Income Account	46000 – Merchandise Sales
Asset Account	12100 – Inventory Asset
Quantity on Hand	0 as of 03/01/2021

Item Type	Inventory Part
Item Name	Propel Mower
Subitem of	Mowers
Description	Self Propelled Mower
Cost	600.00
COGS Account	50000 – Cost of Goods Sold
Tax Code	Tax
Sales Price	1150.00
Income Account	46000 – Merchandise Sales
Asset Account	12100 – Inventory Asset
Quantity on Hand	0 as of 03/01/2021

Item Type	Inventory Part
Item Name	Trimmer
Description	Lawn Trimmer
COGS Account	50000 – Cost of Goods Sold
Tax Code	Tax
Income Account	46000 – Merchandise Sales
Asset Account	12100 – Inventory Asset
Quantity on Hand	0 as of 03/01/2021

Item Type	Inventory Part
Item Name	Gas Trimmer
Subitem of	Trimmer
Description	Gas Powered Trimmer
Cost	300.00
COGS Account	50000 – Cost of Goods Sold
Tax Code	Tax
Sales Price	570.00
Income Account	46000 – Merchandise Sales
Asset Account	12100 – Inventory Asset
Quantity on Hand	0 as of 03/01/2021

Item Type	Inventory Part
Item Name	Battery Trimmer
Subitem of	Trimmer
Description	Rechargeable Battery Powered Trimmer
Cost	200.00
COGS Account	50000 – Cost of Goods Sold
Tax Code	Tax
Sales Price	390.00
Income Account	46000 – Merchandise Sales
Asset Account	12100 – Inventory Asset
Quantity on Hand	0 as of 03/01/2021

Step 3: From the Report Center, export to **Excel** (without spaces between columns) or **print** an Item Listing as of March 1, 2021, for Tomaso's Mowers & More.

TASK 5: CUSTOMIZE THE CHART OF ACCOUNTS

Customize the Chart of Accounts for Tomaso's Mowers & More as follows:

Step 1: Set preferences as follows:

- Display account numbers.

- Select Checking preferences: **Open Make Deposits form with Checking**.

- Deselect: **Warn if transactions are 30 day(s) in the future**.

Step 2: Enter the opening balance for the company Checking account:

- To open the Chart of Accounts, click the **Chart of Accounts** icon in the *Company* section of the Home page.

- Select **Checking** account. **Right-click** to display the pop-up menu.

- Select **Edit Account**.

- When the *Edit Account* window for the Checking account appears, enter Account No.: **10100**.

- Enter Opening Balance: **$2,400** as of **03/01/2021**.

- Click **OK**.

Step 3: Add the following accounts and opening balances to the Chart of Accounts.

This loan will not be paid in one year; therefore, it is a long-term liability.

Account No.	26000
Account Type	Long Term Liability
Account Name	Notes Payable
Account Description	Notes Payable
Tax Line	B/S-Liabs/Eq.:L-T Mortgage/note/bonds pay
Opening Balance	$2,000 as of 03/01/2021

Account No.	12500
Account Type	Other Current Asset
Account Name	Supplies on Hand
Account Description	Supplies on Hand
Tax Line	B/S-Assets: Other current assets
Opening Balance	$500 as of 03/01/2021

Account No.	14000
Account Type	Fixed Asset
Account Name	Store Fixtures
Account Description	Store Fixtures
Tax Line	B/S-Assets: Buildings/oth.depr. assets
Opening Balance	$0 as of 03/01/2021

Account No.	14100
Account Type	Fixed Asset
Account Name	Store Fixtures Cost
Subaccount of	Store Fixtures
Account Description	Store Fixtures Cost
Tax Line	B/S-Assets: Buildings/oth.depr. assets
Opening Balance	$2500 as of 03/01/2021

Account No.	14200
Account Type	Fixed Asset
Account Name	Acc Depr Store Fixtures
Subaccount of	Store Fixtures
Account Description	Acc Depr Store Fixtures
Tax Line	B/S-Assets: Buildings/oth.depr. assets
Opening Balance	$0 as of 03/01/2021

Account No.	64800
Account Type	Expense
Account Name	Supplies Expense
Account Description	Supplies Expense
Tax Line	Other Deductions: Supplies

Step 4: Export to **Excel** or **print** the Chart of Accounts (Account Listing) report for Tomaso's Mowers & More.

Step 5: Export to **Excel** or **print** a Trial Balance report for Tomaso's Mowers & More dated **03/01/2021**.

Step 6: Prepare the following opening adjustments using the Journal:

- Transfer $200 of Uncategorized Income to the Opening Balance Equity account. Use Entry No. **Open ADJ1**.

- Transfer the Opening Balance Equity account balance to the Capital Stock account. Use Entry No. **Open ADJ2**.

Step 7: Export to **Excel** or **print** the Trial Balance report after opening adjustments for Tomaso's Mowers & More dated **03/01/2021**.

TASK 6: RECORD TRANSACTIONS

Tomaso's Mowers & More entered into the following transactions during March 2021.

Step 1: Record the following transactions for Tomaso's Mowers & More. Customers are billed monthly. **Print** checks, purchase orders, invoices, and deposit summaries as appropriate. Use memorized transactions for recurring transactions.

Use Record Deposits window.

Use Write Checks window, then create a memorized transaction.

Use Enter Bills window to record Supplies Expense.

Date	Transaction
03/01/2021	Tomaso Moltissimo invested $10,000 cash in stock of Tomaso's Mowers & More. You invested $5,000 cash in the stock of the business. Deposit the funds into the company Checking account.
03/01/2021	Paid $800 store rent to Hartzheim Leasing (Check No. 601).
03/02/2021	Purchased $300 in supplies on account from Marcus Mower Sales & Repairs.
03/02/2021	Ordered (2) 48" riding mowers, 2 gas powered trimmers, and 3 battery powered trimmers from Astarte Supply.
03/04/2021	Received items ordered from Astarte Supply on 03/02/2021.

Use *Create Invoices* window.

03/05/2021	Sold a 48″ riding mower and a gas powered trimmer to Grady's Bindery on account.
03/07/2021	Received bill from Astarte Supply.
03/09/2021	Ordered 2 self propelled mowers and 1 push mower from Astarte Supply.
03/12/2021	Received only the self propelled mowers ordered on 03/09/2021 from Astarte Supply.
03/13/2021	Received the bill from Astarte Supply for the self propelled mowers only.
03/15/2021	Sold 1 self propelled mower and 1 battery powered trimmer to Mike Stanton on account.
03/16/2021	Sold a 48″ riding mower to Gerry Fowler on account.
03/16/2021	Ordered (2) 48″ riding mowers from Astarte Supply to restock inventory.
03/20/2021	Received and deposited the customer payment from Grady's Bindery (Check No. 401).
03/29/2021	Paid bill from Astarte Supply received on 03/07/2021 and due 04/06/2021. Paid $300 bill from Marcus Mower Sales & Repairs.
03/31/2021	Received and deposited payment from Mike Stanton (Check No. 3001).
03/31/2021	Paid bill for self propelled mowers due 04/12/2021.
03/31/2021	Paid $800 store rent to Hartzheim Leasing.

Step 2:   Export to **Excel** or **print** the Deposit Detail report for March 2021.

Step 3:   Export to **Excel** or **print** the Check Detail report for March 2021.

TASK 7: ADJUSTING ENTRIES

Step 1:   Export to **Excel** or **print** the Trial Balance report for Tomaso's Mowers & More at March 31, 2021.

Step 2:   Make adjusting entries for Tomaso's Mowers & More at March 31, 2021, using the following information.

- **ADJ1**: A count of supplies revealed $350 of supplies on hand.

- **ADJ2**: March depreciation expense for store fixtures was $35.

- **ADJ3**: Interest expense and interest payable at March 31, 2021, on Notes Payable was $15. Add Account No. 21000, Interest Payable.

Step 3:   Export to **Excel** or **print** the Adjusting Journal Entries report at March 31, 2021.

Step 4:   Export to **Excel** or **print** the Adjusted Trial Balance report for Tomaso's Mowers & More at March 31, 2021.

Step 5:   On the Adjusted Trial Balance report, **highlight** the amounts affected by the adjusting entries.

TASK 8: FINANCIAL REPORTS

Step 1:   Export to **Excel** or **print** the following reports for Tomaso's Mowers & More.

- General Ledger for the month of March 2021. (Remember to omit unused accounts with zero balances.)

- Profit & Loss, Standard for the month of March 2021.

- Balance Sheet, Standard at March 31, 2021.

- Statement of Cash Flows for the month of March 2021.

- Accounts Receivable Aging Summary at March 31, 2021.

Step 2:   Using the financial statements, determine the balance of the Supplies Expense account and explain how the account balance was calculated. $_____

Step 3: Using the Balance Sheet, determine the amount of sales tax that Tomaso's Mowers & More collected and owes to the State Board of Equalization. $_____

Step 4: Discuss how the Accounts Receivable Aging Summary report might be used by a small business.

TASK 9: SAVE QUICKBOOKS CASE 10

Save a backup of your QuickBooks Case 10 file using the file name: **YourName QB Case 10 Backup.QBB**. See *Appendix B: Back Up & Restore QuickBooks Files* for instructions.

WORKFLOW

If you are using the Workflow approach, leave your .QBW file open and proceed to QuickBooks Case 11.

RESTART & RESTORE

If you are using the Restart & Restore approach and are ending your computer session now, close your .QBW file and exit QuickBooks. When you restart, you will restore your backup file to complete QuickBooks Case 11.

TASK 10: ANALYSIS AND RECOMMENDATIONS

Step 1: Analyze the financial performance of Tomaso's Mowers & More.

Step 2: What are your recommendations to improve the company's financial performance in the future?

QUICKBOOKS CASE 10 QUICK CHECK

! Ask your instructor if you should Go Digital (Excel* or PDF) or use paper printouts.

NAME:

INSTRUCTIONS:

1. **CHECK OFF THE ITEMS YOU COMPLETED.**
2. **TURN IN THIS PAGE WITH YOUR PRINTOUTS.**

QB CASE 10

- ☐ * Customer List
- ☐ * Vendor List
- ☐ * Item List
- ☐ * Chart of Accounts
- ☐ * Trial Balance
- ☐ * Opening Adjusted Trial Balance
- ☐ Invoices
- ☐ Purchase Orders
- ☐ Checks
- ☐ Deposit Summaries
- ☐ * Deposit Detail
- ☐ * Check Detail
- ☐ * Trial Balance
- ☐ * Adjusting Entries
- ☐ * Adjusted Trial Balance
- ☐ * General Ledger
- ☐ * Profit & Loss
- ☐ * Balance Sheet
- ☐ * Statement of Cash Flows
- ☐ * Accounts Receivable Aging Summary
- ☐ Financial Statement Discussion Questions
- ☐ Analysis and Recommendations

Download Go Digital Excel templates at www.My-QuickBooks.com.

BUILD YOUR DREAM ENTERPRISE

Do you have an interest in being an entrepreneur? Would you like to start your own business? *Build Your Dream Enterprise* QuickBooks cases give you that opportunity. Go to www.My-QuickBooks.com and download the *Build Your Dream Enterprise Case* for Chapter 10.

CHAPTER 11
MERCHANDISING CORPORATION: PAYROLL

SCENARIO

After returning from his vacation, Wil Miles drops by the paint store to visit you and his former business. While the two of you are talking, customers in the store begin asking him for assistance. In cheerful good humor, he offers to tend the store for you while you grab lunch. In fact, he insists.

When you return after lunch, Wil tells you that Katrina Beneficio called, asking when you will have time to finish a paint job for her. Always ready to help, Wil suggests that you finish the Beneficio job while he watches the store.

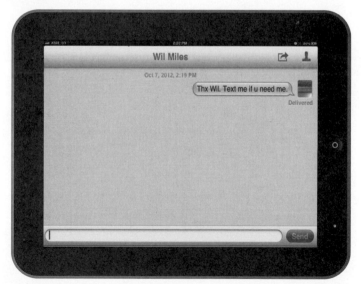

When you return later that afternoon, Wil appears to be thoroughly enjoying himself as he restocks the shelves and waits on customers. By closing time, you and Wil have reached an agreement: you will hire him to manage the store full-time, freeing you to return to your painting. Wil has only one condition—he wants one month of vacation every year.

CHAPTER 11
LEARNING OBJECTIVES

In Chapter 11, you will learn about the following QuickBooks features:

INTRODUCTION

In Chapter 11, you will account for payroll for Paint Palette Store. In Chapter 10, you set up a new merchandising company, Paint Palette Store, in QuickBooks. In this chapter, you will record a bank loan. Then you will set up payroll and record payroll transactions for Paint Palette Store.

> ❗ **Chapter 11 is a continuation of the companies used in Chapter 10.**

OPEN COMPANY FILE

To begin Chapter 11, first start QuickBooks software by clicking on the **QuickBooks desktop icon** or click **Start > Programs > QuickBooks > QuickBooks Premier Accountant Edition 2015**.

WORKFLOW

Use the Workflow approach if you are using the same .QBW file from the prior chapter.

- If your Chapter 10.QBW file is not already open, open it by selecting **File > Open Previous Company**. Select your .QBW file for **Paint Palette Store**.

- Update Company Name to include **YourName Chapter 11 Paint Palette Store**.

RESTART & RESTORE

Use the Restart & Restore approach if you are restarting your work session.

> ❗ **If a login appears, use Admin for User ID and leave the password field blank.**

- Restore your **Chapter 10 Backup .QBB** file using the directions in *Appendix B: Back Up & Restore QuickBooks Files*. Or you can restore the **Chapter 11 DATA STARTER.QBB** file that comes with your text.

- After restoring the file, update Company Name to include **YourName Chapter 11**.

BANK LOAN

Although Paint Palette Store sales appear to be improving, business has been slower than you anticipated. As a result, you need an operating loan in order to pay your bills and Wil's salary.

Paint Palette Store takes out a $4,000 operating loan from National Bank. You intend to repay the loan within one year.

Step 1: Create a new loan account: Note Payable-National Bank.

> A loan to be repaid within 1 year is classified as Other Current Liability.

- Display the **Chart of Accounts**.
- Right-click to display the pop-up menu. Select **New**.
- Select Account Type: **Other Current Liability**.
- Enter Account Number: **26100**.
- Enter Account Name: **Note Payable-National Bank**.
- Enter Description: **Note Payable-National Bank**.
- Enter Tax Line: **B/S-Liabs/Eq.: Other current liabilities**.
- Enter Opening Balance: **$0.00** as of **02/01/2021**.
- Click **Save & Close** to save.

> Because this loan was not an opening balance, the $4,000 is not recorded when the account is established in Step 1. Instead, it is recorded in a separate transaction in Step 2.

Step 2: When the bank deposits the $4,000 loan amount in your Checking account, record the loan as follows:

- From the *Banking* section of the Home page, select **Record Deposits**.
- Select Deposit To: **Checking**.
- Select Date: **02/01/2021**.
- Select From Account: **26100: Note Payable-National Bank**.
- Enter Amount: **4,000.00**.
- **Print** the **deposit summary**.
- Click **Save & Close**.

QUICKBOOKS PAYROLL

Chapter 6 covers payroll using QuickBooks payroll service. Chapter 11 covers QuickBooks manual payroll option.

QuickBooks provides various ways to process payroll. There are two general ways that a company can perform payroll calculations.

1. Use a QuickBooks payroll service.

2. Manually calculate payroll taxes.

Additional information about each option follows.

QUICKBOOKS PAYROLL SERVICES

When you subscribe to a QuickBooks payroll service, QuickBooks automatically calculates tax withholdings. To use the payroll services, you must pay a monthly fee and have an Internet connection.

QuickBooks offers three different levels of payroll services:

Basic Payroll	<ul><li>Create paychecks using automatic calculation of payroll tax deductions.</li><li>Tax forms for filings are not automatically prepared. Entrepreneur must complete the tax forms or work with an accountant on payroll tax filings.</li></ul>
Enhanced Payroll	<ul><li>Create paychecks using automatic calculation of payroll tax deductions.</li><li>Generate payroll tax forms for filings automatically.</li><li>File and pay taxes electronically.</li></ul>
Full Service Payroll	<ul><li>Pay employees using QuickBooks.</li><li>Intuit processes payroll taxes and filings for the entrepreneur.</li></ul>

CALCULATE PAYROLL TAXES MANUALLY

If you do not use a QuickBooks payroll service, you must calculate tax withholdings and payroll taxes manually using IRS Circular E (Publication 15, Employer's Tax Guide). Then enter the amounts in QuickBooks to process payroll.

In Chapter 6, you processed payroll with tax deductions calculated automatically by QuickBooks. In this chapter, you will learn how to enter payroll tax amounts manually instead of using a payroll tax service.

PROCESS PAYROLL MANUALLY

First, enable the full payroll feature for Paint Palette Store by completing the following steps.

Step 1:   Select **Edit** menu > **Preferences**.

Step 2:   Select **Payroll & Employees**.

Step 3:   Select **Company Preferences**.

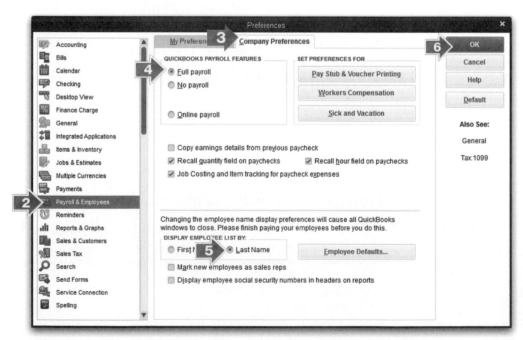

Step 4:   Select **Full payroll** to enable QuickBooks Payroll.

Step 5:   Select Display Employee List by: **Last Name**.

Step 6: Click **OK** to close the *Preferences* window.

To enable manual paycheck entry:

Step 1: Select **Help** menu **> QuickBooks Help**.

Step 2: Type **process payroll manually** in the Search field.

Step 3: Click the **Search** icon.

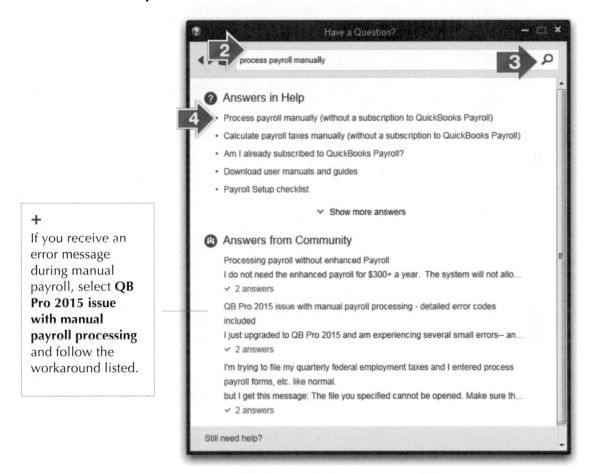

+
If you receive an error message during manual payroll, select **QB Pro 2015 issue with manual payroll processing** and follow the workaround listed.

Step 4: From the topics listed, select **Process payroll manually (without a subscription to QuickBooks Payroll)**.

Step 5: Select **manual payroll calculations** link.

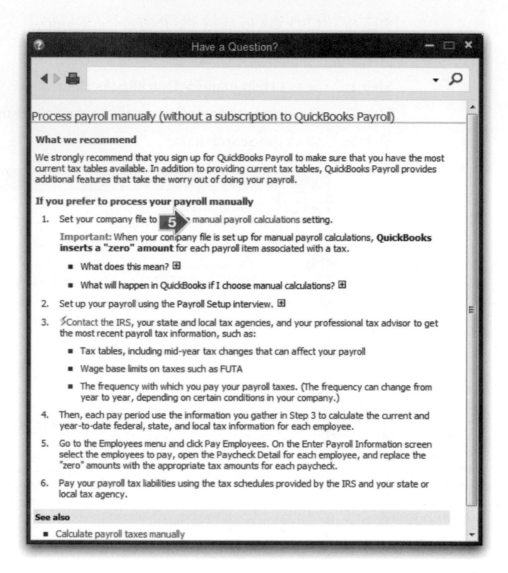

Step 6: When asked Are you sure you want to set your company file to use manual calculations?, select **Set my company file to use manual calculations**.

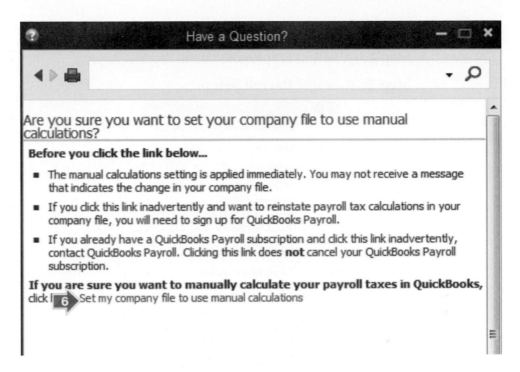

Step 7: Click **OK** when the following QuickBooks Information window appears.

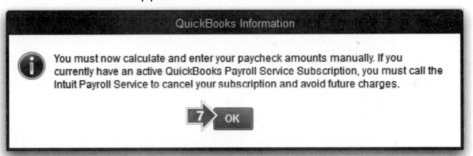

Step 8: The *Employees* section of the Home page should now appear as below.

If the *Employees* section of your Home page does not appear as shown here, close and then reopen the company file.

To set up payroll, complete the following steps.

Step 1: Select **Employees** menu.

Step 2: Select **Payroll Setup**.

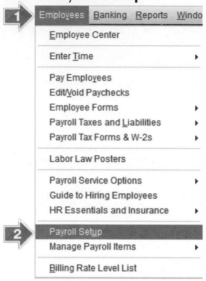

Step 3: After reading the *Welcome to QuickBooks Payroll Setup* window, click **Continue**.

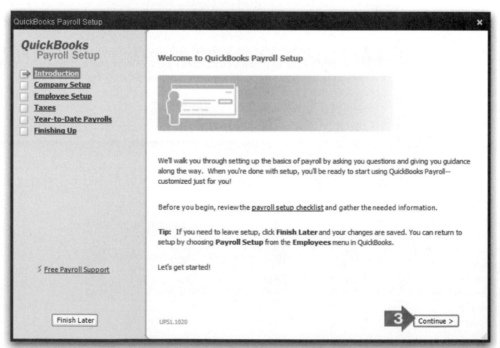

Step 4: When the *Setup Company Compensation and Benefits* window appears, click **Continue**. When the *Add New* window appears, select the following options.

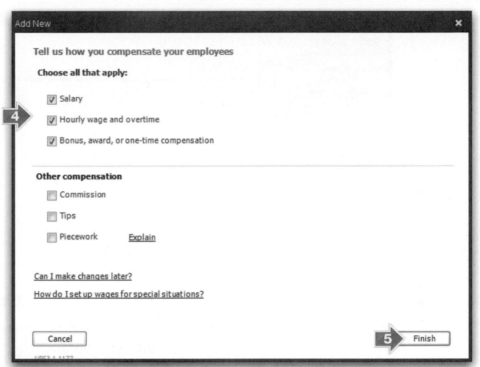

Step 5: Select **Finish**.

Step 6: Click **Continue** when the following *Compensation list* window appears.

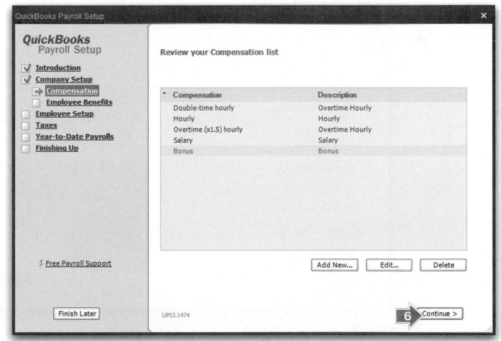

Step 7: Click **Continue** when the *Set up employee benefits* window appears.

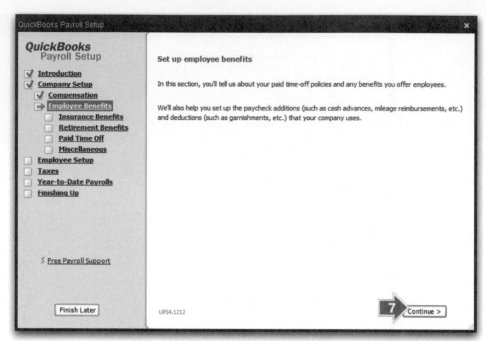

Step 8: Since you are not providing insurance benefits to your employee, select: **My company does not provide insurance benefits**.

+
Set employee defaults for information common to all employees, such as deductions for health insurance.

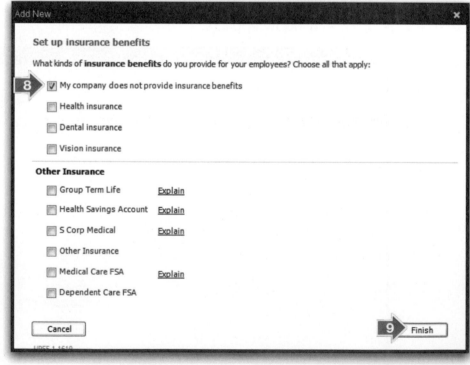

Step 9: Click **Finish**.

Step 10: Click **Continue** when the *Review your Insurance Benefits list* window appears.

Step 11: If your payroll included retirement plan deductions, you would indicate those items on the retirement benefits screen. Since your company does not, select **My company does not provide retirement benefits**.

Step 12: Select **Finish**.

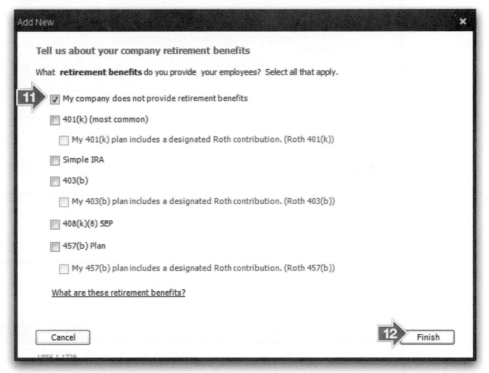

Step 13: Click **Continue** when the *Review your Retirement Benefits list* window appears.

Step 14: When the *Set up paid time off* window appears, select: **My employees do not get paid time off**.

Step 15: Click **Finish**.

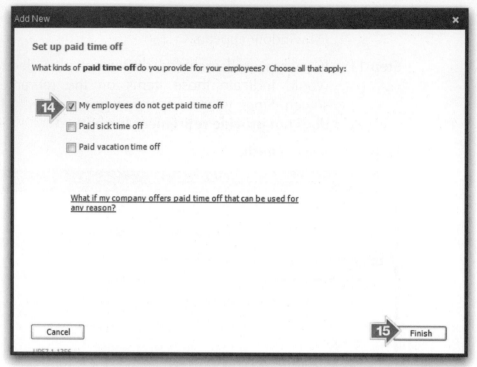

Step 16: Click **Continue** when the *Review your Paid Time Off list* window appears.

Step 17: When the *Set up additions and deductions* window appears, select: **Donation to charity**.

Step 18: Select **Next**.

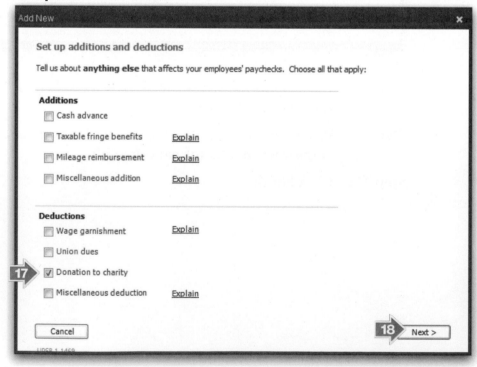

Step 19: When the *Set up the payment schedule for donation to charity* window appears, select: **I don't need a regular payment schedule for this item**.

Step 20: Select **Finish**.

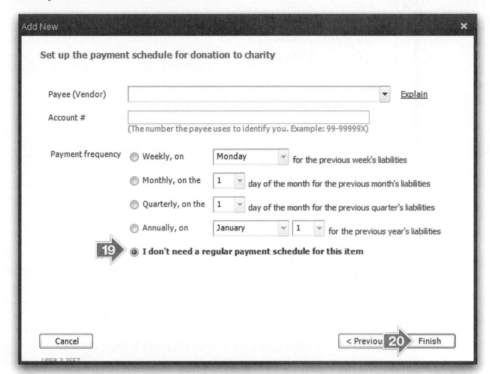

Step 21: Click **Continue** when the *Review your Additions and Deductions list* window appears.

Step 22: Click **Continue** when the *Set up your employees* window appears.

Next, add your new employee, Wil Miles.

Step 1: When the *New Employee* window appears, enter the following information for Wil Miles.

Step 2: Click **Next**.

Step 3: Enter Wil Miles hiring information as follows.

Step 4: Click **Next**.

Step 5:   Enter Wil Miles compensation information as follows.

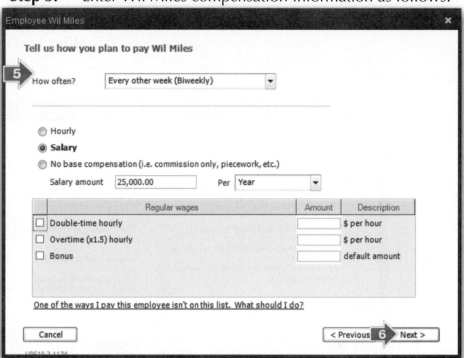

Step 6:   Click **Next**.

Step 7:   When the *Tell us about additional items for Wil Miles* window appears, enter the following.

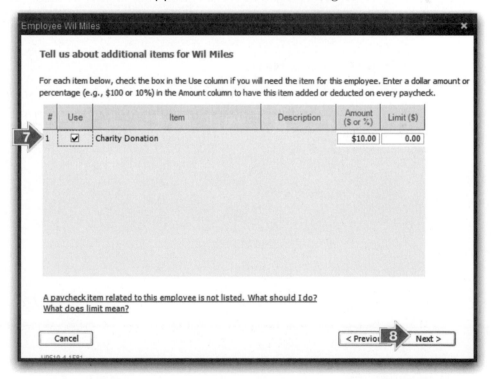

Step 8: Click **Next**.

Step 9: When the *Set up Wil Miles's direct deposit information* window appears, leave **Pay Wil Miles by Direct Deposit** unchecked.

Payroll payments can be set up as direct deposits to a bank account or direct deposits to a pay card, such as a prepaid Visa debit card.

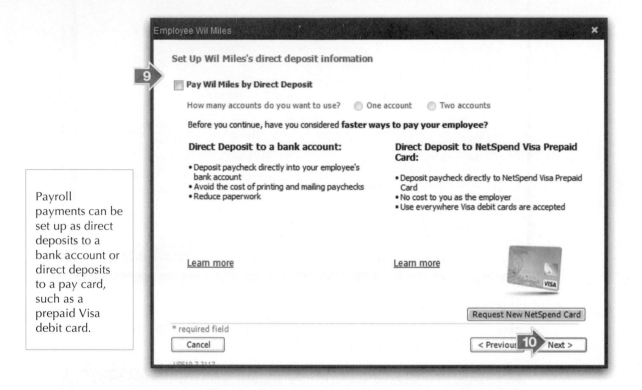

Step 10: Click **Next**.

Step 11: When the *Tell us where Wil Miles is subject to taxes* window appears, enter the following information.

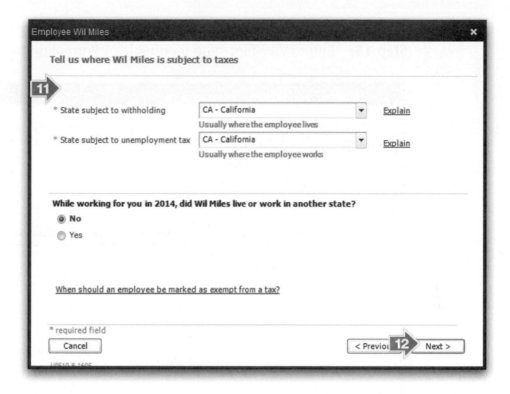

Step 12:   Click **Next**.

Step 13:   Enter Wil Miles federal tax information as follows.

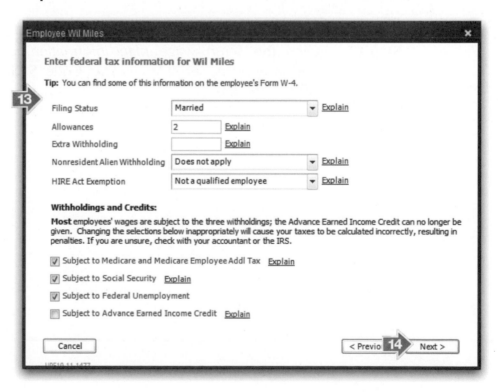

Step 14: Click **Next**.

Step 15: Enter Wil Miles state income tax information as follows.

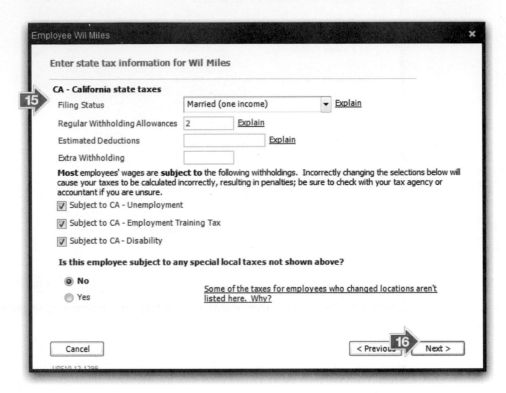

Step 16: Click **Next**.

Step 17: When the *Setup wage plan information for Wil Miles* window appears, select Wage Plan Code: **S (State Plan For Both UI and DI)**.

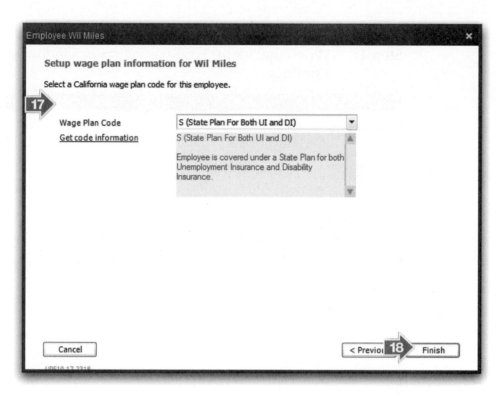

Step 18: Click **Finish**.

Step 19: Review your Employee List, then click **Continue**.

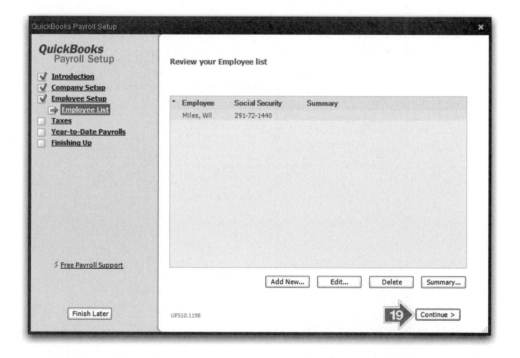

Next, set up your payroll taxes.

Step 1: When the *Set up your payroll taxes* window appears, click **Continue**.

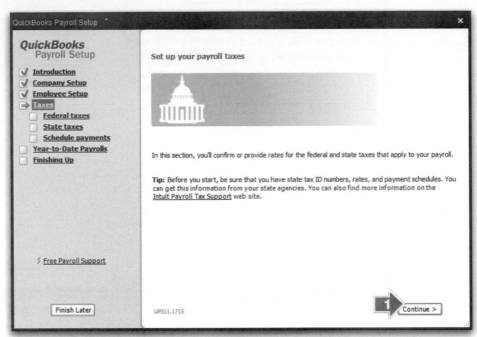

Step 2: Click **Continue** when the *Here are the federal taxes we set up for you* window appears.

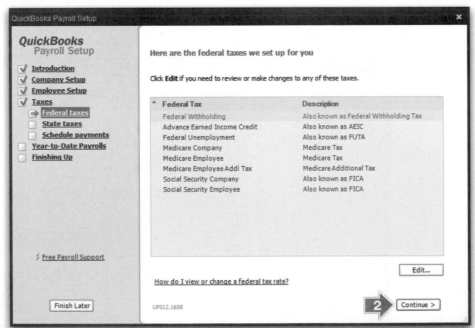

Step 3:   When the *Set up state payroll taxes* window appears, enter the information as follows.

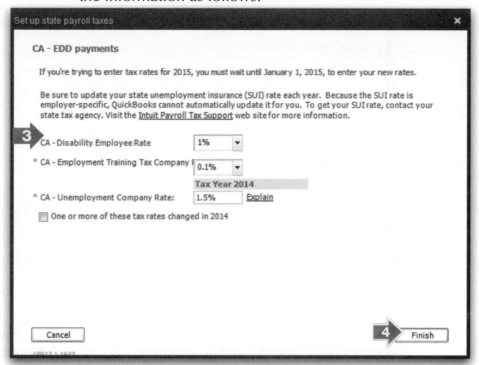

Step 4:   Click **Finish**.

Step 5:   Click **Continue** when the *Review your state taxes* window appears. If necessary, click **Next** if the *Schedule your tax payments* window appears.

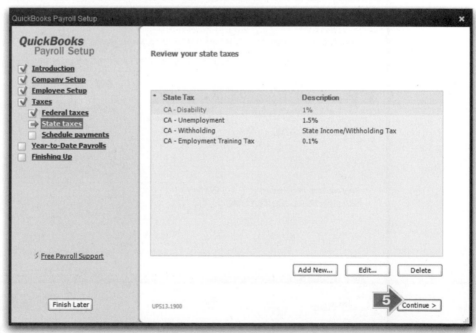

Step 6: Enter the information as follows in the *Set up payment schedule for Federal 940* window.

Step 7: Click **Next**.

Step 8: When the following *Set up payment schedule for Federal 941/944/943* window appears, enter the following information.

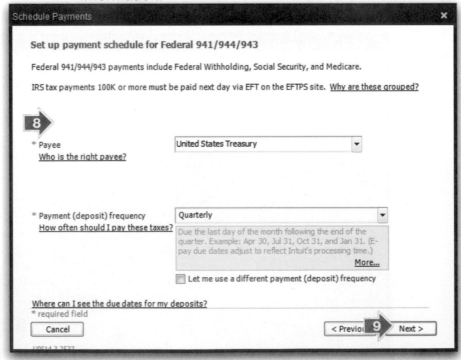

Step 9: Click **Next**.

Step 10: Enter the following in the *Set up payment schedule for CA Withholding and Disability Insurance* window.

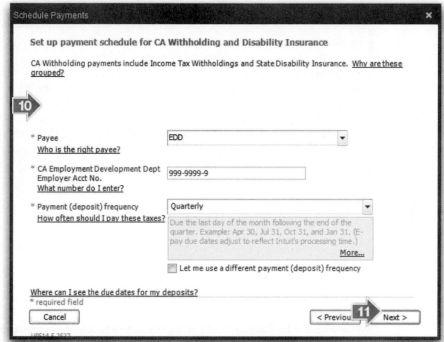

Step 11: Click **Next**.

Step 12: Enter the following in the *Set up payment schedule for CA UI and Employment Training Tax* window.

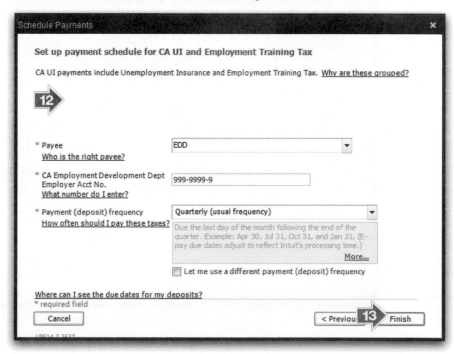

Step 13: Click **Finish**.

Step 14: When the *Review your Scheduled Tax Payments list* window appears, click **Continue**.

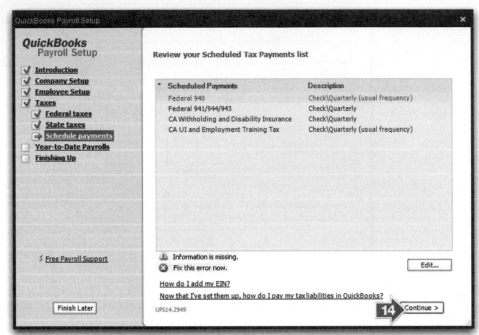

Step 15: Click **Continue** when the *Year-to-date payrolls* window appears.

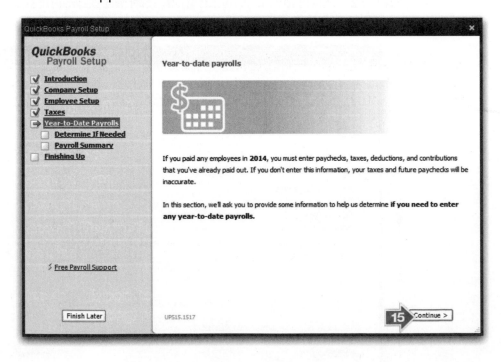

Step 16: When asked if your company has issued paychecks this year, select **No**.

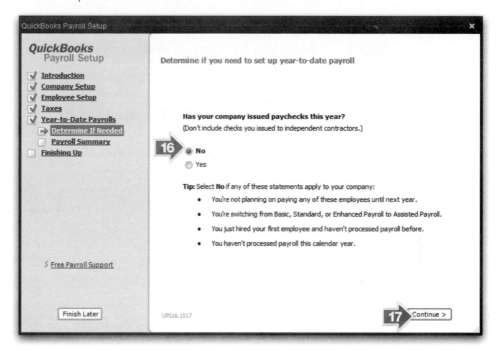

Step 17: Select **Continue**.

Step 18: Click **Go to Payroll Center** when the following *You can now pay your employees!* window appears. The Employee Center should appear.

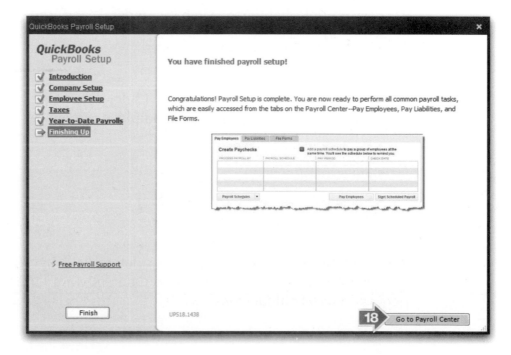

PRINT EMPLOYEE LIST

Print the employee information as follows:

Step 1: From the Employee Center, select **Excel**.

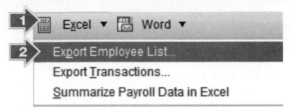

Step 2: Select **Export Employee List**.

Step 3: Export to **Excel** the Employee List. If requested, **print** the Employee List.

Step 4: **Close** the Employee Center.

PRINT PAYCHECKS

As you may recall from Chapter 6, processing payroll using QuickBooks involves the following steps:

1. Create paychecks for the employees.

2. Print the paychecks.

3. Pay payroll liabilities, such as federal and state income tax withheld.

4. Print payroll forms and reports.

When you create paychecks using QuickBooks, you must deduct (withhold) the following items from employees' pay:

- Federal income taxes.

- State income taxes.

- Social security (employee portion).

- Medicare (employee portion).

The amounts withheld for taxes are determined by tax tables that change periodically. Intuit offers two different ways for a company to perform payroll calculations:

1. **Use a QuickBooks payroll service**. For more information about QuickBooks payroll services, select **Employees** menu **> Payroll Service Options > Learn About Payroll Options**.

2. **Manually calculate payroll taxes**. You can manually calculate tax withholdings and payroll taxes using IRS Circular E. Then enter the amounts in QuickBooks to process payroll.

In this chapter, you will learn how to enter payroll tax amounts manually.

Wil Miles was hired by Paint Palette Store on February 1, 2021. He is paid an annual salary of $25,000. Wil will be paid biweekly, receiving a paycheck every two weeks. Therefore, the first pay period ends on February 14 and Wil is paid February 15.

To create a paycheck for Wil Miles:

Step 1: From the *Employees* section of the Home page, click the **Pay Employees** icon.

Step 2: When the following *Enter Payroll Information* window appears, select Bank Account: **Checking**.

Notice the three steps: Enter Payroll Information, Review & Create Paychecks, and Print & Distribute Paychecks.

The Check Date (payday) is the day the check is prepared; the Pay Period Ends date is the last day the employee works during the pay period.

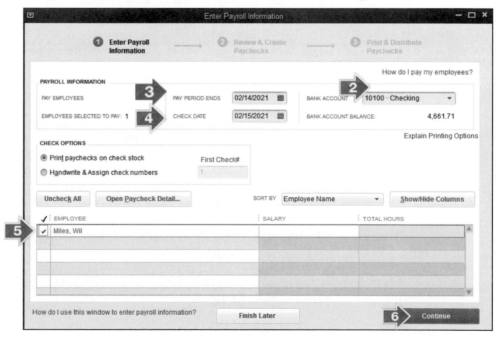

Step 3:   Enter Pay Period Ends: **02/14/2021**.

Step 4:   Enter Check Date: **02/15/2021**.

Step 5:   Select Employee: **Wil Miles**.

Step 6:   Click **Continue**.

Step 7:   When the *Review and Create Paychecks* window appears, select **Wil Miles'** name.

Step 8:   Click **Open Paycheck Detail**.

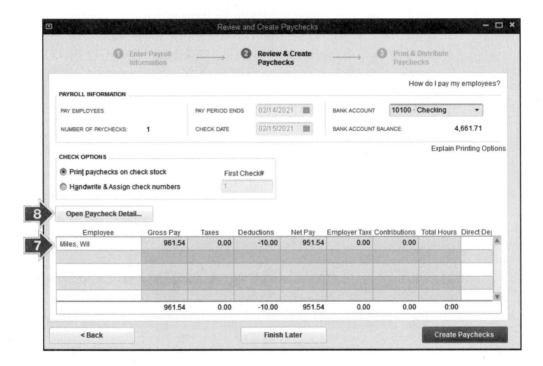

In the *Preview Paycheck* window enter the following information.

Step 1:   In the *Employee Summary* section, the Salary amount of $961.54 and Charity Donation of $-10.00 will automatically appear.

Step 2:   In the *Employee Summary* section, enter Federal Withholding: **-75.00**.

Step 3:   In the *Employee Summary* section, enter Social Security Employee: **-60.00**.

Step 4:   In the *Employee Summary* section, enter Medicare Employee: **-14.00**.

Step 5: In the *Company Summary* section, enter Social Security Company: **60.00**.

Step 6: In the *Company Summary* section, enter Medicare Company: **14.00**. Leave all other amounts at $0.00.

Step 7: Click **Save & Close**.

Step 8: When returning to the *Review and Create Paychecks* window, select Paycheck Options: **Print paychecks on check stock**.

Step 9: Select **Create Paychecks**.

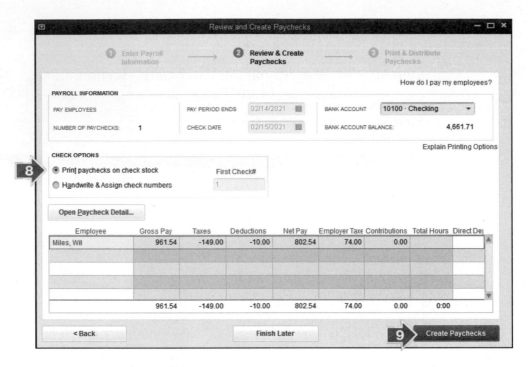

Step 10: When the *Confirmation and Next Steps* window appears, click **Print Paychecks**.

+
When voucher checks are used, paystub information is printed on the voucher. If standard checks are used, print paystubs by clicking **File** menu > **Print Forms > Pay Stubs**.

Step 11: When the *Select Paychecks to Print* window appears, select **Wil Miles**. Enter Check Number **404**. Click **OK**.

Step 12: Select the following print settings:

- Select **Voucher Checks**.

- Select **Print company name and address**.

- Click **Print**.

Step 13: Create and **print** paychecks to pay Wil Miles through the end of March 2021 using the same withholding and matching amounts as for Wil's first paycheck.

Check Number	Check Date	Pay Period
405	03/01/2021	02/15/2021 – 02/28/2021
406	03/15/2021	03/01/2021 – 03/14/2021
407	03/29/2021	03/15/2021 – 03/28/2021

Step 14: Click **Close** to close the *Confirmation and Next Steps* window.

QuickBooks records gross pay (the total amount the employee earned) as salaries expense and records the amounts due tax agencies as payroll tax liabilities.

PRINT PAYROLL JOURNAL ENTRIES

When QuickBooks records paychecks and payroll tax liabilities, it converts the transaction to a journal entry with debits and credits.

To view the payroll entry in the Journal:

Step 1: From the Report Center, select **Accountant & Taxes > Journal**.

Step 2: Select Dates From: **02/01/2021** To: **02/15/2021**. Click **Run**.

Step 3: To view only payroll entries, use a filter. Click the **Customize Report** button in the upper left corner of the *Journal* window.

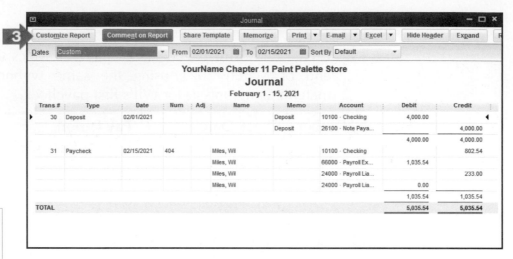

Wil Miles' wages are recorded as payroll expense.

Withholdings from his paycheck, such as amounts owed tax agencies, are payroll liabilities.

Payroll taxes the company must pay, such as employer share of Social Security and Medicare, are recorded as payroll expense.

Step 4: Click the **Filters** tab.

Step 5: Choose Filter: **Transaction Type**.

Step 6: Select Transaction Type: **Paycheck**.

Step 7: Click **OK**.

Step 8: Export to **Excel** or **print** the Journal report.

Step 9: **Close** the *Journal* window, then close the Report Center.

PAY PAYROLL LIABILITIES

Payroll liabilities include amounts Paint Palette Store owes to outside agencies including:

- Federal income taxes withheld from employee paychecks.

- State income taxes withheld from employee paychecks.

- FICA (Social Security and Medicare) taxes, both the employee and the employer portions.

- Unemployment taxes.

By the fifteenth of each month, Paint Palette Store is required to remit federal income tax withheld and the employee and employer portions of Social Security and Medicare taxes from the previous month's paydays. The store plans to make its monthly deposits of these federal taxes by the tenth of each month.

To pay payroll taxes:

Step 1: Click the **Pay Liabilities** icon in the *Employees* section of the Home page.

Step 2: When the *Select Date Range for Liabilities* window appears, enter dates from **02/01/2021** through **02/28/2021**.

Step 3: Click **OK**.

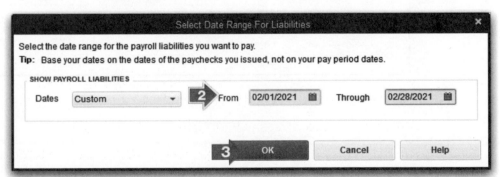

Payroll liabilities are based on check dates rather than pay period. Accordingly, the March 10 payroll liability check covers obligations arising only from the payroll check dated 02/15/2021.

Step 4: When the *Pay Liabilities* window appears, select Bank Account: **Checking**.

Step 5: Select Check Date: **03/10/2021**.

Step 6: Check: **To be printed**.

Step 7: Select the following amounts to pay:

- ✓ Federal Withholding
- ✓ Medicare Company
- ✓ Medicare Employee
- ✓ Social Security Company
- ✓ Social Security Employee

Step 8: Select: **Review liability check to enter expenses/penalties**.

Step 9: Click **Create** to view the check to pay the payroll liabilities selected.

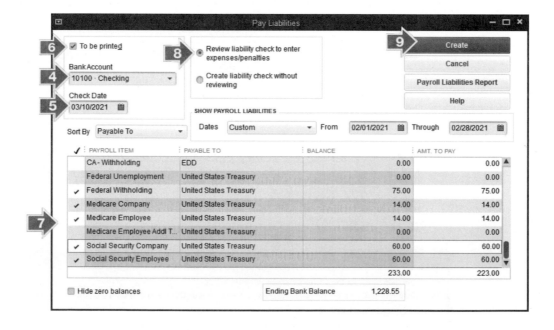

Step 10: To **print** the check:

- Click the **Print** button at the top of the *Liability Check* window.

- Enter the check number: **408**, then click **OK**.

- Select **Voucher** checks.

- Select **Print company name and address**.

- Click **Print**.

Step 11: Record and **print** check No. 409 to pay payroll liabilities for the pay period **03/01/2021** to **03/31/2021** to be paid on **04/10/2021**.

Since payroll liabilities are based on check dates rather than the pay period, the April 10 payroll liability check covers obligations arising from the payroll checks dated 03/01/2021, 03/15/2021, and 03/29/2021.

PRINT PAYROLL REPORTS

QuickBooks provides payroll reports that summarize amounts paid to employees and amounts paid in payroll taxes. Payroll reports can be accessed using the Report Center.

Prepare the Payroll Summary report:

Step 1: From the Report Center select **Employees & Payroll > Payroll Item Detail**.

Step 2: Select Dates From: **01/01/2021** To: **03/31/2021**. Click **Run**.

Step 3: Export to **Excel** or **print** the Payroll Item Detail report.

Prepare the Payroll Summary report:

Step 1: From the Report Center select **Employees & Payroll > Payroll Summary**.

Step 2: Select Dates From: **01/01/2021** To: **03/31/2021**. Click **Run**.

Step 3: Export to **Excel** or **print** the Payroll Summary report.

SAVE CHAPTER 11

Save a backup of your Chapter 11 file using the file name: **YourName Chapter 11 Backup.QBB**. See *Appendix B: Back Up & Restore QuickBooks Files* for instructions.

www.My-QuickBooks.com

Go to www.My-QuickBooks.com to view additional QuickBooks resources including Excel Reports Templates, QuickBooks videos, and QuickBooks Hot Arrows and Hot Topics. The Hot Topics can be viewed on your computer or tablet and feature frequently used QuickBooks tasks.

MULTIPLE-CHOICE PRACTICE TEST

Try the **Multiple-Choice Practice Test** for Chapter 11 on the *Computer Accounting with QuickBooks* Online Learning Center at www.mhhe.com/kay2015.

GO DIGITAL!

Go Digital using Excel templates. See *Appendix D: Go Digital with QuickBooks* for instructions about how to save your QuickBooks reports electronically.

LEARNING ACTIVITIES

Important: Ask your instructor whether you should complete the following assignments by printing reports or by exporting to Excel templates (see Appendix D: Go Digital with QuickBooks).

> **!**
> **Exercise 11.1 is a continuation of Exercise 10.1.**

EXERCISE 11.1: BRITTANY'S YARNS TIME TRACKING

SCENARIO

Brittany, the owner of Brittany's Yarns, has a good friend, Shufang, who enjoys knitting and likes to spend time at the store in the knitting corner. Shufang agrees to watch the store when Brittany is busy or needs to take deposits to the bank. Shufang will not be paid for her time, but Brittany would like to keep track of the hours. You advise Brittany that it is possible to permit Shufang access to the time-tracking feature of QuickBooks but restrict her access to other areas and to closed periods.

TASK 1: OPEN COMPANY FILE

WORKFLOW

If you are using the Workflow approach, you will use the same .QBW file from the prior Exercise 10.1.

- If your Exercise 10.1 QBW file is not already open, open it by selecting **File > Open Previous Company**. Select your **.QBW file.**

- Update Company Name to **YourName Exercise 11.1 Brittany's Yarns**.

RESTART & RESTORE

If you are not using the same computer, you must use the Restart and Restore approach. Restore your **Exercise 10.1 Backup.QBB** file (or use the **Exercise 11.1 DATA STARTER.QBB** file that comes with your text). After restoring the file, update Company Name to include **YourName Exercise 11.1**.

TASK 2: SET UP USER WITH TIME TRACKING

To restrict access when setting up a new user (Shufang):

Step 1: Select **Company** menu > **Set Up Users and Passwords > Set Up Users**.

Step 2: From the *User List* window, click **Add User**.

Step 3: Enter User Name: **Shufang**.

Step 4: Enter Password: **Time**. Confirm password. Click **Next**.

Step 5: Select: **Selected areas of QuickBooks**.

Step 6: Click **Next**.

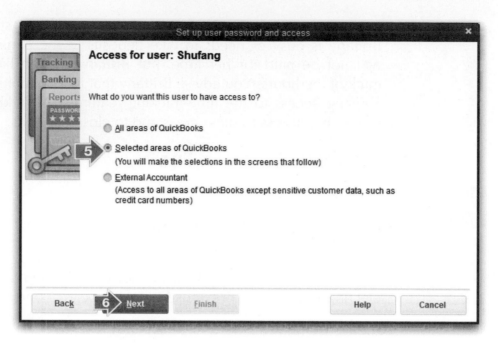

Step 7: Answer **No Access** to questions until you arrive at the *Time Tracking* window.

Step 8: For Time Tracking, make the following selections.

Step 9: Click **Next**.

Step 10: Continue selecting **No Access** until the following window appears.

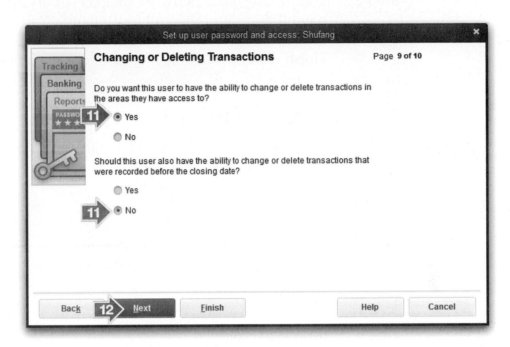

Step 11: To restrict access to closed periods, when the *Set up user password and access: Shufang* window appears, select: **Yes** to answer the first question and **No** to answer the second question.

Step 12: Select **Next**.

Step 13: Click **Finish** to set up Shufang as a new user. If a warning message appears, select **OK** to continue.

Step 14: **Close** the *User List* window.

Shufang will have access to time tracking only and will not have access to other accounting functions or accounting periods prior to the closing date.

TASK 3: SET UP PAYROLL

After you finish setting up Shufang with time-tracking access, Brittany, the owner, decides that it might be a good idea for you to proceed with setting up payroll, just in case she needs this feature in the future.

Step 1: Enable QuickBooks payroll for Brittany's Yarns. (Select **Edit** menu > **Preferences** > **Payroll & Employees** > **Company Preferences** > **Full Payroll**.)

Step 2: Follow the instructions in Chapter 11 to enable manual payroll and set up payroll for Brittany's Yarns. Skip adding specific employee information at this time by selecting **Finish Later** when the *Set up your employees* window appears.

TASK 4: SAVE EXERCISE 11.1

Save a backup of your Exercise 11.1 file using the file name: **YourName Exercise 11.1 Backup.QBB**. See *Appendix B: Back Up & Restore QuickBooks Files* for instructions.

EXERCISE 11.2: WEB QUEST

Learn more about filing payroll Forms 940 and 941 by visiting the IRS website.

Step 1: Go to the www.irs.gov website.

Step 2: **Print** Form 941.

EXERCISE 11.3: WEB QUEST

Employers must give employees Form W-2 each year summarizing wages and withholdings for tax purposes. In addition, employers must file Form W-3 with the Social Security Administration. Form W-3 summarizes the payroll information provided on the W-2 forms.

To learn more about filing Form W-3, visit the IRS website.

Step 1: Go to the www.irs.gov website.

Step 2: **Print** Form W-3.

CHAPTER 11 QUICK CHECK

NAME:

INSTRUCTIONS:

1. CHECK OFF THE ITEMS YOU COMPLETED.
2. TURN IN THIS PAGE WITH YOUR PRINTOUTS.

CHAPTER 11

- ☐   Deposit Summary
- ☐ *   Employee List
- ☐   Voucher Paychecks
- ☐ *   Journal
- ☐   Payroll Liability Checks
- ☐ *   Payroll Item Detail Report
- ☐ *   Payroll Summary Report

EXERCISE 11.2

- ☐   Form 941

EXERCISE 11.3

- ☐   Form W-3

Download Go Digital Excel templates at www.My-QuickBooks.com.

REFLECTION: A WISH AND A STAR

Reflection improves learning and retention. Reflect on what you have learned after completing Chapter 11 that you did not know before you started the chapter.

A Star:

What did you like best that you learned about QuickBooks in Chapter 11?

A Wish:

If you could pick one thing, what do you wish you knew more about when using QuickBooks?

PROJECT 11 RONEN ENTERPRISES

To complete this project, download Chapter 11 Go Digital Reports Excel template at www.My-QuickBooks.com.

Using your company file from Project 10 for Ronen Enterprises, complete the following. (If you experience issues with your file, contact your instructor for a data file.)

1. Download the Chapter 11 Go Digital Reports Excel template. Save the Excel file using the file name: **YourLastName FirstName CH 11**.

2. Update Company Name to include **YourName Project 11**.

3. Enable QuickBooks manual payroll.

4. Set up payroll using the following information. Ronen compensates its employees through salary; hourly wage and overtime; and bonus, award, or one-time compensation. Ronen does not provide insurance benefits, retirement benefits, or paid time off.

Name	Address	Employee Type	SSN	Hire Date	Gender	Pay Frequency	Pay
Meredith Grey	87 Grace Lane Bayshore, CA 94326	Regular	111-22-3333	2/1/2021	Female	Biweekly	Hourly $10.00/hr
Tony Parker	92 Spur Ave Bayshore, CA 94326	Regular	444-55-6666	2/1/2021	Male	Biweekly	Hourly $9.00/hr

Direct deposit?	No
State subject to withholding?	California
State subject to unemployment tax?	California
Live or work in another state?	No
Federal filing status?	Single
Federal allowances?	1
Nonresident alien withholding?	Does not apply
Subject to Medicare, Social Security, and Federal Unemployment?	Yes
Subject to advance earned income credit?	No
State filing status?	Single
State withholding allowances?	1
Subject to CA unemployment, employment training tax, and disability?	Yes
Subject to any special local taxes?	No
Wage plan code?	S

5. Click **Finish Later** after completing Employee Setup and before completing Taxes in Payroll Setup.

6. Using your saved Excel template for Chapter 11, from the Employee Center export to **Excel** the Employee List.

7. Enter the following paycheck and timesheet information.

Bank Account	Checking
Pay Period Ends	02/14/2021
Check Date	02/15/2021

Employee	Pay Period	Hours Worked	Federal Income Tax	Social Security (Emp)	Social Security (Comp)	Medicare (Emp)	Medicare (Comp)	CA Income Tax
Meredith Grey	2/1/2021 – 2/14/2021	40	$80.00	$24.80	$24.80	$5.80	$5.80	$20.00
Tony Parker	2/1/2021 – 2/14/2021	30	$54.00	$16.74	$16.74	$3.92	$3.92	$13.50

8. Prepare voucher paychecks for the employees at February 15, 2021.

9. From the Report Center, export to **Excel** the Payroll Transaction Detail report for February 1-15, 2021.

10. Mark the reports completed on the Excel **11 REPORTS** sheet. Save your Excel file.

11. Save a .QBB backup of your work.

 PROJECT 11 QUICK CHECK
NAME:
INSTRUCTIONS:
1. CHECK OFF THE ITEMS YOU COMPLETED.
2. ATTACH THIS PAGE TO YOUR PRINTOUTS.

! Ask your instructor if you should Go Digital (Excel* or PDF) or use paper printouts.

PROJECT 11
☐ * Employee List
☐ * Payroll Transaction Detail

QuickBooks Case 11 Tomaso's Mowers & More: Payroll

Scenario

> ❗
> **QB Case 11 is a continuation of QB Case 10.**

Tomaso's Mowers & More hired Marcella Kolbe as an office employee. You maintain the payroll records for Tomaso's Mowers & More and print Marcella's payroll checks.

Task 1: Open Company File

Workflow

If you are using the Workflow approach, you will use the same .QBW file from the prior QuickBooks Case 10.

- If your QuickBooks Case 10 QBW file is not already open, open it by selecting **File > Open Previous Company**. Select your **.QBW file.**

- Update Company Name to include **YourName QB Case 11**.

Restart & Restore

If you are not using the same computer, you must use the Restart and Restore approach. Restore your **QB Case 10 Backup.QBB** file (or use the **QB Case 11 DATA STARTER.QBB** file that comes with your text). After restoring the file, update Company Name to **YourName QB Case 11 Tomaso's Mowers & More**.

Task 2: Set Up Payroll

Set up QuickBooks Payroll for Tomaso's Mowers & More by completing the following steps.

Step 1: Enable QuickBooks Payroll for Tomaso's Mowers & More. (From the **Edit** menu, select **Preferences > Payroll & Employees > Company Preferences > Full Payroll > Last Name.**)

Step 2: Follow the instructions in Chapter 11 to enable manual payroll and set up payroll for Tomaso's Mowers & More using the following employee information.

First Name	Marcella
Last Name	Kolbe
Address	58 Appleton Drive
City	Bayshore
State	CA
ZIP	94326
Employee Type	Regular
Social Security No.	343-21-6767
Hire Date	03/01/2021
Gender	Female
Pay Frequency	Weekly
Hourly Regular Rate	$8.00
Direct Deposit	No
State Subject to Withholding	CA
State Subject to Unemployment Tax	CA
Live or Work in Another State	No
Federal and State Filing Status	Single
Allowances	1
Subject to Medicare, Social Security, and Federal Unemployment	Yes
Subject to Advance Earned Income Credit	No
Subject to CA Unemployment	Yes
Subject to CA Employment Training Tax	Yes
Subject to CA Disability	Yes
Subject to Special Local Taxes	No
Wage Plan Code	S
CA Disability Employee Rate	1%
CA Employment Training Tax Rate	0.1%
CA Unemployment Company Rate	1.5%
940 Payee	United States Treasury
940 Payment Frequency	Quarterly
941/944/943 Payee	United States Treasury

941/944/943 Payment Frequency	Quarterly
CA Withholding and Disability Insurance Payee	EDD
CA Employer Acct No.	888-8888-8
CA Withholding Frequency	Quarterly
CA UI and Employment Training Tax Payee	EDD
CA UI and Employment Training Tax Frequency	Quarterly

TASK 3: PRINT EMPLOYEE INFORMATION

From the Employee Center, export to **Excel** or **print** the Employee List.

TASK 4: PRINT PAYCHECKS

Using the following information and instructions in Chapter 11, create and **print** paychecks for Tomaso's Mowers & More employee, Marcella Kolbe. Use voucher style checks.

Check Date	Payroll Period	Hours Worked*
March 5	March 1-3	12
March 12	March 4-10	30
March 19	March 11-17	32
March 26	March 18-24	28
April 2	March 25-31	31

* Enter hours worked in the *Preview Paycheck* window.

Assume the following rates for withholdings:

Federal income tax	20.00%
Social Security (employee)	6.20%
Social Security (company)	6.20%
Medicare (employee)	1.45%
Medicare (company)	1.45%
State (CA) income tax	5.00%

+

To display the QuickMath Calculator:
1. Place your cursor in the federal withholding field, then press the = key.
2. Enter calculations using the * key to multiply.
3. Press **Enter** to enter the amount into the field.

Note that the wage base limit will not be exceeded for Social Security.

> ***Marcella Kolbe's March 12th paycheck is $161.64.***

TASK 5: PAY PAYROLL LIABILITY

On April 10, pay the payroll tax liability for federal income tax, Social Security and Medicare taxes, and the liability for state income tax as of 03/31/2021. **Print** the payroll liability checks.

TASK 6: PRINT PAYROLL REPORT

Export to **Excel** or **print** the Payroll Summary report for Tomaso's Mowers & More for the first quarter of 2021.

TASK 7: SAVE QUICKBOOKS CASE 11

Save a backup of your QuickBooks Case 11 file using the file name: **YourName QB Case 11 Backup.QBB**. See *Appendix B: Back Up & Restore QuickBooks Files* for instructions.

QUICKBOOKS CASE 11 QUICK CHECK

NAME:
INSTRUCTIONS:
1. CHECK OFF THE DELIVERABLES YOU HAVE COMPLETED.
2. TURN IN THIS PAGE WITH YOUR DELIVERABLES.

QB CASE 11
- ☐ * Employee List
- ☐ Paychecks
- ☐ Payroll Liability Checks
- ☐ * Payroll Summary

BUILD YOUR DREAM ENTERPRISE

Do you have an interest in being an entrepreneur? Would you like to start your own business? *Build Your Dream Enterprise* QuickBooks cases give you that opportunity. Go to www.My-QuickBooks.com and download the *Build Your Dream Enterprise Case* for Chapter 11.

NOTES:

CHAPTER 12
ADVANCED QUICKBOOKS FEATURES FOR ACCOUNTANTS

SCENARIO

During the month of January 2020 you continue to operate your painting service while still managing Paint Palette Store. You know that you need to budget for the coming year, providing you an opportunity to develop a business plan for the company.

In the new year, several commercial customers have approached you about custom painting for their offices and restaurants. Moreover, you continue to get referrals from your satisfied customers. The new customers want bids and estimates before they award contracts. Also, since some of these new jobs would require months to complete, you want to use progress billing (bill customers as the job progresses) in order to bring in a steady cash flow for your business.

To streamline your business processes, you use QuickBooks Mobile iPad apps so you can bill and take customer payments on the go.

Furthermore, you continue to provide QuickBooks consulting services for a variety of accounting clients. Therefore, to improve customer service for your QuickBooks clients, you continue to expand your knowledge and learn more about other advanced features of QuickBooks designed for the accounting professional.

CHAPTER 12
LEARNING OBJECTIVES

In Chapter 12, you will learn about the following QuickBooks features:

INTRODUCTION

!
Chapter 12 is a continuation of Exercise 9.5.

This chapter covers some of the more advanced features of QuickBooks software that are of interest to the accounting professional. These features include setting up budgets, progress billing, multiple currencies, remote access for accountants, the accountant's copy of the company file, and the audit trail. Chapter 12 will use the Paint Palette service company file from Chapter 9.

OPEN COMPANY FILE

To begin Chapter 12, first start QuickBooks software by clicking on the **QuickBooks desktop icon** or click **Start > Programs > QuickBooks > QuickBooks Premier Accountant Edition 2015**.

WORKFLOW

Use the Workflow approach if you are using the same .QBW file from Exercise 9.5.

- If your Exercise 9.5 QBW file is not already open, open it by selecting **File > Open Previous Company**.

- Update Company Name to **YourName Chapter 12 Paint Palette**.

RESTART & RESTORE

Use the Restart & Restore approach if you are restarting your work session.

- Restore your **Backup.QBB** file using the directions in *Appendix B: Back Up & Restore QuickBooks Files*. You can restore your Exercise 9.5 Backup.QBB file or restore the Chapter 12.QBB data file that comes with the *Computer Accounting with QuickBooks* text (available on CD or download from the Online Learning Center).

- After restoring the file, update Company Name to **YourName Chapter 12 Paint Palette**.

BUDGETS

As Paint Palette enters its second year of operation, planning for future expansion is important to its continued success. You develop the following budget for 2021.

- January sales are expected to be $3,000. Sales are expected to increase by 5% each month thereafter.

- Paint supplies expense is budgeted at $60 per month.

- The van lease will increase to $300 per month. (Use Account No. 67100.)

To prepare budgets for Paint Palette using QuickBooks:

Step 1:   Select **Company** menu.

Step 2:   Select **Planning & Budgeting.**

Step 3:   Select **Set Up Budgets**.

Step 4: In the *Create New Budget* window, select the year: **2021**.

Step 5: Select budget type: **Profit and Loss**.

Step 6: Select **Next**.

Step 7: Select **No additional criteria**.

Step 8: Select **Next**.

Step 9: Select **Create budget from scratch**.

Step 10: Click **Finish**.

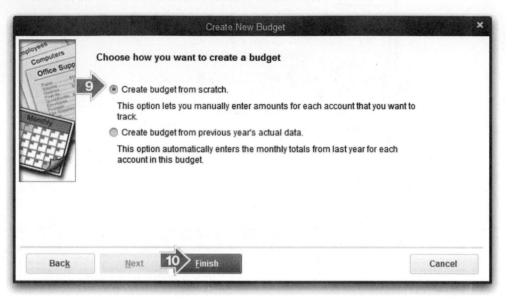

When the following *Set Up Budgets* window appears:

Step 1: Enter **3000.00** for 47900 Sales account in the *Jan21* column.

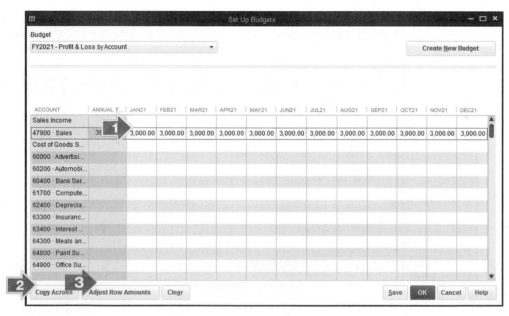

Step 2: Click the **Copy Across** button.

Step 3: Click the **Adjust Row Amounts** button.

Step 4: When the following *Adjust Row Amounts* window appears, select Start at: **Currently selected month**.

Step 5: Select: **Increase each remaining monthly amount in this row by this dollar amount or percentage**.

Step 6: Enter **5.0%**.

Step 7: Check: **Enable compounding**.

Step 8: Click **OK**.

+

Use the **Copy Across** button to fill in the budget amounts for each month.

Step 9: Enter budget amounts for Paint Supplies Expense of $60 per month.

Step 10: Enter Rent Expense for the van of $300 per month.

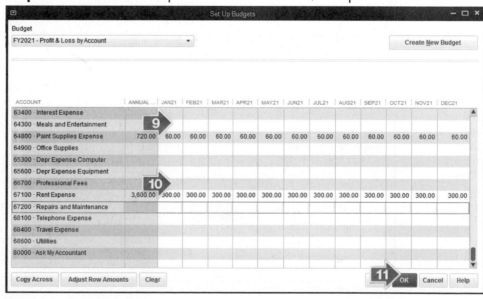

Step 11: Click **OK** to close the *Set Up Budgets* window.

Export to **Excel** or **print** the budget you created for Paint Palette:

Step 1: From the Report Center select **Budgets & Forecasts > Budget Overview**.

Step 2: Select Dates: **01/01/2021** To: **12/31/2021**. Click **Run**.

Step 3: Select: **FY2021 – Profit and Loss by Account > Next**.

Step 4: Select Report Layout: **Account by Month > Next > Finish**.

Step 5: Export to **Excel** or **print** the Budget Overview report.

Step 6: **Close** the *Budget Overview* window.

ESTIMATES

Often customers ask for a bid or estimate of job cost before awarding a contract. Paint Palette needs to estimate job costs that are accurate in order not to *overbid* and lose the job or *underbid* and lose money on the job.

To prepare a job cost estimate for Paint Palette:

Step 1: Click the **Estimates** icon in the *Customers* section of the Home page.

If the Estimates icon does not appear on your screen, select **Edit** menu > **Preferences > Jobs and Estimates > Company Preferences**. Select **Yes** to indicate you create estimates.

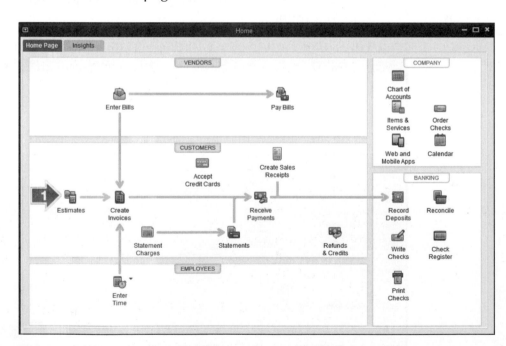

Step 2: When the *Create Estimates* window appears, add a new customer as follows:

- From the drop-down Customer List, select: **<Add New>**.

- Enter Customer Name: **Marcus Café**.

- Enter Company Name: **Marcus Café**.

- Enter Address: **10 Shanghai Blvd, Bayshore, CA 94326**.

- Enter First Name: **Marcus**.

- Click the **Job Info** tab, then enter Job Status: **Pending**.

- Click **OK** to close the *New Customer* window.

> The estimate can be given to a customer when bidding on a job. You can also email estimates to customers using QuickBooks.

Step 3: Next, enter estimate information in the *Create Estimates* window:

- Select Template: **Custom Estimate**.

- Select Date: **01/05/2021**.

- Enter Item: **Labor: Exterior Painting**.

- Enter Quantity **40**.

- Enter a second item: **Labor: Interior Painting**.

- Enter Quantity: **65**.

Step 4: **Print** the estimate, then click **Save & Close** to close the *Create Estimates* window.

PROGRESS BILLING

When undertaking a job that lasts a long period of time, a business often does not want to wait until the job is completed to receive payment for its work. The business often incurs expenses in performing the job that must be paid before the business receives payment from customers. This can create a cash flow problem. One solution to this problem is progress billing.

Progress billing permits a business to bill customers as the job progresses. Thus, the business receives partial payments from the customer before the project is completed.

After you give Marcus Café your estimate of the paint job cost, Marcus awards you the contract. The job will last about three weeks. However, instead of waiting three weeks to bill Marcus, you bill Marcus every week so that you will have cash to pay your bills.

To use progress billing in QuickBooks, first you must turn on the preference for progress invoicing.

To select the preference for progress invoicing:

Step 1:   Select **Edit** menu.

Step 2:   Select **Preferences**.

Step 3:   Select **Jobs & Estimates**.

Step 4:   Select **Company Preferences**.

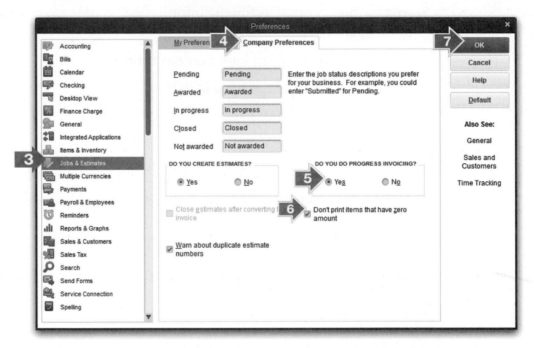

Step 5:   Select **Yes** to indicate you want to use Progress Invoicing.

Step 6:   ✓ Check **Don't print items that have zero amount**.

Step 7:   Click **OK** to save the Progress Invoicing preference and close the *Preferences* window. Click **OK** if a warning window appears.

After selecting the Progress Invoicing preference, the Progress Invoice template is now available in the *Create Invoices* window.

To create a progress invoice:

Step 1: Click the **Create Invoices** icon in the *Customers* section of the Home page.

Step 2: When the *Create Invoices* window appears, select Customer: **Marcus Café**.

Step 3: Select the **Marcus Café** estimate to invoice.

Step 4: Click **OK**.

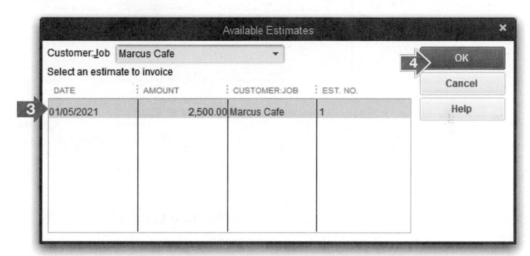

Step 5: When the *Create Progress Invoice Based On Estimate* window appears, select: **Create invoice for the entire estimate (100%)**.

Step 6: Click **OK**.

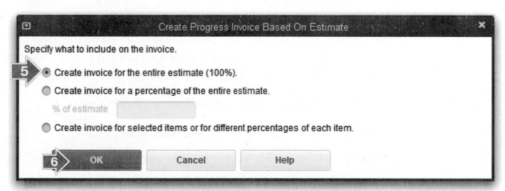

Step 7: When the following *Create Invoices* window appears, the template should now be: **Progress Invoice**.

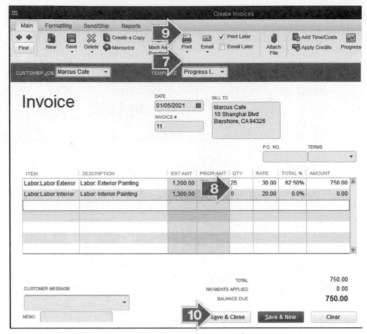

When you selected Create invoice for the entire estimate, QuickBooks automatically entered the items and estimated amounts for the entire job on the progress invoice.

Step 8: Enter the number of hours actually worked on the Marcus Café job.

- Enter Exterior Painting Labor Quantity: **25**.

- Enter Interior Painting Labor Quantity: **0**.

Step 9: **Print** the progress invoice.

Step 10: Click **Save & Close** to close the *Create Invoices* window. If a message appears, click **Yes** to record changes to the invoice.

The following week you complete the exterior painting for Marcus Café and work 6.5 hours on interior painting. Create another progress invoice for Marcus Café by completing the following steps.

Step 1: Display the *Create Invoices* window.

Step 2: Select Customer: **Marcus Café**.

Step 3: Select the **Marcus Café** estimate to invoice, then click **OK**.

Step 4: When the following *Create Progress Invoice Based On Estimate* window appears, select **Create invoice for selected items or for different percentages of each item**.

Step 5: Click **OK**.

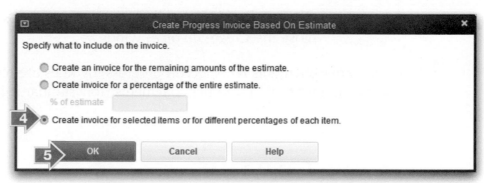

Step 6: When the following *Specify Invoice Amounts for Items on Estimate* window appears, ✓ Check: **Show Quantity and Rate**.

Step 7: ✓ Check: **Show Percentage**.

Step 8: Enter Exterior Painting Quantity: **15**.

Step 9: Enter Interior Painting Quantity: **6.5**.

Step 10: Click **OK** to record these amounts on the progress invoice.

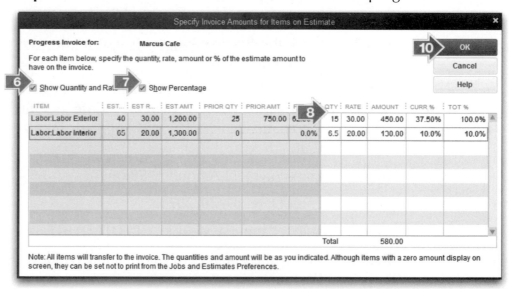

Step 11: When the *Create Invoices* window appears, change the date of the progress invoice to: **01/12/2021**.

Step 12: **Print** the invoice.

 The invoice total is $580.00.

Step 13: Click **Save & Close** to record the progress invoice and close the *Create Invoices* window.

Customer payments received on progress invoices are recorded in the same manner as customer payments for standard invoices (See Chapter 4).

CREDIT CARD SALES

As a convenience to your customers, you agree to accept credit cards as payment for services you provide. Marcus Café would like to make its first payment using a VISA credit card.

In QuickBooks, you record credit card payments in the same manner that you record a payment by check; however, instead of selecting Check as the payment method, you select the type of credit card used.

To record a credit card sale using QuickBooks:

Step 1: Click the **Receive Payments** icon in the *Customers* section of the Home page.

Step 2: When the *Receive Payments* window appears, select Received From: **Marcus Café**. QuickBooks will automatically display any unpaid invoices for Marcus Café.

> If the specific credit card is not listed on the Payment Method List, select **Add New**, then enter the name of the credit card.

Step 3: Enter Payment Amount: **750.00**.

Step 4: Enter Date: **01/30/2021**.

Step 5: Select Payment Method: **CREDIT DEBIT**.

Step 6: When the *Enter Card Information* window appears, select Payment: **Visa**.

Step 7: Enter Card Number: **19585858581958**.

Step 8: Enter Exp Date: **12/2021**.

Step 9: Select **Done**.

Step 10: If not already selected, select outstanding Invoice No. **11**, dated **01/05/2021**.

Step 11: Your *Receive Payments* window should appear as follows. To record the customer payment and close the *Receive Payments* window, click **Save & Close**.

Banks will accept bank credit card payments, such as Visa or MasterCard, the same as a cash or check deposit. You can record the credit card payment as a deposit to your checking account.

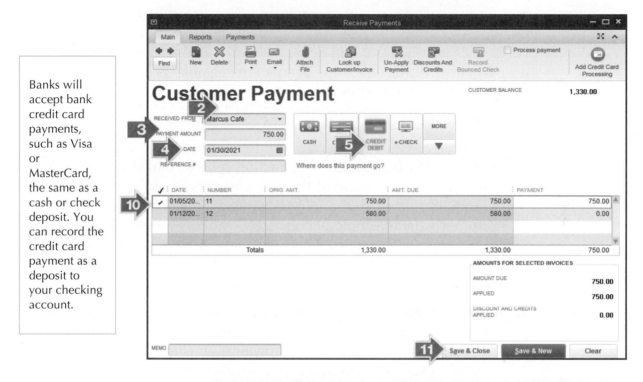

Step 12: Since you are not using the Merchant Account Services, when the credit card payment is deposited at the bank on 01/30/2021, record the deposit just as you would a check or cash deposit.

- Click the **Record Deposits** icon in the *Banking* section of the Home page.

- Select **Marcus Café payment** for deposit. Click **OK**.

- **Print** the deposit summary.

BAD DEBTS

At the time a credit sale occurs, it is recorded as an increase to sales and an increase to accounts receivable. Occasionally a company is unable to collect a customer payment and must write off the customer's account as a bad debt or uncollectible account. When an account is uncollectible, the account receivable is written off or removed from the accounting records.

There are two different methods that can be used to account for bad debts:

1. **Direct write-off method.** This method records bad debt expense when it becomes apparent that the customer is not going to pay the amount due. If the direct write-off method is used, the customer's uncollectible account receivable is removed and bad debt expense is recorded at the time a specific customer's account becomes uncollectible. The direct write-off method is used for tax purposes.

2. **Allowance method.** The allowance method *estimates* bad debt expense and establishes an allowance or reserve for uncollectible accounts. When using the allowance method, uncollectible accounts expense is estimated in advance of the write-off. The estimate can be calculated as a percentage of sales or as a percentage of accounts receivable. (For example, 2% of credit sales might be estimated to be uncollectible.) This method should be used if uncollectible accounts have a material effect on the company's financial statements used by investors and creditors and the company must comply with Generally Accepted Accounting Principles (GAAP).

Paint Palette will use the direct write-off method and record the uncollectible accounts expense when an account actually becomes uncollectible.

When Marcus paid the bill for $750 for Marcus Café, he tells you that his business has plummeted since a new restaurant opened next door. To your dismay, he tells you his café is closing and he will not be able to pay you the remainder that he owes. You decide to write off the Marcus Café remaining $580 account balance as uncollectible.

First, create an account for tracking uncollectible accounts expense and then write off the customer's uncollectible account receivable.

To add a Bad Debt Expense account to the Chart of Accounts for Paint Palette, complete the following steps:

Step 1:   Click the **Chart of Accounts** icon in the *Company* section of the Home page.

Step 2:   Add the following account to the Chart of Accounts.

Account Type	Expense
Account No.	67000
Account Name	Bad Debt Expense
Description	Bad Debt Expense
Tax Line	Schedule C: Bad debts from sales/services

Next, record the write-off of the uncollectible account receivable. There are three different methods to record a bad debt using QuickBooks:

1. Make a journal entry to remove the customer's account receivable (credit Accounts Receivable) and debit either Bad Debt Expense (direct write-off method) or the Allowance for Uncollectible Accounts (allowance method).

2. Use the *Credit Memo* window to record uncollectible accounts.

3. Use the *Receive Payments* window (Discounts And Credits icon) to record the write-off of the customer's uncollectible account.

If you charged sales tax on the transaction written off, use this method.

To record the write-off of an uncollectible account receivable using the *Receive Payments* window, complete the following steps:

Step 1:   Change the preference for automatically calculating payments as follows:

- Select **Edit** menu **> Preferences > Payments > Company Preferences**.

- **Uncheck** the **Automatically calculate payments** preference.

- Click **OK** to close the *Preferences* window.

Step 2:   Click the **Receive Payments** icon in the *Customers* section of the Home page.

Step 3:   When the *Receive Payments* window appears, select Received From: **Marcus Café**.

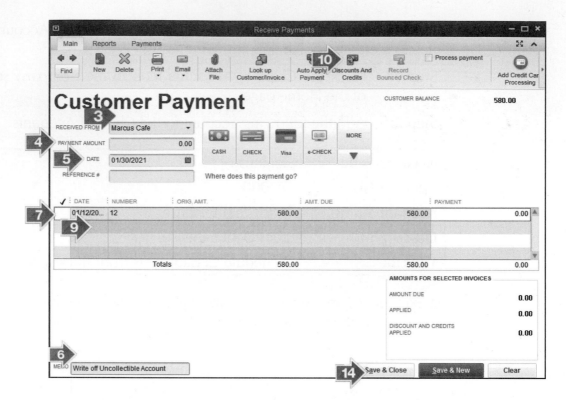

Step 4: Leave the Payment Amount as **$0.00**.

Step 5: Enter Date: **01/30/2021**.

Step 6: Enter Memo: **Write off Uncollectible Account**.

Step 7: Select the outstanding invoice dated: **01/12/2021**.

Step 8: Because the Amount field is $0.00, the following warning may appear. Click **OK**.

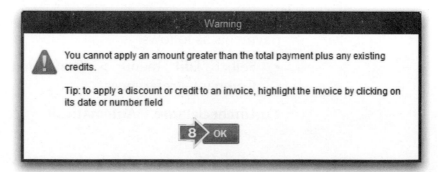

Step 9: Highlight the invoice by clicking on its **Date** field.

Step 10: Click the **Discounts And Credits** icon in the *Receive Payments* window.

Step 11: When the following *Discount and Credits* window appears, enter Amount of Discount: **580.00**.

Step 12: Select Discount Account: **67000 Bad Debt Expense**.

Step 13: Click **Done** to close the *Discount and Credits* window.

Step 14: Click **Save & Close** to close the *Receive Payments* window.

To view the Marcus Café account:

Step 1: From the Report Center select **Customers & Receivables > Customer Balance Detail**.

Step 2: Select Dates: **All**. Click **Run**.

Step 3: To customize the Customer Balance Detail report so the Memo field appears on the report, click the **Customize Report** button to display the *Modify Report* window.

Step 4: Click the **Display** tab.

Step 5: Select Columns: **Memo**.

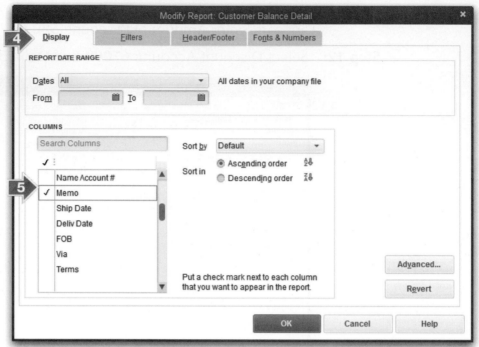

Step 6: Next, to create a filter to display only Marcus Café account information, click the **Filters** tab in the *Modify Report* window.

Step 7: Select Filter: **Name**.

Step 8: Select Name: **Marcus Café**.

Step 9: Click **OK** to close the *Modify Report* window.

Step 10: The *Customer Balance Detail* window should now appear as follows. Note that the bad debt write-off reduced the Accounts Receivable account for Marcus Café by $580. **Double-click** on the entry for 01/30/2021 to drill down to the *Receive Payments* window that displays the entry to write off $580 of the Marcus Café account. **Close** the *Receive Payments* window.

> To record customer NSF checks with insufficient funds that are returned by the bank, see the Quick Guide in Section 3.

> The write-off reduces the Accounts Receivable account by $580.

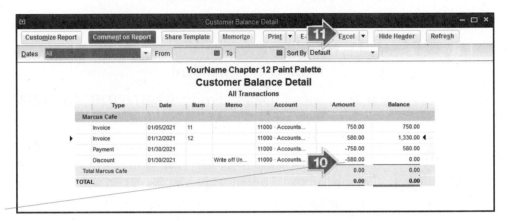

Step 11: Export to **Excel** or **print** the Customer Balance Detail report for Marcus Café.

The Accounts Receivable Aging Summary report (discussed in Chapter 4) provides information about the age of customers' accounts receivable which can be useful for tracking and managing collections.

To reduce uncollectible customer accounts, some companies adopt a policy that requires customers to make a deposit or advance payment before beginning work on a project. In addition, companies often evaluate the creditworthiness of customers before extending credit.

MEMORIZED REPORTS

On March 1, 2021, a potential buyer contacts you, expressing an interest in purchasing your painting service business. The potential buyer offers to purchase your business for a price equal to five times the operating income of the business.

The buyer asks for a copy of the following prior year financial statements for his accountant to review.

- Profit & Loss (Income Statement)
- Balance Sheet
- Statement of Cash Flows

When you prepare the reports, you create memorized reports for future use. To memorize a report, first create the report and then use the memorize feature of QuickBooks.

To create a memorized Profit & Loss report for Paint Palette:

Step 1: From the Report Center select **Company & Financial > Profit & Loss Standard**.

Step 2: Select Dates: From: **01/01/2020** To: **12/31/2020**. Click **Run**.

> *Income for Paint Palette was $31,285. Therefore, the purchase price of the business would be $156,425 (five times income of $31,285).*

Step 3: To memorize the report, select the **Memorize** button at the top of the *Profit & Loss* window.

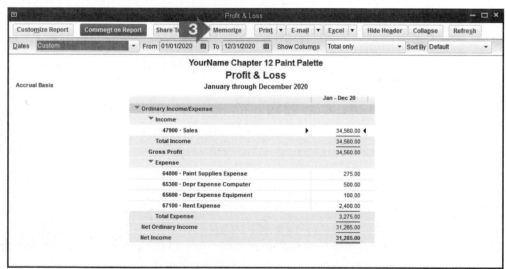

Step 4: When the following *Memorize Report* window appears, enter Memorized Report Name: **Paint Palette Profit & Loss**.

Step 5: Select **Save in Memorized Report Group: Accountant**.

Step 6: Select **OK**.

Step 7: **Close** the *Profit & Loss* window.

Step 8: To use a memorized report, select the **Memorized** tab at the top of the *Report Center* window.

Step 9: Select **Accountant** on the left of the *Report Center* window.

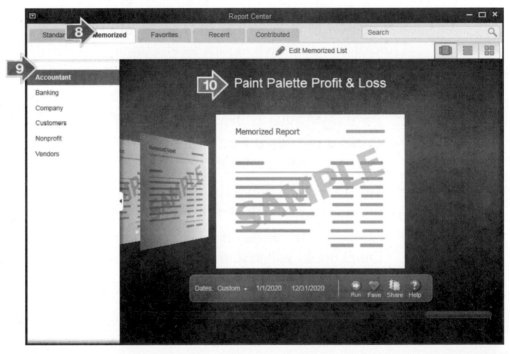

Step 10: When the *Memorized List* window appears, **double-click** on **Paint Palette Profit & Loss** to display the Profit & Loss report.

Step 11: Export to **Excel** or **print** the Profit & Loss report.

Next, create and memorize a Balance Sheet for Paint Palette as of December 31, 2020.

Step 1: Create a Balance Sheet Standard for Paint Palette at December 31, 2020.

Step 2: **Memorize** the Balance Sheet report.

Step 3: Using the memorized Balance Sheet report, export to **Excel** or **print** the Balance Sheet.

Create and memorize a Statement of Cash Flows for Paint Palette for the year 2020.

Step 1: Create a Statement of Cash Flows for Paint Palette for 2020.

Step 2: **Memorize** the Statement of Cash Flows report.

Step 3: Using the memorized Statement of Cash Flows report, export to **Excel** or **print** the Statement of Cash Flows.

In addition to exporting reports to Excel from the *Reports* window, QuickBooks can save reports as electronic files. QuickBooks permits you to select from the following file formats:

- **ASCII text file**. After saving as a text file, the file can be used with word processing software.

- **Comma delimited file.** Comma delimited files can be used with word processing software or database software.

- **Tab delimited file.** Tab delimited files can be used with word processing or database software, such as Microsoft® Access®.

- **Adobe PDF files.** If you have the appropriate software, QuickBooks will save reports as pdf files that are easily emailed.

You can also email reports. Click the **Email** button at the top of the *Reports* window. For example, a client might email reports to the accountant for review.

YOUR DECISION

Based on the financial statement results for Paint Palette, decide whether to sell the painting service business.

Sell painting service?	Yes	No
If you sell, the selling price you will accept:	$_____	
Reason(s) for decision:		

AUDIT TRAIL

The Audit Trail feature of QuickBooks permits you to track all changes (additions, modifications, and deletions) made to your QuickBooks records. When used appropriately, the Audit Trail feature improves internal control by tracking any unauthorized changes to accounting records. The owner (or manager) should periodically review the Audit Trail for discrepancies or unauthorized changes. The Audit Trail report is especially useful if you have more than one user for QuickBooks. This report permits you to determine which user made which changes.

When you export the Audit Trail report to Excel, you can perform further analysis with the Auto Filter feature shown in the following example.

Ima might also try to write off the customer's account as uncollectible in order to ensure the customer does not receive another bill.

To illustrate how an accounting clerk, Ima M. Bezler, might attempt to embezzle funds, assume Ima pockets a customer's cash payment and deletes any record of the customer's bill from QuickBooks.

To test the Audit Trail feature, first record a customer invoice to Katrina Beneficio for $80 using the Intuit Service Invoice template.

Step 1: Using the *Create Invoices* window and the Intuit Service Invoice template, on **02/01/2021** record **2** hours of **mural painting** on the **Katrina Beneficio Vaulted Kitchen job**. **Print** the invoice.

Step 2:   On 02/02/2021, Katrina Beneficio pays her bill in cash. If Ima decides to keep the cash and delete the invoice (so that Beneficio would not receive another bill), the Audit Trail maintains a record of the deleted invoice.

   To delete the invoice, open the Beneficio invoice for $80 and select **Edit** menu **> Delete Invoice**. When asked if you are sure, select **OK**.

The Audit Trail report will list the original transaction (recorded in Step 1 above) and the change to delete the customer's invoice (recorded in Step 2 above).

To prepare the Audit Trail report:

Step 1:   From the Report Center select **Accountant & Taxes**.

Step 2:   Select **Audit Trail**.

Step 3:   Select Dates: **All.**

Step 4:   Select: **Run**.

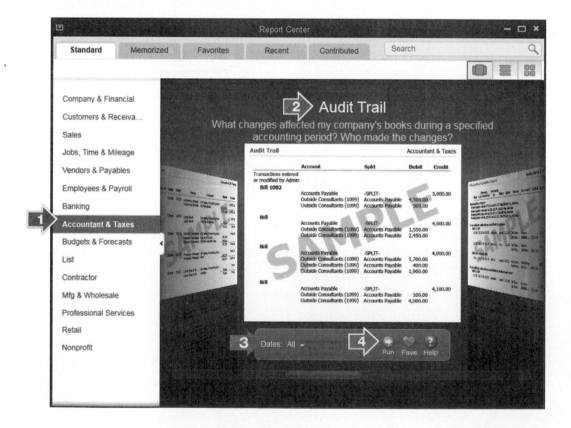

Step 5: To create a filter to display 2021 transactions:

- Select **Customize Report > Filters**.

- Remove Selected Filter: **Entered/Modified Today**.

- Choose Filter: **Date**.

- Select Date From: **01/01/2021** To: **12/31/2021**.

- Click **OK** to close the *Modify Report* window.

Step 6: Click the **Excel** button at the top of the *Audit Trail* window.

Step 7: Select: **Create New Worksheet > Replace an existing worksheet**.

Step 8: Select workbook: **YourLastName FirstName CH12 REPORTS.xls**.

Step 9: Select sheet: **CH12 AUDIT**.

Step 10: Select the **Advanced** tab on the *Send Report to Excel* window.

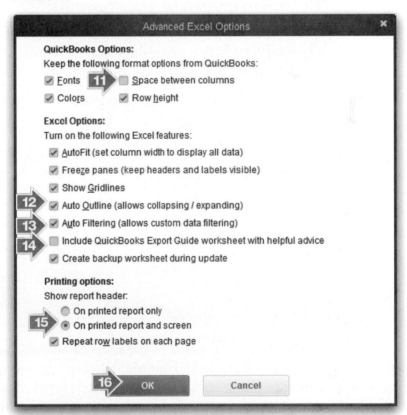

Step 11: *Uncheck:* **Space between columns**.

Step 12: ✓ Check: **Auto Outline (allows collapsing/expanding)**.

Step 13: ✓ Check: **Auto Filtering (allows custom data filtering)**.

Step 14: *Uncheck:* **Include QuickBooks Export Guide worksheet with helpful advice**.

Step 15: Select Show report header: **On printed report and screen**.

Step 16: Select **OK** to close the *Advanced Excel Options* window.

Step 17: Select **Export**.

Step 18: **Highlight** the record of the deleted invoice dated 02/01/2021.

Step 19: **Save** your Excel REPORTS workbook**.**

Notice in the following Audit Trail report exported to Excel including the Auto Filter feature, each column heading becomes a drop-down list. This permits you to sort or select a filter of your choice from the drop-down lists. For example, you could use the Auto Filter to track all items recorded by a specific user (*Last Modified by* field).

As shown in the following Audit Trail report, to track deleted or changed items, you can filter on the status of transactions to display Latest, Prior, or Deleted transactions (*State* field).

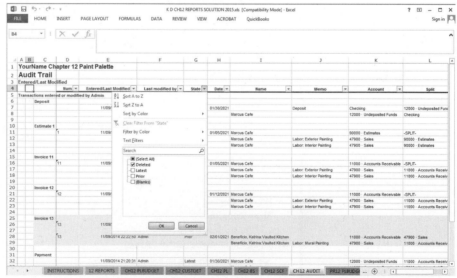

Note that the Audit Trail feature requires more storage for larger files because both original transactions and changed transactions are saved. So the Audit Trail feature may slow processing time.

ACCOUNTANT'S COPY

If an accountant makes adjustments at year-end, QuickBooks can create a copy of the company data files for the accountant to use (Accountant's Copy). The accountant can make adjustments and changes to the Accountant's Copy. Then the Accountant's Copy is merged with the original company data. This permits the entrepreneur to continue using QuickBooks to record transactions at the same time the accountant reviews and makes changes to the records.

To create an Accountant's Copy of Paint Palette:

> The Accountant's Copy can be sent over the Internet to the accountant.

Step 1: Select **File** menu.

Step 2: Select **Send Company File**.

Step 3: Select **Accountant's Copy**.

Step 4: Select **Client Activities**.

Step 5: Select **Save File**.

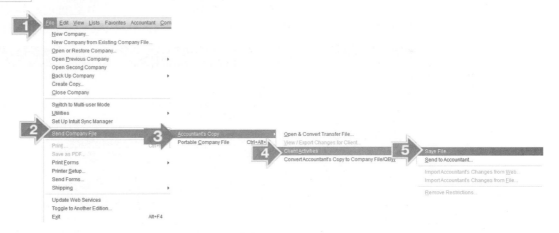

Step 6: After reading the information on the *Save Accountant's Copy* window, select **Accountant's Copy**.

Step 7: Select **Next**.

Step 8: Select Dividing Date: **Custom 12/31/2013**.

Step 9: Select **Next**.

Step 10: When the message appears that QuickBooks must close all windows to prepare an Accountant's Copy, click **OK**.

Step 11: When the *Save Accountant's Copy* window appears:

- Select *Save in* location.

- Enter File name: **YourName Chapter 12**.

- Select Save as type: **Accountant's Copy Transfer Files (*.QBX)**.

- Select **Save > OK**.

QuickBooks will create a copy of the QuickBooks company file for the accountant's temporary use. After the accountant has made necessary adjustments to the Accountant's Copy, the Accountant's Copy is then merged with the QuickBooks company data file, incorporating the accountant's changes into the company's records.

ASK MY ACCOUNTANT

In the Chart of Accounts is an account entitled Ask My Accountant. Entrepreneurs using QuickBooks can use this account to record items when they are uncertain how to record specific items properly. The items can be recorded in this account and the accountant can review these items and record them properly before financial statements are prepared.

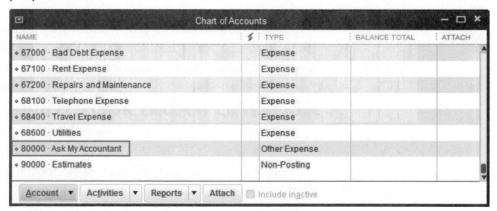

DOCUMENT MANAGEMENT

One challenge for any accounting system is managing numerous and varied documents. QuickBooks now offers a document management feature (Doc Center) to organize your accounting and business documents within QuickBooks software.

Step 1: To view the *Doc Center* window, click on the **Docs** icon in My Shortcuts. You can add documents to the Doc Center in two ways:

1. Add a document on your computer to QuickBooks.

2. Scan a document into QuickBooks using your scanner.

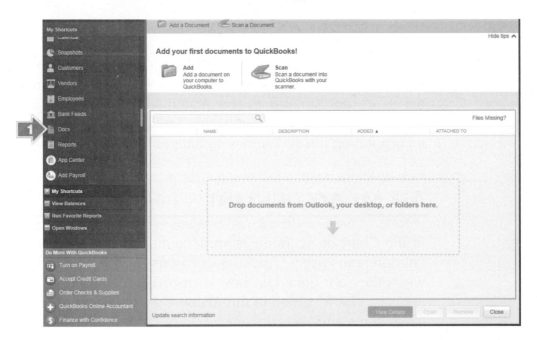

Also, QuickBooks offers you the ability to attach a specific document to a specific transaction. For example, let's say a vendor mails you a hardcopy bill. Wouldn't it be convenient to have an electronic version of the vendor bill attached to the QuickBooks *Enter Bills* form?

As shown in the following example, QuickBooks now permits you to attach the bill you received from a vendor as you enter the bill information into the *Enter Bills* window.

Step 2: To attach a document to a QuickBooks form, open the appropriate QuickBooks transaction or form, such as the following *Enter Bills* form.

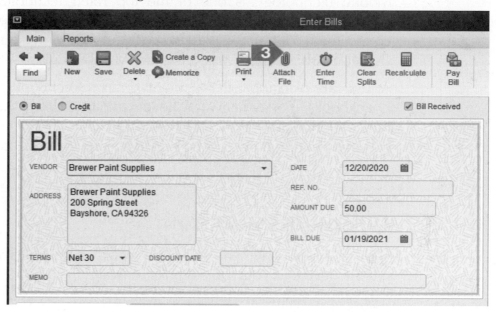

Step 3: Select the **Attach File** icon.

Step 4: When the following *Attachments* window appears, choose from the following options to attach the document:

- **Computer**. Add a document from your computer.

- **Scanner**. Scan a document into QuickBooks with your scanner.

- **Doc Center**. Select a document already uploaded into the QuickBooks Doc Center from your computer or scanner.

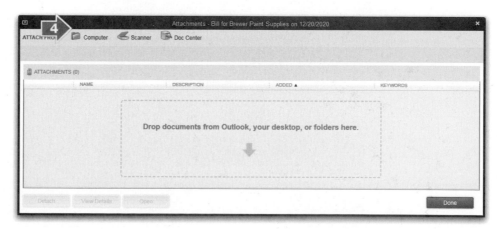

QUICKBOOKS MOBILE APPS

Mobile technology is one of the top rated technology trends in accounting. QuickBooks Mobile Apps use mobile technology to connect you to your QuickBooks software. To view apps, select App Center in QuickBooks software under My Shortcuts.

A QuickBooks app offered by Intuit is QuickBooks GoPayment. Quickbooks GoPayment can be downloaded from the Apps store onto a mobile device, such as your iPad.
customer information can be added on the go and then synced to your QuickBooks software.

QUICKBOOKS GOPAYMENT

QuickBooks GoPayment is an Intuit app that connects you and your mobile device to your QuickBooks software.

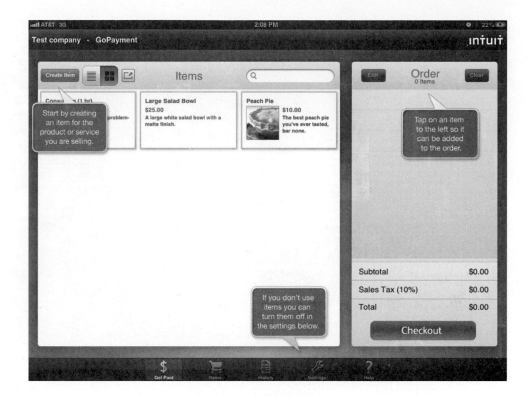

QuickBooks GoPayment permits you to

- Create items that you are selling, including photos of the items.

- Create a sales order by tapping on an item to add it to the sales order.

- Complete checkout for the customer.

- Email the customer a receipt.

You can add and edit items easily, including adding photos of the items to show customers when closing a sale on the go.

QuickBooks GoPayment app permits you to collect customer payments on the go.

A credit card reader connects to your mobile device so you can swipe customer credit cards using your mobile device.

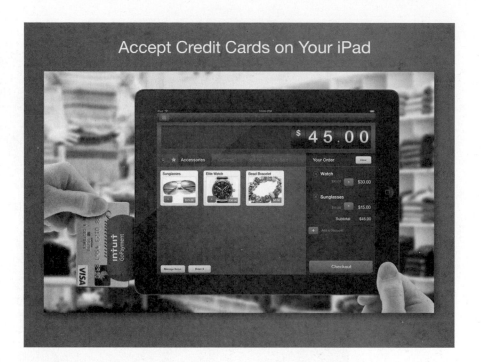

Another payment option is to scan credit cards with your iPhone or iPad camera to process the customer payment.

Get customer sigantures on your iPad or iPhone to complete payment processing. QuickBooks GoPayment generates a customer receipt for the payment that can be emailed to the customer.

QuickBooks GoPayment can sync with your QuickBooks desktop software to record the customer payments.

SAVE CHAPTER 12

Save a backup of your Chapter 12 file using the file name: **YourName Chapter 12 Backup.QBB**. See *Appendix B: Back Up & Restore QuickBooks Files* for instructions.

WWW.MY-QUICKBOOKS.COM

Go to www.My-QuickBooks.com to view additional QuickBooks resources including Excel Reports Templates, QuickBooks videos, and QuickBooks Hot Arrows and Hot Topics. The Hot Topics can be viewed on your computer or tablet and feature frequently used QuickBooks tasks.

MULTIPLE-CHOICE PRACTICE TEST

Try the **Multiple-Choice Practice Test** for Chapter 12 on the *Computer Accounting with QuickBooks* Online Learning Center at www.mhhe.com/kay2015.

GO DIGITAL!

Go Digital using Excel templates. See *Appendix D: Go Digital with QuickBooks* for instructions about how to save your QuickBooks reports electronically.

LEARNING ACTIVITIES

Important: Ask your instructor whether you should complete the following assignments by printing reports or by exporting to Excel templates (see Appendix D: Go Digital with QuickBooks).

EXERCISE 12.1: QUICKBOOKS APPS

The Intuit App Center features apps that work with QuickBooks, including apps that permit you to access your QuickBooks company data on your mobile phone.

Step 1: Select the **App Center** icon under My Shortcuts.

Step 2: From the Apps featured, select your favorite.

Step 3: Summarize for your accounting clients why you consider your choice a worthwhile app for QuickBooks.

EXERCISE 12.2: ACCOUNTANT CENTER

A QuickBooks feature designed for accounting professionals is the Accountant Center. To learn more about this feature:

Step 1: To open the Accountant Center, from My Shortcuts, select **Accountant**.

Step 2: From the *Tools* section of the *Accountant Center* window, select two Accountant tools and write a short email to send to your accounting firm staff summarizing information about how these tools can be used.

EXERCISE 12.3: WEB QUEST

Not ready to file your tax return by April 15? File an extension and postpone filing your tax return until mid October. File Form 4868 by April 15 and send a check for an estimate of the tax you owe to avoid interest and penalties.

To learn more about filing for a tax extension:

Step 1: Go to the IRS website: www.irs.gov.

Step 2: **Print** Form 4868 and instructions for filing a tax extension for an individual income tax return (Form 1040 and Schedule C).

CHAPTER 12 QUICK CHECK

NAME:

INSTRUCTIONS:
1. CHECK OFF THE ITEMS YOU COMPLETED.
2. TURN IN THIS PAGE WITH YOUR PRINTOUTS.

> **!**
> **Ask your instructor if you should Go Digital (Excel* or PDF) or use paper printouts.**

CHAPTER 12
- ☐ * Profit & Loss Budget
- ☐ Estimate
- ☐ Invoice Nos. 11 and 12
- ☐ Deposit Summary
- ☐ * Customer Balance Detail
- ☐ * Profit & Loss
- ☐ * Balance Sheet
- ☐ * Statement of Cash Flows
- ☐ Invoice No. 13
- ☐ * Audit Trail Report

EXERCISE 12.1
- ☐ QuickBooks Apps

EXERCISE 12.2
- ☐ Accountant Center

EXERCISE 12.3
- ☐ IRS Form 4868 and Instructions

 # REFLECTION: A WISH AND A STAR

Reflection improves learning and retention. Reflect on what you have learned after completing Chapter 12 that you did not know before you started the chapter.

A Star:

What did you like best that you learned about QuickBooks in Chapter 12?

A Wish:

If you could pick one thing, what do you wish you knew more about when using QuickBooks?

PROJECT 12 DOMINIC CONSULTING

To complete this project, download the Chapter 12 Go Digital Reports Excel template at www.My-QuickBooks.com.

Using your company file from Project 9 for Dominic Consulting, complete the following. (If you experience issues with your file, contact your instructor for a data file.)

1. Download the Chapter 12 Go Digital Reports Excel template. Save the Excel file using the file name: **YourLastName FirstName CH 12**.

2. Update Company Name to include **YourName Project 12**.

3. Create a Profit and Loss budget for the year 2021.

    ▪ Enter the following budget items and amounts for January 2021.

Account No.	Account	January 2021 Budget Amount
47900	Sales	$4,370.00
64900	Office Supplies (Expense)	$300.00
67100	Rent Expense	$800.00

    ▪ Use a 2% monthly increase for each budget item.

    ▪ Enable compounding.

4. Using your saved Chapter 12 Excel template, export to **Excel** the Profit and Loss Budget Overview report for 2021.

5. Mark the report completed on the 12 REPORTS sheet. Save your Excel file.

6. Save a .QBB backup of your work.

 PROJECT 12 QUICK CHECK
NAME:
INSTRUCTIONS:
1. CHECK OFF THE ITEMS YOU COMPLETED.
2. ATTACH THIS PAGE TO YOUR PRINTOUTS.

> **!**
> Ask your instructor if you should Go Digital (Excel* or PDF) or use paper printouts.

PROJECT 12
☐ * P&L Budget

QUICKBOOKS CASE 12 TUSCANY LANDSCAPES

> **!**
> QB Case 12 is
> a continuation
> of QB Case 9.

SCENARIO

Tuscany Landscapes needs to prepare a budget for 2021.

TASK 1: OPEN COMPANY FILE

WORKFLOW

If you are using the Workflow approach, you will use the same .QBW file from QuickBooks Case 9.

- If your QuickBooks Case 9 QBW file is not already open, open it by selecting **File > Open Previous Company**. Select your **.QBW file.**

- Update Company Name to **YourName QB Case 12 Tuscany Landscapes**.

RESTART & RESTORE

If you are not using the same computer, you must use the Restart and Restore approach. Restore your **QB Case 9 Backup.QBB** file (or use the **QB Case 12 DATA STARTER.QBB** file that comes with your text). After restoring the file, update Company Name to **YourName QB Case 12 Tuscany Landscapes**.

TASK 2: P&L BUDGET

Prepare a budget for Tuscany Landscapes for the year 2021.

Step 1: Prepare a Profit & Loss Budget Overview report for Tuscany Landscapes for the year 2021 using the following information:

- January installation service revenues are expected to be $800. Revenue is expected to increase by 2 percent each month, compounded.

- Supplies for January are budgeted at $60. These costs are expected to increase by 1 percent each month, compounded.

Step 2: Export to **Excel** or **print** the P&L Budget Overview for the year 2021.

TASK 3: MEMORIZE REPORTS

Prepare the following reports for Tuscany Landscapes for the year 2020.

- Profit & Loss, Standard
- Balance Sheet, Standard
- Statement of Cash Flows

Step 1: **Memorize** each report.

Step 2: Export to **Excel** or **print** the reports.

TASK 4: SAVE QUICKBOOKS CASE 12

Save a backup of your QuickBooks Case 12 file using the file name: **YourName QB Case 12 Backup.QBB**. See *Appendix B: Back Up & Restore QuickBooks Files* for instructions.

QUICKBOOKS CASE 12

NAME:

INSTRUCTIONS:

1. CHECK OFF THE ITEMS YOU COMPLETED.
2. TURN IN THIS PAGE WITH YOUR PRINTOUTS.

QB CASE 12

- ☐ * P&L Budget
- ☐ * Profit & Loss, Standard
- ☐ * Balance Sheet, Standard
- ☐ * Statement of Cash Flows

BUILD YOUR DREAM ENTERPRISE

Do you have an interest in being an entrepreneur? Would you like to start your own business? *Build Your Dream Enterprise* QuickBooks cases give you that opportunity. Go to www.My-QuickBooks.com and download the *Build Your Dream Enterprise Case* for Chapter 12.

CHAPTER 13
QuickBooks Live Consulting Project

Scenario

Chapter 13 provides an opportunity to apply the knowledge and skills you have acquired thus far to an authentic QuickBooks project. You will assume the role of a consultant providing QuickBooks consulting services to a client. This project provides an opportunity for realistic, valuable practical experience to better prepare you for professional employment as well as enhance your resume.

The chapter contains a project management framework to guide you through the development of an accounting system for entrepreneurs or not-for-profits using QuickBooks accounting software. The project management approach divides the project into milestones for system development that can be used with various types of organizations, allowing for flexibility to customize the system to meet the specific needs of the entrepreneur or not-for-profit.

The project management framework that you will be using to develop a real QuickBooks accounting system consists of the following seven milestones.

Milestone 1. Develop a proposal. In this milestone, you will identify a real-world client (either a small business or a nonprofit organization) that needs assistance in establishing an accounting system using QuickBooks. After identifying the client, gather information from the client and develop a plan for a QuickBooks accounting system that will meet the client's needs.

Milestone 2. Develop a prototype or sample QuickBooks accounting system for the client. Set up a company in QuickBooks with a sample Chart of Accounts for the client to review. After obtaining approval of the Chart of Accounts from the client and your instructor, enter beginning balances for the accounts.

Milestone 3. Develop sample QuickBooks lists for customers, vendors, items, and employees. Obtain client and instructor approval for the lists and enter the list information.

Milestone 4. Enter sample transactions to test the prototype.

Milestone 5. Identify the reports that the client needs and then create memorized reports using QuickBooks.

Milestone 6. Develop documentation for the project including instructions for future use.

Milestone 7. Present the final project first to your class and then to the client.

This project can be completed individually or in teams. Ask your instructor which approach you will be using.

CHAPTER 13
LEARNING OBJECTIVES

Chapter 13 contains a project management framework consisting of the following seven milestones to develop a QuickBooks accounting system:

INTRODUCTION

This chapter will give you project management tools to develop a real QuickBooks accounting system. You will assume the role of a consultant providing consulting services to a client for developing an accounting system using QuickBooks software. This project provides an opportunity for realistic, valuable practical experience to better prepare you for professional employment and enhance your resume.

Consistent with a sound project management approach, developing a QuickBooks accounting system is divided into seven milestones. Each milestone should be reviewed by your instructor before you proceed to the next milestone. In addition, the QuickBooks Consulting Project Approval form should be signed by the client as each step is completed and approved.

MILESTONE 1
PROPOSAL

For Milestone 1, you will create a project proposal. The purpose of the proposal is twofold. First, it forces you, the consultant, to plan the project from start to finish. Second, the proposal serves to improve communication between you and your client. When the client reads your proposal, there is an opportunity for the client to further clarify any misunderstandings. Furthermore, the client may think of additional information or user requirements that were not mentioned earlier.

Complete the following steps to create a project proposal:

Step 1: Identify a real QuickBooks project.

Step 2: Gather project information and user requirements.

Step 3: Write the project proposal.

IDENTIFY QUICKBOOKS PROJECT

The first step is to identify an actual client who needs a QuickBooks accounting system. The client can be an entrepreneur, small business, or not-for-profit organization. For example, the client can be a friend or relative who operates a small business and needs an updated accounting system. Some colleges have Service Learning Coordinators who assist in matching student volunteers with charitable organizations needing assistance.

GATHER QUICKBOOKS PROJECT INFORMATION AND USER REQUIREMENTS

After identifying the client, the next step is to interview the client to determine specific accounting needs and user requirements. Communication is extremely important to the process of designing and developing a successful accounting system. Listening to the client's needs and then communicating to the client the possible solutions are part of the ongoing development process. If clients are not familiar with accounting or QuickBooks, they may not be able to communicate all of their needs. This requires you to gather enough information from the client to identify both the need and the solution. To make the most effective use of your client's time during the interview, prepare in advance. Before the interview, review all seven milestones of the project to identify the types of information you need to collect. For example, when gathering information for the Customer List, what customer fields does the client need? Also review the QuickBooks New Company Setup (see Chapters 8 and 10) to make certain you ask your client the questions you will need to answer when setting up the new company QuickBooks file for your client.

When collecting information about the Chart of Accounts, first identify the tax return filed by the enterprise. This will help you determine the accounts that are needed for tax purposes. Then, collect information about the assets, liabilities, equity, revenue and expense accounts that the company currently uses. Also, collect information about the beginning balances for accounts with opening balances.

> **!** It is important to inform the client that this is for a class project and all work should be reviewed by his or her own accountant to verify appropriateness.

> **!** All information the client shares with you is confidential and should not be shared with anyone else. If you need to share information of a confidential nature with your instructor, first ask the client's permission.

Prior to your interview, create your own User Requirements Checklist for gathering information from the client. A sample checklist follows.

Milestone 1 User Requirements Checklist	
☐ Organization name	
☐ Type of business (industry)	
☐ Chart of Accounts information ☐ Tax return (Schedule C, Form 1120, Form 1120S) ☐ Beginning account balances	
☐ Customer List information	
☐ Vendor List information	
☐ Employee List information	
☐ Item List information	
☐ Types of transactions to be recorded	
☐ Types of reports needed	
☐ Users of the QuickBooks system and security access	
☐ Other user requirements	

WRITE QUICKBOOKS CONSULTING PROJECT PROPOSAL

After gathering information from the client, write a proposal that describes your plan for designing and developing your project. The proposal is a plan of what you intend to accomplish and how you will accomplish it.

Your proposal should have a professional appearance and tone that communicates to your client your competency and your enthusiasm for his or her project. Components of the proposal include:

1. **Cover Letter.** In the cover letter, you can thank the client for the opportunity to work together on this QuickBooks project, provide a brief introduction about yourself, summarize the main points in your proposal, and provide your contact information if the client has questions.

2. **Executive Summary.** Include the project name, your name, client name, and the date.

   Paragraph 1. Project objectives and initial feasibility assessment.

   Paragraph 2. Possible solutions that would meet project objectives.

   Paragraph 3. Your recommendation for the project and supporting rationale.

   An Executive Summary Template appears on a following page.

3. **Proposal Report.** Include the following headings and sections:

   - **Overview and Objectives.** Briefly describe the client organization and operations. Identify the client's user requirements for an accounting system. For example, the client needs accounting records for tax purposes. Evaluate the feasibility of meeting the organization's needs with QuickBooks and the objectives of this project.

   - **Scope of Services.** Outline the services that you will provide for the client. What accounting features of QuickBooks will be implemented? Accounts receivable? Accounts payable? Specify the services you will provide the client. Will you provide implementation and setup? Conversion assistance?

- **Client Responsibilities.** Clearly specify any responsibilities or information that the client will need to provide.

- **Cost/Benefit Analysis.** Provide a summary of the costs associated with the project that the client might expect to occur. Provide information about the benefits that might be expected, including financial and nonfinancial benefits. For example, estimated time that the client might save in maintaining accounting records.

- **Timeline.** Identify and list the major tasks involved in completing the project. Include a timeline with completion dates for each task. See the sample format below.

Task	Projected Completion Date
1._____	_____
2._____	_____
3._____	_____
4._____	_____
5._____	_____
Etc._____	_____

- **Recommendation.** State your recommendation and provide a short summary including any disclaimers or remaining challenges. End the proposal on a positive, upbeat note.

Submit the proposal to both the client and your instructor. Obtain approval from both the client and your instructor. Ask the client to sign off on the proposal using the approval form that appears at the end of Chapter 13.

Executive Summary [Template]		
Company Name	[Your company name and logo]	
Contact Name	[Your name]	
Date	[Date of proposal]	
For	[Client name]	
Project Name	[QuickBooks project name]	
Objectives	[Paragraph 1 contains a concise summary of the project objectives and the initial feasibility assessment.]	
Possible Solutions	[Paragraph 2 briefly summarizes possible solutions that satisfy the project objectives.]	
Recommendation	[Paragraph 3 contains your recommendation and supporting rationale.]	

MILESTONE 2
COMPANY SETUP

! When creating the Chart of Accounts, refer to the tax form the organization will use. Obtain copies of tax forms at www.irs.gov.

In this milestone, you will set up a prototype or sample company for the client to review and revise.

Step 1: Based on the information collected from the client, set up a new company and customize the Chart of Accounts for the company.

+

Nonprofits use fund accounting. Use subaccounts or the class tracking preference for fund accounting.

Step 2: Submit the Chart of Accounts to your instructor for review and recommendations.

Step 3: Have the client review the Chart of Accounts and make recommendations. Ask the client to sign off on the Chart of Accounts using the approval form.

Step 4: After obtaining approval from both the client and instructor, enter beginning balances for the accounts.

MILESTONE 3
CUSTOMER, VENDOR, EMPLOYEE, AND ITEM LISTS

After the Chart of Accounts has been approved, develop lists (customer, vendor, employee, and item) for the client.

Step 1: After consulting with the client, list the customer information (fields) needed for each customer. If necessary, create user-defined fields in QuickBooks to accommodate the client's needs.

Step 2: List the information needed by the organization for each vendor. Create any user-defined fields that are needed for vendors.

Step 3: List the employee information needed by the organization for each employee. Determine any payroll items needed to accurately record payroll. If applicable, collect payroll year-to-date information.

Step 4: Determine the items (inventory, non-inventory, and service items) required to meet the organization's needs. List the information needed for each item.

Step 5: After obtaining approval for the lists from the client and your instructor, enter information for the following:

- Customer List
- Vendor List
- Employee List
- Item List
- Payroll year-to-date information

MILESTONE 4
TRANSACTIONS

Complete the following steps for Milestone 4.

Step 1: Determine the types of transactions the client will enter in QuickBooks (for example: cash sales, credit card sales, purchase orders).

Step 2: Enter test or sample transactions in QuickBooks. Obtain client and instructor approval of the results.

Step 3: Modify forms as needed to meet the client's needs. For example, if the client needs a *Date* column on the invoice, customize the invoice by following the instructions in QuickBooks Case 9.

Step 4: After obtaining the client's approval for transactions, create memorized transactions for the transactions that will be repeated periodically.

> As you develop the accounting system, you may find that further customization of the Chart of Accounts is needed to meet specific business needs.
> In your final project, highlight any new accounts added.

It is important that you and the client reach an agreement regarding what you will complete before you turn the project over to the client. Discuss with the client whether you will be entering only a few sample transactions or entering all transactions for the year to date. For example, if entering all transactions is too time consuming, you may agree that you will enter only sample transactions and the client will enter the real transactions after you submit the final project.

MILESTONE 5
MEMORIZED REPORTS

Complete the following steps for Milestone 5:

Step 1: Determine which reports the client needs. Review Chapters 4, 5, 6, and 7 to obtain information about the different reports that QuickBooks can generate. You may need to make the client aware of the reports that are available in QuickBooks and then let the client select the reports that would be useful.

Step 2: Obtain client and instructor approval for the reports.

Step 3: After obtaining approval concerning the reports, create and memorize the reports using QuickBooks.

MILESTONE 6
DOCUMENTATION AND CLIENT INSTRUCTIONS

Provide the client with instructions for using QuickBooks Help feature.

Create documentation for the client. Include a history of the project development as well as instructions that the client will need. For example, instructions regarding how and when to back up and restore company files are essential. Providing instructions on how to use memorized transactions and memorized reports is also advisable.

Be prepared for clients to ask if they may call if they need your assistance in the future. Adequate user instructions (Milestone 6) are essential in reducing the client's future dependence on you.

An easy way to provide the client with adequate instructions is to recommend existing training materials to the client and then simply reference pages in the training materials. For example, if the client obtains a copy of this book, you may wish to reference pages of the text for each task the client will be performing.

Other documentation that the client might find useful is the Year-End Guide that appears on a following page. To view the Year-End Guide, select **Help** menu **> Year-End Guide**.

MILESTONE 7
PRESENTATION

There are three parts to this milestone:

Step 1: Make any final changes to your project.

Step 2: Make the project presentation to your class.

Step 3: Make a project presentation to the client.

The presentation to your instructor and classmates is practice for the final presentation to the client. You may want to ask your classmates for suggestions you can incorporate into your final presentation for the client.

A suggested outline for the project presentation follows:

1. **History and Overview.** Provide background about the client and the client's needs as an introduction for your presentation.

2. **Demonstration.** If the room has projection equipment, demonstrate your QuickBooks project. Display memorized transactions, memorized reports, and lists for the class and/or client to view. *Remember to use test/sample data for the class presentation instead of actual client data that is confidential.*

3. **Examples.** Present examples of the documentation and client instructions you are providing the client (see Milestone 6).

4. **Cost/Benefit and Advantages/Disadvantages.** Briefly present advantages and disadvantages of using QuickBooks for this particular project as well as associated costs and benefits.

5. **Summary.** Present concluding remarks to summarize the major points of your presentation.

6. **Questions and Answers.** Provide classmates or the client an opportunity to ask questions about the project. In preparing for your presentation, you will want to anticipate possible questions and prepare appropriate answers.

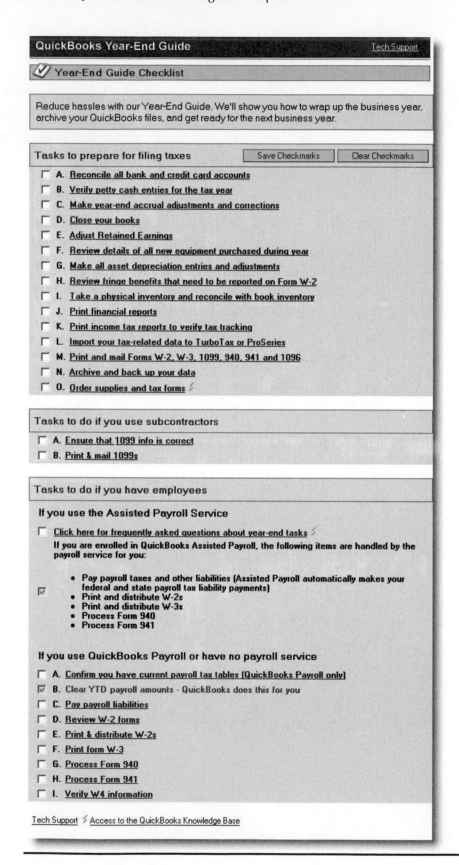

QuickBooks Year-End Guide   Tech Support

✓ Year-End Guide Checklist

Reduce hassles with our Year-End Guide. We'll show you how to wrap up the business year, archive your QuickBooks files, and get ready for the next business year.

Tasks to prepare for filing taxes   [Save Checkmarks] [Clear Checkmarks]

- ☐ A. Reconcile all bank and credit card accounts
- ☐ B. Verify petty cash entries for the tax year
- ☐ C. Make year-end accrual adjustments and corrections
- ☐ D. Close your books
- ☐ E. Adjust Retained Earnings
- ☐ F. Review details of all new equipment purchased during year
- ☐ G. Make all asset depreciation entries and adjustments
- ☐ H. Review fringe benefits that need to be reported on Form W-2
- ☐ I. Take a physical inventory and reconcile with book inventory
- ☐ J. Print financial reports
- ☐ K. Print income tax reports to verify tax tracking
- ☐ L. Import your tax-related data to TurboTax or ProSeries
- ☐ M. Print and mail Forms W-2, W-3, 1099, 940, 941 and 1096
- ☐ N. Archive and back up your data
- ☐ O. Order supplies and tax forms

Tasks to do if you use subcontractors

- ☐ A. Ensure that 1099 info is correct
- ☐ B. Print & mail 1099s

Tasks to do if you have employees

If you use the Assisted Payroll Service

- ☐ Click here for frequently asked questions about year-end tasks

    If you are enrolled in QuickBooks Assisted Payroll, the following items are handled by the payroll service for you:

- ☑ • Pay payroll taxes and other liabilities (Assisted Payroll automatically makes your federal and state payroll tax liability payments)
    • Print and distribute W-2s
    • Print and distribute W-3s
    • Process Form 940
    • Process Form 941

If you use QuickBooks Payroll or have no payroll service

- ☐ A. Confirm you have current payroll tax tables (QuickBooks Payroll only)
- ☑ B. Clear YTD payroll amounts - QuickBooks does this for you
- ☐ C. Pay payroll liabilities
- ☐ D. Review W-2 forms
- ☐ E. Print & distribute W-2s
- ☐ F. Print form W-3
- ☐ G. Process Form 940
- ☐ H. Process Form 941
- ☐ I. Verify W4 information

Tech Support ⚡ Access to the QuickBooks Knowledge Base

QuickBooks Consulting Project Approval

Milestone	Comments	Approved	Date
1. Proposal		_____	_____
2. Company Setup & Chart of Accounts		_____	_____
3. Lists: Customer, Vendor, Employee, & Item		_____	_____
4. Transactions		_____	_____
5. Memorized Reports		_____	_____
6. Documentation		_____	_____
7. Final Presentation		_____	_____

NOTES:

CHAPTER 14
QUICKBOOKS ONLINE ACCOUNTANT

SCENARIO

Your QuickBooks consulting business continues to grow as satisfied clients refer new clients. While most of your clients need the added functionality and features of QuickBooks desktop software, a few clients have asked you about anytime, anywhere QuickBooks Online. Your challenge is to find the best fit to meet your clients' needs while at the same time keeping your consulting service operations streamlined and efficient.

To make informed recommendations to your clients, you realize you need to learn more about the various QuickBooks options offered by Intuit.

CHAPTER 14
LEARNING OBJECTIVES

Chapter 14 contains information about:

ASK MY ACCOUNTANT: WHICH QUICKBOOKS SHOULD I USE?

To meet different QuickBooks users' needs, Intuit offers several different versions of QuickBooks. If you are an accountant advising different clients on the best fit between their needs and QuickBooks version, then a general knowledge of the different types of QuickBooks available becomes vital to provide sound client advice.

In general, QuickBooks versions can be divided into two broad categories:

- **QuickBooks User.** Businesses and organizations that use QuickBooks to maintain their accounting and financial records.

- **QuickBooks Accountant.** Accountants who provide accounting and financial services to multiple clients who use QuickBooks.

Since QuickBooks offers several different options (summarized in the following table), QuickBooks users often turn to their accountants for recommendations about which QuickBooks to use. The QuickBooks version that the client uses dictates which QuickBooks version the client's accountant must use. As the accountant making recommendations, you will need to consider not only how the recommendation affects your client, but also how the recommendation will impact your client services operations.

QuickBooks Versions	Desktop	Online
Client/User	- QuickBooks Pro - QuickBooks Premier - QuickBooks Enterprise	QuickBooks Online
Accounting Firm	QuickBooks Accountant	QuickBooks Online Accountant

When making client recommendations, keep in mind the difference between client needs and wants. Needs are critical; wants are wishes. Stay focused on needs first, so you do not become distracted and sidetracked with client wants, which can keep you from meeting client needs. An easy way to do this is to make two lists with needs on one list and wants on another list. After needs are addressed, then wants can be considered. Prepare your client to face tradeoffs, such as tighter control over data security versus anytime, anywhere access. Your role is to summarize the features and tradeoffs, assisting clients with finding a good fit, even if they do not attain 100% of what they thought they wanted.

How Can Our Accounting Firm Streamline Our QuickBooks Consulting?

Which QuickBooks version your clients use affects your consulting services operations. Some accounting firms relate war stories about clients using an array of QuickBooks desktop software from the 2002 edition and every year to the present edition. This approach to QuickBooks consulting requires the accounting firm to maintain all the various versions of the client software and track which clients use which versions. This can become a logistical nightmare for an accounting firm since it must have not only all the QuickBooks editions operational but also staff trained on the multiple versions.

Other accounting firms take a more streamlined, proactive approach when working with multiple clients that use QuickBooks. These firms recommend to clients which QuickBooks edition to use based on the best fit for the client while still keeping it manageable for the firm. Some accountants move all their clients to the next edition of QuickBooks at the same time. For example, after the 2015 QuickBooks edition is released in fall of 2014 and the accounting firm has thoroughly tested the new edition, the firm moves all clients to QuickBooks 2015 on January 1, 2015. This approach permits the accounting firm to test the new software for possible issues, install updates, and create workarounds before moving clients to the new edition. Since many clients are on a calendar year starting January 1, this timeline permits a nice cutoff. Also, this approach streamlines firm operations since now all clients and the firm are in sync, using the same version of QuickBooks.

This proactive approach requires the accounting firm to communicate clearly with clients, working as a team with clients to prepare and transition them to the new version. Firms that use this proactive approach often state that it requires time and effort to do so, but much less time than trying to maintain multiple versions of QuickBooks for multiple clients. If clients start moving to the new edition as soon as it is released, clients may encounter unexpected issues that the accounting firm has not had time to thoroughly investigate and resolve. Some firms even provide training for clients as they transition them to the new version, summarizing differences and new features to proactively prepare clients for what to expect. This can minimize client errors in working with the new version and save the firm from unexpected disruptions and surprises.

Although features and functionality of QuickBooks options can be expected to change over time, the following sections summarize information about some of the QuickBooks options for clients and accountants. For additional updates about each of these options, see www.Intuit.com.

WHAT ARE MY QUICKBOOKS USER OPTIONS?

QuickBooks is designed for business use, not personal finance. For personal financial records of the business owners, personal financial apps should be used, such as Quicken (Intuit's predecessor to QuickBooks) or Mint (now owned by Intuit).

A QuickBooks user is a business, entrepreneur, or not-for-profit organization that uses QuickBooks to maintain accounting and financial records for that entity. A QuickBooks user has two basic options:

- **QuickBooks Desktop**
- **QuickBooks Online**

If the QuickBooks user selects the QuickBooks desktop option, then there are several additional choices to consider that are summarized next.

QUICKBOOKS PRO, PREMIER, OR ENTERPRISE (DESKTOP)

QuickBooks desktop software can be installed on the hard drive of desktop computers, laptops, or servers controlled by the user (client). If QuickBooks is installed on a network, it can be accessed by multiple QuickBooks users. QuickBooks desktop software can be purchased using three different approaches:

1. **CD.** QuickBooks software is installed from a CD.
2. **Software download.** Since new desktop computers and laptops increasingly do not have CD drives, users can purchase a QuickBooks software key code and download the QuickBooks software using an Internet browser.

3. **Subscription.** Instead of purchasing QuickBooks software, the user can choose to pay a monthly subscription fee to use the software. The QuickBooks software is still downloaded to the desktop computer or laptop, but when the user decides to stop paying the monthly fee, the user's access to the QuickBooks software is blocked.

In general, QuickBooks desktop offers several advantages over QuickBooks Online including:
- Additional features and functionality not offered by QuickBooks Online
- User control over desktop computer access and security
- User control over backups and access to backup data files
- Portability of backup and portable QuickBooks files
- Remote access to QuickBooks desktop
- Navigation features to streamline use, such as the My Shortcuts Icon bar and the Home page with flowcharts
- Intuit offers the following different editions of the QuickBooks desktop software to meet specific user needs, including:
  - *QuickBooks Pro*
  - *QuickBooks Premier*
  - *QuickBooks Enterprise*

QuickBooks Pro is a good option for small businesses that do not require industry-specific features because it is less expensive.

QuickBooks Premier offers more advanced features than QuickBooks Pro and permits you to customize QuickBooks by selecting a version with industry-specific features. QuickBooks Premier has different industry versions from which you can choose including the following.
- Contractor
- Manufacturing and Wholesale
- Nonprofit
- Professional Services
- Retailers
- General Business

QuickBooks Enterprise Solutions is designed for mid-size companies that have outgrown QuickBooks Premier. QuickBooks Enterprise can be used to track inventory at multiple locations and consolidate reports from multiple companies.

QuickBooks Mobile Apps that sync with QuickBooks desktop software include QuickBooks GoPayment, which permits users to collect customer payments on the go with their mobile device and then sync to their QuickBooks desktop system. For more information about QuickBooks Mobile Apps for QuickBooks desktop software see Chapter 12 or access the App Center through the QuickBooks desktop software.

QUICKBOOKS ONLINE

Accessed using a browser and the Internet, QuickBooks Online typically has fewer features and functionality than the QuickBooks desktop version. With QuickBooks Online, there is no software to install on your computer hard drive or local server. The main advantage to QuickBooks Online is its anytime, anywhere use, so long as Internet access is available. Factors to consider when using QuickBooks Online include:

- Internet connection needs to be a secure connection with data in transit encrypted. Using an open WiFi at a café or a hotel when traveling to access QuickBooks Online, while convenient, places data in transit at risk. Your login, password, and confidential financial data could be viewed by others.
- Fewer features and functionality than QuickBooks desktop with features that will continue to change as QuickBooks Online is dynamically updated.
- The convenience of dynamic updates that occur automatically without needing to download and install.

- Loss of control over when updates occur, which may result in the need to learn new updates at unplanned times.

QuickBooks Online Mobile App permits you to access your QuickBooks Online financial records from your iPad, iPhone, or Android device.

WHAT ARE MY QUICKBOOKS ACCOUNTANT OPTIONS?

Designed for accountants serving multiple clients, Intuit offers two QuickBooks Accountant options:

- **QuickBooks Accountant Desktop**
- **QuickBooks Online Accountant**

Which option the accountant chooses is typically dictated by client use because QuickBooks desktop files are not compatible with QuickBooks Online. For example, if all the accounting firm's clients use QuickBooks desktop software, then the accounting firm would use QuickBooks Accountant desktop version. If the clients use QuickBooks Online, then the accountant would need to use QuickBooks Online Accountant. Some accounting firms have clients using QuickBooks desktop versions and other clients using QuickBooks Online, so those accounting firms must use both QuickBooks Accountant desktop and QuickBooks Online Accountant to be able to work with both types of clients.

QUICKBOOKS ACCOUNTANT (DESKTOP)

QuickBooks Accountant desktop is the software packaged free with this text if purchased new. Like QuickBooks desktop software, *QuickBooks Accountant* in the desktop edition is installed on the hard drive of desktop computers, laptops, or network servers. The QuickBooks Accountant edition permits the accountant to toggle between different desktop user editions of QuickBooks. This permits the accountant to view whatever edition of QuickBooks (QuickBooks Pro, QuickBooks Premier, and so on) that a particular client uses. For additional features of QuickBooks Accountant in the desktop edition, see Chapter 12.

QUICKBOOKS ONLINE ACCOUNTANT

QuickBooks Online Accountant is designed for accounting firms that provide services to multiple clients who use QuickBooks Online. QuickBooks Online Accountant is accessed using the Internet and a browser and permits the accountant to collaborate with several different clients, viewing their QuickBooks Online company files. QuickBooks Online Accountant, at this time, does not use the Home page navigational feature. In addition, there are fewer features and functionality with the QuickBooks Online Accountant version than the QuickBooks Accountant desktop version. The main advantage to QuickBooks Online Accountant is the anytime, anywhere access when an Internet connection is available. Of course, since the accountant is responsible for maintaining the confidentiality of client financial data, the Internet connection needs to be a secure connection with data in transit encrypted. Using an open WiFi connection risks data in transit (such as your login, password, and confidential client financial data) being viewed by others. Since accounting firms have a responsibility to maintain client data confidentiality and security, this is a serious concern.

For more information about using QuickBooks Online Accountant:

1. Go to: **www.My-QuickBooks.com**
2. Select: **QB Online**
3. Enter Passcode: **KayQBOA**

SECTION 3
QUICK GUIDE

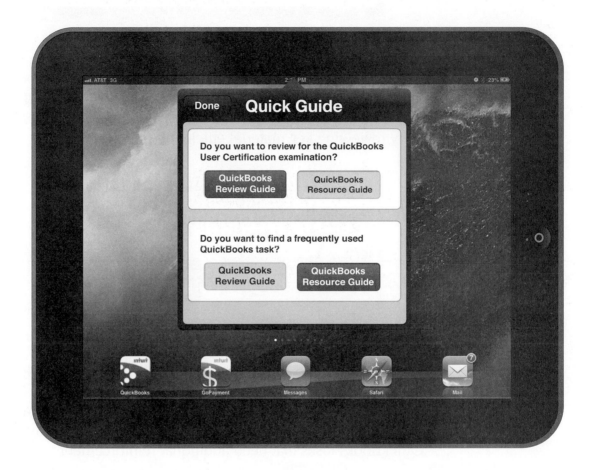

For your convenience, this Quick Guide is designed for you as a quick review guide and resource guide.

QuickBooks Review Guide. A review guide to streamline your prep for the *QuickBooks User Certification* examination.

QuickBooks Resource Guide. A user friendly resource guide for frequently used QuickBooks tasks.

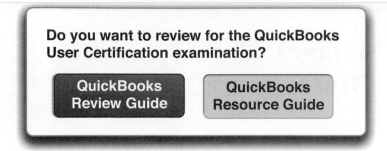

This Quick Guide is a **QuickBooks Review Guide** to streamline your preparation for the QuickBooks User Certification exam. Organized around the 10 domains covered on the QuickBooks User Certification exam, this Quick Guide is designed to guide you in quickly reviewing key material efficiently.

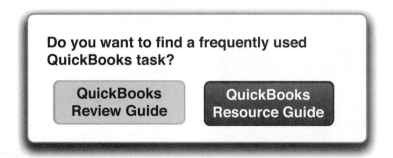

The Quick Guide is also a user friendly **QuickBooks Resource Guide** for frequently used QuickBooks tasks. Tutorials in Chapters 1 through 12 are effective for learning QuickBooks tasks and features. This Quick Guide permits you to locate quickly any key QuickBooks tasks that need additional reinforcement.

Next, learn more about how to use the Quick Guide as a review guide for the QuickBooks User Certification exam and as a QuickBooks Resource Guide.

Quickbooks Review Guide

QUICKBOOKS USER CERTIFICATION EXAM REVIEW GUIDE

After you have completed Chapters 1 through 12 of *Computer Accounting with QuickBooks*, use this Quick Guide to review for the QuickBooks User Certification examination.

WHAT IS THE QUICKBOOKS USER CERTIFICATION EXAMINATION?

The QuickBooks User Certification exam is an online exam that is proctored at authorized testing centers. The exam consists of multiple choice questions or simulations. The QuickBooks User Certification examination is a certification focused on QuickBooks users. The QuickBooks ProAdvisor certification is a different certification that is focused more on accountants who provide advisory services to QuickBooks clients.

WHAT IS ON THE QUICKBOOKS USER CERTIFICATION EXAMINATION?

The QuickBooks User Certification exam covers 10 domains. The following table provides you with information about current coverage of the QuickBooks User Certification exam domains, content and approximate coverage.

	QuickBooks User Certification Domain	Exam %
1	QuickBooks Setup	6%
2	QuickBooks Utilities and General Product Knowledge	10%
3	List Management	6%
4	Items	8%
5	Sales	10%
6	Purchases	10%
7	Payroll	12%
8	Reports	16%
9	Basic Accounting	10%
10	Customization and Saving Time	12%

WHY CONSIDER TAKING THE QUICKBOOKS USER CERTIFICATION EXAMINATION?

Passing the QuickBooks User Certification examination can add another credential to your resume. Employers often look for credentials that indicate skill and knowledge level as a baseline for employment.

HOW CAN THE QUICK GUIDE HELP ME REVIEW FOR THE QUICKBOOKS USER CERTIFICATION EXAMINATION?

This Quick Guide is mapped to the 10 domains of the QuickBooks User Certification exam to streamline your review for the exam.

The Quick Guide domain mapping to the QuickBooks User Certification follows.

Quick Guide	QuickBooks User Certification Domain
1	QuickBooks Setup
2	QuickBooks Utilities and General Product Knowledge
3	List Management
4	Items
5	Sales
6	Purchases
7	Payroll
8	Reports
9	Basic Accounting
10	Customization and Saving Time

WHAT IS AN EFFECTIVE REVIEW ACTION PLAN?

Consider the following action plan to increase the effectiveness of your review. Note that simply reading the instructions assists your review but deeper learning occurs when you actually complete the steps using the QuickBooks software.

1. *Complete* Chapters 1 through 12 of *Computer Accounting with QuickBooks 2015*.

2. *Download* the file: **Section 3 Review DATA STARTER.QBB** from www.mhhe.com/kay2015 or *copy* it from the data file CD.

3. *Restore* the **Section 3 Review DATA STARTER.QBB** file following the instructions in *Appendix B* for restoring a file. When restoring, use the filename **Section 3 Review.QBW**. (If QuickBooks requests a password, leave the Password field **blank**, and click **OK**.)

4. *Read* and then *complete* the steps contained in the QuickBooks Review Guide using the **Section 3 Review.QBW** file. To practice some of the tasks, simply insert realistic data to complete the forms.

   - Consider reviewing the Quick Guide a minimum of three times to improve your retention of the material.

   - Mark any tasks that you found challenging for later practice.

5. Try a practice exam.

   - Take the online practice tests available for each chapter on *Computer Accounting with QuickBooks 2015* Online Learning Center. The practice tests are graded so you can see your practice test score and the correct answers.

   - If you register to take the QuickBooks User Certification exam at www.Certiport.com, you will be provided with a code that permits you to take practice exams before you take the certification examination. Take a practice exam and see how well you do.

HOW DO I OBTAIN MORE INFORMATION ABOUT THE QUICKBOOKS USER CERTIFICATION EXAMINATION?

For more information, see www.certiport.com or go to www.My-QuickBooks.com and click on QB Certified User.

QuickBooks
Resource Guide

QUICKBOOKS RESOURCE GUIDE

This Quick Guide contains step-by-step instructions for frequently used QuickBooks tasks, providing you with a convenient, easy-to-use resource that summarizes essential tasks.

The chapters in *Computer Accounting with QuickBooks* are designed as tutorials for you to initially learn the accounting software, providing numerous screen captures and detailed instructions. To improve long-term retention of your software skills, exercises and projects are designed with fewer instructions to test your understanding and, when needed, to develop your skill at quickly locating additional information to complete the task. JIT Learning, the ability to seek out information as needed, is an increasingly important skill in the rapidly changing business environment, and the design of *Computer Accounting with QuickBooks* seamlessly facilitates your development of this crucial skill.

1. QUICKBOOKS SETUP

2. QUICKBOOKS UTILITIES AND GENERAL PRODUCT KNOWLEDGE

3. LIST MANAGEMENT

7. PAYROLL (EMPLOYEE TRANSACTIONS)

8. REPORTS

9. BASIC ACCOUNTING

10. CUSTOMIZATION/SAVING TIME AND SHORTCUTS

1. QuickBooks Setup

Install QuickBooks Software

To install QuickBooks software, follow the step-by-step directions in *Appendix A: Install & Register QuickBooks Software*.

Register QuickBooks Software

Register QuickBooks software online at the time you install the software, following the directions in *Appendix A: Install & Register QuickBooks Software*.

Failure to register QuickBooks software within the first 30 days will result in the software no longer functioning. To avoid this, register the software at the time you install it. If you fail to register QuickBooks software within 30 days and you are locked out from using the software, select **Help** menu > **Register QuickBooks**. Another option is to uninstall and reinstall the QuickBooks software from your trial version CD that accompanies your text, registering the software when requested.

Start QuickBooks Software

1. Click the QuickBooks desktop icon or click **Start > Programs > QuickBooks > QuickBooks Premier Accountant Edition 2015** (or **QuickBooks Pro 2015**).

2. If necessary, close the *QuickBooks Learning Center* window to begin using QuickBooks.

Set Up New Company

1. Select **File** menu > **New Company**.

2. Select **Detailed Start**. Follow the onscreen instructions to complete the EasyStep Interview to set up a new company. Also see *Chapter 8*.

3. Complete the QuickBooks Setup to add bank accounts, vendors, customers, employees, and items. Also see *Chapter 8*.

Set Up New Company from Existing Company

1. Select **File** menu > **New Company from Existing Company File**.

2. Select **Browse**.

3. Select **a company to copy from**.

4. Enter **a name for the new company**.

5. Select **Create Company**.

6. Select **Save**.

CUSTOMIZE HOME PAGE

1. Select **Edit** menu **> Preferences > Desktop View > Company Preferences**.

2. Select feature icons to appear on the Home page.

SET UP LISTS

1. Select **Lists** menu **> Add/Edit Multiple List Entries**.

2. Select **List** (Customers, Vendors, Service, Inventory or Non-Inventory).

3. **Customize columns** to display.

4. Paste from Excel or type to add or edit the list.

5. Select **Save Changes**.

2. QUICKBOOKS UTILITIES AND GENERAL PRODUCT KNOWLEDGE

HOW TO NAVIGATE QUICKBOOKS

There are three basic ways to navigate QuickBooks:

1. **Home page**.

2. **Menus**.

3. **Icon bar and My Shortcuts**.

See *Chapter 1* for information about the three ways to navigate QuickBooks.

BACK UP COMPANY FILE (.QBB)

Backup company files (.QBB) are compressed company files. Typically, you will want to back up your company at regular intervals. To save a QuickBooks backup company file:

1. Select **File** menu **> Back Up Company > Create Local Backup**.

2. Select **Local backup > Next**.

3. If requested, select location of backup file. Click **OK**.

4. Select **Use this Location**.

5. Select **Save it now > Next**.

6. Select location and backup file name (.QBB). Click **Save**.

Also see *Appendix B: Back Up & Restore QuickBooks Files* and *Chapter 1*.

RESTORE COMPANY FILE (.QBB)

Typically you restore a backup company file when the QuickBooks .QBW file fails. For purposes of this text, you will restore a backup file when you use the Restart and Restore approach. For more information, see *Appendix B: Back Up & Restore QuickBooks Files* and *Chapter 1*.

To restore a QuickBooks backup company file:

1. Select **File** menu **> Open or Restore Company**.

2. Select **Restore a backup copy > Next**.

3. Select **Local backup > Next**.

4. Select location of backup file and backup file name. Select **Open > Next**.

5. Select location and name of restored file. If saving to the hard drive, try saving to your desktop to make it easier to find the .QBW file later. If QuickBooks will not recognize your desktop, then save to the location that QuickBooks defaults to automatically for restoring the file. Make a note of the path and directory.

6. Click **Save**.

7. Click **OK**.

SAVE PORTABLE COMPANY FILE (.QBM)

Portable company files (.QBM) permit you to move your QuickBooks company file from one computer to another. To save a portable QuickBooks company file:

1. Select **File** menu **> Create Copy**.

2. Select **Portable company file > Next**.

3. Enter the location and filename, then click **Save**.

4. Select **OK** to close and reopen your QuickBooks company file.

OPEN PORTABLE COMPANY FILE (.QBM)

To open a QuickBooks portable company file:

1. Select **File** menu **> Open or Restore Company**.

2. Select **Restore a portable file > Next**.

3. Select the location and portable company file name (.QBM) to open. Select **Open > Next**.

4. Enter the QuickBooks working file name (.QBW) and location.

5. Click **Save**.

CHANGE COMPANY NAME

1. Select **Company** menu **> My Company**. Or select **My Company** from My Shortcuts Icon bar.

2. Select **Edit** icon.

3. Update Company Name.

4. Click **OK**.

VIEW VERSION AND RELEASE NUMBER

1. With QuickBooks software running, press the **CTRL** and **1** keys at the same time (**CRTL+1**).

2. In the Product field of the *Product Information* window, find the version and release. (Example: QuickBooks Accountant 2015 R3P indicates the version is QuickBooks Accountant 2015. R3P indicates it is release 3.)

UPDATE QUICKBOOKS SOFTWARE

To update QuickBooks software, first download the updates and then install the updates. To download the updates:

1. Verify that you have an Internet connection.

2. Select **Help** menu **> Update QuickBooks**.

3. Click the **Options** tab.

4. If you would like QuickBooks to automatically update each time you connect to the Internet, select **Yes** for Automatic Update.

5. In the *Updates* section of the *Options* screen, select Updates: **Maintenance Releases**, **Help**, **Accountant**, **Data Protect**. Ask your instructor if you should select Payroll updates to download. If you

download payroll updates, your answers may not match the text answers for payroll assignments.

6. To download an update, select **Update Now** tab **> Get Updates**. If asked if you want to update QuickBooks, click **Yes**.

To install the QuickBooks update:

1. **Close** QuickBooks software, then **reopen** QuickBooks software.

2. At the prompt to install the update, select **Yes**.

3. After the update completes, **restart** your computer.

UPDATE QUICKBOOKS COMPANY FILE

To update your company file created using a previous version of QuickBooks (for example, to update a QuickBooks company file created in QuickBooks 2014 to QuickBooks 2015):

1. Back up your company file.

2. Using QuickBooks 2015 software, select **File** menu **> Open or Restore Company**.

3. Select **Restore a backup copy > Next**.

4. Select **Local backup > Next**.

5. Select location of backup file and backup file name. Select **Open > Next**.

6. When asked if you want to update the file, enter **YES** and click **OK**.

USE SINGLE-USER AND MULTI-USER MODES

1. If you are in multi-user mode, to switch to single-user mode select **File** menu **> Switch to Single-user Mode > Yes**.

2. If you are in single-user mode, to switch to multi-user mode select **File** menu **> Switch to Multi-user Mode > Yes**.

OPEN COMPANY FILE (.QBW)

To open a QuickBooks company file (.QBW) that is on the hard drive (C:) or that has been restored to the C: drive:

1. After QuickBooks software is open, select **File** menu **> Open or Restore Company**.

2. Select **Open a company file (.QBW) > Next**.

3. Select the company file and location. Click **Open**.

CLOSE QUICKBOOKS COMPANY FILE (.QBW)

1. Select **File** menu.
2. Click **Close Company**.

EXIT QUICKBOOKS SOFTWARE

1. Select **File** menu.
2. Select **Exit**.

PASSWORD PROTECT QUICKBOOKS

1. Select **Company** menu > **Set Up Users and Passwords** > **Set Up Users**.
2. Select **Add User** (or Edit User).
3. Enter **User Name**.
4. Enter **Password**.
5. Confirm **Password**.
6. Select **Next**. Select the appropriate QuickBooks user access settings.
7. Click **Finish**.

CUSTOMIZE QUICKBOOKS WITH PREFERENCES

To customize QuickBooks to fit your accounting software needs, you can select preferences as follows:

1. Select **Edit** menu > **Preferences**.
2. From the left scroll bar *Preferences* window, select the category:
   - Accounting
   - Bills
   - Calendar
   - Checking
   - Desktop View
   - Finance Charge
   - General
   - Integrated Applications
   - Items & Inventory
   - Jobs & Estimates
   - Multiple Currencies
   - Payments
   - Payroll & Employees

- Reminders
- Reports & Graphs
- Sales & Customers
- Sales Tax
- Search
- Send Forms
- Service Connection
- Spelling
- Tax: 1099
- Time & Expenses

3. Select the **My Preferences** tab or the **Company Preferences** tab.

4. Enter the preference settings you desire to customize QuickBooks.

5. When finished selecting preferences, click **OK**.

3. LIST MANAGEMENT

MANAGE QUICKBOOKS LISTS

QuickBooks uses lists to record and organize information about:

- Customers
- Vendors
- Items (such as services, inventory, and non-inventory)
- Employees
- Other

There are several different ways to manage lists in QuickBooks. For example, the Customer list can be accessed from the Customer Center and the Vendor list accessed from the Vendor Center. Another option is to manage lists using the Add/Edit Multiple List Entries window as follows.

ADD NEW ENTRIES

To add new entries using the *Add/Edit Multiple List Entries* window:

1. Select **Lists** menu **> Add/Edit Multiple List Entries**.

2. Select a type of list (such as Vendor) from the **List** drop-down menu.

3. **Customize Columns** to display in the list.

4. Enter or paste from Excel to add to the list.

5. Click **Save Changes**.

DELETE ENTRIES

To delete entries from a list using the *Add/Edit Multiple List Entries* window:

1. Select **Lists** menu **> Add/Edit Multiple List Entries**.
2. Select a type of list (such as Customer) from the **List** drop-down menu.
3. Select the entry to delete.
4. **Right-click > Delete Line**.
5. Click **Save Changes**.

Note that typically entries related to transactions, such as customer entries related to invoices, cannot be deleted.

EDIT ENTRIES

To edit entries in a list using the *Add/Edit Multiple List Entries* window:

1. Select **Lists** menu **> Add/Edit Multiple List Entries**.
2. Select a type of list (Customer, Vendor, and so on) from the **List** drop-down menu.
3. **Customize Columns** to display in the list.
4. Enter changes to the list entries.
5. Click **Save Changes**.

MERGE ENTRIES

To merge or combine entries on a list:

1. Select type of list (Customer, Vendor, Employee, or Item) from the **List** drop-down menu.
2. If your list has two names for the same vendor, for example, but one is misspelled, select the misspelled vendor name on the list, **right-click** then select **Edit**.
3. Type the correct name.
4. Click **OK**.
5. Click **Yes** when asked if you would like to merge this entry with the other entry with the same name.

After merging, only the correct name will appear on the list. QuickBooks will also merge the transactions for the two entries. Note that when merging accounts for the Chart of Accounts, only accounts with the same type (Income, Expense, and so on) can be merged.

IMPORT LISTS FROM EXCEL

To import lists of customers, vendors, accounts, or items from Microsoft Excel into QuickBooks:

1. Back up the QuickBooks company file.

2. Select **File** menu **> Utilities > Import > Excel Files**.

3. When the *Add/Edit Multiple List Entries* window appears if you select **Yes**, QuickBooks will take you to the **Lists** menu **> Add/Edit Multiple List Entries** to add/edit multiple lists. Further instructions follow in the next section.

4. If you select **No**, the *Add Your Excel Data to QuickBooks* window will appear.

5. From the *Add Your Excel Data to QuickBooks* window, click **Advanced Import** button.

6. Select the **Set up Import** tab **> Select A File > Mappings**.

7. Click the **Preference** tab. Select how to handle duplicates and errors.

8. Click **Preview**. Make appropriate corrections.

9. Click **Import**.

Another way to import data into Excel is using the Add/Edit Multiple List feature:

1. Select **Lists > Add/Edit Multiple List Entries.**

2. Select List (Customers, Vendors, Service, Inventory or Non-Inventory).

3. **Customize Columns** to display.

4. Paste from Excel or type to add or edit the list.

5. Select **Save Changes.**

You can also import data from Excel from the specific center. For example, to import the Customer List from Excel:

1. From the **Customer Center**, click the **Excel** button.

2. Select **Import from Excel**.

3. When the *Add/Edit Multiple List Entries* window appears, if you select **Yes**, QuickBooks will take you to the **Lists** menu **> Add/Edit Multiple List Entries** to add/edit multiple lists.

4. If you select **No**, the *Add Your Excel Data to QuickBooks* window will appear. From this window, select the appropriate **type of data you want to add to QuickBooks** button.

5. Follow the onscreen instructions to copy your data into a spreadsheet formatted to work with QuickBooks.

6. Save the Excel file.

EXPORT LISTS TO EXCEL

You can export data to Microsoft Excel for customers, vendors, inventory items, transactions, payroll summary, and reports. For example, to export customer data to a new Excel workbook:

1. Click **Customers** on the Icon bar.

2. Display the **Customer List**.

3. Click the **Excel** button. Select **Export Customer List**.

4. Select **Create new worksheet > in new workbook > Export**.

5. When the Excel file opens, save the Excel file.

See *Appendix D* for more information about how to export to Excel and replace an existing worksheet.

4. ITEMS

HOW TO USE QUICKBOOKS ITEMS

The QuickBooks Item list is used to track items purchased and sold. Types of items include:

- Service
- Non-inventory Part
- Inventory Part
- Inventory Assembly
- Group
- Discount
- Sales Tax

USE DIFFERENT TYPES OF ITEMS

When adding items to the Item list, the appropriate type of item is selected. This cannot be changed later. The three main types of items frequently used are service, non-inventory part, and inventory part.

- **Service item**: Use this item type for services you purchase or sell, such as labor, consulting hours, or professional fees.

- **Non-inventory part item**: Use this item type for goods you buy but don't need to track the quantity, such as office supplies or materials for a specific customer job that you will charge back to the customer.

- **Inventory part item**: Use this item type for goods you purchase, track as inventory, and resell to customers.

ADD ITEMS

1. From the **Company** section of the Home page, click the **Items & Services** icon.

2. **Right-click** to display the pop-up menu. Select **New**.

3. Enter item information.

4. To enter another item, click **Next**.

5. When finished, click **OK**.

EDIT ITEMS

1. From the **Company** section of the Home page, click the **Items & Services** icon.

2. After selecting the item you would like to edit, **right-click** to display the pop-up menu. Select **Edit Item**.

3. Edit item information.

4. When finished, click **OK**.

ENTER AN ITEM SELLING FOR A SPECIFIED PRICE

When a specific item is typically sold at the same specified price, that price can be entered in the Item list. This specified sales price will automatically appear on invoices when this item is selected.

To enter an item that sells at a specified price:

1. From the **Company** section of the Home page, click the **Items & Services** icon.

2. **Right-click** to display the pop-up menu. Select **New**.

3. Select **Item Type**.

4. Enter item information.

5. Enter **Sales Price**. When the Sales Price is entered in the Item list, then this sales price will automatically appear on invoices when this item is selected. Note that this automatic price can be changed on the invoice when needed for a specific sale.

6. To enter another item, click **Next**.

7. When finished, click **OK**.

ENTER AN ITEM SELLING FOR DIFFERENT PRICES

When a specific item is typically sold at different prices, the price for that item can be left blank in the Item list. When the item is selected for sale on an invoice, the sales price will automatically appear as $0.00. Then you enter the price required for the specific sale on the invoice.

To enter an item that sells for different prices:

1. From the **Company** section of the Home page, click the **Items & Services** icon.

2. **Right-click** to display the pop-up menu. Select **New**.

3. Select **Item Type**.

4. Enter item information.

5. Enter **Sales Price: 0.00**. When a Sales Price of $0.00 is entered for an item in the Item list, then $0.00 will automatically appear as the sales price on invoices when this item is selected. You can enter whatever price is required for the specific sale on the invoice.

6. To enter another item, click **Next**.

7. When finished, click **OK**.

5. SALES (CUSTOMER TRANSACTIONS)

USE THE CUSTOMER CENTER

1. Click **Customers** on the Icon bar.

2. From the Customer Center, you can view your Customer: Job list, enter new customers, edit current customers listed, enter new transactions,

print or export to Excel, view transactions and contacts.

ENTER CUSTOMER INFORMATION

1. Click **Customers** on the Icon bar.
2. Select **New Customer & Job > New Customer**.
3. Enter customer information.
4. Click **OK** to save and close the window.

ADD NEW JOB

1. Select the specific customer from the Customer List in the Customer Center.
2. With the customer selected, **right-click** to display the pop-up menu. Select **Add Job**.
3. Enter the Job Name and other job information.
4. Click **OK** to save and close the window.

INVOICE CUSTOMERS

1. From the **Customers** section of the Home page, click the **Create Invoices** icon.
2. Enter invoice information.
3. Click the **Print** icon to print the invoice or the **Email** icon to email the invoice.
4. Click **Save & New** to enter another invoice or **Save & Close** to close the window.

RECEIVE CUSTOMER PAYMENTS

1. From the **Customers** section of the Home page, click the **Receive Payments** icon.
2. Enter receipt information.
3. Click **Save & New** to enter another receipt or **Save & Close** to close the window.

DEPOSIT CUSTOMER PAYMENTS

1. From the **Banking** section of the Home page, click **Record Deposits**.
2. Select **Payments to Deposit**, then click **OK**.

3. Select **Bank Account**. Enter **Date** and deposit information.

4. Click **Print** to print the deposit summary.

5. Click **Save & Close**.

CREATE SALES RECEIPTS

1. From the **Customers** section of the Home page, click the **Create Sales Receipts** icon.

2. Enter receipt information.

3. Click **Save & New** to enter another receipt or **Save & Close** to close the window.

CREATE STATEMENTS

1. From the **Customers** section of the Home page, click the **Statements** icon.

2. Select Statement Date, Statement Period, and Customer(s).

3. If requested, in the *Select Additional Options* section you can choose to show invoice item detail on the statement.

4. Click **Print** to print the invoice or **Email** to email the invoice.

5. Click **Close** to close the window.

CREATE PROGRESS INVOICE

1. Select **Edit > Preferences > Jobs & Estimates > Company Preferences.** Select Do you create estimates? **Yes.** Select Do you do progress invoicing? **Yes.**

2. From the **Customers** section of the Home page, click the **Create Invoices** icon.

3. Select Template: **Progress Invoice**.

4. Select appropriate Customer and Job.

5. When asked, select appropriate estimate.

6. Enter the quantity or percentage of work completed to be billed.

7. Click **Save & New** to enter another receipt or **Save & Close** to close the window.

RECORD A CUSTOMER CREDIT

1. From the **Customers** section of the Home page, click the **Refunds & Credits** icon.

2. Select the appropriate Customer and Job.

3. Enter credit information.

4. Click **Save & New** to enter another receipt or **Save & Close** to close the window.

ACCOUNT FOR BOUNCED NSF CHECK

When a customer check is returned by the bank because the customer has insufficient funds to cover the check, you must account for:

- The returned check
- Any bank fees you are charged by the bank
- Any fees you charge the customer for the NSF check

How you account for an NSF check depends upon which QuickBooks version you use. If you are using a QuickBooks version that has a bounced check feature, complete the following steps to account for the NSF check.

1. From the **Customers** section of the Home page, select the **Receive Payments** icon.

2. From the *Receive Payments* window, select the customer payment associated with the bounced check. For example, find the customer payment for **Abercrombie, Kristie: Remodel Bathroom** on **12/15/2019** for **$7633.28**.

3. The Pmt. Method must have **Check** selected for the **Record Bounced Check** icon to be active in the *Receive Payments* window.

4. With the customer transaction for the bounced check appearing in the *Receive Payments* window, select the **Record Bounced Check** icon. (Note: if your *Receive Payments* window does not display a Bounced Check button: (1) the Pmt. Method was not Check, or (2) your QuickBooks version may not offer this feature.)

5. In the *What did the bank charge you for this bounced check?* section of the *Manage Bounced Check* window, enter amount for **Bank Fee**.

6. Enter **Date**.

7. Enter Expense Account: **60600 – Bank Service Charges**.

8. In the *How much do you want to charge your customer?* section of the *Manage Bounced Check* window, enter amount for **Customer Fee**.

9. Select **Next**.

10. A *Bounced Check Summary* window should appear summarizing what will happen in QuickBooks when you record the bounced check. QuickBooks will perform a series of steps to account for the bounced check:

    - The original customer invoice is marked unpaid.
    - The customer payment is stamped: Bounced Check.
    - The customer's bounced check that was deposited in your account will be deducted from your bank account. (A journal entry is made to increase accounts receivable and decrease your Checking account.)
    - The fee the bank charges you for bounced checks will be deducted from your bank account. (A journal entry is made to increase the Bank Service Charge Expense account and reduce your Checking account by the amount you are charged for the bank's NSF fee.)
    - A new invoice is created to charge the customer for the bounced check fee.

An example *Bounced Check Summary* window follows.

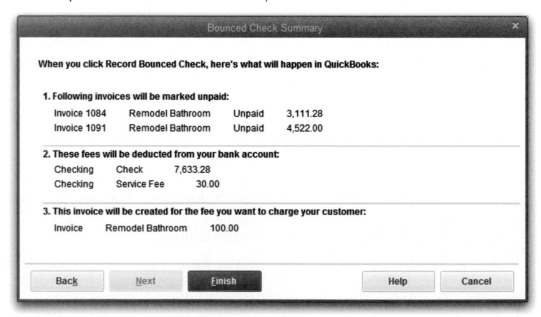

11. Select **Finish**.

12. Select **Save & Close** to close the *Receive Payments* window.

To create a collection letter to send the customer regarding a bounced check:

1. From the Customer list in the **Customer Center**, select the customer to receive the bounced check collection letter.

2. At the top of the Customer Center, click the **Word drop-down arrow > Prepare Letter to [Customer Name]**.

3. In the *Choose a Letter Template* window, select **Bounced Check**.

4. Follow the onscreen instructions in the Letter and Envelopes wizard to create the customer's bounced check letter.

If your version of QuickBooks does *not* have the bounced check feature, approaches to account for the NSF check include the following:

- Create a credit memo for the NSF check and offset it against the corresponding customer invoice
- Create a new invoice for the NSF check including the bounced check fee charged the customer

The following instructions are an example of how to use a new invoice to account for an NSF check if your QuickBooks version does *not* have the bounced check feature.

First, create an item for tracking bounced (NSF) checks:

1. From the **Company** section of the Home page, select **Items & Services**.

2. Select **Item** button **> New**.

3. Select Type: **Other Charge**.

4. Enter Item Name/Number: **Bounced Check**.

5. In the Amount or % field, leave: **0.00**.

6. In the Account field, select: **Checking**.

7. Click **Next** to enter another item. Leave the *New Item* window open.

Next create an item to track bad check charges that you charge customers for bounced checks.

1. With the *New Item* window still open, select Type: **Other Charge**.

2. Enter Item Name/Number: **Bad Check Charge**.

3. In the Amount or % field, leave: **0.00**.

4. In the Account field, select: **<Add New>**.

5. Select Account Type: **Income**.

6. Enter Account Name: **Returned Check Charges**.

7. Select **Save & Close** to close the *Add New Account* window. The Account field should now display Returned Check Charges.

8. Click **OK** to close the *New Item* window.

The next task is to re-invoice the customer for the bounced check plus any returned check charges.

1. From the **Customers** section of the Home page, select **Create Invoices**.

2. From the customer drop-down list, select the customer and job related to the bounced check.

3. Select Item: **Bounced Check**.

4. In the Amount field, enter the amount of the bounced check. Note that this will reduce your bank account by the amount of the bad check.

5. Move to the second line item. Select Item: **Bad Check Charge**.

6. In the Amount field, enter the amount of returned check charges you want to recover from the customer.

7. The rest of the invoice can be completed as you normally would.

8. Select **Save & Close**.

Another related task is to see that any NSF fees the bank charges your company are recorded when you reconcile your company bank statement.

6. PURCHASES (VENDOR TRANSACTIONS)

USE THE VENDOR CENTER

1. Select **Vendors** on the Icon bar.

2. From the Vendor Center, you can view your Vendor list, enter new vendors, edit current vendors listed, enter new transactions, print or export to Excel, view transactions and contacts.

ENTER VENDOR INFORMATION

1. Select **Vendors** on the Icon bar.

2. From the **Vendor Center**, click the **New Vendor** button > **New Vendor**.

3. Enter vendor information.

4. Click **OK** to save and close the window.

ENTER ITEMS

1. From the **Company** section of the Home page, click the **Items & Services** icon.

2. **Right-click** to display the pop-up menu. Select **New**.

3. Select type of item.

4. Enter item information.

5. To enter another item, click **Next**.

6. When finished, click **OK**.

CREATE PURCHASE ORDERS

1. After entering items into the Item List, to record the purchase of inventory, from the **Vendors** section of the Home page, click **Purchase Orders**.

2. Enter purchase information.

3. To enter another purchase order, click **Save & New**.

4. When finished, click **Save & Close**.

RECEIVE ITEMS

1. From the **Vendors** section of the Home page, click **Receive Inventory**.

2. Select **Receive Inventory with Bill** or **Receive Inventory without Bill**.

3. Select the vendor. If asked if you want to match against outstanding purchase orders, click **Yes**.

4. Enter the remaining information.

5. To enter another item received, click **Save & New**.

6. When finished, click **Save & Close**.

ENTER BILLS AGAINST INVENTORY

1. From the **Vendors** section of the Home page, click **Enter Bills Against Inventory**.

2. Select the vendor and choose the Item Receipt that corresponds to the bill.

3. Enter the remaining information.

4. To enter another bill, click **Save & New**.

5. When finished, click **Save & Close.**

ENTER BILLS

1. From the **Vendors** section of the Home page, click **Enter Bills**.

2. Select the vendor.

3. Enter bill information.

4. Select Expenses or Items tab and select the appropriate account.

5. To enter another bill, click **Save & New**.

6. When finished, click **Save & Close.**

PAY BILLS BY CHECK

1. From the **Vendors** section of the Home page, click **Pay Bills**.

2. Select **Show all bills**.

3. Select bills to pay.

4. Enter **Payment Date**.

5. Select Method: **Check**. Select appropriate Checking account.

6. Click **Pay Selected Bills**.

PRINT CHECKS

1. Select **File** menu > **Print Forms** > **Checks** (or click the **Print Checks** icon in the **Banking** section of the Home page).

2. Select **Bank Account**.

3. Enter **First Check Number**.

4. Select checks to print.

5. Click **OK**.

6. Select **Check Style**.

7. Click **Print**.

WRITE CHECKS

1. From the **Banking** section of the Home page, click **Write Checks**.

2. Select **Bank Account**.

3. Enter **Check Date** and remaining check information.

4. Enter **Account** and **Amount**.

5. Select **Print Later**.

6. Click **Print** to print the checks.

PAY WITH CREDIT CARD

1. From the **Vendors** section of the Home page, click **Pay Bills**.

2. Select **Show all bills**.

3. Select bills to pay.

4. Enter **Payment Date**.

5. Select Method: **Credit Card**. Select appropriate account.

6. Click **Pay Selected Bills**.

PAY WITH DEBIT CARD

1. From the **Vendors** section of the Home page, click **Pay Bills**.

2. Select **Show all bills**.

3. Select bills to pay.

4. Enter **Payment Date**.

5. Select Method: **Check**.

6. Select **Assign check number**.

7. Select appropriate Checking account.

8. Click **Pay Selected Bills**.

9. Assign check number **DC** for Debit Card. Click **OK**.

PAY WITH ONLINE BANK PAYMENT

1. From the **Vendors** section of the Home page, click **Pay Bills**.

2. Select **Show all bills**.

3. Select bills to pay.

4. Enter **Payment Date**.

5. Select Method: **Online Bank Pmt**. Select appropriate account.

6. If appropriate, select **Include reference number**.

7. Click **Pay Selected Bills**.

RECORD VENDOR CREDIT

To record a vendor credit:

1. From the **Vendors** section of the Home page, click **Enter Bills**.

2. Select **Credit** (instead of Bill) near the top of the *Enter Bills* window.

3. From the drop-down list, select the appropriate **vendor**.

4. Enter the **credit amount**.

5. Select the **account** used to record the initial expense or item.

6. To enter another vendor credit, click **Save & New**.

7. When finished, click **Save & Close** to save the credit memo.

To apply the credit memo against a specific bill:

1. From the **Vendors** section of the Home page, click **Pay Bills**.

2. Select the bill that you would like to apply the credit to.

3. If the amount of the credit needs to be adjusted, select **Set Credits**.

4. Enter amount of credit in the **Amount To Use** column for the bill(s).

5. Click **Done** to close the *Discount and Credits* window.

6. Select any other bills to pay.

7. Click **Pay Selected Bills**.

8. Select **Done** or **Print Checks** to close the *Payment Summary* window.

HOW TO SET UP, COLLECT AND PAY SALES TAX

To set up sales tax:

1. Select **Edit** menu > **Preferences** > **Sales Tax** > **Company Preferences** (or from the **Vendors** section of the Home page, select **Manage Sales Tax** > **Sales Tax Preferences**).

2. Select Do you charge sales tax? **Yes**.

3. Select **Add sales tax item**. Enter and save sales tax item information for each county or sales tax district where you collect sales tax.

4. Select your most common sales tax item from the drop-down list.

5. Select Accrual or Cash Basis as appropriate for When Do You Owe Sales Tax?

6. Select appropriate answer for When Do You Pay Sales Tax?

7. Click **OK** to close the *Preferences* window.

8. When entering customer information into the Customer list, select the appropriate sales tax settings for the specific customer from the *New/Edit Customer* window by selecting **Sales Tax Settings** tab **> Tax Code > Tax Item**.

To collect sales tax:

1. When using the *Create Invoices* or *Create Sales Receipts* windows, enter the customer information and items sold. The Tax column should automatically reflect the sales tax settings entered in the Customer list for the specific customer.

2. If necessary, select the appropriate sales tax item from the Tax drop-down list on the *Create Invoices* or *Create Sales Receipts* windows.

To pay sales tax:

1. From the **Vendors** section of the Home page select **Manage Sales Tax > Pay Sales Tax.**

2. From the *Pay Sales Tax* window, enter the **Pay From Account**.

3. Select **Check Date**.

4. Select **Show sales tax due through** date.

5. Check the sales taxes to pay.

6. Click **OK**, then print checks to pay sales taxes.

RECONCILE BANK STATEMENT

1. From the **Banking** section of the Home page, click **Reconcile**.

2. Select **Bank Account**.

3. Enter **Statement Date** and **Ending Balance**.

4. Enter **Service Charges** and **Interest Earned**.

5. Click **Continue**.

6. Check deposits and checks that appear on the bank statement.

7. Click **Reconcile Now**.

7. PAYROLL (EMPLOYEE TRANSACTIONS)

WAYS TO PROCESS PAYROLL WITH QUICKBOOKS

There are two general ways that a company can process payroll using QuickBooks:

- Manually calculate payroll taxes.
- Use a QuickBooks payroll service.

QuickBooks offers three different levels of payroll services:

1. **Basic Payroll.** Basic payroll service creates paychecks using automatic calculation of payroll tax deductions. Tax forms for filings are not automatically prepared so the entrepreneur must complete the tax forms or work with an accountant on payroll tax filings.

2. **Enhanced Payroll.** Enhanced payroll service creates paychecks using automatic calculation of payroll tax deductions and generates payroll tax forms for filings automatically.

3. **Full Service Payroll.** Full service payroll automatically calculates payroll tax deductions and processes payroll taxes and filings for the entrepreneur.

HOW TO SET UP PAYROLL

1. Select **Edit** menu > **Preferences** > **Payroll & Employees** > **Company Preferences** > **Full Payroll**.

2. Enter **Employee Defaults**.

3. Click **OK** to close the *Preferences* window.

4. Select **Employees** menu > **Payroll Setup**.

5. Complete the QuickBooks Payroll Setup.

See *Chapters 6 and 11* for more information about payroll setup.

ADD PAYROLL ITEM

1. Select **Employees** menu > **Manage Payroll Items** > **New Payroll Item**.

2. Select **EZ Setup** > **Next**.

3. Select type of payroll item, such as Insurance Benefits. Click **Next**.

4. After the Payroll Setup Interview loads, select the appropriate payroll items, such as Health Insurance. Click **Next**.

5. Answer any remaining questions about the payroll item(s).

6. Select **payees**, appropriate **accounts**, and **payment frequency**.

7. Click **Finish**.

EDIT PAYROLL ITEM

To edit a payroll item:

1. Select **Employees** menu **> Manage Payroll Items > View/Edit Payroll Item List** to open the Payroll Item list.

2. Select the specific payroll item you would like to edit. **Right-click** and select **Edit**.

3. If necessary, edit the name of the payroll item. Click **Next**.

4. Answer the questions regarding the payroll item, then click **Next**.

5. Click **Finish**.

Next, enter employee information as needed for payroll item deductions.

ENTER EMPLOYEE INFORMATION

1. Select **Employees** on the Icon bar.

2. From the **Employee Center**, click the **New Employee** button.

3. Enter employee information.

4. Click **Next** to enter another employee or click **OK** to save and close the window.

TRACK TIME FOR PAYROLL

1. From the **Employees** section of the Home page, select **Enter Time** icon **> Use Weekly Timesheet**.

2. Select **Employee Name**.

3. Select **Week**.

4. Enter time worked (if needed, select customer and service item).

5. To enter another timesheet, click **Save & New**.

6. Click **Print** to print the timesheets.

7. When finished, click **Save & Close**.

TRACK TIME FOR INVOICING CUSTOMERS

See the preceding Track Time for Payroll for instructions on entering time using the weekly timesheet.

To transfer time worked to customer invoices:

1. From the **Customers** section of the Home page, select **Create Invoices.**

2. Select the customer and job from the Customer: Job drop-down list.

3. If necessary, select **Add Time/Costs**.

4. When the *Billable Time/Costs* window appears, click: **Select the outstanding billable time and costs to add to this invoice?** Click **OK**.

5. Select **Time** tab. Select time to transfer to the invoice and appropriate options. Click **OK**.

6. Complete the rest of the invoice.

7. When finished, click **Save & Close.**

TRACK SICK AND VACATION TIME

To track sick and vacation time for employees, when setting up payroll, select the appropriate options for sick and vacation time. To adjust sick or vacation time for a specific employee:

1. Select **Employees** on the Icon bar.

2. From the Employee list, double-click on the employee's name to open the *Edit Employee* window.

3. Select **Payroll Info** tab.

4. Select Sick Hourly, Sick Salary, Vacation Hourly or Vacation Salary from the Item Name drop-down list.

5. Choose the **Accrual period** from the drop-down list.

6. Select other sick and vacation options as needed.

7. When finished, click **OK** to close the *Sick and Vacation* window.

8. Click **OK** to close the *Edit Employee* window.

SET UP PAYROLL SCHEDULES

1. From the **Employees** section of the Home page, select **Payroll Center**.

2. If this is the first scheduled payroll, from the **Pay Employees** section, select **Start Scheduled Payroll > Set up Now**.

3. If a payroll schedule already exists and you are adding another payroll schedule, from the **Pay Employees** section, select **New** from the Payroll Schedules drop-down.

4. In the *New Payroll Schedule* window, enter the name for the payroll schedule.

5. Enter how often you will pay employees on this schedule.

6. Select what date should appear on paychecks for this pay period.

7. Click **OK**.

PAY EMPLOYEES

1. From the **Employees** section of the Home page, click **Pay Employees**.

2. In the **Pay Employees** section of the *Employee Center: Payroll Center* window, select **Start Scheduled Payroll** or **Start Unscheduled Payroll**.

3. In the *Enter Payroll Information* window, enter **Pay Period Ends** and **Check Date**.

4. Select **Employee name**. Select **Open Paycheck Detail**.

5. Enter withholding and deduction amounts. Select **Save & Close**.

6. Continue until all employee paychecks are completed. Then click **Continue**.

7. Click **Create Paychecks**.

8. Click **Print Paychecks** to print the paychecks.

PAY PAYROLL LIABILITIES

1. From the **Employees** section of the Home page, select **Pay Liabilities**.

2. In the **Pay Liabilities** section, select payroll liabilities you would like to pay.

3. Select **View/Pay**.

4. Select **E-payment** or **Check**.

5. When finished, click **Save & Close.**

PREPARE PAYROLL FORMS

1. From the **Employees** section of the Home page, select **Process Payroll Forms**.

2. Select **Federal form** or **State form**. Click **OK**. (Forms available to select depends upon the payroll service.)

3. Choose the form you want to use.

4. Click **OK**.

8. REPORTS

USE THE REPORT CENTER

You can access the Report Center in the following ways:

1. Select **Reports** from the Icon bar, My Shortcuts.
2. Select **Reports** menu **> Report Center**.

After opening the Report Center to display a report:

1. Select the report type.

2. Select the report.

3. Select **Date**.

4. Click **Run**.

CUSTOMIZE REPORTS

1. From the **Report Center**, display the desired report.

2. Select **Customize Report** near the top of the report window.

3. Select from **Display**, **Filters**, **Header/Footer**, and **Fonts & Numbers** tabs to customize your report.

4. Select **OK**.

EXPORT REPORTS TO EXCEL

To export reports to Microsoft Excel:

1. Using the **Report Center**, display the desired report.

2. Click the **Excel** button at the top of the report window.

3. Select **Create New Worksheet** or **Update Existing Worksheet** as appropriate.

4. If you are replacing a worksheet in an existing worksheet, select Replace Existing Worksheet. Select the appropriate workbook and sheet. (Excel

templates can be downloaded from www.My-QuickBooks.com. For more information about how to Go Digital with your QuickBooks assignments, see the Instruction worksheet in the template or *Appendix D: Go Digital with QuickBooks*.)

5. If you would like to add Auto Outline or Auto Filtering to your Excel worksheet, select **Advanced**. Select **Auto Outline** and/or **Auto Filtering**. Select **OK**.

6. Click **Export**.

7. When the Excel file opens, save the Excel file.

MEMORIZE REPORTS

1. From the **Report Center**, display the report that you wish to memorize.

2. Select **Memorize** at the top of the report window.

3. In the *Memorize Report* window, enter the **Name** you wish to use for the report.

4. Select **Save in Memorized Report Group** and specify the group.

5. Click **OK**.

6. Close the report window.

PRINT TRIAL BALANCE

1. From the **Report Center**, select **Accountant & Taxes > Trial Balance**.

2. Select **Dates**.

3. Click **Run** icon.

4. Click **Excel** or **Print**.

PRINT GENERAL JOURNAL

1. From the **Report Center**, select **Accountant & Taxes > Journal**.

2. Select **Dates**.

3. Click **Run** icon.

4. Click **Excel** or **Print**.

PRINT GENERAL LEDGER

1. From the **Report Center**, select **Accountant & Taxes > General Ledger**.

2. Select **Dates**.

3. Click **Run** icon.

4. Select **Customize Report > Advanced**. Select to show only accounts **In Use**.

5. Click **Excel** or **Print**.

PRINT INCOME STATEMENT

1. From the **Report Center**, select **Company & Financial**.

2. Under the **Profit & Loss (Income Statement)** section, select **Profit & Loss Standard**.

3. Select **Dates**.

4. Click **Run** icon.

5. Select **Customize Report > Display** tab. Select the type of Report Basis needed for your income statement: **Accrual** or **Cash**. Click **OK**.

6. Click **Excel** or **Print**.

PRINT BALANCE SHEET

1. From the **Report Center**, select **Company & Financial**.

2. Under the **Balance Sheet & Net Worth** section, select **Balance Sheet Standard**.

3. Select **Dates**.

4. Click **Run** icon.

5. Click **Excel** or **Print**.

PRINT STATEMENT OF CASH FLOWS

1. From the **Report Center**, select **Company & Financial**.

2. Under the **Cash Flow** section, select **Statement of Cash Flows**.

3. Select **Dates**.

4. Click **Run** icon.

5. Click **Excel** or **Print**.

9. BASIC ACCOUNTING

BASIC FINANCIAL STATEMENTS

Three basic financial statements often used when evaluating an organization's performance are:

1. Income statement (also called Profit and Loss or P & L). The income statement measures revenues and expenses over a period of time, such as one year.

2. Balance sheet (also called a statement of financial position). The balance sheet measures assets (items with future benefit), liabilities (obligations), and owner's equity (the residual left when liabilities are subtracted from assets).

3. Statement of cash flows. The statement of cash flows has three main sections: cash flows from operations, cash flows from financing activities, and cash flows from investing activities.

To create these three main financial statements, see preceding *Domain 8 Reports*.

DIFFERENCE BETWEEN CASH AND ACCRUAL

The cash basis and accrual basis are two different ways of measuring revenues and expenses. The cash basis uses cash inflows and cash outflows. For example, an income statement on the cash basis measures cash inflows received for revenues and cash outflows paid for expenses.

The accrual basis uses the matching principle to measure revenues and expenses. In general when the accrual basis is used, revenues are recorded when the goods or services are provided to the customer (earned). Expenses are matched against revenues earned.

To select Accrual basis for a report:

1. From the **Report Center**, open the desired report, such as the income statement.

2. Select **Customize Report > Display** tab.

3. Select Report Basis: **Accrual**.

4. Select **OK**.

5. **Print** or **export** the report to Excel.

To select Cash basis for a report:

1. From the **Report Center**, open the desired report, such as the income statement.

2. Select **Customize Report > Display** tab.

3. Select Report Basis: **Cash**.

4. Select **OK**.

5. **Print** or **export** the report to Excel.

ENTER NEW ACCOUNTS

1. From the **Company** section of the Home page, click the **Chart of Accounts** icon.

2. **Right-click** to display the pop-up menu. Select **New**.

3. Enter **Type of Account, Account Number, Name, Description,** and **Tax Line**.

4. Click **Save & New** to enter another account.

5. Click **Save & Close** to close the *Add New Account* window.

ENTER BEGINNING ACCOUNT BALANCES

1. If the account has a beginning balance, when entering the new account, from the *Add New Account* (or *Edit Account*) window, select the **Enter Opening Balance** button.

2. Enter the **Opening Balance** and the **As of Date** for the beginning balance.

3. Click **OK**.

PRINT CHART OF ACCOUNTS

1. From the **Report Center**, select **Accountant & Taxes > Account Listing**.

2. Enter **Date**, select **Run**, then **Excel** or **Print**.

JOURNAL ENTRIES

1. Select **Accountant** menu > **Make General Journal Entries**. (For QuickBooks Pro, select **Company** menu > **Make General Journal Entries**.)

2. Enter **Date, Entry Number, Accounts,** and **Debit and Credit** amounts.

3. Click **Save & New** to enter another journal entry.

4. Click **Save & Close** to close the *Make General Journal Entries* window.

ADJUSTING ENTRIES

1. Select **Accountant** menu **>** **Make General Journal Entries**.

2. Enter **Date, Entry Number (ADJ#), Accounts,** and **Debit and Credit** amounts.

3. **Check** the Adjusting Entry checkbox.

4. Click **Save & New** to enter another journal entry.

5. Click **Save & Close** to close the *Make General Journal Entries* window.

CORRECTING ENTRIES

To correct an error, make two correcting entries in the Journal:

1. Eliminate the effect of the incorrect entry by making the opposite journal entry.

   For example, assume the Cash account should have been debited for $200.00 and the Professional Fees Revenue account credited for $200.00. However, the following incorrect entry was made for $2,000.00 instead of $200.00.

Debit	Cash	2,000.00
Credit	Professional Fees Revenue	2,000.00

   To eliminate the effect of the incorrect entry, make the following entry:

Debit	Professional Fees Revenue	2,000.00
Credit	Cash	2,000.00

2. After eliminating the effect of the incorrect entry, make the following correct entry that should have been made initially:

Debit	Cash	200.00
Credit	Professional Fees Revenue	200.00

In addition to correcting entries, QuickBooks provides a number of additional ways to correct errors. For more information about correcting errors in QuickBooks, see *Appendix C: QuickBooks Issue Resolution*.

CLOSING

Before closing a fiscal period, prepare adjusting entries and print all reports needed. To close the fiscal period:

1. Select **Edit** menu **> Preferences > Accounting > Company Preferences.**

2. In the Closing Date section, select **Set Date/Password**.

3. Enter the **Closing Date**. If desired, enter and confirm the **Closing Date Password**.

4. Click **OK**.

10. CUSTOMIZATION/SAVING TIME AND SHORTCUTS

MEMORIZE TRANSACTIONS

1. Enter the transaction into the appropriate form (Enter Bill, Create Invoice, and so on).

2. Select the **Memorize** icon.

3. Enter **Name** for the memorized transaction.

4. Select **How Often**.

5. Select **Next Date**.

6. Click **OK**.

SET UP MULTIPLE USERS WITH ACCESS

1. Select **Company** menu **> Set Up Users and Passwords > Set Up Users.**

2. Select **Add User** (or **Edit User**).

3. Enter **User Name**.

4. Enter **Password**.

5. Confirm **Password**.

6. Select **Next**. Then complete the following QuickBooks user access settings.

7. Click **Finish**.

CREATE CUSTOM FIELDS

1. Open the appropriate list, such as customer, vendor, or employee list.

2. With your cursor over the list, **right-click** and select **New** or **Edit**.

3. Select the **Additional Info** tab **> Define Fields**.

4. In the *Label* column of the *Set up Custom Fields for Names* window, enter the name you wish to use for the custom field.

5. Select Use for: **Customer**, **Vendor** and/or **Employee**.

6. Click **OK** to close the *Set up Custom Fields for Names* window.

7. Click **OK** to close the customer, vendor, or employee window.

CUSTOMIZE AN INVOICE

First, create a copy of an existing invoice template:

1. From the **Customers** section of the Home page, select **Create Invoices**.

2. Select the **Create a Copy** icon near the top of the *Create Invoices* window.

3. If a *QuickBooks Information* window appears informing you that a duplicate invoice has been created, click **OK** to close it.

Next, customize the layout of the duplicate invoice template:

1. Select the **Template** that you wish to customize.

2. Select the **Formatting** tab near the top of the *Create Invoices* window.

3. Select the **Customize Data Layout** icon.

4. Select Basic Customization, Layout Designer, or appropriate tabs (Header, Columns, Prog Cols (Progress Invoice Columns), Footer, or Print) to customize your invoice.

5. When finished, click **OK**.

REVIEW NOTES:

SECTION 4
QUICKBOOKS EXTRAS

A

INSTALL & REGISTER QUICKBOOKS SOFTWARE

B

BACK UP & RESTORE QUICKBOOKS FILES

C

QUICKBOOKS ISSUE RESOLUTION

D

GO DIGITAL WITH QUICKBOOKS

E

QUICKBOOKS & MY MAC

F

WWW.MY-QUICKBOOKS.COM

APPENDIX A

INSTALL & REGISTER QUICKBOOKS SOFTWARE

INSTALL QUICKBOOKS SOFTWARE

To install your QuickBooks trial version software that accompanies *Computer Accounting with QuickBooks*:

Step 1: Close any open programs and disable your antivirus software.

Step 2: Insert the QuickBooks trial version CD in your CD drive or download the software using a browser. Check the Online Learning Center (OLC) Student Version for the software download link and directions.

Step 3: Follow the onscreen instructions that the QuickBooks Installer provides.

Step 4: When requested, enter the License and Product number (located on the back of the disk jacket for the QuickBooks software CD or provided with your ebook).

Step 5: Register the QuickBooks trial version within 30 days. Then you will have use of the trial version for 140 days. Note that you might want to wait to install the software until you need it for your QuickBooks course.

For more accountant resources, select **Help** menu **> Ask Intuit > Download & Install**.

REGISTER QUICKBOOKS SOFTWARE

You can use the QuickBooks trial version for 30 days without registering. Three ways to register your QuickBooks trial version are:

1. Register the software when you install it.

2. Select **Help** menu **> Register QuickBooks**.

3. Register your QuickBooks software by phone at 888-246-8848 or 888-222-7276 and select the appropriate menu option.

If you fail to register QuickBooks software within 30 days and you are locked out from using the software, select Help menu > Register QuickBooks. If that is unsuccessful, try uninstalling and reinstalling the QuickBooks software from your trial version CD that accompanies your text.

!
If you already have another version of QuickBooks software installed on your computer, you can select to replace it with the newer version or to install both versions. If your QuickBooks software fails to install, try uninstalling any prior versions of QuickBooks and then reinstalling QuickBooks 2015 software.

!
Register your QuickBooks software! Failure to register your QuickBooks trial version software will result in the software no longer functioning.

VIEW QUICKBOOKS SOFTWARE RELEASE NUMBER

Periodically, QuickBooks software is updated with releases. Releases are intended to correct software issues. To view your QuickBooks software release number, complete the following steps:

Step 1: With QuickBooks software running, press the **Ctrl** key and the **1** key at the same time.

Step 2: When the *Product Information* window appears, you will find the Release number on the Product line after QuickBooks Accountant 2015. In the following *Product Information* window, R3P indicates this is Release 3.

Step 3: Select **OK** to close the *Product Information* window.

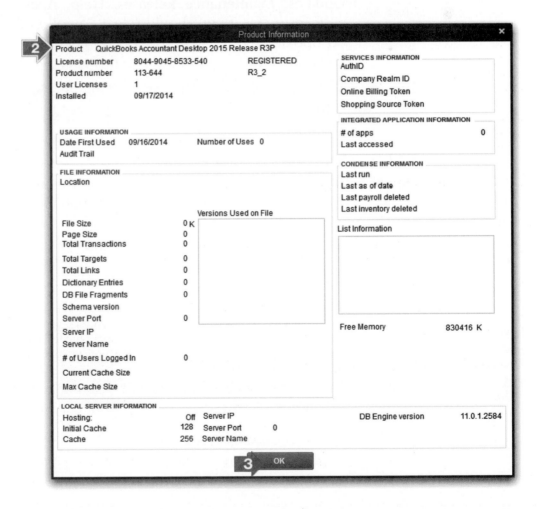

UPDATE QUICKBOOKS SOFTWARE

To update QuickBooks software automatically when the software updates become available:

Step 1: Establish your Internet connection.

Step 2: Select **Help** menu **> Update QuickBooks**.

Step 3: Click the **Options** tab.

Step 4: If you would like QuickBooks to automatically update each time you connect to the Internet, select **Yes** for Automatic Update.

Step 5: From the *Updates* section of the *Options* screen, select Updates: **Maintenance Releases**, **Help**, **Accountant**. Ask your instructor if you should select Payroll updates. If you do update payroll, some of your QuickBooks assignment answers may differ from those in this text.

Step 6: To download an update, select **Update Now** tab **> Get Updates**. If asked if you want to update QuickBooks, click **Yes**.

Step 7: **Close** the *Update QuickBooks* window.

Step 8: To complete the update installation, **close** and then **reopen** QuickBooks software. If asked if you want to install updates, select **Yes**.

!

NOTE: QuickBooks typically reminds you that a new release is available to install when you close and reopen QuickBooks. So when you close and then reopen QuickBooks, you may be asked if you want to install updates. Select **Yes**. If you do not close QuickBooks but leave it running, QuickBooks may not automatically remind you that there are new updates to install. In that case, you will need to periodically use the **Update Now** tab.

OPEN QUICKBOOKS DATA STARTER FILES

QuickBooks QBB files are provided with *Computer Accounting with QuickBooks* for use as company data starter files. If you have an error in your QuickBooks company file that you cannot locate or correct, you can use the .QBB data starter files provided with the text to restart with correct account balances.

The .QBB data starter files are provided on the data file CD packaged with your text and as a download on the *Computer Accounting with QuickBooks* Online Learning Center.

QUICKBOOKS DATA STARTER FILES (CD ACCOMPANYING TEXT)

To use the data starter files (.QBB) on the CD that accompanies *Computer Accounting with QuickBooks*:

Step 1: Insert the data starter file CD into your CD drive.

Step 2: Follow the onscreen instructions.

Step 3: Copy the .QBB data starter files to your desktop.

Step 4: Follow the instructions in the text to open and use the .QBB data starter files.

QUICKBOOKS DATA STARTER FILES (ONLINE LEARNING CENTER)

To download and use the QuickBooks .QBB data starter files provided on the Online Learning Center:

Step 1: Go to www.mhhe.com/kay2015.

Step 2: From the Student Edition of the Online Learning Center, locate the data starter files.

Step 3: Follow the instructions to download and unzip the data starter files.

Step 4: Save the data starter files to your desktop or removable media.

Step 5:   Restore the data starter files following the instructions in *Chapter 1* or *Appendix B: Back Up & Restore QuickBooks Files*.

APPENDIX B
BACK UP & RESTORE QUICKBOOKS FILES

In Appendix B, you will learn about:

QUICKBOOKS FILE VERSIONS

QuickBooks software uses a company file to store information about a specific enterprise. Thus, you can use the QuickBooks software installed on your computer with many different company files. This is similar to using Microsoft Excel software, for example, with many different Excel data files.

The different versions of QuickBooks company files are summarized in the following table.

Extension	QuickBooks Company File
.QBW	**QuickBooks for Windows**. You can think of this file as a QuickBooks working file. This is the file version that you use to enter transactions and data. It is usually saved to the hard drive of your computer.
.QBB	**QuickBooks Backup**. A QuickBooks Backup file should be created at regular intervals in case your .QBW file fails or is destroyed. The .QBB file version is a compressed file and cannot be opened directly. Furthermore, you cannot enter transactions directly into a .QBB file. Instead, you must unzip the file first by restoring the file into a .QBW file version.
.QBM	**QuickBooks Mobile**. A QuickBooks Mobile file, also called a QuickBooks Portable file, is used to move a QuickBooks file to another computer. Like the .QBB backup file version, the .QBM file version is compressed and must be unzipped and restored into a .QBW file version before it can be used to enter data.
.QBX	**QuickBooks Accountant**. A QuickBooks Accountant Copy is identified with a .QBX extension. This version of the company file is given to the accountant. The accountant can make changes, such as adjusting entries, to the .QBX version of the company file while the .QBW company file is used to continue entering transactions.

QUICKBOOKS FILE MANAGEMENT

QuickBooks file management involves managing your QuickBooks company files to ensure the security and integrity of your QuickBooks accounting system.

For a business, there are two approaches to QuickBooks file management:

1. Workflow
2. Restart and restore

 ## WORKFLOW

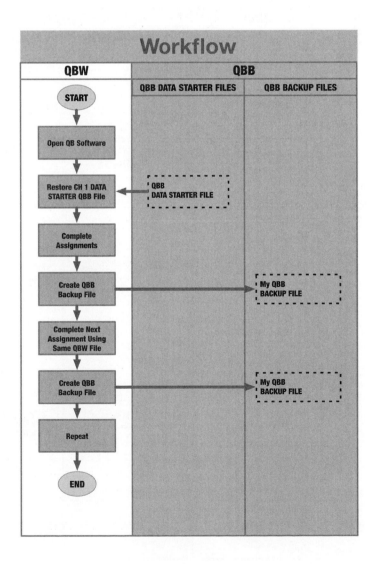

In a typical business workflow, you use the same .QBW computer file on the same computer. Sound file management includes making backups as part of a disaster recovery plan. A good backup system is to have a different backup for each business day: Monday backup, Tuesday backup, Wednesday backup, and so on. Then if it is necessary to use the backup file and the Wednesday backup, for example, fails, the company has a Tuesday backup to use. Furthermore, it is recommended that a business store at least one backup at a remote location.

RESTART & RESTORE

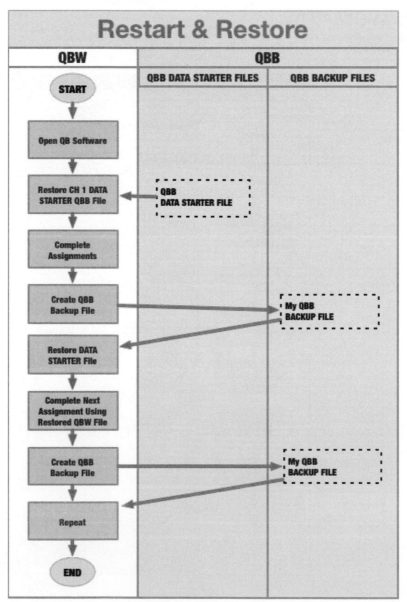

If a company's .QBW file fails, then you must restart by restoring your most recent .QBB file version. The backup file (.QBB) is compressed and must be converted to a working file (.QBW) before you can use it to enter data or transactions.

Backup BACK UP QUICKBOOKS FILES

To save a backup (.QBB) file:

Step 1: With your QuickBooks file (*.QBW) open, click **File**.

Step 2: Select **Back Up Company**.

Step 3: Select **Create Local Backup**.

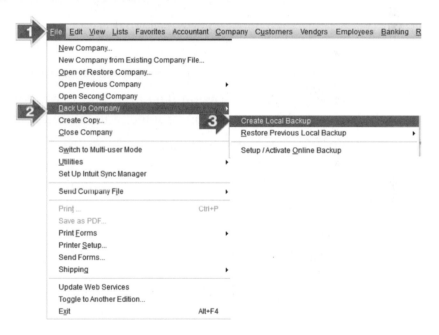

Step 4: When the following window appears, select **Local backup**.

Step 5: Select **Next**.

You can schedule a backup every time you close a QuickBooks company file or at regular intervals.

Backup files can also be saved using QuickBooks Online Backup service.

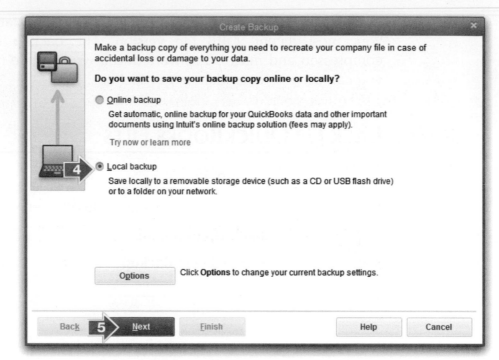

Step 6: If the following *Backup Options* window appears, click the **Browse** button to select a location to save the backup.

Step 7: To make it easier to find your backup files, select **Desktop**. To organize your backup files, consider creating a QBB Backup folder on your desktop and then saving your QBB files to that desktop folder.

Step 8: Click **OK** to close the *Browse for Folder* window. Click **OK** again to close the *Backup Options* window.

Step 9: Select **Use this Location** if a *QuickBooks* warning window appears.

Step 10: Select **Save it now**.

Step 11: Select **Next**.

Step 12: When the following *Save Backup Copy* window appears, the *Save in* field should automatically show: **Desktop**.

Step 13: Update the *File name* field. For example, as shown below the *File name* field is updated to **YourName Chapter 1 (Backup)**. Depending on your operating system settings, the file extension .QBB may appear automatically. If the .QBB extension does not appear, ***do not type it.***

Step 14: The *Save as type* field should automatically appear as **QBW Backup (*.QBB).**

Step 15: Click **Save**.

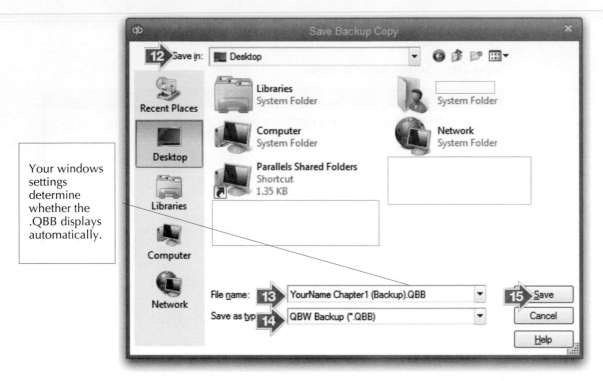

Your windows settings determine whether the .QBB displays automatically.

Step 16: When the following message appears, click **OK**.

RESTART & RESTORE QUICKBOOKS FILES

To restore a backup .QBB file:

Use your .QBB backup file, copy a .QBB backup file from the data file CD, or download a .QBB backup file from the Online Learning Center.

Step 1: From the Menu bar, click **File**.

Step 2: Select **Open or Restore Company**.

Step 3: Select **Restore a backup copy**.

Step 4: Click **Next**.

For your convenience, QuickBooks backup (*.QBB) data files accompany *Computer Accounting for QuickBooks*. You will find the data files on the CD packaged with your text. Before using the data files on the CD, you must copy the files to your desktop or removable media.

Or you can download the backup data files from the Online Learning Center at www.mhhe.com/kay2015.

Step 5: When the following *Open or Restore Company* window appears, select **Local backup**.

Step 6: Click **Next**.

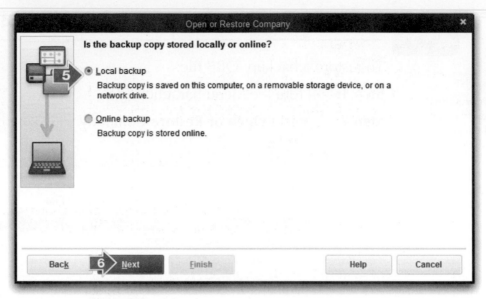

Step 7: Identify the location for the data starter file. If you copied the Chapter 1 DATA STARTER file to your desktop, select the *Look in* **field** to find the location of the .QBB file on your desktop.

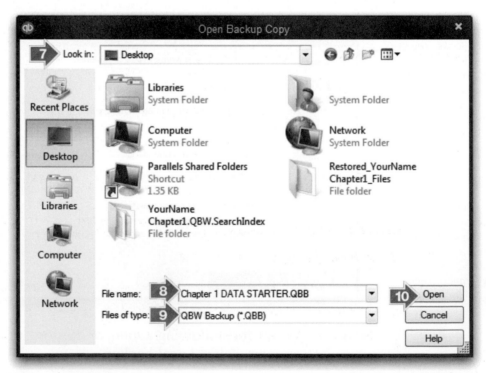

Step 8: Select the data starter file, such as **Chapter 1 DATA STARTER.QBB.**

Step 9: The *Files of type* field should automatically display: **QBW Backup (*.QBB)**.

Step 10: Click **Open**.

Step 11: When the following window appears, click **Next**.

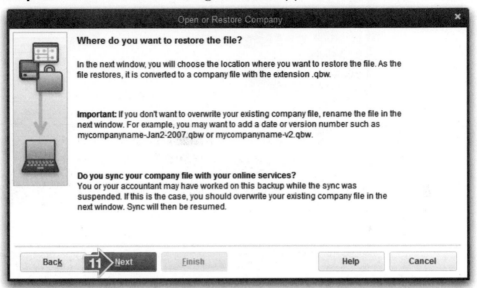

Step 12: Identify the file name and location of the new company file (.QBW) file. You can save the .QBW (working file) on your desktop. Select the location to save in: **Desktop**. (Another option is to save your QBW files to Users > Public > Public Documents > Intuit > QuickBooks > Company Files. Be sure you have permissions to save to a folder.)

Step 13: Enter the QBW File name, such as **YourName Chapter 1**. Insert your name in the file name so you can identify your files.

Step 14: The *Save as type* field should automatically appear as **QuickBooks Files (*.QBW)**.

Step 15: Click **Save**.

QBW files can also be saved to your storage device if there is adequate storage space.

Step 16: Click **OK** if the following window appears.

If an *Update Company* window appears, select **Yes**.

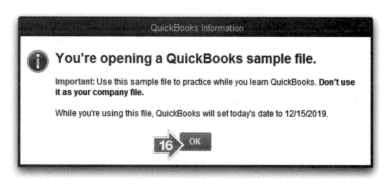

Step 17: Click **OK** if the following *QuickBooks Information* window appears.

Step 18: If the *Accountant Center* window appears, **uncheck Show Accountant Center when opening a company file**. **Close** the *Accountant Center* window.

PORTABLE QUICKBOOKS FILES

QuickBooks portable files (.QBM) are used to move QuickBooks company files.

To save a portable .QBM file:

Step 1: Select **File** menu > **Create Copy**.

Step 2: When the *Save Copy or Backup* window appears, select **Portable company file > Next**.

Step 3: When the *Save Portable Company File* window appears:

- Select *Save in* field: **Desktop**.

- Enter the file name: **[YourName Chapter or Exercise No.] (Portable)**.

- Click **Save**.

Step 4: When the *Close and reopen* window appears, click **OK** to close and reopen your company file before creating a portable company file. Click **OK**.

To open a portable .QBM file:

Step 1: Select **File > Open or Restore Company**.

Step 2: Select **Restore a portable file**. Click **Next**.

Step 3: Identify the location and file name of the portable company file.

- Select *Look in* field: **Desktop**.

- Select the file.

- The *Files of type* field should automatically appear as .QBM.

- Click **Open**.

Step 4: When the *Open or Restore Company* window appears, click **Next**.

Step 5: When the *Save Company File as* window appears:

- Select the *Save in* field: Desktop.

- Enter the file name.

- **QuickBooks Files (*.QBW)** should appear automatically in the *Save as type* field.

- Click **Save**.

APPENDIX C
QuickBooks Issue Resolution

Appendix C QuickBooks Issue Resolution provides you with information about the following frequently asked questions (FAQs) and issue resolution tips:

QUICKBOOKS ISSUE RESOLUTION STRATEGY

WHY ARE QUICKBOOKS ISSUE RESOLUTION SKILLS VALUABLE?

As the rate of change in technology accelerates, issue resolution skills become even more valuable. Ask yourself this question: *If you were an employer, would you want to hire someone who is always interrupting other employees' work to ask technology questions or someone who has well honed issue resolution skills? Which employee would you hire?*

WHAT IS A QUICKBOOKS ISSUE RESOLUTION STRATEGY?

When you encounter a QuickBooks issue, try the following strategy to develop your QuickBooks issue resolution skills:

1. Reread the directions in your text, checking off the step-by-step instructions as you complete each step. QuickBooks is unforgiving if you skip a step or two.

Appendix

2. Review *Appendix C: QuickBooks Issue Resolution* for FAQs.

3. Search the QuickBooks Help & Live Community and www.quickbooks.com/support for answers to your questions

4. Go to www.My-QuickBooks.com to check for the latest update information or known issues.

5. Contact your instructor in a professional manner. Try using the following ABC approach when you email your professor with a QuickBooks question.

   A. State the specific issue that you are experiencing. Be explicit and include screen captures in your email of any warnings or error messages. Refer to specific text pages if applicable.

   B. List the specific action steps you have taken to attempt to resolve the issue. This should follow the order of the first three steps listed above. State the result of the action and/or why it did not work.

   C. Provide your instructor with any additional information that might be helpful in resolving the QuickBooks issue.

QUICKBOOKS HELP & LIVE COMMUNITY

QUICKBOOKS HELP

To search QuickBooks Help to troubleshoot the QuickBooks issue you are experiencing:

1. Select **Help** menu > **QuickBooks Help.**

2. Type your question into the Search field.

3. Click the **Search** icon.

4. Click on a search result to view the Help information.

QUICKBOOKS LIVE COMMUNITY

QuickBooks Live Community is an award winning feature that permits QuickBooks users to post questions and answers to a QuickBooks Live Community. To search QuickBooks Live Community to troubleshoot the QuickBooks issue you are experiencing:

1. Select **Help** menu > **QuickBooks Help.**

2. Type your question into the Search field.

3. Click the **Search** icon.

4. View **Answers from Community**.

5. Click on a search result to view the Help information.

Another way to search for answers to receive results from Intuit, Live Community, and Internal Revenue Service, all at the same time is as follows:

1. Select **Help** menu > **Ask Intuit**.

2. When the website opens, type your question into the search field.

3. Click **Search**. Results are displayed under three tabs:

    -   Intuit Results
    -   Community Results
    -   IRS Results

4. Select the appropriate results tab.

If you do not find an answer to your question in your searches, to post a question to QuickBooks Live Community:

1. Select **Help** menu **> QuickBooks Help**.

2. Select Still Need Help?

3. Select **Ask our community of experts**.

4. Type your question. Click the **Ask** button.

QuickBooks Installation FAQs

How Do I Install My QuickBooks 140-Day Trial Version?

 For instructions to install your QuickBooks 140-day trial version software, see *Appendix A: Install & Register QuickBooks Software.*

My Text Does Not Have the 140-Day Trial Software

Only new copies of the textbook purchased from bookstores or online vendors come with the 140-day trial version. This is a trial version of the software that will allow you to complete the text assignments.

QuickBooks Registration FAQs

!
Register your QuickBooks software! Failure to register your QuickBooks trial version software will result in the software no longer functioning.

QuickBooks Keeps Prompting Me to Register

If QuickBooks prompts you to register your version of QuickBooks, please do so. Follow the prompts using the information on your CD jacket.

Why Am I Asked for a Validation Code?

A validation code is necessary only when registering the full version of QuickBooks. Please register the trial version when prompted at installation or when reminded using the codes on the CD jacket. If you decide to purchase the full version later, you will need the validation code at that time.

QuickBooks Expired before 140 Days

If QuickBooks tells you that your trial version has run out before the 140 days have passed, it may be due to one of the following:

1. The trial version was not registered when prompted.

2. The date on the operating computer has been set forward and is now past 140 days since installation.

3. The trial version came with a used textbook and has already been registered and used for its allotted time.

Software FAQs

QuickBooks Gives Me a "Failed" Message

When trying to open a QuickBooks file, if an *Error: Failed* window appears, try one of the following solutions:

1. Make sure that you are opening the file correctly: select **Open or Restore Company > Restore a backup copy**. QuickBooks (.QBB) data files are compressed and cannot be opened simply by double-clicking on the file.

2. The files might have been corrupted at download and you might need to restart with a new downloaded file. Delete the files you downloaded onto your computer. Go to the Online Learning Center and download the files again. Instructions for accessing the Online Learning Center are provided in *Appendix A: Install & Register QuickBooks Software*.

3. If you receive an error message that your QuickBooks file needs to be rebuilt, select **File menu > Utilities > Rebuild Data**.

4. If the previous solutions do not work, you may need to repair QuickBooks. To repair QuickBooks, insert the QuickBooks software CD in the CD drive of your computer. For some Windows operating systems, you can select **Start > Settings > Control Panel > Add/Remove Program > QuickBooks > Repair**.

QuickBooks Has Locked Me Out

If you did not register your trial version of QuickBooks at installation or when prompted, you will eventually be locked out of the software. If this happens, go to **Help** menu > **Register QuickBooks**. Complete the registration process. If this solution is not successful, try uninstalling QuickBooks software, reinstalling the software, and then registering QuickBooks.

QUICKBOOKS HAS LOCKED UP OR FROZEN

If QuickBooks locks up, try one of the following solutions:

1. Shutdown QuickBooks software using the Task Manager. Press the CTRL+ALT+DELETE keys at the same time. Select **Task List** (or **Start Task Manager**) **> Applications** tab **> QuickBooks > End Task**.

2. Reboot your computer. QuickBooks uses a large amount of memory when operating. If your system does not have adequate memory, this can cause your computer to freeze. Rebooting may take care of this problem.

DATA FILE FAQS

HOW DO I USE THE DATA FILES?

For step-by-step instructions to use the .QBB backup data files that accompany *Computer Accounting with QuickBooks*, see *Appendix B: Back Up & Restore QuickBooks Files*.

The data files are available on a CD that accompanies the text or can be downloaded from the text Online Learning Center at www.mhhe.com/kay2015.

The data files can be restored and used when your data file is corrupted or contains an irresolvable error.

WHEN MY DATA FILES OPEN THE HOME PAGE DOESN'T APPEAR

Occasionally when opening a data file, an additional window will appear on the screen based on what you last had open when you were using QuickBooks. Simply close the window and click **Home** on the Icon bar to display the Home page.

THE DATA FILES TAKE A LONG TIME TO DOWNLOAD

If the data files are slow to download directly from the Data CD, try the following:

1. Copy the files to your desktop first. If you are downloading to a removable drive that is almost full, it may take a long time to download the files.

2. Make sure you are restoring the data file as directed in *Appendix B: Back Up & Restore QuickBooks Files*. You cannot open the data files by double-clicking on the file. Instead, you must restore the file using QuickBooks software.

3. Close other programs running on your computer that might be slowing your computer down.

4. Reboot your computer.

WHAT DO I DO IF THE DATA FILES ARE ZIPPED?

Unzip compressed backup data files from the Online Learning Center at www.mhhe.com/kay2015 as follows:

1. Double-click the file link on the Online Learning Center.

2. From the File Download menu, select **Save**.

3. Choose the folder to save the file, and click **Save**.

4. From the File Download menu, choose **Open Folder**.

5. **Right-click** on the zipped file and choose **Extract All**.

6. The files within the zipped file will then appear within that folder. If necessary, choose which file to unzip and double click.

Some versions of Windows will open up an Extraction Wizard. If so, simply follow the defaults and choose **Show extracted files** to view and open files.

BACK UP & RESTORE FAQS

HOW DO I BACK UP OR RESTORE?

Detailed backup and restore instructions are provided in *Appendix B: Back Up & Restore QuickBooks Files*.

Depending on your classroom situation, there are two different approaches to completing the assignments: Workflow or Restart & Restore. The Workflow approach is similar to the workflow that most businesses use. In a typical business environment, you would continue to use the same .QBW file, backing up periodically. This is a good option if you will be using the same computer throughout your entire course.

If you will be switching between campus and home computers, then you may want to use the Restart & Restore approach, where you will make a backup data file each time you complete a chapter. Then when you change computers, you will restore the backup file to restart your work in QuickBooks. You can use your own backup data file or use the data files that are provided on the data file CD or the Online Learning Center.

Additional information about the Workflow and Restart & Restore approaches are contained in *Appendix B*.

MY QUICKBOOKS FILE WON'T OPEN

If you are trying to open a backup file from the student CD or after downloading the file from the Online Learning Center, you cannot simply double click on the backup file to open it. In order to open a backup file you must restore the backup using QuickBooks software.

See *Appendix B: Back Up & Restore QuickBooks Files* for step-by-step directions on opening and using your backup files.

TEXT INSTRUCTION FAQS

THE TEXT INSTRUCTIONS DO NOT MATCH MY SCREEN

If your screen does not match the text instructions, it may be due to software updates. To see the latest updates and changes, go to www.My-QuickBooks.com or the Online Learning Center (select Text Updates).

THE TEXT SCREEN CAPTURES DO NOT MATCH MY SCREEN

If your screen or printed report does not match those in the text, it may be due to differences in software systems. The text is created using Windows 7 operating system and QuickBooks Accountant 2015. If your QuickBooks software is a different version or your operating system is different, this may explain the discrepancy.

I THINK I FOUND AN ERROR IN THE TEXT

Every effort is made to eliminate all errors in the text; however, if you think you found an error, it might have already been discovered. Go to www.My-QuickBooks.com, the QuickBooks student website, for the latest updates. Or go to the Text Updates section of the Online Learning Center to see the latest updates and changes. If the discrepancy is not listed in the text updates, please speak with your instructor for assistance.

CORRECTING ERRORS

QuickBooks provides a number of ways to correct errors. When you discover an error often determines how you correct the error. For example, if you make an error when you are entering information into an onscreen check form, you can correct the error using the Backspace key. However, if you do not discover the error until after the check is saved, you should void the check and prepare a new check.

CORRECTING ERRORS BEFORE DOCUMENT IS SAVED

In general, errors detected before the document is saved can be corrected in one of the following ways:

1. **Backspace key:** Deletes characters to the left of the cursor in the current field you are entering.

2. **Delete key:** Deletes characters to the right of the cursor.

3. **Undo command:** Before you press the *Enter* key, you can undo typing on the current line.

4. **Clear button:** On some onscreen forms, a Clear button appears in the lower right corner of the window. Clicking this button clears all fields on the screen.

5. **Revert command** (Edit menu): Reverts the entire screen back to its original appearance.

BACKSPACE

The Backspace key is used to correct errors that occur when you are entering data. For example, if you mistype a company name on a check, you can use the Backspace key to delete the incorrect characters. Then enter the correct spelling.

Assume you need to write a check to Davis Business Associates for professional services performed for your company.

To use the Backspace key to correct an error on a check:

1. With the Rock Castle Construction Company file open, click **Write Checks** in the **Banking** section of the Home page to display the *Write Checks* window.

2. When the *Write Checks* window appears:
   - Select **Print Later**.
   - Select from the *Pay to the Order of* drop-down list: **Davis Business Associates**.
   - Type the street address: **1234 Brentwodo**.

3. The correct address is 1234 Brentwood. Press the **Backspace** key **twice** to erase "**do**."

4. Type "**od**" to finish entering Brentwood.

UNDO

The Undo command can be used to undo typing before you press the Enter key.

To use the Undo command:

1. With the same *Write Checks* window still open and the check for Davis Business Associates displayed, type the city and state for the Davis address: **Bayshore, CA**.

2. After you type the address, Mr. Castle tells you the address is San Diego, CA, not Bayshore. To use the undo command, click **Edit** on the Menu bar. Then click **Undo Typing**. Bayshore, CA, will be deleted.

3. Next, enter the correct city and state: **San Diego, CA**.

The Backspace key erases the character to the *left* of the cursor. The Delete key erases the character to the *right* of the cursor.

Use the data file for any of the Chapters 1 through 7 company files.

Davis Business Associates should automatically appear in the *Address* field.

The Undo command is useful if you want to delete an entire line of typing.

CLEAR

A Clear button is usually located in the lower right corner of an unsaved onscreen form. If you start entering data and want to clear all the fields in the onscreen form, click the **Clear** button.

After an onscreen form has been saved, the Clear button changes to a Revert button.

The Clear command also appears on the Edit menu. This command can be used before a document, such as a check, has been saved.

To illustrate, assume that you decide to wait to pay Davis Business Associates until it completes all the work it is performing for you. Therefore, you want to erase everything that you have entered on the check.

To use the Clear function:

1. With the *Write Checks* window still open and the check for Davis Business Associates displayed, click **Edit** on the Menu bar.

2. Click **Clear**. The *Write Checks* window returns to its original appearance with blank fields. The information you entered about Davis Business Associates has been erased.

The Clear command on the Edit menu and the Clear button on the onscreen form perform the same function: both clear the contents of an onscreen form that has not yet been saved.

CORRECTING ERRORS ON SAVED DOCUMENTS

Once a document has been saved, you can use one of three approaches to correct the error:

1. **Display** the document, correct the error, then save the document again.

2. **Void** the erroneous document, then create a new document.

3. **Delete** the erroneous document, then create a new document.

You can only use the **Undo** command *before* moving to a new field.

The Revert button permits you to revert the onscreen form back to its appearance when you opened the saved onscreen form. This feature can be used before the onscreen form has been resaved.

If the correction involves a check (Write Checks, Pay Bills, or Create Paychecks), display the check in the *Write Checks* window by clicking **Previous** or select **Edit** menu > **Find**.

ENTER CORRECTIONS IN SAVED ONSCREEN FORM

To enter corrections in a saved onscreen form, complete three steps:

1. Display the erroneous onscreen form. For example, display an incorrect invoice in the *Create Invoices* window.

2. Correct the error by entering changes directly in the onscreen form.

3. Save the onscreen form.

VOID

You cannot correct deposits using this approach. If you attempt to make changes to a saved deposit, you will receive a warning that you must delete the deposit and then reenter the appropriate information.

The Void command will void a document and remove its effect from your accounting records. For example, if you void a check, the check amount is no longer deducted from your checking account. The check will still appear in your QuickBooks records, but it is labeled Void.

To void a document in QuickBooks, first display the document on your screen. Then select **Edit** from the Menu bar. The Edit menu will change depending upon the document that has been opened. For example, if you open a check, the Edit menu will display "Void Check." If you open an invoice, then the Edit menu will display "Void Invoice."

To void a check in QuickBooks:

1. With the *Write Checks* window open, enter the following information for Davis Business Associates:

Date	12/15/2019
Check Amount	$200.00
Account	Professional Fees

!

Notice that VOID now appears in the Memo field of the check and the amount of the check has been changed to $0.00.

2. Click **Save & Close** to save the check.

3. Next, you decide to void the check and pay Davis Business Associates at a later time. Display the check for Davis Business Associates on 12/15/2019 for $200.

4. Click **Edit** on the Menu bar.

5. Click **Void Check**.

The voided check will remain in your QuickBooks records but the amount of the check will not be deducted from your checking account.

To void an invoice:

1. Open any invoice.

2. Click **Edit** menu.

3. If you wanted to void the invoice, you would click Void Invoice. For this activity, close the Edit menu by clicking anywhere outside the Edit drop-down menu.

> Notice that the Edit menu now displays Void Invoice instead of Void Check.

DELETE

The difference between the Delete command and the Void command is that when the Delete command is used, the document is deleted and completely removed from your QuickBooks records. The document is no longer displayed in the QuickBooks records.

When the Void command is used, the document's effect upon your accounts is removed from your accounting records, but the voided document still appears in the QuickBooks records marked "VOID."

When the Delete command is used, the document is removed from your accounting records. The audit trail maintains a record of all changes made to your QuickBooks records, including deleted documents, but the document itself does not appear in your QuickBooks system.

> To delete an invoice, simply display the invoice onscreen, then click Edit. Instead of Delete Check appearing on the Edit menu, Delete Invoice will appear.

To delete the Davis Business Associates check:

1. Display the voided check to Davis Business Associates.

2. With the check displayed on your screen, click **Edit** menu.

3. Click **Delete Check** to delete the check. Now this check will no longer appear in your QuickBooks accounting records.

4. Click **OK** when asked if you are sure you want to delete the check.

5. Close the *Write Checks* window.

The Delete command removes the document from your records. If you want to maintain a record of the document but simply remove its effect from your records, use the Void command. The Void command provides a better trail of changes made to your accounting records.

PRINTER FAQS

THE PRINTER WON'T PRINT

If the printer will not print try the following:

1. Verify the printer has paper.

2. Verify the printer is not out of ink or toner.

3. Verify the paper is loaded correctly in the printer.

4. Print a test page to verify the printer is functioning.

5. Verify the latest print drivers are installed on your computer. If necessary, refer to the printer manufacturer website.

MY COMPUTER CANNOT CONNECT TO THE PRINTER

If you receive an error message that your computer cannot connect to the printer, try the following:

1. The printer may be turned off. Verify the printer is turned on.

2. Try using another printer on the network.

ADDITIONAL ISSUE RESOLUTION RESOURCES

Look to these additional resources for issue resolution assistance:

1. Student website: www.My-QuickBooks.com. Check the QuickBooks student website for the latest updates.

2. Online Learning Center: www.mhhe.com/kay2015. Look here for FAQs and text updates.

3. QuickBooks Support: support.quickbooks.intuit.com. Look here to search the QuickBooks support database for articles and community posts that might answer your questions.

4. Customer Support: 888-246-8848. Call toll free and select Customer Support to talk to an Intuit specialist.

APPENDIX D
GO DIGITAL WITH QUICKBOOKS

In Appendix D, you will learn about:

INTRODUCTION

Now you can Go Digital with QuickBooks. *Computer Accounting with QuickBooks* offers you three options for going Digital with your QuickBooks assignments.

!
Ask your instructor if you are to Go Digital with QuickBooks. If so, ask which option you should use: Option 1, 2 or 3.

Option	QuickBooks Electronic Deliverables
Option 1 **Excel**	**Microsoft Excel Spreadsheets** Go Digital using Excel templates at www.My-QuickBooks.com. Then send your instructor your assignments electronically. When using the Excel option, you create QuickBooks reports and export to the Excel REPORTS templates provided for you at www.My-QuickBooks.com.
Option 2 **PDF**	**Adobe® PDF Files** Print your assignments to PDF files and then send the PDF files to your instructor via e-mail or courseware, such as Canvas.
Option 3 **QBB**	**QuickBooks Backup QBB Files** Using the memorized reports feature in QuickBooks software, save your reports electronically in QuickBooks. Then send your .QBB backup file to your instructor electronically.

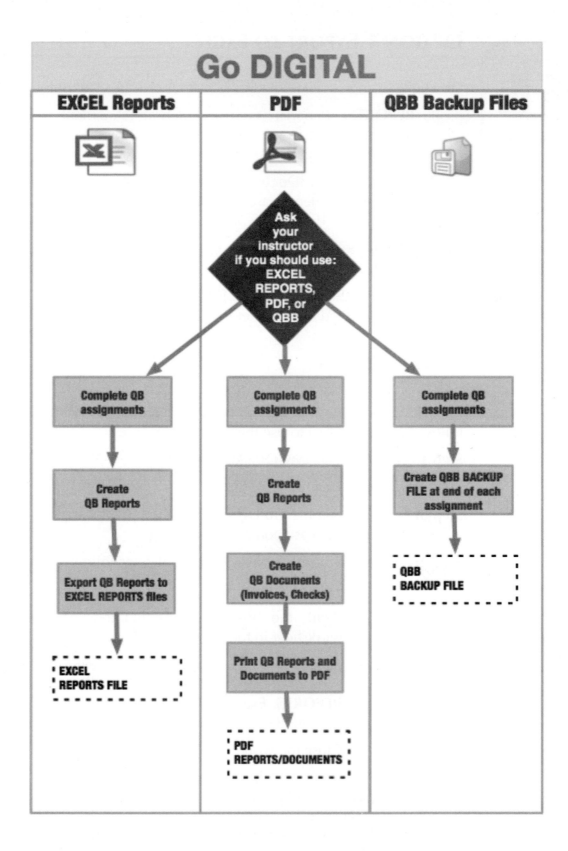

OPTION 1 EXPORT TO EXCEL

Go Digital using Excel. QuickBooks creates two types of output:

A. REPORTS. Reports, such as income statement and trial balance, are created using the QuickBooks Report Center. QuickBooks reports can be exported to Excel.

B. DOCUMENTS. Documents, such as invoices, checks and purchase orders, are created using onscreen forms. QuickBooks does ***not*** export documents to Excel.

Excel REPORTS templates are provided for you at www.My-QuickBooks.com for QuickBooks reports exported to Excel.

Assignments on the Quick Check list marked with an * are REPORTS that can be exported to the Excel REPORTS template.

Instructors:
Excel
REPORTS
workbooks
can be graded
with the
QuickBooks
Grade
Assistant.

EXCEL REPORTS

For this option, export your QuickBooks reports to Go Digital Excel REPORTS templates provided at www.My-QuickBooks.com. Just follow the steps below to use this easy option.

Step 1:   Go to **www.My-QuickBooks.com**.

Step 2:   Select the **QB2015** link.

Step 3:   **Download** the **Go Digital Excel REPORTS template** for the chapter or case you are completing.

Step 4:   Prepare the Excel REPORTS template as follows:

- **Open** the Excel REPORTS template workbook.

- **Read** the instructions contained on the first worksheet in the Excel template.

- Select **File > Save As**. Use the file name: **[YourLastName FirstName] [CH/CASE][No.] REPORTS**. Example: YourLastName FirstName CH1 REPORTS.

- **Close** the workbook.

Step 5:   Follow your text instructions until you are instructed to export a report to Excel. Assignments that can be exported to Excel are identified on the Quick Check list with an *. When your *Computer Accounting with QuickBooks* text

+
To keep your Desktop neat, consider adding a Folder to your Desktop: *QB Excel Reports Templates*. Then download the Excel Reports Templates to that folder.

asks you to prepare a report, select **Reports** in the *My Shortcuts* section of the Icon bar to display the Report Center.

Step 6: Select the report category and the specific report you would like to create.

Step 7: Select **Date** and **Run**.

Step 8: With the report displayed onscreen, select **Excel**.

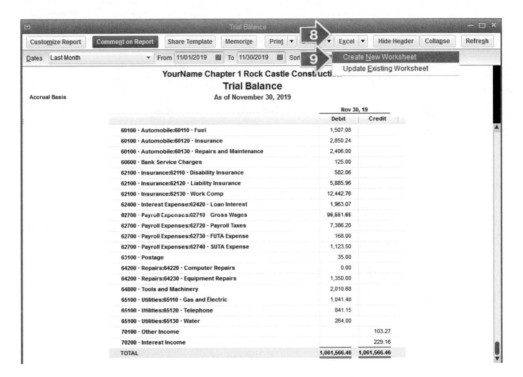

Step 9: Select **Create New Worksheet**.

Step 10: Select **Replace an existing worksheet**.

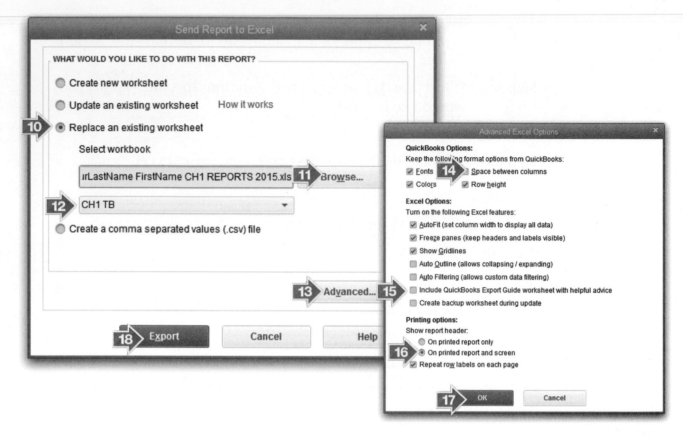

Step 11: **Browse** for the appropriate Excel REPORTS template containing your name in the filename (Example: **YourLastName FirstName CH1 REPORTS**).

Step 12: Select the correct **sheetname** from the drop-down list (Example: **CH1 TB**).

Step 13: Select **Advanced**.

Step 14: *Uncheck* **Space between columns**.

Step 15: *Uncheck* **Include QuickBooks Export Guide worksheet with helpful advice.**

Step 16: Select Show report header: **On printed report and screen**.

Step 17: Click **OK.**

Step 18: Click **Export**.

Step 19:   If the *Export Report Alert* window appears, select **Do not display this message in the future**.

Step 20:   Select **Yes**.

Excel should open on your screen with your QuickBooks report inserted.

Step 1:   Select the **REPORTS** sheet tab.

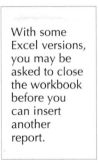

With some Excel versions, you may be asked to close the workbook before you can insert another report.

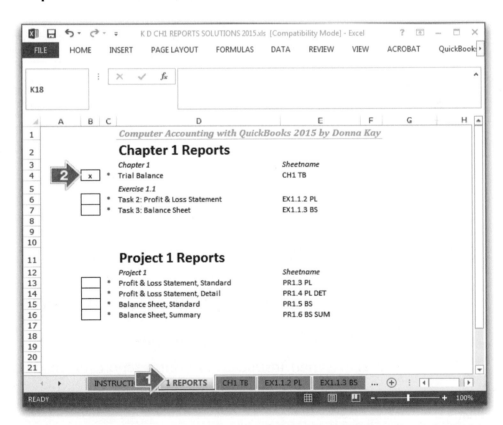

Step 2:   Mark the report sheet you completed by inserting an "**x**".

To avoid losing points, make certain you mark completed assignments with an "x" by the sheetname on the Quick Check list.

Step 3: Save your **REPORTS** Excel workbook using the filename: **[YourLastName FirstName] [CH/CASE][No] REPORTS**.

 To avoid losing points, make certain your first name and last name are included in the Excel workbook file name.

Step 4: Ask your instructor if you should email the Excel spreadsheet or upload to your courseware.

Step 5: Items that are not an Excel report are not marked with an * on the Quick Check list. If there is no Excel report for the document, such as checks, *ask your instructor* if (1) you are to omit the items that cannot be exported as Excel reports or (2) use PDF for documents.

OPTION 2 EXPORT TO PDF

To create PDF electronic deliverables, you will print your reports to an electronic Portable Document Format (PDF) file. If you have PDF software available on your computer, select the PDF option from the drop-down printer list.

> **!**
>
> Before using this option, open a QuickBooks document, select **Print**. Verify that your printer drop-down list has an option to print to PDF. If there is no PDF option, download and install PDF software.

!
Some documents can be printed as PDF files by selecting **File** menu > **Save as PDF** or **Print > Save as PDF**.

Follow the steps below to use this option.

Step 1: When instructed to print a report (or onscreen document) in the text, from the Report Center, display the report you wish to create.

Step 2: Select **Print**, then make the appropriate selections.

Step 3: Select the drop-down list to view the installed printers.

Select the PDF software option. (If there is no PDF option, download and install PDF software. Google for free PDF software options.)

Step 4: Select **Print**.

Step 5: Enter a file name using your initials and Chapter, Exercise, Project, or Case number.

Step 6: Select **Save**.

Step 7: Ask your instructor if you should email the PDF files as attachments or upload to your courseware.

OPTION 3 USE QBB FILES

For this option, you will use the memorized reports feature of QuickBooks to save your reports. Then send your .QBB company file electronically to your instructor. To use the .QBB option, follow the steps below.

First, create a new Memorized Report Group. You will create one report group for each chapter. Thus, you will have a Report Group for Chapter 1, another one for Chapter 2, and so on.

Step 1: Select **Reports** menu.

Step 2: Select **Memorized Reports**.

Step 3: Select **Memorized Report List**.

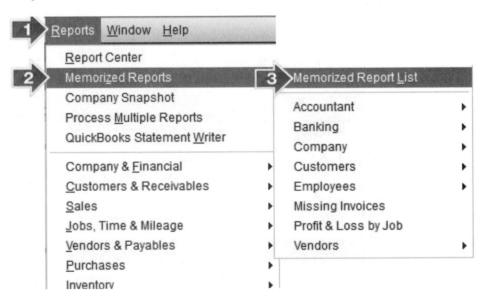

Step 4:   From the following *Memorized Report List* window, select **Memorized Report**.

Step 5:   Select **New Group**.

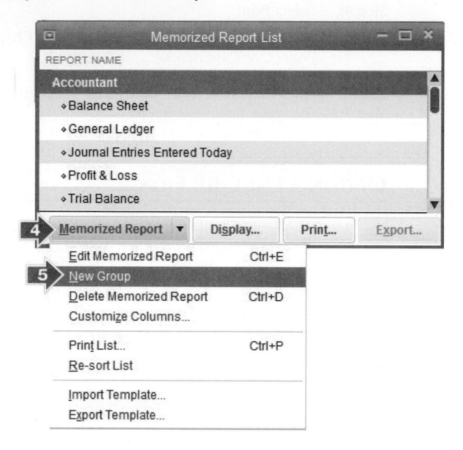

Step 6:   Enter Memorized Report Group name: **Chapter** and the chapter number.

Step 7:   Click **OK**.

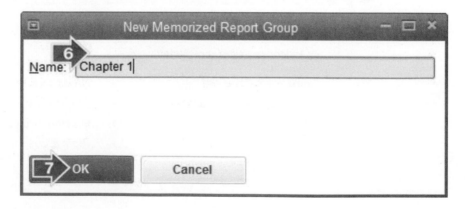

You will complete Steps 1 through 7 each time you begin a new chapter.

Next, for each chapter, add memorized reports to the Report Group:

Step 1: When instructed to print a report in the text, from the Report Center, display the report you wish to create.

Step 2: Select **Memorize**.

Step 3: Enter Name as follows, specifying chapter or exercise, number, and name of report.

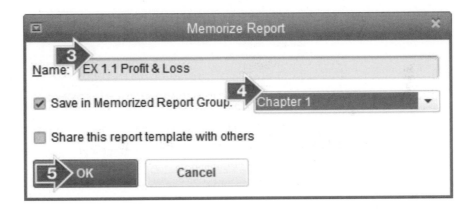

Step 4: Select **Save in Memorized Report Group**. Select the report group for the appropriate chapter.

Step 5: Click **OK**.

Step 6: The memorized report should now appear in the chapter report group.

Step 7: Memorize each of the reports requested in the chapter, exercise, or project.

Step 8: After memorizing all the report assignments for a chapter, back up your QuickBooks file. See *Appendix B: Back Up & Restore QuickBooks Files* for step-by-step directions for backing up QuickBooks files.

Step 9: Ask your instructor if you should deliver your .QBB file using email or upload to your courseware.

NOTES:

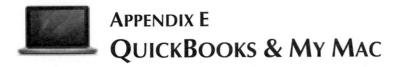

APPENDIX E
QuickBooks & My Mac

Would you like to use QuickBooks on an Apple computer? Ways to use QuickBooks with a Mac are:

1. **QuickBooks for Windows software running on a Mac.** You have several options for installing QuickBooks for Windows on a Mac. You can use the Mac's Bootcamp feature. Another option is to use virtualization software, such as Parallels to operate QuickBooks for Windows on a Mac. To learn more about these options, visit www.My-QuickBooks.com.

2. **QuickBooks for Mac software.** QuickBooks for Mac software runs on Apple computers. However, the features of QuickBooks for Mac software differ from QuickBooks for Windows. See www.quickbooks.com for highlights of differences between QuickBooks for Windows and QuickBooks for Mac.

3. **QuickBooks Online Accountant.** See *Computer Accounting with QuickBooks* Chapter 14 for more information about using QuickBooks Online and QuickBooks Online Accountant that you can access through a browser.

APPENDIX F
WWW.MY-QUICKBOOKS.COM

Go to www.My-QuickBooks.com to view the QuickBooks website that accompanies *Computer Accounting with QuickBooks*.

www.My-QuickBooks.com includes:

- **Go Digital Reports Excel Templates.** Use these Excel templates to create digital QuickBooks reports instead of paper printouts for your assignments.

- **QuickBooks User Certification Information.** Learn more about how you can obtain the QuickBooks User Certification.

- **QuickBooks Videos.** View videos on QuickBooks topics such as back up, restore, and much more.

- *Computer Accounting with QuickBooks* **Updates**. Check out the latest updates to stay current with the latest updates for QuickBooks software and this text.

- **QuickBooks for Mac.** Explore different approaches and ideas for using QuickBooks for Mac.

- **And More....**

INDEX

-Q-

-R-

-S-